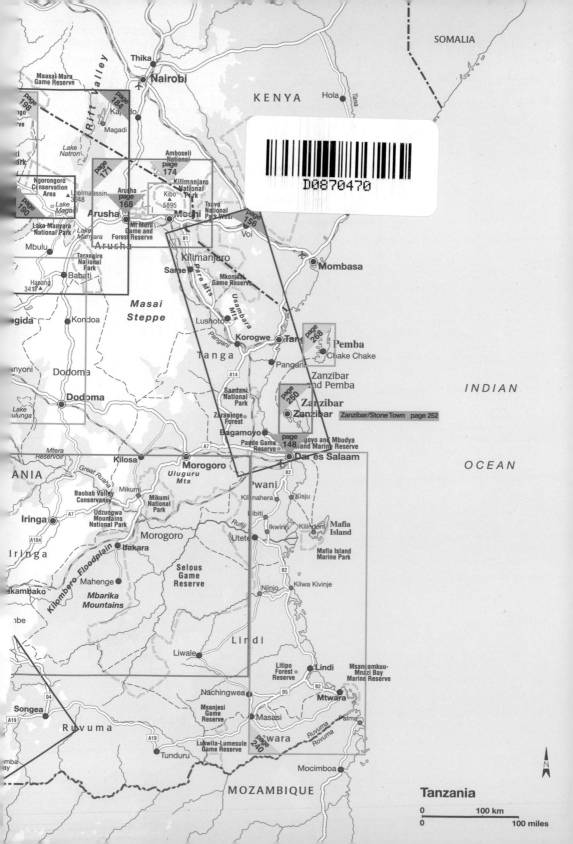

SOMALIA

KENYA

Thika

Nairobi

Maasai Mara Game Reserve

Rift Valley

page 198

page 184

Kajiado

Magadi

Hola

Tana

Lake Natron

Amboseli National page 174

Ngorongoro Conservation Area

Lbolmalassin 3648

page 190

Lake Magadi

Arusha page 168

Kibo 5895

Kilimanjaro National Park

page 171

Tsavo National Park West

page 156

Voi

Lake Manyara National Park

Mbulu

Arusha

Lake Manyara

Mt Meru Game and Forest Reserve

Moshi

Mombasa

Tarangire National Park

Babati

Same

Kilimanjaro

B1

Mkomazi Game Reserve

Hanang 3417

Pare Mts

Usambara Mts

Masai Steppe

Kondoa

Lushoto

Pemba

Pangani

Korogwe

Tanga

page 268

Chake Chake

Dodoma

Tanga

Pangani

Zanzibar and Pemba

Dodoma

A14

page 250

Lake ulunga

Saadani National Park

Zanzibar

Zanzibar

Zanzibar/Stone Town page 252

Mtera Reservoir

Zaraninge Forest

Bagamoyo

page 148

Kilosa

A7

Pande Game Reserve

Ngoyo and Mbudya Island Marine Reserve

Morogoro

Dar es Salaam

INDIAN

OCEAN

ANIA

Great Ruaha

Uluguru Mts

Pwani

B2

Iringa

Mikumi

Mikumi National Park

Kilmahera

Kisju

Baobab Valley Conservancy

A7

Udzungwa Mountains National Park

Dibiti

Ikwiriri

Kilingoni

Mafia Island

A104

Morogoro

Rufiji

Iringa

Ifakara

Utete

Mafia Island Marine Park

akambako

Mahenge

Mbarika Mountains

Selous Game Reserve

Njinjo

Kilwa Kivinje

B2

be

Lindi

Liwale

Litipo Forest Reserve

Lindi

Msangamkuu-Mnazi Bay Marine Reserve

D4

Nachingwea

B2

Songea

A19

Msanjesi Game Reserve

B5

Mtwara

wara

Masasi

Palma

Ruvuma

A19

Lukwila-Lumesule Game Reserve

page 240

Ruvuma

Rovuma

mba ay

Tunduru

Mocimboa

MOZAMBIQUE

N

Tanzania

0   100 km

0   100 miles

INSIGHT GUIDES
TANZANIA
& ZANZIBAR

Discovery
CHANNEL

APA·PUBLICATIONS L

Part of the Langenscheidt Publishing Group

INSIGHT GUIDE
TANZANIA & ZANZIBAR

Editorial
Project Editor
Melissa Shales
Managing Editor
Clare Griffiths
Series Editor
Dorothy Stannard

Distribution

UK & Ireland
GeoCenter International Ltd
Meridian House, Churchill Way West,
Basingstoke, Hampshire RG21 6YR
Fax: (44) 1256 817988

United States
Langenscheidt Publishers, Inc.
36–36 33rd Street, 4th Floor, Long Island
City, New York 11106
Fax: 1 (718) 784 0640

Australia
Universal Publishers
1 Waterloo Road
Macquarie Park, NSW 2113
Fax: (61) 2 9888 9074

New Zealand
Hema Maps New Zealand Ltd (HNZ)
Unit D, 24 Ra ORA Drive
East Tamaki, Auckland
Fax: (64) 9 273 6479

Worldwide
**Apa Publications GmbH & Co.
Verlag KG (Singapore branch)**
38 Joo Koon Road, Singapore 628990
Tel: (65) 6865 1600. Fax: (65) 6861 6438

Printing

Insight Print Services (Pte) Ltd
38 Joo Koon Road, Singapore 628990
Tel: (65) 6865 1600. Fax: (65) 6861 6438

ABOUT THIS BOOK

The first Insight Guide pioneered the use of creative full-colour photography in travel guides in 1970. Since then, we have expanded our range to cater for our readers' need not only for reliable information about their chosen des-tination but also for a real under-standing of the culture and workings of that destination. Now, when the internet can supply inexhaustible (but not always reliable) facts, our books marry text and pictures to provide those much more elusive qualities: knowledge and discern-ment. To achieve this, they rely heavily on the authority of locally based writers and photographers.

Insight Guide: Tanzania and Zanz-ibar is structured to convey an understanding of the country and its peoples as well as to guide readers through its many sights and activities:

♦ The **Features** section, indicated by a yellow bar at the top of each page, covers the natural and cul-tural history of the country in a series of informative essays.

♦ The main **Places** section, indi-cated by a blue bar, is a complete guide to all the sights and area worth visiting. Places of speci interest are coordinated by numb with the maps. A wildlife gaze with stunning photography cluded in this section for fie armchair reference.

♦ The **Travel Tips** listings with an orange bar, pr handy point of reference the-minute information around, hotels, shops, re and lots more.

and project editor on *Insight Guide: Kenya*. Pike has travelled extensively in Africa since 1984.

The chapters on Dar es Salaam, Tanzania's major city, and the North Coast were written by freelance travel writer and broadcaster **Mary Johns**. This was her first foray into the world of guidebooks.

Christine Otieno, who wrote the modern history chapter Tanzania Today, was formerly BBC chief correspondent in Tanzania, and is now based in Kampala, Uganda.

Claire Foottit, an Edinburgh-based freelance journalist specialising in Africa, wrote the chapter Safari, the essay on geography, The Lie of the Land, and the Arusha and Kilimanjaro chapter.

Tony Fishlock, a partner in www.allabouttanzania.com, contributed the piece on coral diving, which outlines the best dive sites around the islands of Unguja, Pemba and Mafia.

The rest of the book was written by **Philip Briggs**, a South African travel writer who has written guides to many African countries and contributes regularly to a number of leading South African and British wildlife periodicals.

The comprehensive Travel Tips section was written by **Jason Mitchell** and **Christina Park**.

Two photographers, **Martin Harvey** and **Ariadne van Zandbergen**, have contributed significantly to this guide, while picture research was by **Hilary Genin** and **Corrie Wingate**. The book was proofread by **Neil Titman** and indexed by **Helen Peters**. This edition was edited by **Rachel Fox** and updated by **Nina Springle**, a writer living in Zanzibar.

The contributors

A dedicated team in the UK, Kenya, South Africa and Tanzania worked hard to create *Insight Guide: Tanzania & Zanzibar*.

Clare Griffiths was the managing editor for this title, while the project editor was **Melissa Shales**. Shales is a London-based freelance travel writer and editor specialising in Africa. She has written or edited guides for most of the major publishers. Previous work for Insight includes titles on Turkey and Istanbul, and *Discovery Travel Adventure: African Safari*. Shales wrote much of the history section and the chapters on the Northern Safari Circuit, Zanzibar and Pemba.

Jeffery Pike, who wrote two of the history chapters and the wildlife gazetteer, is another Insight regular

Map Legend

▬ ·· ▬	International Boundary
▬ ▬ ▬	Province Boundary
⊖	Border Crossing
▬ • ▬	National Park/Reserve
▬ ▬ ▬	Ferry Route
✈ ✈	Airport: International/Regional
🚍	Bus Station
❶	Tourist Information
✉	Post Office
✝ † ⛪	Church/Ruins
†	Monastery
☾	Mosque
✡	Synagogue
🏰	Castle/Ruins
🏠	Mansion/Stately home
∴	Archaeological Site
∩	Cave
🗿	Statue/Monument
★	Place of Interest

The main places of interest in the Places section are coordinated by number with a full-colour map (e.g. ❶), and a symbol at the top of every right-hand page tells you where to find the map.

Maps

CONTENTS

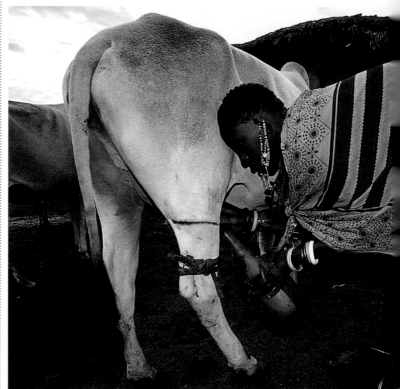

A Maasai
woman milks
her cow at
dawn

THE BEST OF TANZANIA

Bigger than France and Germany combined, Tanzania has a history
as long and as fascinating as its physical assets are wild and wonderful.
Here, at a glance, are our recommendations for an unforgettable trip

SPECTACULAR GAME VIEWING

- **The Great Migration** Every year, between December and July, close to 6 million hooves pound the endless plains as animals join in the massive migration through Serengeti National Park in search of fresh grass. *See page 196.*
- **Ruaha National Park** Game viewing begins as soon as the plane touches down, Ruaha being so full of wildlife. The shores of the Ruaha River are a permanent hunting ground for lion, leopard, jackal, hyena and the rare African wild dog. *See page 224.*
- **Lake Manyara National Park** Home to Tanzania's famous tree-climbing lions, dense populations of buffalo and elephant, as well as a dazzling array of bird life. *See page 186.*
- **Tarangire National Park** Huge herds of elephants rival the park's ancient baobab trees as its most celebrated feature. *See page 183.*
- **Ngorongoro** Ngorongoro is a huge caldera (collapsed volcano). The crater is the habitat for around 20,000 large animals, including some of the world's last black rhinoceros. *See page 191.*

ADVENTURE ACTIVITIES

- **Balloon Safari** Flights by balloon take off as dawn breaks over the Serengeti, illuminating the amazing natural habitat of the most famous game reserve in the world. *See page 198.*
- **Paragliding** Just some of the areas to fly over are the Usumbaras, the Rift Valley and numerous hills around Mount Meru. *See page 310.*
- **Kite surfing** A fusion of wakeboarding and windsurfing, this is the newest extreme sport catching on in East Africa. *See page 310.*
- **Equestrian Safaris** Galloping alongside a

herd of zebra or wildebeest as they race across the open plains is a life-long dream for many riders. Horse safaris make that dream a reality with well-schooled mounts, professional equipment and the luxury of infinite space. *See page 310.*

LEFT: kingfisher in Lake Manyara National Park.
ABOVE RIGHT: a balloon safari at daybreak over the Serengeti is an unforgettable experience.

CULTURE

● **Swahili Coast** The Islamic Swahili trading nation dominated Tanzania's coast for centuries. There are reminders of this great civilisation in Kilwa, Bagamoyo, Tanga and Pangani, and all over the Zanzibar Archipelago. *See pages 239, 155, 160 and 249.*

● **Maasailand** Engaruka is the lost city in the shadow of the Great Rift Wall, where Maasai mix irrigation, farming and traditional herding. In Mkuru, short camel treks give visitors a glimpse into nomadic culture as they climb nearby Ol Donyo Landaree. *See pages 169 and 192.*

● **Lake Eyasi** The Hadza bushmen are some of the last hunter-gatherers in Africa. Morning hunts with the Hadza warriors armed with bows and arrows, honey-gathering, walks to find healing plants and food, and traditional dances are all part of this cultural tourism experience. *See page 189.*

● **Tingatinga** At its best, Tingatinga painting is vibrant and appealing in its simple depictions of Tanzania's animals and people, sometimes with political undertones. It is essentially African, when so much other artwork is derived from Western ideas with Western tastes in mind. *See page 69.*

● **Bullfighting** Thought to be a legacy of Portuguese rule in the 16th century, bull-fighting contests take place between August and November on Pemba Island. *See page 306.*

HISTORY

● **Olduvai Gorge** Considered by many to be the "Cradle of Mankind", this is the site of many ground-breaking archaeological discoveries: fossil remains of hominids dating back 1.75 million years, and extinct animals including a sabre-toothed cat, lion-like creature, two species of elephant, a massive giraffe and a giant pig. *See pages 19 and 194.*

● **Bagamoyo** Once the centre of the slave and ivory trade, Bagamoyo was the last stopping point on the continent for caravans of slaves before being shipped off to the Middle East and beyond. *See pages 155.*

● **Kondoa Rock Paintings** A fascinating treasury of prehistoric rock art that decorates the granite faces and overhangs of north-central Tanzania. *See page 215.*

● **Kilwa** Kisiwani Island was once the trading centre of the Swahili Empire. The ruins of the settlement still remain and are considered to be one of the most important Swahili historical sites in East Africa. *See page 239.*

● **Ismilia Stone Age Site** Situated west of Iringa, this ancient site is one of the richest sources of early Stone Age tools in the world. *See page 230.*

ABOVE: Hadza tribespeople. **ABOVE RIGHT:** Kondoa rock paintings reflect the life of the hunter-gatherer. **RIGHT:** young Maasai woman in traditional dress.

8

WATER SPORTS

- **Deep-sea Fishing**
The waters between
Unguja and Pemba
Islands, and around
Mafia Island, offer
some of the best
fishing in the world.
*See pages 133 and
324.*
- **Inland Fishing** Catch
trout in the rivers
around Mount
Kilimanjaro and
Mount Meru, tiger
fish in Kimlombero
and Great Ruaha,
and Nile perch in the
Great Lakes. *See
page 133.*
- **Diving** The best dive
sites are Mnemba
Atoll, Mafia Marine
Park and Misali
Island. *See page 270.*

- **Snorkelling** The
pristine reef at
Chumbe Island
Marine Sanctuary is
home to over 200
species of coral and
provides sanctuary to
over 400 species of
fish. *See page 262.* ●
Canoeing Experience
game viewing by
water while canoeing
through Arusha
National Park. *See
page 309.*
- **Dhow Safaris** Step
back in time on one of
these handcrafted,
wooden sailing boats
around Unguja Island.
See page 309.

SCENERY

- **Kitulo National
Park** A botanist's
paradise, Kitulo hosts
"one of the greatest
floral spectacles in the
world" annually from
November to April.
See page 234
- **Lake Natron** The
area around this soda
lake at the base of the
Ol Donyo Lengai
volcano has a desolate
and almost lunar
beauty. *See page 199.*
- **Mahale Mountains
National Park** A
chain of dramatic

peaks draped in lush
vegetation is the
habitat for over 1,000
chimpanzees. *See
page 210.*
- **Amani Nature
Reserve** This
primeval forest offers
wonderful vistas of
woodland vegetation,
Colobus monkeys and
a magnificent array of
bird life. *See page161.*
- **Empakaai Crater**
The views from the
rim of this volcanic
crater are astounding;
the Rift Valley and
the cones of Lengai
and Karamasi, Lake
Natron, Meru and
Kilimanjaro. *See page
192.*
- **Zanzibar's Beaches**
Dazzling white sand
and impossibly blue
sea: heaven for sun
worshippers.

OFF THE BEATEN TRACK

- **Mkomazi Game
Reserve** Together
with Tsavo National
Park, the reserve is
one of the largest
protected areas in
Africa. *See page 162.*
- **Gombe Stream
National Park**
Gombe is home to the
chimpanzee colony
made famous by
British researcher,
Jane Goodall. *See
page 209.*
- **Katavi National
Park** A huge, almost
untouched wilderness
awaits the few visitors
who make it here. *See
page 210.*

- **Selous
Game
Reserve** A
visit here
offers
exciting
game
viewing in
isolated
surroundings. *See
page 221.*
- **Livingstone
Mountains** This low-
altitude mountain
chain borders Lake
Nyasa in Tanzania's
southwest corner and
is home to the Kisi
people, famous for
their earthenware
pottery. *See page 237.*

ABOVE: fishing off the Zanzibar coast. **ABOVE RIGHT:**
chimps in Gombe Stream. **RIGHT:** Lake Natron.

FESTIVALS

- **Mwaka Kogwa** is a four-day celebration of the Shirazi New Year that takes place at the end of July. The biggest celebrations are held in the southern village of Makunduchi on the island of Unguja. *See page 265.*
- **Sauti za Busara Music Festival** runs over six days in February celebrating the best of East African music and performance with a rich and vibrant mix of styles. *See page 72.*
- **ZIFF Festival** embraces the arts and culture of the Dhow countries. The centrepiece is an international film programme as well as workshops, a literary forum and live performance. *See page 253.*
- **B Connected Festival** is part of the Music May Day festivities, designed to celebrate young artistic talent. Parallel festivals are held all over the world to promote connections between countries. *See page 302.*
- **Bagamoyo Arts Festival** Bagamoyo is Tanzania's arts capital and for five days it buzzes with traditional music, dance, acrobatics, theatre, art and sculpture. *See page 302.*

ABOVE RIGHT: Tanzania's arts festivals are vibrant and colourful.
RIGHT: Mount Meru, a challenge for hikers.

MOUNTAIN CLIMBING AND HIKING

- **Kilimanjaro** This is Africa's highest mountain and one of the highest walkable summits on the planet. *See page 174.*
- **Meru** Africa's fifth-highest peak offers amazing views of Mount Kilimanjaro and the Momela Lakes from the top. *See page 170.*
- **Usambara Mountains** A hiker's paradise, with dozens of treks through the stunning mountainous district of Lushoto. *See page 162.*
- **Udzungwa Mountains** Five trails cover the slopes, offering varying levels of difficulty. *See page 226.*

FAMILY HOLIDAYS

With careful planning, Tanzania can be a wonderful experience for children.

Zanzibar's Beaches The idyllic beaches on the north and east coasts are ideal for children – the soft sand and warm, calm sea will keep them content for hours on end. *See page 266.*

Wet 'n' Wild, Dar es Salaam Located 24 km/13 miles north of Dar, this aquatic park has all the usual stuff that kids love: slides, flumes and pools *See page 153.*

Dar es Salaam Annual Charity Goat Race This event is great fun for all the family. As well as galloping goats, the festivities include fancy dress, live music arts and crafts, and plenty of good food. *See page 307.*

Jozani Forest and Kirk's Red Colobus Monkeys For older children, the chance to see rare and endangered species is a thrilling and educational experience. A guided walk explores the ecosystem of the forest. *See page 263.*

Safari Blue is a trip to the Menai Bay Conservation Area, south of Unguja Island. It includes dhow sailing, dolphin watching and snorkelling. *See page 310.*

Health For advice on health precautions before and during your holiday, *see Travel Tips, page 314 .*

THE STUFF OF LEGENDS

*Tanzania is one of the most complex, romantic, friendly
and scenically stunning countries in Africa*

Tanzania has some of the finest game parks in the world, Africa's highest mountains, superb white-sand beaches and coral reefs and delightfully friendly and hospitable people. Even the names are the stuff of legend: the great Serengeti plains; Lake Victoria, birthplace of the Nile; the towering bulk of Mount Kilimanjaro; the red-clad Maasai cattle herders; the spice islands of Zanzibar and Pemba. Traders sailing the East African coast named the Swahili people and provided the inspiration for the tales of Sinbad the Sailor, while Sultan Said built glamourous baths for his Persian wife, Sherezade. Inland, the great Victorian explorers, Burton, Speke, Livingstone and Stanley, led convoys of porters across the vast terrain. Imagination can run riot here; the reality more than matches the fantasy.

Most tourists come for two things – the wildlife and the beach. Both are extraordinary, but those who take the time to look further will also find a rich culture and history stretching back nearly 4 million years to man's first upright steps.

As a country, Tanzania is new, created only in 1964 by the merging of mainland Tanganyika and offshore Zanzibar. Little more than a century before that, the whole region, plus a chunk of southern Kenya, northern Mozambique and Malawi, belonged to Zanzibar – which in turn was part of the vast Omani Empire. However, only the coast and islands were developed; the Swahili traders never tried to conquer or develop the hinterland, seeing it simply as a vast natural storehouse of their main cash crops – ivory and slaves.

With independence, the balance of power has shifted, purely on weight of numbers: about 39 million on the mainland to just over 1 million on the islands. There is still a great divide between the two main cultures, and the link remains fragile. Economic power remains in the east. Dusty little Dodoma may be the official capital of the country, purely because it is in the centre of the country, but it is largely ignored, even by the politicians, who prefer to hang out with the money in Dar es Salaam.

President Nyerere's post-independence government gave Tanzania a true sense of nationhood: the country has over 120 different tribal groups, each with its own language and traditions, but no one tribe is large enough to dominate the others. Tanzania is striving to develop its tourism industry without destroying the natural beauty on which it is based. The nation is looking forward optimistically; the sense of hope, a rarity in troubled Africa, is enticing.   ❏

PRECEDING PAGES: hippos huddle together in the drying river,
Katavi National Park.
LEFT: sea-kayaking off Tondooni Beach, Pemba.

Decisive Dates

*c.*3.6 million years ago *Australopithecus Afarensis* leaves footprints in the Laetoli mud.

*c.*2 million years ago *Australopithecus Boisei* living at Olduvai Gorge; *Homo habilis* first appears.

*c.*1 million years ago *Homo erectus* appears.

*c.*130,000 years ago The first signs of modern man, *Homo sapiens*.

*c.*10,000 years ago Identifiable Bushman people in central Tanzania create early rock art at Kondoa.

*c.*1000 BC Cushitic tribes begin to move in from the Ethiopian highlands.

THE HISTORIC ERA

*c.*AD 60 Author of the *Periplus of the Erythraean Sea* gives the first recorded account of the East African coast in a guide to Indian Ocean shipping.

*c.*AD 150 In his *Geography,* Ptolemy mentions the island of Menouthesias (Zanzibar).

2nd–4th centuries AD Indian and Persian ships trading along Tanzanian coast. The first Bantu-speaking peoples arrive from West Africa.

7th century AD Islam is brought south by traders and early Arab settlers.

11th century First Nilotic people move south into Tanzania from Egypt and the Sudan.

1107 Earliest known mosque is built at Kizimkazi on Unguja Island, Zanzibar, by Shirazi settlers.

1332 An Arab traveller, Ibn Battuta, visits the prosperous trading port of Kilwa.

15th century There are 30 Swahili city-states along the East African coast, each ruled by a Sultan. Zanzibar is visited by Chinese admiral Cheng Ho.

EUROPEANS ARRIVE

1489 Pedro de Covilhan sails south from Alexandria along the East African coast.

1497–98 Portuguese explorer Vasco da Gama finds the sea route around the Cape of Good Hope to India, visiting Zanzibar on his way home.

1503 The Portuguese capture Unguja Island, the *Mwinyi Mkuu* becomes a subject king and allows Portuguese ships free passage, food and water.

1506 The Portuguese capture Pemba.

1510 When the locals refuse to pay their tribute, the Portuguese, led by Duarte de Lemos, loot and plunder Unguja and Pemba.

1560 The Portuguese build a small chapel and fort on the west coast of Unguja. The fledgling settlement eventually becomes Zanzibar Town.

1591 Sir James Lancaster visits Zanzibar in the British ship the *Edward Bonaventure.*

OMANI RULE

1650 The Omani Arabs sail south to help the *Mwinyi Mkuu* overthrow the Portuguese in Zanzibar.

1668 The Omanis gain control of the whole coast, apart from Mombasa and Stone Town.

1695 The last Portuguese settlers on Pemba leave.

1698 The Omanis drive the Portuguese from Mombasa and Zanzibar. Queen Fatuma, a Portuguese supporter, is taken to Muscat where she spends 12 years in exile while her son, Hassan, takes the title, paying tribute to the Omanis. The Omanis rule through a series of local governors.

18th century The Omanis raid inland Africa for non-Muslim slaves for their plantations and sale overseas. Numbers of slaves rise from about 500 a year to 8,000 a year at the beginning of the 19th century.

Early 19th century The Maasai arrive in Tanzania, taking over the northern highlands.

1827 First clove plantations created in Zanzibar.

1840 Sultan moves the capital of Oman from Muscat to Zanzibar. By now, at least 40,000 slaves a year are being traded along the coast.

1840s Ngoni (Zulu) people arrive from the south, terrorising much of southern Tanzania and disrupting the balanced system of chiefdoms. The first European missionaries, Johann Krapf and Johannes Rebmann, arrive at Mt Kilimanjaro.

1858 Burton and Speke "discover" Lake Tanganyika; Speke finds Lake Victoria; Livingstone reaches Lake Nyasa.
1871 Livingstone and Stanley famously meet.
1873 Slave trade abolished; David Livingstone dies.

THE COLONIAL YEARS

1885 Karl Peters's German East Africa Charter Company (DOAG) forms bogus treaties with several inland tribes and is mandated by the German government to administer the territory.
1890 Britain and Germany carve up Africa. Britain gets Uganda and Malawi; Zanzibar and the coast becomes a British Protectorate; the rest of Tanzania becomes a German colony, German East Africa.
1905–7 The Maji Maji Rebellion in southern Tanzania is crushed. It is the last of several unsuccessful uprisings against the Germans.
November 1914 British and Indian expeditionary force arrives; World War I reaches East Africa.
November 1918 German commander, Paul Lettow-Vorbeck, surrenders undefeated to the British.
1919 Treaty of Versailles gives Rwanda and Burundi to the Belgians and mandates rule of the rest of German East Africa to the British.
1929 The Tanganyika African Association (TAA) marks the start of the nationalist independence campaign.
1939–45 Nearly 100,000 Tanganyikans fight as Allied troops in Europe during World War II.
1947 The UN affirms Tanganyika's status as a Trustee Territory, to be administered by Britain.
1954 The TAA is rebranded as the overtly political Tanganyika African National Union, led by Nyerere.

INDEPENDENCE

9 December 1961 Tanganyika gains full independence, with Julius Nyerere as prime minister.
1962 Tanganyika becomes a republic, with Julius Nyerere the first executive president.
1963 Zanzibar is given independence.
1964 Sultan of Zanzibar is deposed in a bloody revolution; Nyerere and the Zanzibari leader, Karume, sign the Act of Union, creating modern Tanzania from Tanganyika and Zanzibar.
1967 The Arusha Declaration sets out Nyerere's vision of African Socialism, leading to the disastrous policy of *Ujamaa* collective villages.

PRECEDING PAGES: President Nyerere takes the salute while celebrating 10 years of independence.
LEFT: medieval picture of an Arab dhow.
RIGHT: Nyerere becomes the first prime minister of newly independent Tanganyika in 1961.

1977 With Tanzania now among the world's poorest countries, *Ujamaa* is abandoned.
1979 Tanzania invades Uganda and topples the brutal dictator, Idi Amin.
1985 Nyerere resigns. Ali Hassan Mwinyi becomes president.
1995 Mwinyi retires. Benjamin Mkapa becomes president. The World Bank and IMF to help rebuild the economy on a Western, capitalist model.
1998 An Al-Qaeda bomb explodes outside the US Embassy in Dar es Salaam, killing 11 people.
1999 Tanzania is one of the first countries to be awarded Highly Indebted Poor Country (HIPC) status, qualifying for billions of dollars of debt relief.

2003 The new US embassy opens in Dar es Salaam – five years after its bombing.
2005 Violence mars the Zanzibar elections as Karume returns to power amid allegations of vote-rigging. Jakaya Kikwete becomes president.
2005–6 A large part of Tanzania's massive external debt is cancelled.
2007 The Africa-America Institute (AAI) awards Tanzania the Africa National Achievement Award for its progress in education, conservation and business development.
2008 President Kikwete is elected Chairman of the African Union. Prime Minister Lowassa stands down after the Richmond Development energy scandal and is replaced by Mizengo Pinda. ❑

THE EARLIEST INHABITANTS

Tanzania's human history goes back nearly 4 million years to mankind's first steps, and is being pushed back further with every new find

The earliest history of human beings is pieced together from a handful of bones and a few broken tools scattered across thousands of miles, from South Africa to the Gobi Desert, and a biological and social study of our nearest relations, primates such as chimpanzees and gorillas. One new find, a skull or set of fossilised footprints, can rewrite the books. At best, it is an inexact science.

Yet one thing cannot be disputed – as things stand at present, many of the key discoveries on which we base our knowledge of our earliest ancestors have been made by one family, the Leakeys *(see page 23)* in East Africa – in Ethiopia, at Koobi Fora on Kenya's Lake Turkana, and, above all, in the Olduvai Gorge in northern Tanzania *(see page 194)*. Perhaps more than any other place on earth, Olduvai has a claim to be the Garden of Eden, perhaps because it is genuinely the birthplace of mankind, or simply because the gorge has conveniently exposed the ancient fossil beds to modern science.

First steps

It is now commonly accepted that man's earliest roots do lie in Africa, and that we are not descended from apes, but share a common ancestor from some 20 million years ago. The apes evolved into forest dwellers, while humans, who lived more vulnerably in the open, learned first to stand upright, for better vision, thus freeing their hands to use tools. With no natural defences against predators or weapons for hunting, the use of strategy and tools became essential for survival. And as social creatures, the use of language for communication was an inevitable mark of progress.

The earliest proto-humans were first identified in South Africa in 1924. Technically classified as hominid (man-like) primates, these

Australopithecines (literally "southern apes") seem to have been the first to walk upright. The oldest found so far is *A. ramidus*, discovered in Ethiopia in 1995, who lived around 5 million years ago. *A. Anamensis,* found in northern Kenya, and *A. Afarensis,* identified in Ethiopia, seem to have lived at roughly the same time,

around 4¼ to 3 million years ago. They stood 1.2–1.4 metres (3ft 8in–4ft 7in) high and had a chimp-like face. They left no stone tools, but probably used sticks. The oldest known evidence of man in Tanzania is two sets of footprints at Laetoli, near Olduvai, discovered by Mary Leakey in 1976, thought to have been made by *A. Afarensis* around 3.6 million years ago. They have been covered over again for preservation, but there is a cast in the Olduvai Gorge Museum.

The fossil record actually within the 50-km (30-mile) long Olduvai Gorge begins around 2 million years ago with *A. Boisei*, also known as *Zinjanthropus* ("nutcracker" man), first discovered by Mary Leakey in 1959. This was a

LEFT: Olduvai Gorge in northern Tanzania has yielded much information about the origins of human beings.
RIGHT: a 1.8-million-year old *Australopithecine* skull, unearthed by Mary Leakey.

much larger and more robust species, with a bigger brain and teeth as large as a modern gorilla's. However, it also appears to be a line that later died out and is not a direct ancestor of modern man.

The first true humans

In 1964, Louis Leakey, Phillip Tobias and John Napier announced another milestone in evolutionary understanding when they found and named *Homo habilis* ("handy" man). Originally thought to be a true ancestor to modern man, this has now been disproved, with several similar species found at other dig sites.

H. habilis, who lived about 2 million years ago, had a significantly larger brain (around 600 cubic cm /36 cubic in) and was the earliest species known to manufacture stone tools, such as rudimentary choppers, scrapers and chisels. Another million years went by, and finally the first serious contender for our direct ancestors arrived at Olduvai. *Homo erectus* ("upright" man), who survived until some 25,000 years ago, was taller and more upright with a 950-cubic cm (58-cubic in) brain. His face was flatter, with an external nose, and a smaller jaw, making him look far more recognisably human. He used an increasingly sophisticated range of

Human remains are not the only fascinating finds at Olduvai Gorge. Once the site of a freshwater lake, the area was teeming with wildlife, much of it now extinct. The black rhino, hare, guinea fowl and gazelle have been around in a readily identifiable form for the past 4 million years. In the earliest days, they would have been joined by the pygmy giraffe, giant tortoise, three-toed horse and horse-like chalicothere. Two million years ago, the hyena made its first appearance, along with early species of elephant, hippo, lion and the long-horned buffalo. One million years ago, you could have seen giant baboons, a now extinct zebra and an early form of wildebeest.

purpose-built tools, controlled fire, ate meat regularly and had become an expert hunter.

H. erectus is also the first species to be found outside Africa, as far afield as Europe and the Far East, suggesting that by now man was beginning to travel, although he didn't venture beyond warm, open, grassy environments until about 50,000 years ago.

Thinking man

Evolution rarely seems to follow a straight line and for a time, *H. erectus* lived side by side with our nearest ancestor, *Homo sapiens* ("thinking" man), who first appeared on the scene about 130,000 years ago. *H. sapiens* is significantly taller but less bulky than his pre-decessors, with a much larger brain (about 1,300 cubic cm/79 cubic in). His success has led not only to total domination of the plant and animal kingdoms, but the eventual extinction, en route, of all other hominid species. Although we now come in all shapes, sizes and colours, these genetic variations are relatively young, and DNA evidence is pointing ever more strongly to modern man having spread across the planet from Africa.

By the Acheulian era (*c*.100,000–50,000 years ago), man was crafting elegantly designed, highly efficient hand axes, cleavers,

The Bushmen

Throughout sub-Saharan Africa, the oldest surviving aboriginal people belong to the Khoisan (Bushman) races, small, relatively sharp-featured, slightly yellowy-skinned people whose culture and "click" language are thought to date back 40,000 years. Even today, the last few groups live as nomadic hunter-gatherers, providing us with a direct link to the late Stone Age. However, as other groups have dominated, they have been integrated, enslaved, exterminated or simply pushed back to the inhospitable fringes of the continent, such as the southern Namib and Kalahari deserts.

scrapers and knives. Fine collections have been found at Olduvai and Isimila, near Iringa, in central Tanzania *(see page 229)*, an erosion gully that was once the shore of a large fresh-water lake. By 10,000 years ago, these tools had been refined into microliths, small, ultra-efficient flakes of stone, used for spears, arrows or as knife blades inserted into a wooden han-dle. Families lived in rock shelters, their walls frequently decorated with pictures of animals, hunting and dancing.

LEFT: Louis and Mary Leakey excavating Olduvai Gorge in 1961.
ABOVE: reconstruction of *Australopithecine* hunters.

In Tanzania, they are represented by the Hadza people, who live in the remote Lake Eyasi region *(see page 189)*, and the Sandawe, who live in the area around Kondoa *(see page 215)*, famed for its ancient rock art. Other than the click, these groups have virtually no lin-guistic links in common with the southern San, so if they are related, the split seems to have occurred many thousands of years ago.

The Cushites

Over the past 3,000 years, the pace of change has quickened as wave after wave of invaders have arrived and taken root, leading to the com-plex web of people that now inhabit Tanzania.

First to arrive were the Cushitic tribes, who began to drift south from Ethiopia about 3,000 years ago. With them, they brought agriculture. These were more settled people, living in villages and clearing the bush to plant millet and vegetables, while their herds of domestic cattle, sheep and goats competed for grazing with the local wildlife. The balance between man and nature began to shift. The Cushites settled the fertile northern highlands, pushing the nomadic hunter-gatherers south to the lowland plains. Of the true Cushitic people, only the Iraqw (in the area between Ngorongoro and Lake Manyara) remain *(see page 62)*.

The Bantu-speakers

The Bantu people come originally from West Africa. About 2,000 years ago, they began to move south and east across the continent, blocked only by the Sahara to the north. They have meandered across the continent ever since, with the Ngoni fleeing north from Zulu aggression in the 19th century. Even the massive shifts of 20th-century refugees continue the theme.

Physically, the Bantu people have the familiar "African" stocky build and broad features. Linguistically, they are linked from South Africa to Kenya, although there are hundreds of different languages and dialects. Even Swahili, the coastal lingua franca that is Tanzania's national language, is connected. Today, 95 percent of the population speaks a Bantu language.

Like the Cushites, the Bantu-speakers are farmers and cattle herders, living in villages, with a strong family and clan structure. Where they gained superiority over all existing inhabitants was in their ability to work metal. Their iron tools were not only infinitely more effective weapons, but enabled them to cultivate more difficult ground, clearing woodland and invading the less hospitable reaches that had, until now, been the preserve of the hunter-gatherers.

Iron was so important that the ironworkers became the local aristocracy, appointing administrators to rule their web of chiefdoms. They were also traders, with the early long-haul trade in salt and iron gradually being joined by gold, ivory and slaves.

The Nilotic tribes

The last major black group to reach Tanzania was the Nilotic people who came south from Egypt and the Sudan, the first arriving in about the 11th century AD. The Nilotic people fall into three main branches. The "highland" branch, represented by the Datoga people, settled the area around Ngorongoro, before being pushed back to Lake Eyasi. The "river-lake" people (the Luo in Kenya) infiltrated the area around Lake Victoria. Both have been partially assimilated by the local Bantu population, learning to farm and fish as well as herding cattle. The last to arrive, in the early 19th century, were the "plains" people – the Maasai.

The glamourous Maasai, readily recognisable for their tall, slender physique, aristocratic features, trademark red robes and intricate bead jewellery, have resolutely refused to give up the cattle with which they identify so strongly, despising agriculturists. Their continued expansion and their rapidly growing population keep them in dispute with their neighbours today.

The coast

Meanwhile, since the 5th century AD, the coast and islands have seen a very different type of invader, looking for trade not land. Here, where the Bantu met the Arabs and created the Swahili culture, there has been a written history and a sophisticated material culture for more than a thousand years.   ❑

LEFT: extinct animals on display at the Olduvai Gorge.

The Leakeys

L ouis Leakey was born in 1903, in Kenya, the son of English missionaries working with the Kikuyu tribe. Brought up with the local children, he was initiated into the tribe along with his playmates at the age of 13. Always fascinated by early history, he studied anthropology and archaeology at Cambridge in the 1920s, returning to East Africa to conduct digs in several areas. He carried out his first serious excavation of Olduvai Gorge in 1931.

In 1933, he met Mary Nicol, an English scientific illustrator, who was the daughter of a popular landscape painter. Mary had spent much of her childhood in the Dordogne region of France, becoming fascinated by the rich prehistory of the area. She never took a degree, but followed a number of university courses and was, in later life, inundated with honorary degrees. The two married in 1936, after Louis's divorce from his first wife, Frida. Together, they began a serious study of Olduvai, which resulted in a string of discoveries that completely rewrote man's evolutionary history.

Mary's first major discovery was the first fossil skull of the extinct Miocene primate, *Proconsul*, in 1948. In 1959, she discovered *Australopithecus Boisei*, shooting the family to international stardom. In 1964, Louis led the team that found and identified *Homo habilis*.

During World War II, Louis became involved in intelligence work, and in 1945 he became the curator of the Coryndon Museum (now the National Museum of Kenya). In 1947, he organised the first Pan-African Congress of Prehistory. Always a flamboyant man, he was an excellent speaker and fundraiser who used his increasing international fame to generate finance not only for the family's archaeological expeditions, but a series of other ventures, including Jane Goodall and Diane Fossey's acclaimed primate studies and his own anthropological work. During the last years of his life he suffered from increasingly poor health, and died in England in 1972, aged 69.

Meanwhile, Mary, who is generally recognised to have been the better scientist, remained in her husband's shadow, quietly getting on with excavating Olduvai and surrounding archaeological sites. With their three children grown up and her

marriage disintegrating due to Louis's womanising and global wandering, she moved almost full-time to Olduvai in the 1960s, living there for the next 20 years. In 1976, she discovered the 3.6 million-year-old Laetoli footprints.

In 1983, Mary retired to Nairobi where she remained until her death, aged 83, in 1996. However, this was not the end of the story. Their middle son, Richard, led his first fossil-hunting expedition in 1964. Two years later, he started work with the National Museum of Kenya and began a series of excavations at Koobi Fora on Lake Turkana in northern Kenya, where he added significant new species to the early catalogue of hominids.

In 1966, he married an archaeologist, Margaret Cropper, who also began to work in the family "firm". In 1970, after their divorce, he married a primate researcher, Meave Epps. He, like his father, has been distracted by other things, heading the National Museum of Kenya, the Kenya Wildlife Services, and eventually the entire Kenyan Civil Service, before taking a seat in parliament in 1997.

However, Meave has continued to work as a palaeoanthropologist, discovering *Australopithecus Anamensis* in 1995 and *Kenyanthropus platyops* in 2001, the same year their daughter, Louise, completed her PhD in palaeontology. The dynasty looks set to continue. ❏

RIGHT: Louis Leakey, father of a respected archaeological dynasty.

SWAHILI TRADERS

*The arrival of the Arabs created a new world with the introduction
of Islam, high culture and international trade*

There has been trade along the East African coast since at least the 4th century BC. In about AD 60, an anonymous Greek author wrote the *Periplus of the Erythraean Sea*, a guidebook to the Indian Ocean shipping routes. In about AD 150, Ptolemy discussed the region in his *Geography*. Both mention the island of Menouthesias, thought to be Zanzibar.

By the 2nd century AD, Indian and Persian ships were trading regularly along the Tanzanian coast. It was also about this time that the Bantu colonised the region. When the first Arab traders arrived a century later, they were firmly entrenched enough for the region to be named *Zinj el Barr* (Land of the Blacks). However, it was far from being a single country. Instead, the coast and islands were split into numerous small kingdoms. The ruler of Zanzibar was known as the *Mwinyi Mkuu* (Great Lord).

From the 7th century AD onwards, Arab traders brought Islam to the coast. A century later, they began to settle and intermarry with the local people. Legend has it that the first to arrive were the Sultan of Shiraz and his six sons, who fanned out to colonise Mombasa, Pemba and Kilwa. Over the years, the Bantu, Arab and Shirazi languages, customs and blood mingled to form a distinct new people, their name, Swahili, taken from the Arabic word *sahil* (sail).

Close to the wind

Life was governed by the trade winds. The Arab dhows, their design little altered today, would head south on the northeast monsoon between October and February, carrying trade goods such as cloth, beads and porcelain, returning north on the southwest monsoon between March and September, laden with gold, ivory and slaves. It was a pattern that was to continue in a recognisable form, with similar

LEFT: Khalifa bin Haroub (seated), Sultan of Zanzibar from 1911 to 1960.
RIGHT: Swahili girl standing amidst the crumbling colonial buildings of Bagamoyo.

cargoes, right up to the birth of the steamship and the nominal abolition of the slave trade in the late 19th century.

The area and trade flourished, with enough wealth for all and little squabbling by rival power bases. By the 11th century, there were significant cities on Zanzibar and Pemba.

Zanzibar's earliest surviving building is the Kizimkazi Mosque, dated to 1107.

By the end of the 12th century, Kilwa had become a major port, its initial wealth founded on trading gold with the southern city-state of Sofala (in present-day Mozambique). Kilwa and, in later years, Mombasa, dominated the coast, but 13th-century chronicles also talk of Zanzibar as a wealthy city with fine stone houses. By the early 15th century, direct trade with China was sufficiently important for Admiral Cheng Ho to make an official visit, returning home with a giraffe as a present to the Emperor from the Sultan of Malindi. The Chinese trade stopped abruptly in 1443 when the Ming Emperor cut China off from foreign trade, but trade with India and the Middle East remained buoyant. With riches enough for all, life continued to be peaceful, with little squabbling between the various kingdoms.

The equilibrium was rudely shattered in 1498 by the arrival of the Portuguese, with their superior ships and firepower.

Search for the sea route

With the Renaissance in full swing back home, Europe was rich and self-indulgent, looking for ways to spend money. Luxuries, from silk to spices, came from the East and reached Europe

the hard way, by sea to Arabia, then by camel caravan to the Mediterranean. Much of the journey was through territory now held by the hostile Ottoman Empire, and supplies were precarious. There was a fortune waiting for those who could find a shipping route to India.

The Portuguese and Spanish were the first to try. Christopher Columbus sailed west and inadvertently discovered America in 1492. Vasco da Gama was more successful. In 1497 he rounded the Cape of Good Hope and, with the aid of the amenable but short-sighted Sultan of Malindi, who lent him his finest pilot, discovered the secret of the trade winds. On 20 May 1498, da Gama arrived in Calicut, in

southern India, where he remained for three months, causing mayhem. On the way home he stopped in Zanzibar.

Other ships soon followed, and the Portuguese were permitted to build repair bases on both Zanzibar and Pemba. In 1503, however, their ambition got the better of good relations. Ship's captain Rui Lorenço Ravasco attacked Zanzibar, capturing 20 dhows and killing some 35 people. To stop the carnage, the *Mwinyi Mkuu* had to agree to pay tribute, provide fresh food and water and free access to all Portuguese shipping. In 1505 the Portuguese captured Sofala, with its lucrative gold trade, established a military garrison and trading post at Kilwa, and sacked Mombasa. They took over Pemba in 1506, and by 1511 had spread north to grab Muscat and Hormuz on the Gulf of Arabia. By 1525, they controlled the whole of the African coast from the Red Sea to Sofala, while mirror colonies in India ensured their total domination of Indian Ocean shipping routes.

It was not always plain sailing, however, with a constant rumble of protest. In 1510 they brutally suppressed uprisings on both Pemba and Unguja. In 1512 they realised that Kilwa was of no use to them, as they already controlled the gold trade, and withdrew, leaving the city virtually bankrupt. The traders of Kilwa, in search of a way to rebuild their fortunes, looked to the interior for luxury trade goods including ivory, rhino horn and beeswax. Eventually they linked up with the Yao people who were moving north from Mozambique, hungry for iron and cloth. The first of Tanzania's infamous caravan routes was born.

Omani revolution

By the end of the 16th century, the British were also taking a keen interest in the area. In November 1591 the *Edward Bonaventure*, under the command of Sir James Lancaster, sailed into Zanzibar. It was the first of an increasing number of British ships stopping off for supplies and repairs. Relations remained outwardly friendly, but Portugal now faced a potential rival with serious military muscle. In 1593 they built a fort at Chake Chake on Pemba and began work on the imposing Fort Jesus in Mombasa. In the end, however, the British remained on friendly terms. It was the subject Arabs who proved to be the real threat. In 1622 the Omanis succeeded in throwing the

Portuguese out of Hormuz. In 1631 Pemba helped Mombasa regain its independence. In 1650 the Omanis retook Muscat. Two years later, they sailed south to "liberate" Unguja while Pemba attacked pro-Portuguese Kilwa. The Portuguese won that encounter and struggled on, propped up by a series of increasingly feeble alliances, for another 50 years. However, it signalled the beginning of the end.

In 1682 the Christian, pro-Portuguese Queen of Pemba was thrown out by her own people, and the Portuguese were pushed off the island altogether in 1695. The following year the Omanis besieged Mombasa, and in March 1696

A trading nation

The Arabs paid relatively little attention to their new possessions in the early years, while the enfeebled Yarubi dynasty struggled to hang onto power at home. On Zanzibar, the first obvious sign of the new occupation was the immediate building of a formidable fort on the site of the Portuguese church, right next to – and totally dominating – the palace of the *Mwinyi Mkuu*. The next, as it was forbidden to enslave Muslims, was the huge growth of the slave trade to provide workers for the Omani date plantations. Old trading centres such as Kilwa were revived, and new towns, including

attacked Zanzibar, killing hundreds. By 1698 Mombasa had fallen, closely followed by Zanzibar. Portugal's only remaining property on the East Coast was Mozambique.

The revolution was over, but far from helping the coastal states regain their independence, the Queen of Zanzibar was taken to Muscat, where she lived in exile for the next 12 years, while her son was installed as a puppet king. Real power was in the hands of the Omani governor. East Africa had new imperial masters.

LEFT: French impression of an African slave market.
ABOVE: rare photo of chained slaves awaiting sale in 19th-century Zanzibar.

Tanga, Bagamoyo and Dar es Salaam, sprang up along the coast.

In 1744 the Yarubis were finally overthrown by the dynamic trading Bu Said dynasty. Minor members of the family were installed as governors of many regions, including Zanzibar, but elsewhere, local governors had enough autonomy to give them ideas above their station. In 1753 the rival Mazrui family, governors of Mombasa, broke away, declared independence and attacked Zanzibar, which managed to repel the invasion and stay loyal to Oman.

It was nearly 50 years before the Omanis were able to reclaim Mombasa, while Sofala, the traditional gold port, was in the hands of the Portuguese. Zanzibar filled the gap, rapidly becoming the commercial and political hub of the coast. Meanwhile, the Arabs and Swahilis began to venture further inland, taking control of the previously African-operated slave and ivory caravans to maximise profits. New markets opened up when the Dutch and French arrived to buy slaves for their plantations in Indonesia, Mauritius and Réunion.

Although they had banned slavery at home in 1772, the British proved happy to deal with slavers, signing a Treaty of Commerce and Navigation with Oman in 1798 in order to block Napoleon's proposed takeover of the

Middle East. The British East India Company set up shop in Muscat, and from then on the British played an increasingly important role in the administration of the coast.

Sultan Said

One of the longest-living and influential of the Omani rulers, Sultan Said came to the throne in 1804, aged 13, initially reigning with his cousin, Bedr, as regent. In 1806, suspicious that his life was in danger, he acted first, had Bedr killed and assumed full power. From the first, he showed himself to be an astute player of international power politics. In 1822 he took the first official step towards breaking the power of the

slave trade, by signing a British accord abolishing the transport of slaves beyond the so-called Moresby Line. This still allowed traffic between Zanzibar and Oman, but supposedly stopped sales to the rest of the Indian Ocean.

Five years later, Said made his first visit to Zanzibar, where he founded huge clove plantations, not only providing a lucrative new market for slaves, but annexing a considerable portion of Indonesia's spice trade. Meanwhile, French and Dutch slave ships continued to trade freely. The number of slaves passing through Zanzibar each year went up from 3,000 in the 1780s to 13,000 in the 1840s.

Sultan Said signed trade agreements with the United States (1833), Great Britain (1839), France (1844) and the Hanseatic League (1859), and set up diplomatic relations with the United States, France and Great Britain.

In 1837, with British help, Said overthrew the Mazruis and brought Mombasa back into the empire. In December 1840 he moved his capital to Zanzibar, leaving his son, Thuwaini, as Governor of Oman. Within a couple more years, Arab traders had set up trading posts at Tabora on Lake Tanganyika and Buganda on Lake Victoria. They went on to open up routes to Mt Kenya, southern Ethiopia and the Congo.

Said also encouraged the immigration of Asian businessmen, from small shopkeepers to the wealthy financiers who ran his customs and tax departments. From 1840 to 1860 the number of Asians in Zanzibar grew from around 300 to around 5,000. As they were heavily involved in financing, if not running, the slave trade, they also followed the caravan routes, setting up shops and trading posts, and founding many of Tanzania's small towns. Wherever the caravans went, the area came under the nominal control of Zanzibar, creating an empire that covered most of Central Africa, although it was used as a supply depot and never developed.

In 1845 the British forced another supposed reduction in the slave trade on the Sultan. This time the trading limits were set between Lamu and Kilwa, cutting off trade with Oman. The ban was policed by a British naval blockade which proved so effective that over the next 20 years the number of slaves passing though Zanzibar rose to 20,000 a year. ❑

LEFT: Tippu Tip was the most notorious of all the slavers to traffic out of Zanzibar.

Slaves and Spice

T he history of slaving in Africa is at least 2,000 years old. The Romans had black slaves; it is known that the Bantu enslaved the Bushmen as they expanded across the continent during the 1st millennium AD; and the international slave trade with Arabia dates back to the 4th century AD. It is inextricably intertwined with the other luxury goods – ivory, gold and spice.

Slaves were used to work the gold mines in what is now Zimbabwe, while the inland tribes around Lakes Tanganyika and Nyasa, the inland termini of the Tanzanian caravans, set up profitable careers as ivory and people hunters, leading to the virtual extinction of elephants, bitter tribal clashes and the depopulation of some areas. In exchange, the local chiefs received iron, copper, salt, guns, cloth and beads.

The slaves, who were captured in raids or simply sold by their families, were used as porters to carry the ivory to the coast. The vast majority (up to nine out of ten) are thought to have died on the tortuous journey cross-country. Those who survived were sold on as part of the cargo, sent primarily to Arabia and Persia. In total, about 1½ million people are thought to have been sold through the slave markets in Zanzibar, Bagamoyo and Kilwa.

The other highly prized cargoes, including rhino horn, animal pelts, tortoiseshell, ambergris and, of course, ivory, were traded on to China and India, in exchange for spices, silk and porcelain. These in turn were traded in Europe for guns, cloth and beads. The odd East African slave fetched up as a curiosity in a European home, but Zanzibar was never part of the American slave trade, which was almost entirely fuelled by West Africa.

Zanzibar's spice plantations were a by-product of this lucrative triangular trade. Not only did the Arabs realise that they could cut out the long, expensive sea voyages to the Far East, but that those surplus slaves, used as porters on the caravans, could be readily employed on the islands. Clove trees, originally from Indonesia, were smuggled out to Mauritius in the mid-18th century, and were first brought to Zanzibar from Réunion in 1812 by an Arab plantation owner, Saleh bin Haramil al Abray.

In 1822 European opposition to the slave trade began to bite when the Sultan was persuaded by

British Captain Fairfax Moresby to limit the international passage of slaves to Oman, cutting off the lucrative French and Dutch islands. In 1827 Sultan Said annexed al Habray's plantations along with other land and set up 45 commercial clove plantations, decreeing that all Zanzibaris should plant three clove trees for every coconut palm. Failure resulted in confiscation of their land.

In 1873, amidst growing international pressure fuelled by missionaries' heart-rending tales of the slave caravans, the British finally persuaded the Sultan to ban the sale of slaves altogether.

The slave trade simply went underground, and was carried out in remote corners of the island

such as Mangwapani. The practice was eventually only abolished in 1919, when the British took complete control of the island.

Meanwhile, a hurricane effectively wiped out Unguja's plantations in 1872. They never fully recovered, and today around 80 percent of Zanzibar's cloves are grown on Pemba. The trade is in crisis: the government of Zanzibar operates a state monopoly with an artificially low price, and growers can make far more money smuggling cloves to Kenya – a situation that has caused huge political discontent. In 2007, the government announced its intention to gradually privatise the clove trade in an effort to revive what was once the islands' main foreign exchange earner. ❑

RIGHT: spices on sale in modern Zanzibar.

STANLEY IN AFRICA.

IMPERIAL AMBITIONS

*Faced by European military might, the Sultan of Zanzibar could only stand
aside and watch as the British and Germans carved up his empire*

Although Vasco da Gama had opened the floodgates to European involvement on the coast nearly 350 years before, it was not until the 1840s that any Westerners ventured more than a few miles into the East African interior. By then, Europe's second wave of empire building was getting under way.

In 1788 the Africa Association (later merged with the Royal Geographical Society) was founded in Britain, with the aim of exploring and exploiting the continent. In South Africa, the British were dogging the heels of the Boers, as they colonised the interior, finding rich farmland and mineral resources. The businessmen, bedazzled by Portuguese tall tales of gold nuggets as big as fists lying on the ground waiting to be picked up, were beginning to take an interest in the seemingly endless wealth pouring into Arab coffers. The Church, having abolished slavery at home, was beginning to take a serious interest in cutting it off at the roots.

It was the Victorian age of optimism, adventure and, above all, arrogant certainty about the superiority of Western ideas. The mood of the age – as far as Africa was concerned – was neatly summed up by David Livingstone's assertion that he was going out to spread "civilisation, commerce and Christianity". The three Cs went neatly hand in hand into the unknown.

The great explorers

The first European to venture into the Tanzanian hinterland was a German missionary, Johann Krapf, sent out to East Africa by the English Church Missionary Society in 1844. Two years later, he was joined by Johannes Rebmann, who "discovered" Mt Kilimanjaro in 1848. In 1856 the Royal Geographical Society dispatched an official expedition in search of the White Nile, led by the mismatched and quarrelsome Lieutenants Richard Burton and

PRECEDING PAGES: an 1872 German version of the famous meeting between Livingstone and Stanley.
LEFT: Henry Morton Stanley.
RIGHT: Vasco da Gama.

John Hanning Speke. They reached the Lake Tanganyika terminus of the slave caravan route in January 1858. Burton then had to turn back, due to ill health, but Speke continued north to find and name Lake Victoria. He returned in 1860 with a Scottish explorer, James Grant, and the two actually found the source of the Nile.

Proving it was more difficult, and Speke died amidst professional ridicule, led by Burton *(see The Riddle of the Nile, page 204)*.

Meanwhile, the celebrated Scottish explorer Dr David Livingstone was turning his attention to East Africa. He arrived in Zanzibar in January 1866, funded by the British government to solve the question of the source of the Nile once and for all. Convinced it was to be found at Lake Tanganyika, he headed south, eventually finding the source of the Lualaba, which he remained convinced until his dying day would prove to be the Nile. His journeys took him far off the beaten path and kept him totally out of touch for several years. With alarm bells ringing back home, three separate expeditions set out to find him. The first, led by the American journalist Henry Morton Stanley, actually did so in 1871 *(see box below)*. The second, led by Lieutenant Llewellyn Dawson, met Stanley in Bagamoyo in 1872, heard the news and went home. The following year, when Livingstone had failed to appear, a third expedition, led by Lieutenant Verney Lovett Cameron, set out from Zanzibar. By this time, it was too late.

Livingstone had grown weak from dysentery and died on 2 May 1873, in the village of Chitambo (in modern Zambia). Two of his servants, Susi and Chumah, buried his heart under

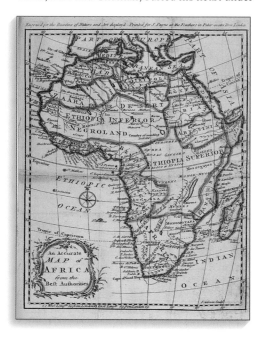

a tree, dried his body and carried it to Zanzibar, a journey of several months. En route, they met Cameron, who decided to keep going, and became the first European to cross Africa from east to west. Livingstone was finally buried in Westminster Abbey on 18 April 1874.

A divided kingdom

At court, life was getting fraught. Sultan Said died at sea in 1856, leaving behind three of his sons to slug it out for control: Thuwaini, governor of Oman, Majid, governor of Zanzibar, and Barghash, who had no real claim to the throne but was with his father when he died.

Barghash's first hasty bid for the throne was abortive, and after much posturing, the kingdom was split, with Thuwaini ruling Oman and Majid becoming the Sultan of Zanzibar. Barghash staged a second unsuccessful coup in 1859 with the help of his sisters Salme *(see page 252)* and Khole, then spent the next two years in exile in India. In 1861 the British Governor General of India, Lord Canning, was asked to mediate in the dispute. He decreed that the two states should be split, with Zanzibar paying an annual tribute to Oman, but existing as a sovereign state with the Sultan at its head. The role of the traditional *Mwinyi Mkuu* was completely sidelined, and the last of the line, Ahmed, died almost unnoticed in 1873.

In 1866 Sultan Thuwaini was murdered, Majid promptly stopped paying tribute and, from then on, Oman withdrew from international affairs, only re-emerging in the 1970s. Zanzibar was left on its own. In 1870 Majid died, and Barghash finally gained the throne he had coveted for so long.

STANLEY AND LIVINGSTONE

In 1866 Livingstone was charged by the Royal Geographical Society with resolving the hotly debated source of the Nile. By 1869, however, the mystery of Livingstone's whereabouts had become more topical than the riddle he had been sent to resolve. The *New York Herald*, hoping for the scoop of the decade, contacted a young reporter named Henry Morton Stanley with a telegram bearing the plain instruction, "Find Livingstone".

Two years later, Stanley arrived at Ujiji where, he later recalled, "The great Arabs, chiefs and respectabilities... disclosed to me the prominent figure of an elderly white man clad in a red flannel blouse, grey trousers, and a blue cloth, gold-banded cap. All around me was the immense crowd, hushed and expectant, and wondering how the scene would develop itself... I could do no more than exercise some restraint and reserve, so I walked up to him, and, doffing my helmet, bowed and said in an inquiring tone: "Dr Livingstone, I presume?" Smiling cordially, he lifted his cap, and answered briefly: "Yes."

Stanley recorded his mission to find Livingstone in his book *How I Found Livingstone*. After Livingstone's death, Stanley decided to continue his research on the Congo and the Nile. His journey to the sources of the Nile, *Through a Dark Continent*, was published in 1878.

The builder king

Barghash was undoubtedly one of Zanzibar's most influential rulers. Zanzibar town had been growing by leaps and bounds, but there was no town planning or even basic sanitation. The place was awash with disease, and the stench could be smelt miles out to sea. Influenced by the British Vice-Consul, Sir John Kirk, who was also a doctor, Barghash built the town a fresh water supply, as well as building his family a series of opulent palaces, based on the luxurious royal residences he had seen in India.

Only two years into his reign, Zanzibar was hit by a freak hurricane that decimated the

above all, there was no real will to crack down on the thriving underground traffic. However, it was the beginning of the end.

In 1875 Barghash was invited on a state visit to Britain to ratify the treaty. Between various engagements, he became fascinated by the wonders of modern technology and, on his return home, set to work to provide his city with paved roads, electric street lighting, telephones, a telegraphic link to Europe, an ice factory and a police force. He also bought a fleet of steamships, which could be used free by pilgrims travelling to Mecca for the haj, as well as for commerce.

clove plantations on Unguja, although those on Pemba remained largely intact. Barghash decided to replant, and the slave trade sprang into overdrive to provide the workers. It was the last straw. In 1873, faced by a total British blockade, he was eventually persuaded by Sir John Kirk to sign a treaty closing the slave market and protecting liberated slaves. It wasn't perfect – the treaty didn't free all slaves; Zanzibaris were still permitted to import slaves from the mainland as domestic workers; and

He also appointed a British officer, William Lloyd Matthews, as Commander-in-Chief of a revamped army, aiming to take greater control of his vast mainland empire. However, he had left it too late. The European empire builders were on their way.

German East Africa

In 1885 a German doctor, Karl Peters, arrived in Zanzibar disguised as a mechanic. From here he headed into the interior, armed with a series of official-looking treaties. As far as the many local chiefs who signed them were concerned, they were merely treaties of "Eternal Friendship". What they actually did was hand their

LEFT: 1763 map of Africa.
ABOVE: John Hanning Speke.
RIGHT: David Livingstone.

lands over, lock, stock and barrel to Dr Peters's Society for German Colonisation. They weren't worth the paper they were written on, and the land technically still belonged to the Sultan, but they were sufficiently impressive for Peters to get a German imperial charter from Bismarck for his Deutsche Ostafrikanische Gesellschaft (the German East Africa Charter Company), with official sanction to colonise and run German East Africa. The speed with which he moved was phenomenal, and the Sultan could only watch as his empire was stripped from him.

In dismay, Barghash turned to his supposed British allies. The ensuing series of high-level

European summits neatly sliced his empire up between the British, Germans and Portuguese, leaving Zanzibar only the islands and a 16-km (10-mile) wide strip along the coast, although Germany took Dar es Salaam. In 1887 the British leased the northern part of the strip (now the Kenya coast), which included Mombasa; the Tanzanian portion was ceded to the Germans.

Barghash died in 1888. The following year, his successor, Khalifa, agreed to abolish slavery within his territories, before dying the following year. In 1890, Sultan Ali bin Said signed a treaty forbidding the sale or purchase of slaves. The same year, with Karl Peters attempting to claim Uganda, the British and Germans held a

final summit, recognising German control over mainland Tanganyika, giving Britain Kenya and Uganda and formalising Zanzibar's position as a British Protectorate. In 1891 Zanzibar got its first constitutional government, with General Sir Lloyd Matthews as First Minister. European control of East Africa was complete, and with the loss of slaving revenues and the mainland ports of Mombasa and Dar es Salaam now coming to the fore, Zanzibar began to slide slowly but inexorably into the atmospheric backwater it remains today.

German occupation

On the mainland, the Germans moved swiftly, efficiently and often harshly to consolidate their new possession. Local resistance began in the Pangani area in 1888 and spread to Tanga and Bagamoyo before it was eventually suppressed.

In May 1889 an Imperial Commissioner, Major Von Wissmann, was appointed with the aim of suppressing the uprisings. In 1891, the German government took over administration of the colony from the charter company.

Administrative towns were set up across the country, connected by a network of roads and railways. German missionaries were encouraged to settle, with their stations becoming a focus for new rural settlements. Local people were moved into less productive areas, allowing the Germans to develop the fertile agricultural land. Those who managed to stay on their lands were forced to grow cash crops, often at the expense of their own foodstuffs.

In 1891 the Germans killed peaceful envoys from a southern Hehe chief, Mkwawa, due to a misunderstanding, sparking off a war that lasted until 1898. In 1892 the Kilimanjaro area erupted into violence, and in 1894 it was the turn of the German garrison at Kilwa to come under fire. Other uprisings were more localised and caused little harm to the Germans, until the devastating Maji Maji Wars of 1905–7.

The Germans had been forcing the Matumbi Highlanders to grow cotton on unsuitable soil. Sparked by a rumour that a potion had been discovered that would turn the white man's bullets to water before they could strike, they rebelled. It was the first uprising to cross tribal boundaries and spread throughout the south. By the end, 100,000 people had died in bitter fighting, and the Germans' scorched-earth policies led to a three-year famine.   ❑

Missionaries

Perhaps the most crucial – and least acknow-ledged – role in the colonisation of Africa was that of the missionaries, who were amongst the earliest and most dedicated European explor-ers. Even the Portuguese and Spanish navigators sailed with priests, the call of the Catholic Mon-archs and the Inquisition ringing in their ears. In Tanzania, Krapf and Rebmann, the first Westerners to venture into the interior, were sent there by the English Church Missionary Society. Livingstone was actually an employee of the London Missionary Society, although he proved to be far more effi-cient as an explorer, leaving others to follow behind to do the conversions. The first German governor used Lutheran and Moravian missionaries to open up the Mbeya region to colonisation.

The relationship between the missionaries, the traders and the administration was always a prag-matic one. The missionaries believed sincerely that the way to God was through Western civilisation and that commerce would help produce the desired result. They also were prepared to use any means to justify the end result.

From the first, they found the slave trade abhor-rent and campaigned rigorously against it. Living-stone's graphic first-hand accounts of conditions on the caravans led to a huge anti-slaving cam-paign back in Britain and the near saint-like status he still enjoys in Tanzania today. However, he and most of his colleagues used Zanzibar as a base and supply depot; they were happy to accept the generous hospitality of the Sultan and travelled long distances under the protection of Arab slavers. Livingstone even stayed in the home of the infa-mous slave trader Tippu Tip.

From the point of view of local tribes, the mis-sionaries were generally welcomed, first as a curiosity, but then for the benefits they brought with them. The chiefs frequently used these edu-cated Westerners as translators, scribes and advis-ers during negotiations. Some actively became involved in trading such items as much sought-after cloth, and were welcomed for the wealth their activities provided. Others were seen as political allies and buffers against intertribal violence.

LEFT: the British destroying the last vestiges of slavery in the 1890s.
RIGHT: 19th-century missionaries set up a bush school on the mainland.

Life was not all plain sailing. Some missions faced a rougher reception, particularly in areas where the traditional priests had great power. One of the forces behind the Maji Maji Rebellion *(see page 36)* was a last-ditch attempt to reassert tra-ditional religious views. Its disastrous outcome led directly to a mass conversion of the south, as the disillusioned people resigned themselves to colo-nial rule, and gratefully took the missionaries' food during the ensuing famine.

The missionaries were most persuasive when the message came from other African converts, such as freed slaves from the model village in Mbweni set up by Universities' Mission in Central

Africa *(see page 260)* or graduates of St Andrew's College, the country's first really good school, also founded by the UMCA, in 1869. Then, people could see the tangible benefits of adopting this foreign God in exchange for food, clothes, education and health care. Above all, they were the only people to give the Africans the type of education necessary to lead a modern life. It was, to a great extent, mission-educated men who created the Tanganyikan civil service, the first nationalist movements and the first independent government. Today, although the coast and islands remain essentially Islamic, the vast majority of mainlanders are Christian, although many hedge their bets, worshipping their traditional gods alongside Christ. ❑

Zeichnung von P. Simm

PINK ON THE MAP

World War I had repercussions far beyond Europe: in East Africa,
dogged German resistance was followed by 40 years of British colonial rule

When the Austrian Archduke Franz Ferdinand was assassinated by Serbian nationalists in Sarajevo, a major European conflict was clearly imminent. Kaiser Wilhelm II immediately affirmed German support for Austria-Hungary, while France and Russia rushed to stand behind the Serbians – but for six weeks Britain was indecisive about entering the war. However, it did not escape the notice of the British War Ministry that Germany's far-flung colonies were essentially isolated from Germany, defended only by small garrisons.

Although the British Empire already comprised nearly one-quarter of the globe, Britain's greed for territory was unabated. The decision to enter the war on the side of Serbia, Russia and France was partly prompted by the expectation of easy pickings that could be assimilated into the British Empire at little cost.

In 1914 German East Africa was surrounded on the map by a pink sea of British colonial territories – Kenya and Uganda to the north, Rhodesia to the south and the islands of Zanzibar and Pemba to the east. To the west lay the Belgian Congo. Germany's forces in East Africa were not only surrounded by Allied troops but also heavily outnumbered.

An inspired Prussian

The German commander, Oberst (Colonel) Paul von Lettow-Vorbeck, had fewer than 4,000 men under his command. They included several hundred German officers and non-commissioned officers, and a handful of European volunteers, but the bulk of his force were *Askari*, native African recruits. If the British expected German East Africa to capitulate without a fight, however, they had reckoned without the skill and daring of Lettow-Vorbeck, the descendant of distinguished Prussian army officers and an inspired commander. Far from

LEFT: a 1915 cartoon shows the British in their surprising struggle to defeat Germany in East Africa.
RIGHT: Colonel Paul von Lettow-Vorbeck, commander of the German forces in East Africa.

capitulating, or even taking a defensive stance, Lettow-Vorbeck launched a series of effective attacks on the railway in Kenya, and even attempted to capture Mombasa, although he was beaten back.

In November 1914 a large British and Indian invasion force landed at Tanga with orders to

"secure German East Africa". Although they heavily outnumbered Lettow-Vorbeck's troops, they were poorly organised and indecisively led. They walked into a German trap, suffered heavy casualties and retreated to their landing craft, leaving behind large quantities of weapons and ammunition which Lettow-Vorbeck gratefully seized. Unsurprisingly, the British government hushed up this humiliating defeat until long after the end of the war.

Encouraged and rearmed, Lettow-Vorbeck proceeded to make raids into Kenya and Rhodesia, attacking and laying waste to a number of forts, 20 trains, several bridges and many miles of British railway line.

In 1916 Britain launched another major attack on German East Africa, led by the Boer General Jan Christian Smuts. But even with 40,000 troops under his command, including reinforcements from the Belgian Congo, Smuts was unable to rout Lettow-Vorbeck's 4,000.

By 1917, with the British attacking from Kenya and Rhodesia, the Belgians from the Congo, and the Portuguese from Mozambique, the overwhelming odds began to tell on the German commander. Running low on ammunition, food and supplies, Lettow-Vorbeck resorted to guerilla warfare. His *Askari* showed him how to live off the land, and how to make

their own clothing and medicines. Munitions were acquired by surprise attacks on Portuguese forts on the Mozambique border. The unique combination of Prussian tactics and discipline and *Askari* knowledge of the African bush made Lettow-Vorbeck's force perhaps the finest guerrilla army in military history.

The aftermath of war

In November 1918 Lettow-Vorbeck was planning a large-scale attack on a British command centre in Rhodesia when news arrived of the Armistice in Europe. He reluctantly surrendered to the British, undefeated after a brilliant four-year campaign. The East African cam-

paign had weakened the country disastrously. Apart from the many thousands of Europeans and Africans killed in the fighting, food production had been disrupted, and famine (especially severe in the Dodoma region) claimed many more lives. The 1919 Treaty of Versailles assigned Germany's former African territories to the new League of Nations. Ruanda-Urundi (now Rwanda and Burundi) was handed to Belgium; the rest of German East Africa was renamed Tanganyika and mandated to Britain. In theory, under the League of Nations mandate, it was to be managed by the British in the interests of the "native inhabitants". In practice, Tanganyika became another country coloured pink on world maps, administered by the Colonial Office in London.

In 1925 Sir Donald Campbell was appointed governor. Adapting the former German policy of "indirect rule", he included tribal leaders in local decision-making, while denying them access to central government. Chiefs were nominated to preside over "native" courts, collect taxes, recruit labour and enforce other colonial edicts. In some areas this worked fairly well. In others, tribal leaders commanded little respect among their "subjects", and were unable or unwilling to perform their duties.

Food boom

The British devoted much energy to organising agriculture, concentrating on export crops, produced both on plantations, owned and managed by Europeans, and on peasant farms. To encourage locals to commit themselves to growing cash crops, the British persuaded village families to move to the plantations by building schools and health facilities near by, and offered technical support and price inducements for cultivation on family land.

These incentives greatly increased the production of export crops – but also led to a dangerous neglect of food production for local use. With most of its fertile land devoted exclusively to cash crops, Tanganyika suffered several serious food shortages during the inter-war years. Although the new plantation communities may have disrupted traditional social systems, they did foster the formation of African associations and community collectives, which later provided the foundation for political organisation. Some groups, such as the Bahaya Union in Bukoba, sprang up in agricultural communities. Others began in towns: the Tanganyika African Association was formed in Dar es Salaam in 1929 and later spread to rural areas. In time, these groups became more political, and joined the campaign for self-government.

Growing prosperity

World War II strengthened the Tanganyikan economy as dramatically as World War I had weakened it. The country saw no fighting, so food production continued unabated – while international food prices soared. An increased world demand for sisal, cotton and pyrethrum (an insecticide made from chrysanthemums) also boosted exports. Tanganyika's revenue from overseas trade grew by 600 percent between 1939 and 1949.

After the war, the League of Nations evolved into the United Nations, and in 1947 Tanganyika's status was affirmed as a UN Trustee Territory. Implicit in the trusteeship was the goal of self-government: observed by visiting UN missions, the British colonial administration was expected to work to that end. The governor, Sir Edward Twining, took steps towards self-rule by making "native" authorities responsible for devising and implementing development plans, with funds available from government agencies. He went further and set up local councils on which Europeans, Asians and Africans would take equal numbers of seats – even in areas with small or non-existent European or Asian populations.

These plans were at best ineffective. More often they provoked serious and even violent opposition, which soon found a collective voice in one organisation: the Tanganyika African National Union (TANU). The Tanganyika African Association (TAA) had begun life as a social organisation, but in the post-war years it became a focus for nationalist feeling. In 1953 a former schoolteacher, Julius Nyerere *(see page 47)*, was elected its president, and immediately redrafted its constitution. In 1954 the TAA became the TANU, an overtly political organisation with the slogan *Uhuru na Umoja* (Freedom and Unity). Nyerere embarked on a vigorous recruitment campaign, and within a

> ### GROUNDNUT SCHEME
>
> The disastrous attempt in 1947 by the British to farm groundnuts in Tanganyika lasted three years and made a loss of £35 million.

year TANU had become the largest political organisation in Tanganyika. It entered candidates for the 1958 elections for the Legislative Council, an advisory body that had always been dominated by non-Africans. Governor Twining continued to reserve two-thirds of the council seats for Europeans and Asians, and voter registration was restricted, yet TANU picked up a large share of the popular vote and won five seats. As tensions mounted, the British government replaced Twining with a new governor, Sir Richard Turnbull, with instructions

to guide Tanganyika towards independence. His first act was to scrap the tripartite (European-Asian-African) council. In the 1960 elections, with no restrictions along ethnic lines, TANU candidates were returned in all but one seat. The message to Britain was clear. Hasty constitutional reform instituted a Government of Internal Affairs, dominated by TANU. By May 1961, the governor had lost all effective power. Tanganyika was effectively self-governing, with Julius Nyerere as its chief minister.

On 9 December, the Union flag was replaced by a new green, black and gold flag. Tanganyika had achieved full independence, without a shot being fired or a single life being lost. ❏

LEFT: farming in the 1950s; a worker carries millet home for processing.
RIGHT: independence celebrations in 1961.

INDEPENDENCE

The post-independence era was dominated by one man, as Julius Nyerere's radical policies rapidly defined the character of the new country

Prime Minister Nyerere had big plans for the newly independent Tanganyika. His first aim was to forge a sense of national unity. To this end, he made Swahili the national language and ordered that it should be taught in all schools. Swahili, already widely spoken among the country's many different ethnic groups, soon became the lingua franca, even in areas where it had not been much used before.

But that was just the beginning. Nyerere planned to make Tanganyika economically self-sufficient. Internally, he was determined that rural Africans should not be oppressed by a rich elite. Internationally, his stance was theoretically non-aligned, yet he expressed support for the disenfranchised Africans in South Africa, Angola and Mozambique. It was not long before his leftist egalitarian ideals caused watchful concern among some Western states.

In December 1962 Tanganyika became a republic within the Commonwealth, and Julius Nyrere smoothly progressed from being prime minister to president.

Revolution in Zanzibar

Although Tanganyika was independent, Zanzibar was still a British Protectorate. In 1962 a constitutional conference in London thrashed out a plan for independence for the island, with the Sultan as head of state. Elections the following year left legislative power in the balance: the predominantly Arab Zanzibar National Party (NZP) held most of the seats in the Legislative Council, although the left-wing Afro-Shirazi Party (ASP), led by Sheikh Abeid Amani Karume, won 54 percent of the popular vote.

When independence arrived in December 1963, tension between the two factions was mounting. Within a month, it erupted into bloody revolution. The Sultan was deposed and driven into exile. Most of the island's Arab population fled or were killed. The NZP was ousted by the revolutionary council of the ASP, with Abeid Karume as prime minister. As old scores were settled, an estimated 12,000 Arabs and 1,000 Africans lost their lives.

Most of the world, including Britain and the US, refused to recognise Karume's left-wing

regime. Feeling vulnerable, he looked to his nearest neighbour. In April 1964, Karume and Julius Nyerere signed an Act of Union between Zanzibar and Tanganyika, creating the United Republic of Tanzania, with Nyerere as president and Karume vice-president.

The Arusha Declaration

Re-elected for a second term in 1965, Nyerere soon fell out with Britain. He loudly condemned what he saw as the tacit British acceptance of the Unilateral Declaration of Independence (UDI) in Rhodesia. In return, Britain suspended economic aid to Tanzania. Increasingly frustrated at Tanzania's slow eco-

LEFT: political rallies can be volatile in Tanzania.
RIGHT: stop and search by revolutionaries during the 1963 Zanzibar Revolution.

nomic growth, Nyerere made radical plans to make his country self-supporting. The 1967 Arusha Declaration outlined his vision of African Socialism, nationalising banks, plantations and major industries, and redistributing individual wealth through selective taxation.

The cornerstone of the new policy was a system of co-operative farming that combined Maoist collectivist principles with the traditional African village. The watchword was *Ujamaa* (familyhood).

> **POLITICAL INTERESTS**
>
> In order to prevent the growth of a wealthy elite, under the Arusha Declaration politicians were forbidden to own more than one house or car, or to receive a second income from any source.

meant that the ambitious production targets were still not being met. From 1973 compulsory resettlement drove literally millions of people into the villages, with dramatic results. By 1977 more than 13 million (about 85 per-cent of the population) had been resettled into more than 8,000 *Ujamaa* villages. The effects were socially invigorating but economically disastrous.

Rural collectivisation gave millions access for the first time to clean water, health care and education, giving Tanzania one

Families were to move voluntarily into large villages in which food and basic commodities would be produced collectively for the community. The state would provide incentives including piped water, electricity, schools and clinics, but the villages would be effectively self-governing.

Collapse of *Ujamaa*

After three years, the number of people working in collectivised villages had grown to only 500,000 − less than 4 percent of the total population. To hurry things along, Nyerere added more incentives in the form of financial and technical assistance. However, a widespread reluctance to move to the collectives

of the highest literacy rates in Africa, but agri-cultural productivity actually dropped. The villages tended to be overcrowded, and the surrounding lands were usually incapable of supporting large populations. Water supplies were often inadequate to support the large herds of cattle and goats, and Tanzania's frequent droughts only exacerbated the situation.

By 1977 it was clear that rural collectivisation had failed to produce a viable economy. Reluctantly, the *Ujamaa* policy was abandoned, and Tanzania was obliged to accept loans from donor countries and the International Monetary Fund (IMF), with all the political and economic strings they entailed.

International relations

Despite its economic problems, Tanzania was not entirely inward-looking during the 1970s. It gave safe haven to African National Congress (ANC) members wanted by South Africa's apartheid government. Nyerere urged neighbouring countries to boycott South African goods and refrain from investing in South African companies. He also gave active support to the independence movements in Angola, Mozambique and Rhodesia, even offering a home and training camps for the freedom fighters. When Zambia closed its border with Rhodesia, the Tanzanians and Chinese built the Tazara railway from Lusaka to Dar es Salaam to give the copper mines access to a port.

Since 1967 Tanzania, Kenya and Uganda had been members of the East African Community (EAC), a free-trade zone which shared some services, including immigration, telecommunications and an airline. But ideological differences between the three members soon emerged, as Tanzania embraced socialism, Kenya adopted a capitalist stance and Uganda was oppressed by the erratic dictator, Idi Amin. Things came to a head in 1977, in a dispute over the funding of the jointly run East African Airways (EAA). Kenya unilaterally seized all the planes, and Tanzania retaliated by closing the border with Kenya. The EAA was effectively dead, and the Tanzania–Kenya border remained closed until 1983, when the assets of the EAA were finally settled.

Relations with Amin's Uganda were even worse. When Tanzania gave refuge to Ugandan dissidents including Milton Obote (the former president) and Yoweri Museveni (the current president), Amin retaliated by invading Tanzania, bombing the lake ports of Bukoba and Musoma and occupying the region east of the Kagera River. Tanzania had virtually no regular army, but a people's militia was assembled, and in January 1979 a hastily trained Tanzanian force of over 20,000 invaded Uganda, routing the disaffected Ugandan army and marching into Kampala. Amin fled into exile, initially to Libya, while an occupying force of 12,000 Tanzanian

> ### THE UNSUNG WAR
> Despite being the only African country ever to win a war, Tanzania does not celebrate the victory over Amin's Uganda, and has erected no monuments.

troops kept the peace in Uganda. Elections in 1980 returned Milton Obote as president for a second time. The Tanzanian troops withdrew the next year. Although the West – and most of Africa – were glad to see the end of Amin's regime, no other country contributed to the war effort or towards the estimated US$500 million war cost.

Political upheaval

In 1975 a law was passed making TANU the national political party. Tanzania was now officially a one-party state – although Zanzibar still

had its own semi-autonomous government, controlled by the Afro-Shirazi Party. A pragmatic merger took place in 1977, TANU and the ASP combining to form Chama Cha Mapinduzi (CCM), the Party of the Revolution.

Nyerere was duly re-elected president in 1980. But by now the failure of *Ujamaa*, the collapse of the EAC and the war against Uganda had brought the economy to its knees. Poverty and corruption were rife; the infrastructure was crumbling, and improvements in education and health care were being eroded.

Western governments, the World Bank and the IMF were all prepared to help – but only if Tanzania undertook major social and economic

LEFT: most people were forcibly rehoused in a push to make the *Ujamaa* villages successful.
RIGHT: any means of transport available was used to take Tanzania's scratch army across to Uganda.

reforms, including liberalisation and privatisation. Julius Nyerere refused to compromise his socialist principles, but in 1985 he relinquished the presidency – the first post-independence African president to do so voluntarily.

Economic about-turn

The new president, Zanzibari Ali Hassan Mwinyi, spent the next 10 years trying to revive Tanzania's economy with IMF-sanctioned austerity measures: spending cuts, privatisation, encouraging foreign investment and anti-corruption policies.

> **OPEN FRONTIERS**
>
> In 1998 an East African passport was introduced, allowing citizens of Tanzania, Kenya and Uganda to cross borders freely.

The results were not instantaneous, but since that time Tanzania has maintained an annual growth rate of 5–6 percent. Mwinyi could not entirely eradicate corruption, although a purge of the civil service was remarkably effective. One of his notable achievements was the abolition of the one-party state.

Parliamentary opposition

In 1995 Mwinyi retired after two terms in office, and the first multi-party election in decades took place. The CCM won 186 of the 232 National Assembly seats, and Benjamin Mkapa became president. The major opposition party, the Civic United Front (CUF), accused the CCM of vote-rig-

ging in Zanzibar – and international observers agreed that the electoral process was badly flawed. Having failed to get a rerun of the election, the CUF boycotted the National Assembly. Tension between the government and the opposition continued until 1998, when the CUF ended its three-year boycott of parliament and reached an uneasy truce with the CCM.

In August 1998, international terrorism reached Tanzania when an Al-Qaeda-backed bomb exploded outside the US Embassy in Dar es Salaam, killing 11 people. Many more died in a similar explosion in Nairobi.

Meanwhile, President Mkapa was forced to address a number of difficult domestic problems, particularly the country's debt-saddled economy (most of the debt was cancelled by the US in 2002). In an effort to balance the budget and increase state revenue, he downsized the civil service and brought in stringent laws against tax evasion. He also cracked down on gold and gemstone smuggling in Dar es Salaam and Magauzo, which had for years diverted a significant amount of government revenue.

With varying degrees of success, Mkapa strived to attract international investment and revive trade relations in the former East African Community, with a long-term aim to forge an EU-style common market and common currency.

In 2005 Jakaya Kikwete was elected as president of Tanzania. In Zanzibar, a repeat of the previous election's violence and allegations of corruption and vote-rigging saw Karume re-elected for what will be his final term by law.

Kikwete's government has received praise, both at home and abroad, for addressing issues of corruption, social justice and education, and for encouraging new investment. Kikwete recently launched a national campaign on voluntary HIV/Aids testing; he and his wife were the first to be tested in Dar es Salaam.

However, Tanzania remains one of the poorest countries in the world, and the tension in Zanzibar has yet to be resolved after almost two years of talks ended in stalemate. Pressure is on Kikwete to step in and find a solution to the impasse using his experience in power-sharing negotiations after the Kenyan election riots. ❏

LEFT: Jakaya Kikwete, president of Tanzania.

President Nyerere

Julius Nyerere, known to the Tanzanians as Father of the Nation and *Mwalimu* (Teacher), is regarded with an almost reverent respect for his success in freeing his people from ethnic and civil conflict. Yet he also attracts resentment for relocating 85 percent of the population in an attempt to develop a new brand of socialism, and for his responsibility in creating many of Tanzania's economic difficulties.

He was born in March 1922 in Butiama, the son of a Zanaki chief. From the start he showed a remarkable intellect. He shone at primary school went onto Tanganyika's only secondary school and Makerere University in Uganda, from where he graduated with a teaching degree. This was followed by three years studying economics and history at the University of Edinburgh in Scotland.

Although Nyerere began his working life as a teacher, he soon turned into a full-time politician. In 1953 he became the president of the Tanganyikan Africa Association which, under his leadership, gradually evolved into the Tanganyika African National Union (TANU), with the slogan "Freedom and Unity". By 1957 TANU was the largest political organisation in the country, and Nyerere was the voice of Tanganyika's bid for independence from colonial government.

He became chief minister in 1960 and guided his country to independence on 9 December 1961.

Passionate about eradicating the structure of colonial rule, Nyerere wanted to introduce a sense of national identity and pride in the emerging nation and a fairer system of sharing for his people. He made Swahili the national language, even going so far as to have Shakespeare translated. He also persuaded neighbouring Zanzibar to unite with Tanganyika, creating the country of Tanzania.

In 1965 Nyerere was officially acknowledged as head of a one-party state, and started to introduce a form of communism that was basically Chinese but embraced the African ethos of hard work, equality and *Ujamaa*, which means familyhood.

Two years later, his Arusha Declaration was designed to create a nation which would feed and educate itself and offer equality to all. His idea was to establish large *Ujamaa* villages which would combine productivity and the distribution of the nation's resources, replacing the many small, rural villages which were too scattered to allow a proper supply of water, education and health services.

In the end, 85 percent of the people were moved compulsorily, causing huge resentment. Education, health care and access to water did improve, but the villages were ultimately unable to produce enough food to feed themselves, and rural poverty became rife.

On the international scene, he was regarded as a political mover and shaker. He was one of the founders of African nationalism and one of the continent's greatest statesmen. A leading supporter of the freedom struggle in Zimbabwe and anti-apartheid movements in South Africa, he was

instrumental in overthrowing Idi Amin's stranglehold on Uganda, and campaigned for developing world debt relief. He strongly supported unity and cooperation between the regions, consistently maintaining that he would like to see Tanzania and its neighbours work together to form an East Africa Federation.

By 1985, however, Tanzania's economy was in dire straits. Nyerere took responsibility for his actions, telling his people, "I failed. Let's admit it." He resigned in favour of Ali Hassan Mwinyi, but continued to exercise political influence in Tanzania and across Africa until 1990, when he retired back to the place of his birth with his wife and seven children. He died in October 1999. ❑

RIGHT: Julius Nyerere, first president of Tanzania.

TANZANIA TODAY

Tanzania may be a tourist's paradise, but its people are
held back by poverty, disease and a lack of education

Tanzania is being hailed by foreign donors and investors alike as a bastion of peace and stability in East Africa and a nation full of promise and hope. High accolades indeed, but they don't erase the stark facts that Tanzania faces a great many problems.

In 2005 President Kikwete was elected as Mkapa's successor, with the Chama Cha Mapinduzi (CCM) taking the majority of seats in the National Assembly. While there were the usual cries of foul play from the Civic United Front (CUF), they eventually recognised Jakaya Kikwete as president after their requests for a new vote in several seats were refused.

Things weren't quite so calm during Zanzibar's election, and there were outbreaks of violence during voter registration. The heavy military presence during and immediately after the elections all but stifled any protests attempted by CUF supporters, who refuted its fairness. Several election observers agreed.

The poverty line

Meanwhile, other matters demand urgent attention. Tanzania is one of the poorest countries in the world, with a per capita GNP of US$350 per year. Over half of the population live below the internationally recognised poverty line of US$1 per day. About 30 percent of the population living in abject poverty. It is also highly dependent on agriculture, which provides 50 percent of the GDP and employs over 80 percent of the workforce. The majority of Tanzania's poor live in rural areas and are dependent on subsistence farming as a means of income.

Although poverty has in the past been a largely rural phenomenon, the number of urban poor is growing, as is evident from the mushrooming slums on the outskirts of the country's commercial capital, Dar es Salaam. According to the United Nations Development Programme (UNDP), Tanzania's ranking in terms of human

PRECEDING PAGES: painting an advert in Mwanza.
LEFT: Tanzania's young people face a difficult future.
RIGHT: voting in a general election.

development achievements has been slipping in recent years, with the majority of the poor lacking the necessary skills to exploit any new economic opportunities and increase their standard of living. They are also hampered by the lack of access to social services, especially in rural areas – only about 60 percent of Tanzani-

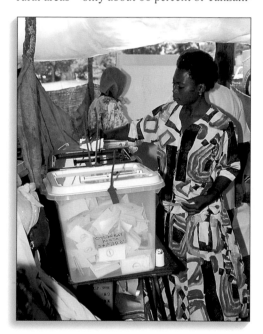

ans have access to safe drinking water. Preventable diseases such as malaria, tuberculosis, diarrhoea and waterborne infections continue to kill in large numbers.

Aids

The other major killer is Aids. Official figures indicate that around 1.6 million people are living with HIV/Aids in Tanzania (the real figure may be far higher). Since 2005 there has been a massive multi-sectorial response to the epidemic using donor and public sector funding. In 2007 President Kikwete inaugurated an HIV testing campaign by being publicly tested himself. In addition, 400,000 people have been provided with antiretroviral treatment and another 1.2 million have been enrolled in specialist healthcare.

Despite this campaign, Aids prevalence remains at a fairly constant level, and the disease is having a devastating effect. Reliable figures are hard to find but it is reckoned that the epidemic has left nearly 1 million children orphaned and vulnerable, and this figure is only likely to increase. Every year thousands more young people join the ranks of Dar es Salaam's street children.

However, evidence of the thriving economy is scarcely visible in rural areas, most of which still suffer from few or substandard facilities. Likewise, the expansion in employment opportunities is clearly helping those who already have an education and vocational skills. The poorest of poor have received few, if any, of the benefits. Their lot has not improved with economic growth and may even have got worse. Much of the new investment comes from abroad; large-

> **POVERTY IN PARADISE**
>
> Tanzania is one of the poorest countries in the world, with a per capita GNP of US$350 per year. Over half the population live on less than US$1 a day, and nearly 30 percent of people live in abject poverty.

Debt relief

Since 2000, Tanzania has qualified for total debt relief from the World Bank, the International Monetary Fund and the African Development Bank. As a result, the official economic figures look good. From 2001 to 2006 Tanzania's GDP growth rate increased while inflation fell. Foreign Direct Investment (FDI) was also on the rise and financed about 20 percent of Tanzania's investment. Between 2004 and 2005 per capita income increased by nearly 13 percent. These are impressive figures, and economic growth is clearly visible in large cities such as Dar es Salaam, where infrastructure and facilities are slowly improving.

scale developers are able to undercut local small businesses. The poorest sections of society are losing their traditional livelihoods while profits leave the country.

Mining

Tanzania has great mining wealth, with gold and tanzanite leading the mineral deposits. It also has the third-largest gold mine in Africa. Its largest mine, situated in Bulyanhulu, is Canadian-owned, and after an initial investment of US$280 million the mine produces about 400,000 ounces of gold a year. This has taken Tanzania's annual gold output to more than 1 million ounces a year. Tax revenues collected from gold mining in 2005 were over US$200 million, and with the operations of the mine in Bulyanhulu, the figure is set to rise. In 2004/2005 non-traditional exports fetched a record US$1.11 billion of the US$1.43 billion total export earnings, with minerals, dominated by gold, accounting for 60 percent of the income.

This highly impressive dollar figure may point to Tanzania's rapidly growing economy, but what has this accolade of "third-largest gold producer in Africa" done for the people of Bulyanhulu? In 1996 controversy soon followed the newly acquired Canadian mine,

so much support that it prompted the World Bank to investigate the allegations. (In 2007, some of these investigations had still not been completed.) Meanwhile, the small-scale local miners in Bulyanhulu suddenly had their livelihood taken from them. For them, the boost the new mine gave to the Tanzanian economy meant absolutely nothing but bad news. The miners lost their jobs, local unemployment soared and so did the poverty level.

Human rights groups have argued that mining companies are morally obliged to share part of their handsome profits with the local miners they dislodge from the land, and with the

with allegations from a local human rights organisation of crimes against the local artisan miners who occupied the land before it was sold to the company. The allegations ranged far and wide, the most damning being an accusation of burying up to 60 miners alive as the land was cleared of artisan miners following its sale to the Canadian firm. Both the owners of the mine and the Tanzanian government vehemently denied the allegations.

However, the human rights group garnered

local communities in which the mines are situated. Local MPs have added their voices to these demands, asking that mining companies adopt a system of profit redistribution similar to that used by Tanzania's national parks. Parks pay a quarter of their revenue to the local population as a measure of compensation for restrictions on land use. President Mkapa called on large-scale miners to "foster constructive cooperation and partnership with small-scale miners". However, there was no compulsion for them to do so and relations do not appear to have improved: in 2007, about 1,000 miners on strike over pay, health and risk allowances were fired by the mining corporation.

LEFT: colourful street scene in downtown Dar es Salaam.
ABOVE: children gather for a Qur'an class.

Tanzanite

In the region of Mererani, not far from Bulyanhulu, still in northern Tanzania, are the tanzanite mines. Tanzanite, a purple-blue semi-precious stone found only in Tanzania *(see page 78)*, is exported mainly to the US, Japan and Europe. The US alone buys 80 percent of production. The porous nature of the Tanzanian mining industry has resulted in untold lost revenues. In 2007 the Tanzanian government received an estimated US$20 million in tanzanite sales, yet the US alone recorded sales of over US$500 million. Much of the difference was in smuggled gems.

Uncollected revenue is not the only problem to dog the industry. In 2001, a Wall Street article alleged a link between tanzanite and Osama bin Laden's Al-Qaeda network. The article claimed that sales from the gem were used to finance the network. America, still reeling from September 11, 2001, immediately slapped a ban on the gem. An unlikely source of support for tanzanite came from the Americans themselves when a study, funded by the United States Agency for International Development (USAID), said they could find no link between the gem and al-Qaeda or any other terrorist organisation. The ban was lifted and it should have been business as usual.

However, tensions were already simmering between local artisan miners and the largest mining company of tanzanite in Tanzania, a South African-owned firm. There was a series of riots and sometimes bloody clashes.

It is a familiar story: the influx of foreign companies into Tanzania's mining industry may have been good for the economy, but it does little to improve the standard of living for the local miners. If anything it pushes them further into poverty with unfair competition. The whole basis of the industry works against them. Attractive tax exemptions from the government to the foreign firms, their sophisticated methods of mining, their purchase of land that the miners had traditionally been using are all to the advantage of the foreigners.

Power and corruption

Energy generation is one of Tanzania's recurring problems. In times of low rainfall, the low water levels in the reservoirs supplying the hydro-electric power stations cause frequent power cuts. To combat this problem, the Tanzanian government contracted US-owned Richmond Development to provide emergency power generation in times of drought. A huge scandal erupted in late 2007 when it was revealed that, despite being paid a whopping US$100,000 a day by the government, Richmond Development provided no power at all before the water levels rose. The then prime minister Edward Lowassa advised the government to extend the contract despite the fact that he knew Richmond Development had sold its contract to another company. As a result, President Kikwete sacked Lowassa and reshuffled the entire cabinet in an attempt to stamp out the corruption tainting his government.

Education

Universal free primary school education was first introduced by President Nyerere in the 1970s but harsh economic reality soon put an end to this vision. The standard of education fell, and the transition rate from primary to secondary school dropped. Eventually the policy had to be abandoned.

Under Mkapa's presidency (1995–2005), reforms of the education system achieved only patchy results but more progress has been made in recent years. In 2006, primary enrolment rates were up to 96 percent. The pass rate of pupils completing primary education also significantly improved from a dismal 22 percent in 2000 to a more respectable 62 percent in 2006. This has been achieved through a wide range of measures including better curriculum content and enhanced teacher training, as well as greater community participation in managing school affairs.

While slightly improved, secondary enrolment statistics are less impressive. However, 1,500 new secondary schools have been built, and a new 40,000-student science

TOURISM IN AFRICA

President Kikwete said in 2008 that Africa must develop its infrastructure if it is to unite as a continent and benefit from the boom in global tourism.

by the government for students in education to get more teachers into classrooms quickly. As momentum gathers from this long overdue expansion of the education system, a clearly defined strategy will be necessary to maintain quality and to give more of Tanzania's young people the opportunity to fulfil their potential.

The future

Through the implementation of solid policy reform over the last 15 years, Tanzania has made an impressive turn-around in terms of

university is under construction in Dodoma. These developments have attracted significant amounts of aid from donor nations such as the US and the UK.

The massive demand for more education, whilst encouraging, poses significant challenges. Even though the pupil-to-books ratio has significantly improved, it is still far below adequate levels. And the huge increase in student applications far outstrips the supply of teachers. Full scholarships have been offered

LEFT: dock workers in Dar es Salaam.
ABOVE: a government Aids awareness poster in the battle against rising rates of HIV.

economic and social change. Yet there is no room for complacency: much needs to be done before these changes translate into tangible improvements in the quality of life for most of its people. President Kikwete has acknowledged that tourism has a crucial role to play, although it needs careful monitoring to ensure that it brings real and sustainable benefits to local communities and their environment.

With the immense challenges that the Aids epidemic brings and the dire need for large capital investment into infrastructure and public amenities, Tanzania must remain steadfast and accountable to achieve well rounded sustainable development. ❑

PEOPLE

*In an African success story, Tanzania's many different tribes and cultures
have developed a harmonious and hospitable way of life*

A pair of Maasai warriors draped in red-checked togas, metal-tipped wooden spears clutched protectively to their sides, stroll loose and languid down Arusha's Sokoine Avenue, animatedly conversing in their guttural Maa mother tongue. An annoying bleeping sequence forms a half-recognisable tune as one of the warriors fumbles deep in his toga to pull out a compact, squeaky new plastic box. He lifts the gadget to his ear, presses a button and barks a colloquial Kiswahili greeting – "Mambo!" – then, on recognising his caller, switches over to Tanzania's second national language, English: "Me? Ah, I'm well, very well, thank you!"

It is such mildly surreal encounters that subvert Western preconceptions about African modernity and traditionalism to reveal Tanzania's true human essence. Superficially, the country can often come across as a mass of seemingly irreconcilable contradictions. This proudly unified nation is comprised of more tribes than any other African country, a land where Islam and Christianity coexist alongside ancient animist cultures, while its people are steeped in conservatism yet eager to embrace the latest technology.

Tanzania's "safari capital" of Arusha must surely have the highest pro rata concentration of four-wheel drives, internet cafés and satellite televisions in equatorial Africa. And yet, only 20 km (12 miles) out of town, the road to the country's renowned northern game reserves speeds through open plains where traditionally attired pastoralists cling defiantly to a lifestyle little changed from that of their forefathers.

The peopling of Tanzania

Where between these two opposite worlds does one locate the real Tanzania? Tanzania's modern population – just over 40 million – consists

---

PRECEDING PAGES: Maasai warriors; Stone Town street scene, Zanzibar.
LEFT: woman in Kilwa Kivinje, south coast.
RIGHT: Iraqw marriage skirts can be turned upside-down and held taut, and can be used as a drum.

of at least 120 tribes (a word used widely within Tanzania) of diverse origin. The country's oldest inhabitants, though numerically insignificant today, are the Hadza of Lake Eyasi *(see page 189)*, the sole cultural heirs to the nomadic hunter-gatherers who once roamed much of the Tanzanian interior, leaving behind a rich artis-

tic legacy in the form of numerous rock paintings scattered through the hills of Kondoa district. In about 1000 BC, the first agriculturists arrived in the region, Cushitic speakers represented today by the Iraqw, who live in the highlands around Karatu and Mbulu, and claim distant Arabian ancestry.

The pivotal event in the populating of modern Tanzania was the arrival, some 2,000 years ago, of Iron Age Bantu-speaking agriculturists from West Africa. In most parts of the region, the Stone Age hunter-gatherers were displaced by, or absorbed into, these more technologically advanced migrant societies. Today, the country's most populous tribes, such as the

Sukuma of Lake Victoria, the Nyamwezi of Tabora, the Chagga of Kilimanjaro and the Hehe of Iringa, all speak languages of the Bantu family. While most such tribes have ancient roots within Tanzania, others are more recent arrivals – the Ngoni, for instance, are refugees from South Africa who settled around Songea in the 1850s.

For visitors, the most charismatic of Tanzania's people are its traditional pastoralists, in particular the Maasai of the northern Rift Valley and Ngorongoro Highlands, who seem to epitomise the soul of ancient Africa. Ironically, the Maasai are among the most recent arrivals

to Tanzania, having crossed the modern-day border with Kenya in the early 19th century, at the end of an all-conquering southward migration through the Rift Valley. The Datoga of the central Rift Valley, like their Maasai neighbours, are dedicated cattle herders who speak a Nilotic tongue and migrated south from western Ethiopia, but they were resident in Tanzania hundreds of years before the Maasai.

The coastal people

The coast, like the interior, has been subject to numerous intra-African and local population movements over the centuries. But nearly

THE IRAQW

The Iraqw, who inhabit fertile areas of Arusha province, are the only true Cushitic tribe left in Tanzania, with an estimated population of around 500,000–600,000. Their houses are built cave-style on hillsides, with thick wooden frameworks covered in mud planted with grass. The home is large and open, with the men sleeping on one side and women and children on the other. Society is run by a series of councils for youths, women, men and elders, in which the men's council has the final say. Although regarded as equal, all tribesmembers are divided into black, red and white, according to the tone of their skin, with paler skin equating to greater physical beauty.

1,500 years of trade links with Arabia and Asia have also left their mark on the coastal Swahili. Over the centuries, merchants from all over the world settled in East Africa's trade ports and intermarried with the indigenous African inhabitants. Kiswahili, the main coastal tongue, is a virtual linguistic mirror of this maritime history and trade: a Bantu language whose vocabulary is liberally spiced with words derived from Arabic and Hindi, and more recently Portuguese, German and English.

Having spread along the coast as the lingua franca of medieval commerce, Kiswahili played a similar role along the 19th-century slave caravan routes into the interior. Today, it is the first official language of Tanzania, spoken as a first or second language by around 95 percent of the populace and a similar proportion of Kenyans, and it still performs its traditional role as a trade language in bordering parts of Mozambique, Malawi, Zambia, Burundi, Rwanda and Uganda.

Religion

The most significant Arab implant in Tanzanian culture has been religious. Numerous ruined medieval mosques, some dating back to the 12th century, line the country's coastline, while its modern ports are uniformly possessed of a

are likely to express surprise, if not outright shock, at any visitor who professes to the unfamiliar concept of atheism.

In keeping with this atmosphere of religious tolerance, many practising Muslims or Christians in Tanzania adhere concurrently to apparently conflicting animist beliefs. Traditional healers and spiritualists are frequently consulted in times of ill heath or misfortune; in the Islamic port of Tanga, the football team routinely prepares for a crunch match by leaving a sacrifice to the powerful spirits that inhabit the nearby Amboni Caves.

Exotic religions hold little sway among the

deep and pervasive Islamic mood. In the 19th century, Islam followed Kiswahili along the caravan routes, taking root in important trade depots such as Ujiji and Tabora.

In general, however, the interior is essentially Christian in feel, the result of various missions established throughout the interior from the late 19th century onwards. Tanzanians of Islamic and Christian persuasion generally live side by side without noticeable rancour, though both

LEFT: bringing home the herds at dusk, near Tarangire National Park.
ABOVE: American Maryknoll priest at the Easter Sunday service, Issenye.

pastoralists of the Rift Valley. The Maasai traditionally worship a dualistic deity, Engai, who resides in the tempestuous volcanic crater of Ol Doinyo Lengai near the Kenyan border *(see page 199)*. Mount Hanang, in the central Rift Valley *(see page 217)*, is the home of Aseeta, the God of the Datoga, who has little influence over earthly affairs, but monitors them through his all-seeing eye, the sun.

Of all Tanzania's people, the Barabaig, a subgroup of the Datoga, have proved least mutable to evangelical persuasion – 99 percent of them adhere exclusively to their traditional beliefs.

MAASAI COWS

The Maasai believe that every cow in the world is theirs by godly ordain, and recognise cattle as the only real measure of material wealth. Since cows have no value once dead, they are slaughtered for eating only on special occasions. The traditional Maasai diet is a mouth-watering blend of fermented cow's blood and milk, although this is no longer consumed regularly. The Maasai view tribes who hunt, fish or eat vegetables with absolute contempt, and their proprietorial claim on every last breathing cow has often made life difficult for neighbouring pastoralists. Such attitudes have mellowed recently, but intertribal cattle raids still occur occasionally on territorial boundaries.

Food

For most Africans, the wide selection and easy availability of foodstuffs in Western societies is difficult to comprehend. In rural Tanzania, choice of food more or less amounts to whatever one can cultivate or lay one's hands on – indeed, one of the first questions rural Tanzanians like to ask foreigners is what crops they grow in London, Paris, New York, or from wherever the visitor hails. Thus, in coastal areas and around lakes, the main source of protein is fish, while people living away from water generally herd cattle and goats, and keep poultry.

In most parts of Tanzania, the main staple is *ugali*, a stiff porridge made from maize meal. Served in a large solid heap, the *ugali* is customarily hand-rolled into mouth-sized balls by the diner, then dunked into a bland, watery stew of meat, fish or beans, often accompanied by a local vegetable very similar to spinach. Until the European introduction of maize, the staple would have been millet, still regarded by the Iraqw as an "oath" plant, used when making solemn vows from marriage to curses.

In moister and more fertile areas – parts of the Lake Victoria hinterland, for instance, and the slopes of Kilimanjaro – *ugali* is replaced by *batoke*, a dish made with cooked plantains. A popular snack throughout Tanzania, the local equivalent of a quick burger, is *chipsi mayai* (literally chips eggs), basically an omelette made with thick potato chips.

More interesting to most foreign palates is traditional Swahili food. Fish and shellfish feature strongly, and rice becomes the main carbohydrate. Thanks to centuries of Arabic, Asian and Portuguese trade and influence, it is distinguished by the liberal use of spice (in particular peri-peri) and coconut milk.

Swahili cooking is also permeated with the culinary influence of the many Indians who are settled along the coast, and in many instances the line between traditional Swahili and Indian dishes is blurred. Indians have also settled all over the Tanzanian interior, and tourists in need of a decent meal should always consider seeking out Indian eateries in smaller towns where there is not a huge choice of restaurants.

The British colonial influence is discernible less perhaps in the "steak, chips and one vegetable" style of menu favoured by many midrange hotels than in the breakfast fry-ups offered by the majority of lodges.

Traditional medicine

Many Tanzanians depend on their surroundings as a source not only of food, but also of *dawa* (medicine). To outsiders, the relationship between Western and traditional medicine can be difficult to comprehend, especially as it varies regionally and from one individual to the next.

But while Westernised clinics are increasingly visited to treat serious diseases such as malaria and Aids, traditional healers still play an important role, particularly in rural society,

> **GRUBBING FOR FOOD**
>
> Even insects are not safe from the cooking pot. Termites and flying ants are popular, eaten raw or fried in butter. Other edible insects include locusts, grasshoppers, mopane worms and lake flies.

A moderate nation

Within East Africa, Tanzanians are regarded as egalitarian and peaceful people, somewhat fuddy-duddy, and not publicly demonstrative, but imbued with a deeply ingrained sense of tolerance, justice and respect for other cultures. Without wishing to reinforce national stereotypes, few outsiders who have spent significant time here would strongly disagree with these sentiments. Tanzania's transition to independence occurred with a unique absence of

where many ailments are alleviated using medicine made from herbs, bark and other organic materials. In some areas, for instance, the bark of the striking sausage tree is boiled in water to cure cramps, while the stem is used to treat pneumonia. The bark of the whistling thorn – a common tree in the Serengeti – is said to alleviate diarrhoea, and throughout East Africa, frayed ebony stems serve as handy organic toothbrushes for many people.

LEFT: Maasai man and boy in their traditional red robes.
ABOVE: cooking up a barbecue in Stone Town, Zanzibar.

bloodshed, as did its subsequent evolution from benign dictatorship to full democracy. It is one of the few African countries to enter its fifth decade of independence without ever having experienced a coup, sustained civil unrest, or the rule of an unpopular leader who refused to stand down.

A principled stance on international politics was reflected in staunch support of the ANC at the height of apartheid, and the strong denouncement and eventual overthrow of the bloodthirsty Ugandan dictator Idi Amin. Tanzania, poor though it is, has opened its arms to around half a million refugees fleeing recent regional conflicts, mainly in the Democratic

Republic of Congo and Burundi. Their presence has caused little internal tension, although the long-term goal of the Tanzanian government is to see them repatriated.

Tanzania's pervasive sense of nationhood is generally attributed to two main factors. The first, ironically, is the country's very cultural diversity. Elsewhere in Africa, national politics is often dominated by the jostle for supremacy between two numerically dominant tribes. In Tanzania, the most populous tribe accounts for less than 15 percent of the populace, so that tribal self-interest plays no significant role in determining national affairs. The other factor

maa villages. The result was a disaster, since many of the villages lay in areas without sufficient water or arable land to support a large community. Tanzania, already one of the least developed African colonies, retreated further into economic torpor, to be ranked among the world's 10 poorest countries.

Following Nyerere's voluntary retirement from the presidency in 1985, Tanzania has undergone a dramatic economic transformation *(see page 46)*. Its sustained growth rate since 2000 has been among the highest on the continent, and the healthy aura of commercial bustle that envelops Dar es Salaam today would render

is the guiding influence of first president Julius Nyerere – affectionately remembered by the name *Mwalimu* (Teacher) – whose actions, words and policies repeatedly stressed the importance of nationhood over more parochial concerns. Tanzanians generally hold their tribal roots in deep regard, but as a source of cultural pride rather than political divisiveness.

Economic ups and downs

Nyerere, for all his virtues, was the instigator of the misguided *Ujamaa* (familyhood) scheme of centralised collective villages *(see page 44)*, implemented in 1967. By the mid-1970s some 85 percent of the rural population lived in *Uja-*

the city virtually unrecognisable to anybody who last visited it during the economic nadir of the mid-1980s. Yet it is difficult to determine the extent to which the bustling city centre, with its smartly dressed businessmen, burgeoning shopping malls and fancy restaurants, reflects an improvement in the lot of the average Tanzanian. The outskirts of Dar es Salaam are lined with slums. The city's population far exceeds that of the next ten largest urban centres in the country combined. The vast majority of Tanzanians live rurally as subsistence farmers, fisherfolk or livestock herders, and poverty is manifest. Unemployment is high in rural areas, and the majority of employed workers and subsistence farmers survive below the breadline. Meanwhile, the population has virtually trebled in number since independence – and continues to grow rapidly. Inadequate health-care facilities have been stretched thinner in recent years by the Aids pandemic – average life expectancy currently stands at below 50 years. Education, too, is far from being a given: only around 62 percent of children complete primary education. Of these, fewer than one in 10 complete secondary school. The dropout rate among girls is particularly high, especially in rural areas, where large families with limited resources accord priority to the education of their male progeny.

The traditional division of day-to-day labour varies significantly from one tribe to the next, but rural Tanzanian women typically bear the full burden of rearing children, housekeeping, raising crops and fetching water. Some case studies show women doing up to 85 percent of the work required to support the family.

Polygamy, customary in most traditional societies, is on the decline, partly due to the infiltration of Christianity, partly for economic reasons, though the pastoralists of the Rift Valley remain actively polygamous, while also (almost uniquely among Tanzanians) practising initiation rites centred on the genital mutilation of pubescent girls.

The role of women

Even after years of socialist, supposedly egalitarian rule, the inferior education and literacy rate of modern Tanzanian women is reflected by their low profile in national politics and the formal business sector. It is a disparity rooted in traditional tribal structures, which are almost exclusively patrilineal and governed by males.

FAR LEFT: Bugwandega primary school, built by the villagers, near Shinyanga.
LEFT: drawing water from the well.
ABOVE: applying medicine made from cow's blood to a child's eyes, near Dodoma.

A modern phenomenon, and a major factor in the spread of the HIV virus, is prostitution, which is rife in most towns, linked to the economic necessity for many men to seek employment away from their family home.

While it would not do to gloss over the economic and social concerns raised above, it should be stressed that similar problems are endemic throughout the world's poorest continent. What distinguishes Tanzania – a colonial creation in which disparate tribes were forced to coexist within arbitrarily imposed national borders – is the way it has transcended its hotchpotch tribal beginnings to become a genuinely united and forward-looking nation. ❑

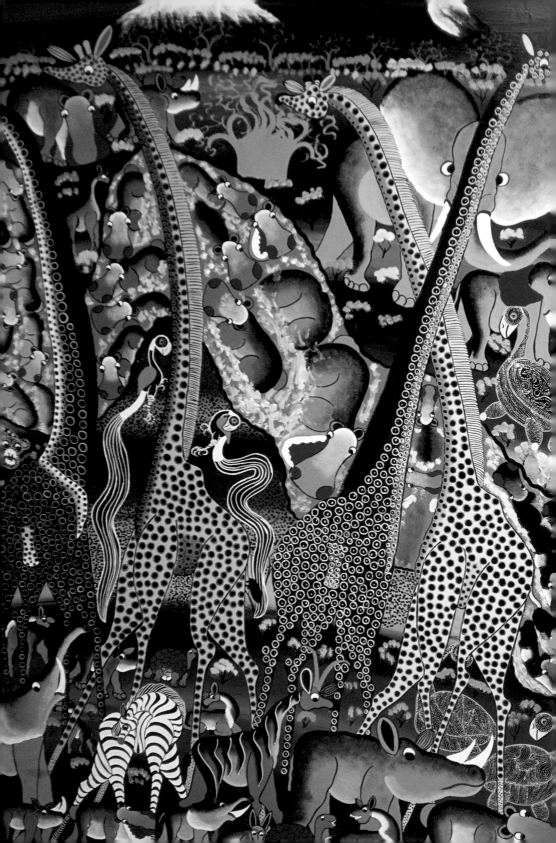

MUSIC, DANCE AND ART

Few of Tanzania's arts are sophisticated, but everything, from the music to the paintings, is bright with colour and full of life

usic leads to dancing and dancing to art, and in Tanzania they are all vibrant and colourful, if perhaps, to the Western eye, a little naive. Music, dance and art are inextricably linked in Tanzania. Indigenous painting and carving is relatively undeveloped in comparison to music and dance. Although there are renowned examples, specifically Tingatinga painting and Makonde carving, the growth of fine art has been heavily influenced by the dictates of the tourist market. This has had a negative impact on artistic quality, but nevertheless has secured a livelihood for the many craftsmen who satisfy a voracious demand for souvenirs.

Tingatinga

Tanzania's most notable artist is Edward Saidi Tingatinga, whose story began in the first half of the last century. He was born in 1932 in Namonchelia (now Nakapanya in the Ruvuma region) to a poor peasant family, and worked variously on the sisal plantations, in gardens, as a street vendor and an embroiderer. He started painting in 1968, using a brush and oil paints to depict animals and African scenes on hardboard.

His paintings began to sell in Dar es Salaam, and in time the National Arts Company agreed that Tingatinga should supply some of his paintings. The prices doubled, and he quit his day job to become a full-time artist and train young relatives as apprentices. Tingatinga died aged 40 from gunshot wounds as he was chased by police in a stolen car, abruptly ending the brief period during which he produced African naive art but arguably increasing the popularity of his work.

His students continued to paint in his style, and currently around 50 artists work at the Dar es Salaam factory alone. This art co-operative was formed with government backing. Each year on Christmas Day the artists clean his burial ground and cook food as a sacrifice.

LEFT: Tingatinga painting in Stone Town; more than any other style, these vivid cartoons have become the trademark of Tanzania.
RIGHT: Tingatinga painter at work, Stone Town.

Tingatinga's work is characterised by a highly decorative, patterned finish, usually in square format worked in enamel and high-gloss oil paints. Each picture tells its own story, often of rural life and sometimes with political undertones. It has a simplicity which borders on animation, a cross between Grandma Moses and Walt Disney.

Stylised birds, fish or animals may be depicted against Mount Kilimanjaro in the background, or perhaps a decorative pattern of dots.

The early paintings were quite simple and usually tended to feature just one African creature on a flat, monotone background. However, since his death, imitators have appeared in several parts of the country, and the style has developed towards the extremely colourful and complex ones that we see everywhere, aimed specifically at the tourism market.

Much of the work has little artistic merit but provides a cheerful reminder of Tanzania, and can now be found in many parts of the country, including Zanzibar.

The art of women

Painting is almost exclusively a male preserve, whilst crafts are the domain of women. Tourists can find a natural development of this cultural tradition at the Bagamoyo Living Art and Handicraft Design Centre, on the north coast, where women produce excellent weaving, tie dye, batik, pottery and printed fabrics.

The women use indigenous materials, with an emphasis on traditional design, and their work is a classic illustration of practical culture becoming an art form.

Further up in the Usambara Mountains, walking tours offer visitors the chance to visit

Wood

As in many African countries, woodcarving is a staple of traditional craft. However, it can be difficult to distinguish between imported lookalikes and genuine local products. Probably the majority of "curios" on sale in Tanzania come from elsewhere in Africa, such as Kenya, South Africa and Zimbabwe, all of which have older tourist trades and infinitely more sophisticated craft traditions. Once you have established its provenance, you need to look carefully at the quality of the workmanship and also at the wood itself. Real ebony is exceptionally heavy and black inside as well. However, the wood

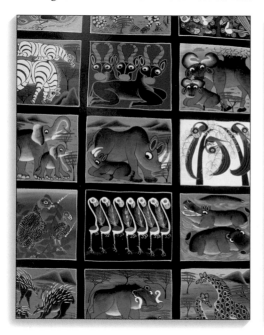

mountain villages like Kileti where around 30 potters work. They are all women, as decreed by ancient sacred tenets. Their knowledge is passed from generation to generation, and men are forbidden to participate. A typical pot takes a week to prepare, starting with a 2-km (1-mile) walk to dig the clay, which the potter carries back to her village on her head. The clay is broken up, mixed with water and pounded to a smooth consistency, and the pots are made from a clay ball which has been pushed and pulled into shape. Bigger pots have coil after coil of clay added to the rim. The surface is decorated with gourd scrapers and fired inside a mound of firewood.

is now endangered due to extensive cutting, and if you do decide to buy a piece, limit yourself to one object only or buy "fake" ebony.

Probably the best and most imaginative wood-carving in East Africa is produced by the Makonde people from southern Tanzania and northern Mozambique, who have been practising their craft for about 300 years. Some carvers still work on the Makonde Plateau, but many have gravitated to Dar es Salaam and Arusha.

One style of carving consists of distorted and highly stylised people, usually a mother and her children. These would have been carried by the male carver for good luck. More common are those with *ujamaa* motifs and those known as *shetani*, which include grotesque figures based on Makonde spirits. *Ujamaa* carvings look like totem poles made up of interlocking people and animals. Made from a single piece of wood, they contain up to 50 figures and can stand several metres high.

The Swahili tradition

The doorway was always the most elaborate feature in a Swahili home, but during the 1800s craftsmen in Zanzibar developed a style and tradition of carving wooden doors that has no parallel in any other part of the world. They

boxes and tables. If you have the money, you can even commission a four-poster bed.

Where to shop

Excellent-quality modern wood products can be obtained at most of the major souvenir shops, such as Cultural Heritage in Arusha or Zanzibar Gallery in Stone Town. In Dar es Salaam, try the markets outside The Slipway, or shops along Samora Avenue, south of the Askari Monument. There are also many crafts stalls along Ali Hassan Miringyi Boulevard. However, the best place in the country to see the diversity of these high-quality artefacts is at

combined Indian methods with Islamic decorative styles and the home-grown Swahili tradition. When a house was built in Zanzibar, the door was the first part to be erected, and the greater the wealth and social position of the owner, the larger and more elaborate the door. There are still around 560 carved doors in Stone Town, and others to be found in areas such as Bagamoyo, Kilwa and Pemba. The ornate geometric and floral decoration that typifies Swahili design can also be found on chests, jewellery

the Mwengi Craft Market *(see page 153)* on the outskirts of Dar es Salaam. Craftspeople from all over the country sell their wares in a little enclave of stalls stacked high with carvings.

There are spears, life-size warriors, masks, giraffes, lions. You name it, they've carved it – anything from a tiny hippo for about £1 (US$1.60) to life-size African women and warriors for £150,000 (US$240,000). This is as much a workshop as a showcase. The air is thick with sawdust, craftsmen sculpt under the trees, and as you visit each hut you can hear the tapping of their work and watch the women polish the finished products. Other souvenirs, from slippers to drums or jewellery, are also on

FAR LEFT: Tingatinga painting.
LEFT: Makonde carver at Mwengi Market.
ABOVE: intricately carved door in Stone Town.

display. Prices are very reasonable, and the quality is generally excellent. Larger objects can be shipped.

The rhythm of dance

Of all the arts, music and dance have progressed most naturally and creatively. Traditional dance rhythms have been maintained, while new forms emerge as musicians and dancers are influenced by modern, Western sounds. The Swahili word for dance is *ngoma*, which also means drums. Of all the country's traditional

Zanzibar. This evening show involves a singer backed by a 40-piece orchestra of drums, horns and strings. Women in evening wear slowly approach the singer, dancing as they ascend and offering money to sponsor lines they feel speak to their own lives. The music itself is a mix of Indian, Arabian and African.

Sauti za Busara, a music festival that attracts musicians and spectators from across the globe to Zanzibar, is a huge event in the Tanzanian calendar. Held in the

instruments, the drum is supreme, used to announce arrivals and departures and to keep morale up in farming societies through a dance called *Gobogobo*.

Among the many other musical instruments new to Western ears on display in the National Museum in Dar es Salaam are the *kalimba* (a type of thumb piano), *kayamba* (shakers), rattles, bells and *silva* (horns). Dance in Tanzania serves as a way of communicating with ancestors as well as a means of entertainment and a way of expressing emotion. Although performances for tourist groups tend to dilute the message, most traditional movements and rhythms remain the same. *Taarab* is popular in

Old Fort along Stone Town's waterfront during the first week of February, Sauti za Busara is foremost a celebration of Tanzanian music in all its diversity. Don't expect much sleep – performances begin early in the morning and run throughout the day and night.

Mwaka Kogwa *(see page 265)*, in southern Zanzibar, is a colourful dance and music festival celebrating the Shirazi New Year (in July). It features mock fights with banana stems which enable the fighters to vent their grievances and enter the new year with a pure heart.

Dancing with masks is not common except in the southeast, where the Makonde and the Makua use masked dancing to celebrate coming-out ceremonics for children. Just south of Bagamoyo, on the road to Dar es Salaam, Chuo cha Sanaa is a theatre and arts college which sometimes gives performances of traditional drumming and dancing. Enquiries should be made at the school.

Bring on the band

Many displays of traditional music and dance in Tanzania have moved on in a way that art and crafts have not. During the colonial era, British and German military bands had an influence, and brass instruments were combined with traditional instruments, creating rhumba bands.

specific national style of music. Lyrics are more important than the music, and a topical message is often incorporated. It is folk music in the making; this song from Remmy Ongala is typical of modern music with a message:

A bicycle has no say in front of a motorbike.
A motorbike has no say in front of a car.
A motorcar has no say in front of a train.
The poor person has no rights.
I am poor. I have no right to speak.
Poor and weak before the powerful.
Weak as long as the powerful likes.

The Tanzanians are natural and enthusiastic dancers. *Sedema* is a type of music during

There is also a Tanzanian new wave of dance called *mchirku* which is big in the cities. Comprising seven or eight teenagers, three or four drums, a tambourine and keyboard, it is rhythmic and raucous, and was banned in the 1970s for its lewd lyrics and erotic dance style. It's now heralded as a new Tanzanian sound.

The local dance-band scene is also thriving. Since the late 1960s the radio has exclusively featured Tanzanian bands on its Swahili programme, and this in turn has helped develop a

which the musicians dance as they play and the audience copies them. It has traditional origins and was taught by a *ngoma* (drummer). In its original form, the dancers were bare-chested, carried a spear and had bells on their ankles. Jazz is also popular. The first local jazz band goes back to the 1940s, and you'll find many jazz musicians in Dar es Salaam, where, once again, the dance tradition is strong.

This interlinking of dance, music and art makes Tanzania's deep traditional culture very accessible. To enjoy it is to learn about Tanzanian history and lifestyle, and to discover a people with a big heart and capacity to live to the full. ❏

FAR LEFT: traditional dancers in Zanzibar.
LEFT: Makonde mask.
ABOVE: traditional musicians at Saba Saba Festival.

THE LIE OF THE LAND

From the blinding white of coral sand to the snows of Kilimanjaro, Tanzania has some of Africa's most varied and dramatic natural environments

anzania is remarkable for the extraordinary variety of its topography, giving it one of the greatest ranges of biodiversity in Africa. The Serengeti, Ngorongoro and the Selous are all World Heritage Sites. Ancient pre-Cambrian basement rocks of gneisses, schists and granite, which form the large central plateau of the Maasai steppe, rise from 1,000 to 1,500 metres (3,300 to 4,900 ft) in the Serengeti.

Next door, violent volcanic activity over 20 million years has formed the Great Rift Valley and its associated mountains – including Africa's highest mountain, Kilimanjaro. Along the narrow coastal belt are the younger sediments of the Jurassic, Cretaceous and Tertiary periods, while offshore there are even coral atolls.

Valley deep, mountain high

The Great Rift Valley, which stretches from Turkey through Africa to Mozambique, divides into two branches in Tanzania. The western arm, which forms a natural boundary between the Democratic Republic of Congo, Zambia and Malawi, is marked by the vast freshwater lakes – Victoria, Tanganyika, Rukwa and Nyasa (Lake Nyasa and Malawi are the same lake, but both names are used; Malawi was previously called Nyasaland). The eastern arm is clearly visible in parts, with dramatic escarpments, as can be seen from the road to Serengeti, flanking the alkaline lakes Manyara and Eyasi, and rising sharply to the Ngorongoro Highlands.

The Ngorongoro Crater has been dubbed the eighth wonder of the world, not only as the world's largest complete volcanic caldera, born of a mountain that may have been higher than Kilimanjaro, but as a natural amphitheatre, 16 km (10 miles) wide, with a staggering concentration of 30,000 animals.

The north of the country is dominated by the domed peaks of Kibo – 5,890 metres (19,320 ft) – and Mawenzi – 5,140 metres (16,860 ft) –

on Kilimanjaro, which rises like a giant sugar-loaf from the flat plains, making it the world's highest free-standing mountain. Kibo's crater is 200 metres (656 ft) deep and contains active fumeroles. Ol Donyo Lengai, the Maasai "Mountain of God", near Lake Natron on the Kenyan border, is still active. Other rift moun-

tains, such as Meru – 4,560 metres (14,960 ft) – are deemed to be dormant, not having erupted within the past 200 years.

Elsewhere, mountain ranges include the Monduli, west of Arusha; the Pare and Usambara of the Eastern Arcs, to the southeast of Kilimanjaro; the Uluguru, east of Morogoro; the Ugzungwa, southwest of Mikumi; and the Mahale on the shores of Lake Tanganyika.

Rivers

Southern Tanzania is characterised by a fairly flat ancient landscape with poor soils and deciduous woodland, interspersed with sand rivers that flood during the rainy season, clearly

LEFT: hot-air balloon at dawn, over the Serengeti.
RIGHT: elephants roaming in the shadow of Mount Kilimanjaro.

seen in the Selous Game Reserve, which has a network of sand rivers the size of Wales linking to the Rufiji River.

Surprisingly, wetland areas cover about 10 percent of the country. Apart from the Great Lakes, several major rivers flow into the Indian Ocean. The Pangani drains the Kilimanjaro region; the Great Ruaha and Kilombero join the Rufiji, with a catchment area in the southern highlands; while the Ruvuma (sometimes called the Ruva) forms the boundary with Mozambique.

> ## A GRAND DESIGN
>
> Covering an area of 945,100 sq. km (364,900 sq. miles), including the Zanzibar archipelago and Mafia Island, Tanzania is over four times the size of Britain.

The Malagarasi, which feeds Lake Tanganyika, also forms the Malagarasi swamps, which are of international significance as Tanzania's first Ramsar site – conforming to international agreements set out in Ramsar, Iran, on the conservation of wetlands.

The soda lake, Natron, in the far north, has been earmarked as a second Ramsar site, due to its importance as a breeding ground for the deep rose-pink lesser flamingos.

Other significant wetland areas include the Kilombero Valley, south of the Udzungwa Mountains and the only home to the Kilombera weaver, and Kagera west of Lake Victoria on the Ugandan border.

The human population

Tanzania's complex underlying geology and water resources have both played a significant role in the geographical distribution of the country's humans and wildlife. The third important factor is the climate. East Africa has two rains a year and does not have a long dry season. In Tanzania, the significance of this is apparent in the shorter, sweeter grasses found in the Serengeti and the Maasai steppe, which can support higher densities of wildlife – hence there are more animals and a greater variety of species in East Africa than southern Africa. The southern part of Tanzania falls into the miombo woodland belt which continues south into Zambia, Zimbabwe and Botswana. This area has one rainy season, and consequently game densities are less high, and there are fewer species.

Tanzania's human population is mainly rural. Around 80 percent of the population is employed in the agricultural industry, which focuses on the upland areas where rich, volcanic soils and two growing seasons support high population densities.

The semi-arid lowlands are far more sparsely inhabited, by pastoralists such as the Maasai and Datoga, and are also where the major wildlife areas are concentrated. However, in recent years an increase in population has led to more permanent settlement in the marginal areas, giving rise to increasing soil erosion and potentially serious conflicts over water usage.

Another major factor influencing population distribution is the presence of the tsetse fly, which causes sleeping sickness. The "fly-belt" is a vast area that cannot be inhabited or farmed by humans. The wildlife in these areas is in effect preserved by the presence of the pest.

There are a few large urban centres, such as Dar es Salaam, Arusha, the capital Dodoma and Zanzibar Town on Unguja Island, in Zanzibar. Other significant regional towns include Tanga, Mwanza, Morogoro, Tabora and Iringa.

Commercial farming

Expansive, bright-green tea plantations dominate much of the Usambara and Tukuyu regions, at an altitude of around 2,130 metres (7,000 ft). At a lower altitude are the Robusta coffee farms around Bukoba, and the Arabica coffee farms found in the Moshi and Usa River area near Arusha, on the foothills of Kilimanjaro. Other crops are grown alongside the coffee, such as beans, bananas – 10 types, from the tiny, sweet, yellow, finger bananas to the large, green *matoke* which is used as a savoury staple – and increasingly a variety of horticultural products. Fruit and vegetables for the local market range from strawberries to Arusha tomatoes. A new commercial crop is flowers, grown both for seed production and for export as cut flowers to Europe.

POPULATION

Officially at just over 40 million, Tanzania's population is made up of some 120 tribal groups. No one group has supremacy.

until the market collapsed due to competition from synthetic materials. There are still several large plantations, but the area has also diversified into horticultural production to meet the demand of the domestic market around Dar es Salaam. Although only 4 percent of the land is given to crop production, there is enormous potential to increase yields and expand the areas under cultivation through irrigation; but this in turn needs to be balanced against traditional agricultural practices and the impact on the wetland areas.

There are wheat farms to the north of Arusha region and on the slopes of the Ngorongoro Highlands, while extensive maize production is found in the drier areas. Other cash crops include tobacco, grown by local smallholders, and pyrethrum. Cotton is produced inland from Tanga and Dar es Salaam, along the Rufiji River and south down the coast as far as Kilwa. Rice and cotton are also grown in the Shinyaga area near Lake Victoria. The Morogoro region was once the world's largest producer of sisal,

On Lake Victoria, sardine fishing is an important industry at Kibirizi and Kigoma. While tilapia is the preferred fish for eating, Nile perch, which was introduced into the lake in 1956, accounts for 75 percent of the catch.

All things nice

Along the coast, commercial coconut plantations are harvested for copra, which produces coconut oil, coconut meal for livestock and a host of other by-products.

Cloves, coconut and spice plantations dominate the Zanzibar archipelago. The island of Pemba is the world's largest producer of cloves, where some trees are as high as 24 metres (79 ft).

LEFT: aerial view of the Kigosi-Moyowasi swamp system, near Kigoma.
ABOVE: banana plantation near Lake Nyasa.

During the clove-picking season, from July to December, the air is thick with the pungent scent of cloves. Other spices include nutmeg, lemon grass, vanilla and ginger, and local factories produce clove and lemon-grass oil. In the northeast of Unguja Island, around Matemwe, the local women cultivate seaweed in the shallows for export to the Far East. At the coast there's also a healthy domestic market for deep-sea fish, such as marlin and tuna, as well as more easily caught sea creatures from octopus to crabs or snapper.

Forests in Tanzania account for about 37 percent of the land area, but deforestation is

graphite, tin and copper. Mining areas are found around Shinyaga, and gold has recently been discovered in Mwanza. Mwadui has the largest pipe diamond mine in Africa. Alexandrite is mined in Tunduru, rubies in Morogoro and emeralds, rubies and rhodolite in Tanga.

Tanzanite, the mauve semi-precious stone the colour of jacaranda flowers, is mined in the hills near Kilimanjaro Airport *(see box below and page 54)*. Low-grade coal is mined in the south, and sources of power include hydroelectric schemes on the Rufiji River, together with natural gas deposits found in the Rufiji delta.

increasingly a problem, as land is cleared for agriculture, firewood and charcoal. In the mountainous regions, commercial timber is an important commodity; camphorwood, teak, mahogany and ebony are produced. At the coast, mangrove swamps are extensive in the Kilwa and Rufiji areas, where they are harvested for mangrove poles which are much in demand by the building industry, while the bark is used for tanning leather.

Mining

In recent years there has been a significant increase in mineral exploration and production, with the ancient rocks yielding gold, diamonds,

TANZANITE

First discovered in 1967 by a Maasai herder, tanzanite was given to a ruby prospector, Manuel d'Souza. He took it to Tiffany's, the New York jewellers, who named and popularised the stone. Gemologically, tanzanite is called blue Zoisite, but it was renamed to avoid the similarity with the word "suicide". A hydrated calcium aluminium silicate mineral, it is technically only semi-precious, but as it is rarer than diamonds, and the pale-brown stone, when heated, becomes a glorious purple-blue, it is highly sought after. The only mine in the world producing tanzanite is at Mererani, 40 km (25 miles) southeast of Arusha. The stones are available at good curio shops in Arusha.

National Parks

Remarkably, 25 percent of Tanzania's land has been set aside as national parks, game reserves, game controlled areas and wildlife management areas – a reflection of the diverse range of habitats and the value placed on wildlife for tourism and hunting.

The northern circuit, operating out of Arusha, is the most developed; it includes the Serengeti, Ngorongoro Crater, Lake Manyara and Tarangire, together with Mount Kilimanjaro and Arusha. The southern circuit, visited from Dar es Salaam, focuses primarily on the Selous, Ruaha and Mikumi.

Due to the tremendous topographical variation, virtually all the major habitats found elsewhere in Africa are represented in Tanzania, the only major exception being arid desert. The major division of ecological zones primarily relates to altitude. Within a small area there can be a variety of habitats – for example, Lake Manyara National Park contains only about 100 sq. km (39 sq. miles) of land around the lake, but the habitats range from the rift wall to the groundwater forest, acacia woodland, open grassland, the lake shore, swamp areas and the lake itself.

Lowland eco-zones

There are varying definitions of habitat type – some sources suggest six major ecological zones, while others expand the list to around 13 or more. However, they may be broadly defined as acacia savanna grassland; miombo woodland; lowland rainforest; riverine and evergreen forest; montane forest; heath and moorland; and highland desert.

The **acacia savanna grassland** is rich in flora, with some 2,500 plant species. It forms the backbone of the central plateau and northern ranges of grassland. The Serengeti plains are dominated by the red oat grass, *Themeda triandra*, and the sedges of *Sporobolus ioclada* and *Kyllinga* species. Wooded grassland is extensive, with many regional variations, and is dominated by trees from the acacia or *Combretum* family. (Tanzania has more than 40 indigenous acacia.) A typical combination, as found in parts of the Serengeti, is a woodland dominated by *Acacia tortilis* and *Commiphora schimperi*, with other common species being *A. drepanolobium, A. seyal, A. melacocephala* and *A. pseudofistula*. Interestingly, the grassland areas are dependent upon being grazed – by both wild and domestic animals. If grazing was removed from the equation, the grassland would naturally revert to acacia woodland.

The south of the country is extensively covered by **miombo woodland**, dominated by some 15 species of *Brachystegia*, tall deciduous trees with an open canopy. They shed their leaves during the six months of the dry season, while the tall grasses are prone to bush fires.

THE FEVER TREE

Acacia xanthophloea, better-known as the fever tree, was given its ominous name by early travellers. The trees are commonly seen along watercourses, which provided good shade and water for pitching camp. These areas were also rampant breeding grounds for mosquitoes, and travellers soon linked their bouts of malaria to camping in these regions. Initially they thought the fever was caused by the trees, whose yellow powdery bark seemed to signal danger. One of the most attractive of the acacias, it is easily recognised by its (harmless) yellow bark and flat-topped crown. The tree has developed a shallow root system to avoid being waterlogged in clay soils.

LEFT: the Rift Valley escarpment.
RIGHT: yellow-barked acacia (fever tree) and wild date palm, in the Seronera River Valley, Serengeti.

Lowland rainforest is found in the Eastern Arc Mountains, and typified by the lower eastern slopes of the Usambaras, characterised by *Anthocleista grandiflora, Cephalosphaera usambarensis* and *Anisophyllea obtusifolia*. The Usambaras have the greatest altitudinal range of unbroken forest cover in East Africa, from the lowland forest communities at below 250 metres (820 ft) through to montane species. They support one of the richest biological communities in Africa. Of the 276 forest trees recorded, 50 are endemic. Remarkably, over 100 species of trees and shrubs in the area have been selected for their importance in terms of biodiversity.

Riverine and evergreen forest follows the major rivers and is also found at the foot of the escarpment at Manyara, fed by springs from the foot of the scarp. Here, there are magnificent stands of tall, mature trees, among them *Trichilea emetica, Antiaris toxicaria, Bridelia micrantha* and *Ficus sycamorus*, with an understorey of *Croton macrostachys* and *Rauvolfia caffra*. Other species include the *borassus* and *phoenix* palms.

Gombe Stream and the Mahale Mountains still possess fragments of the original West and Central African forests, which became isolated during the climate changes over the past 8,000

years. Among trees common to the West African forest which can be seen are species of *Anthocleista, Elaesis, Myrianthus, Pseudosponias* and *Pyncanthus*.

Mountain vegetation

Montane forest is found between the 1,200-metres (3,937-ft) contour and the treeline at 3,000-metres (9,843-ft) and shows variations, with a greater number of species in areas of higher rainfall. On the slopes of Kilimanjaro, the most common tree around Marangu is *Macaranga kilimandscharica*, which has a smooth grey bark and heart-shaped leaves. The forest on the western and northern slopes receives less rain. Here the dominant trees are juniper, *Juniperus procera*, the olives, *Olea africana* and *O. kilimandscharica*, and *Nuxia congesta,* which is often draped with moss and lichen and has attractive clusters of white flowers which bloom at the start of the rains. One of the tallest trees is the *Podocarpus milanjianus*, a conifer which can grow to 30 metres (100 ft), together with the ivy, *Ilex mitis*, and the camphorwood, *Ocotea usambarensis.*

A dense understorey of shrubs and wild flowers contains familiar species such as Busy Lizzies and begonias, popular as house plants. Giant tree ferns grow up to 6 metres (20 ft) high

Erica arborea and *E.excelsa*, the yellow flowers of *Hypericum revolutum* and the papery, everlasting daisy-like flowers of *Helichrysum*. A yellow protea, *Protea kilimandscharica*, and the red-hot poker, *Kniphofia thomsonii*, are also easily recognised.

On the moorland, lobelias reach 3 metres (10 ft) high, among tussocks of grass, *Pentaschistis minor*, and mauve-flowered herbs like *Satureia biflora* and *S. kilimandscharica*. Some species, like *Lobelia deckenii* and *Senecio kilimanjari,* are endemic to Kilimanjaro. The lobelia has adapted to the sub-zero conditions by closing its open leaves over its rosette buds at night.

in wetter parts of the forest, while orchids, African violets and balsams are also commonly seen. In the upper reaches, stands of the feathery giant heather tree, *Erica excelsa*, grow 3 metres (10 ft) high, with pink or white flowers, and giant groundsel, *Senecio johnstonii*, has cabbage-like leaves and small clusters of yellow flowers.

Typical **heath and moorland** vegetation (from 2,800 metres/9,200 ft to 4,000 metres/13,100 ft) is characterised by giant heathers,

FAR LEFT: baobab in Ruaha National Park.
LEFT: tropical montane forest on the slopes of Mt Meru, northern Tanzania.
ABOVE: giant lobelia growing on Kilimanjaro.

The **highland desert** (4,000 metres/13,200 ft to 5,000 metres/16,400 ft) freezes at night, while daytime temperatures can soar to 40°C (104°F). Evaporation is high and water retention in the soil is poor, particularly when the soil is frozen. Yet some 55 plant species have adapted to these bleak conditions. Among them, coloured lichens cling to the lava rocks, free-rolling moss balls wrap themselves around a nodule of soil, and rosette plants like *Haplocarpa rueppelii* and *Haplosciadium abyssinicum* also flourish. Other plants have adapted by coating their leaves in silvery hairs, which reflect the sun and trap a layer of air around the leaves which reduces temperature loss. ❑

SAFARI

*In Swahili, safari simply means "journey"; today the word
is synonymous with the thrill of seeing Africa's great wildlife*

Images of the grand hunting safari, complete with an entourage of porters, still abound in Tanzania, immortalised by the adventures of glamorous big-game hunters such as Ernest Hemingway. Hunting and photographic safaris are still the mainstay of Tanzanian tourism, but their origins may be found in far more ancient interaction between humans and wildlife.

Food or commerce?

It was probably man's urge to hunt that led to the very first development of tools, from scrapers used to skin an animal to arrowheads for shooting them. Some of the early rock-art sites scattered around Tanzania depict men hunting. Although now on the verge of extinction, scattered groups of nomadic hunter-gatherers still exist around the margins of Lake Eyasi, southwest of Ngorongoro. Retaining an intimate knowledge of their environment and hunting terrain, the nomadic Hadza *(see page 189)* use different plant poisons to lethal effect on their poison arrows, and employ agility and cunning in the hunt. They are skilled trackers, reading game trails like a map, but will also use certain trees as a lookout point. At times they will even imitate an animal as part of the chase, for example, donning a headdress of impala horns when stalking impala.

Other tribal groups, such as the pastoralist Maasai, have happily coexisted in harmony with the wildlife over the years, referring to them as their second cattle, and only resorting to hunting for food in times of severe hardship. Yet traditionally, young *moranis* (warriors) had to kill a lion as part of the ritual to attaining manhood and status, although this is no longer a prerequisite.

The ivory trade stretches back to the days of ancient Rome. Arab caravans were certainly operating from the 7th century. By the time the

British arrived, the slaughter of elephants for their ivory had become part of a sophisticated trading network, with the ivory conveniently transported to the coast by the slaves the traders had captured en route.

The Arabs supplied guns to the African hunters, and it is estimated that in the 1850s

30,000 elephants were being killed a year in Kenya, Uganda and Tanzania. By the 1880s, this had risen to between 60,000 and 70,000.

Trophy hunting

The advent of trophy hunting started with the Victorian big-game hunters, who moved up from southern Africa where much of the game had been decimated, lured by the big tuskers and large herds of East Africa.

In 1902 Frederick Courteney Selous made his first expedition to East Africa. In 1909 he returned to set up a hunting expedition for the American President, Theodore Roosevelt. The scale of this safari, to collect specimens for the

---

LEFT: the black rhino has a triangular lip, designed for browsing; the wide-mouthed white rhino, a grazer, is extinct in Tanzania.
RIGHT: a traditional hunter on Yellow Mountain.

Smithsonian and American Museum of Natural History in New York, took on epic proportions, and covered a nine-month period and four countries. The attendant press entourage gave international publicity to African safaris, initiating the beginning of the commercial hunting safari in Africa. Meanwhile, Selous himself made the transition from hunter to safari guide, and began, through his writings, to influence world opinion on the need to conserve wildlife.

Great white hunter

The commercial hunting safari was thus established. For the most part, however, the profes-

sional hunters were men who appreciated the wildlife, revelled in the excitement of the bush, and simply took hunting clients to earn a living. Unfortunately, they were often too efficient. The pioneering pilot, Beryl Markham, tells of watching the elephants gather round the big tuskers to hide them from her spotter plane.

Meanwhile, these romantically rugged figures became further glamourised and embellished by films like *King Solomon's Mines*, filmed in the 1950s, the writings of hunting fanatic Ernest Hemingway, and the filming of *Kilimanjaro*. White hunters became enveloped in the mantle of Hollywood.

Selous was by no means the only hunter to become an ardent conservationist. Another was Constantine Ionides, more renowned for his passion for snakes, who gives an interesting account of the early hunting days in his autobiography, *A Hunter's Story*.

Drawn to Tanzania by a passion for hunting, he joined the 6th King's African Rifles, arriving in 1925. After a short spell in the army, he turned to hunting and poaching elephants, where he was not averse to bribing chiefs and officials when in pursuit of big ivory. Ionides then worked as a white hunter, taking hunting safaris, where the emphasis was on tracking the game and finding suitable specimen trophies for the client, without the frills of drinks on ice and gourmet cuisine. He aptly describes the development of the role of the white hunter today as combining the social skills of a travelling hotel manager with those of a hunter.

From the 1920s onwards, land had been set aside for Game Parks and Reserves. Ionides joined the Game Department in 1933; at that time six European game rangers and around 120 African scouts were responsible for the entire country. Their remit was to conserve the game, protect human life and property from attacks by wildlife and control hunting.

The modern hunt

Apart from a seven-year period from 1973 when a complete moratorium was imposed, the hunting safari has been a highly profitable industry for Tanzania. Licensed hunting began in 1984, when the government issued 10 hunting concessions through the Tanzania Wildlife Corporation (TAWICO), which was subsequently privatised. The Game Department is the government arm responsible for controlling hunting, issuing hunting concessions and regulating game quotas. There are 39 companies and 110 hunting blocks. Among the largest are Robin Hurt Safaris, Tanzania Game Tracker Safaris and Game Frontiers Safaris. They all strive to maintain high ethical standards. Tanzania Game Tracker Safaris states: "We are committed to maintaining a long tradition of ethical hunting, and not merely providing opportunity for indiscriminate killing of animals."

The annual hunting season runs from 1 July

LAND FOR ANIMALS

Today, wildlife areas – National Parks, National Reserves, Game Controlled Areas and Wildlife Management Areas – account for a massive 25 percent of Tanzania.

Nothing but pictures

The development of the photographic safari derived from the hunting safaris, replacing the gun with the camera and attracting an increasing number of tourists on different budgets. The big five of the photographic safari are still those that were the prime hunting trophies in the past – elephant, lion, leopard, buffalo and rhino.

While some companies retain the classic style of the traditional mobile camp complete with gourmet catering, others operate a less

to 31 December. Restrictions on certain species are laid down by the international monitoring agency, the Convention on International Trade in Endangered Species (CITES). Hunting is big business – overseas clients hunting buffalo, elephant, lion and leopard pay thousands of dollars for the privilege. The government gains in the region of US$18 million a year in trophy fees and other associated fees. Additional money is paid to local communities, and there are significant tips for the trackers.

LEFT: trophies are a large part of the testosterone-fuelled pleasures of big-game hunting.

ABOVE: cheetahs use a vehicle as a convenient lookout.

lavish set-up, with basic camping facilities. Increasingly, new types of permanent and sophisticated accommodation have appeared from the permanent tented camp to lodges and opulent hotels decked out in a 1930s theme. Books have been written on safari style, catering for a new fashion of Western tourist, reinventing the romantic notions conjured up by Hollywood, where accommodation has become as important as the wildlife.

While the National Parks are all dedicated to photographic safaris, in the Game Reserves and Wildlife Management Areas certain lands are allocated as hunting zones. With the advent of walking safaris in the community lands adjacent to the parks in northern Tanzania, there has been a conflict of interests between the operators of hunting and photographic safaris, giving rise to a need for more stringent zoning of activities and, quite possibly, for buffer zones between them. Not only do many photographic tourists dislike the whole concept of hunting, but the proximity of guns makes the animals infinitely less approachable. Those looking for good pictures are likely to be very disappointed.

Community involvement

An interesting phenomenon is that both hunting and photographic safaris have increasingly

become involved with the local communities. Quite rightly, some of the revenue received from hunting and photographic tourism is ploughed back into community development, building schools, providing bursaries for education, health care and waterpoints.

On walking safaris in Maasai areas, tourists are guided by the Maasai, learning about the environment and the traditional uses of plants, as well as glimpsing Maasai culture at first hand. With the hunting safaris, local people are employed as trackers, and meat is distributed to neighbouring villages. This has resulted in a shift in the attitude of local people from seeing wildlife as a pest to valuing it as a resource.

Hunter as conservationist?

The role hunting plays in wildlife conservation is a contentious issue, especially among those who are against hunting in any shape or form. But whatever one's personal views, there is no doubt that in Tanzania it brings in vital revenue which can be ploughed back into conservation projects.

The Game Department does not have the financial resources to patrol effectively the vast areas under its jurisdiction, and is heavily reliant on assistance from the private sector.

Safari operator Richard Bonham, who runs a lodge and walking safaris in the Selous Game Reserve, believes hunting is a valuable conservation tool, saying: "About 80 percent of the Selous's revenue is derived from trophy hunters in comparison to photographic safaris."

He observes that the anti-hunting lobby is breaking one of the first rules of nature, and it's important to understand the big picture. "Nature is unemotional and they are throwing emotion into it," says Bonham. He explains the economic bottom line, that if a lion is shot on lion control, the lion brings in no revenue, and it costs the Game Department money to carry out the operation. That same lion can bring in US\$4,000–5,000 if shot by a trophy hunter. In the Selous, the combined income from hunting and photographic safaris makes the wildlife resource viable.

This view is echoed by Charl Beukes from Tanzania Game Tracker Safaris, who says, "Hunting certainly plays a major part in the conservation of wildlife. You're not going to get photographic safaris going into the remote areas. Logistically it's too hard, and they can't charge enough. But you can charge enough on a hunting safari to cover the costs, and as you have a presence in an area it's a deterrent towards poaching." This works during the hunting season, but for six months of the year, the hunters do not have a presence. Many hunting companies are affiliated to non-governmental organisations like the Friedkin Conservation Fund, which assists the Tanzanian government with anti-poaching measures and provides tangible economic benefits to the local communities, funded from hunting wildlife in a sustainable manner.

Poaching

During the 1970s and '80s, as elsewhere in Africa, Tanzania's elephant population was decimated in the ivory wars. Some herds were poached to within 20 percent of their former size. At its worst, in the Selous Game Reserve, 20,000 elephants were slaughtered over a two-year period. Poaching was out of control, and the government did not have the resources to combat it. The timing coincided with the anti-hunting ban in Tanzania, giving the poachers carte blanche in the hunting areas.

Fortunately, the international outcry resulted in the CITES imposing a moratorium on the ivory trade in 1989, when the African elephant was placed on the critical endangered species list, which gave a total ban on trading

70 percent of Tanzania's total rhino population. The larger white rhinos have long since vanished, and the black rhino population is so fragmented and dispersed that there have been suggestions that the only way to create a viable breeding pool is to create a sanctuary within the Selous.

In 1994, the Sand Rivers Rhino Project was established by Richard Bonham and the late Elizabeth Theobold to protect rhinos from poaching. The project, now named the Selous Rhino Trust (www.selousrhinotrust.org), has grown in scale and received major funding from the European Union.

in elephant products. In late 2002, a limited trade in ivory was reinstituted. There have been some reports of a slight increase in poaching, although not on the same level as in the past.

On the endangered list

The current situation with black rhino is more fragile. It is estimated that there are only about 100 animals in the Selous, and they constitute

LEFT: a government bonfire of animal products captured from poachers and illegal traders.
ABOVE: game viewing by Landrover in the Serengeti National Park.

The rhino are difficult to see, a reflection of poaching avoidance and the dense, riverine gullies in which they live. Trackers with global positioning systems (GPS) have only a 50 percent chance of finding rhino evidence along a 1,000-km (620-mile) transect.

Since the carnage of the 1970s and '80s, poaching remains a problem, but it is not on the same gross scale as before. However, there has been an increase in the local bushmeat trade, particularly of smaller species such as antelope, where the indiscriminate killing gives great cause for concern. Undoubtedly, the future of Tanzania's wildlife remains balanced in the hands of man. ❑

MAMMALS

Tanzania offers some of the world's finest game-viewing,
with an extraordinarily rich array of wildlife

There are more large mammals in East Africa than virtually anywhere else on earth – more than 80 species in Tanzania alone. (By "large", zoologists mean anything from the size of a domestic cat.) There are plenty of smaller ones, too, although most of these are nocturnal and can be difficult to spot. Everyone wants to see Africa's big five – elephant, rhino, lion, leopard and buffalo – and Tanzania contains them all. But in your eagerness to tick them off, don't ignore the less dramatic creatures: the dogs and the smaller cats, the monkeys and the mongooses, and above all the antelopes – nearly 40 different species, from the imposing eland to the tiny dik-dik.

The list that follows contains more than 50 mammals – the species you are most likely to encounter on safari – with descriptions to help you identify each one, and suggestions as to where you might see them. Many mammals are restricted to one type of vegetation or habitat; others are more versatile and are found throughout the country. Some occur in a variety of subspecies, which we do not have space to describe. For more information, and details of *all* the Tanzanian mammals, you should buy an up-to-date field guide to the region *(see Further Reading at the end of Travel Tips)*.

Elephant *(Loxodonta africana)*

The largest of all land mammals, the African elephant can grow to 3.4 metres (11 ft) at the shoulder and weigh 6,300 kg (over 6 tons). Females live in loose-knit herds, in which the oldest cow plays matriarch. Males usually leave the family at around age 12, to drift between herds, roam singly or form bachelor groups. Elephants are active 16–20 hours a day, eating, drinking, bathing or travelling in search of food – they can eat up to 150 kg (330 lb) of vegetation in 24 hours. For more information, *see the feature on page 107*.

Hippopotamus *(Hippopotamus amphibius)*

This huge mammal (up to 2,000 kg/2 tons) is found in most of Tanzania's large rivers and lakes, in herds of 10 or more presided over by a dominant male, who defends his territory fiercely. Hippos' skin is very thin and has no sweat glands – which means they can easily dehydrate and overheat, so they spend the day submerged in water, often with only their eyes, ears and nostrils showing. Evenings and early mornings are the time to see them on land, when they follow well-worn trails to and from their nocturnal grazing.

Hook-lipped rhino *(Diceros bicornis)*

The black rhino (though it is grey), has been poached almost to extinction for its horn for use in traditional medicine and as dagger handles in Yemen. Black rhinos prefer savanna with thickets, where they browse on leaves, twigs and branches with their muscular upper lip. In arid areas they can go without drinking for four days. Tending to be solitary, they gather in temporary groups at waterholes, and a calf will stay with its mother for up to four years. There are no white rhinos left in Tanzania.

Lion *(Panthera leo)*

Tawny or fawn in colour, with manes ranging from gold to black on the male, the lion is the largest of Africa's three big cats, and also the most sociable. Prides consist of six to a dozen females and their cubs, with one or more dominant males. Most of the hunting is done by females, working as a team usually at night, but males will normally be first to eat at a kill. Some prides specialise in hunting buffalo or giraffe, but most feed on impala, zebra or wildebeest, seizing the prey by the throat and suffocating it.

Leopard *(Panthera pardus)*

The elegant leopard is larger than the other spotted cats, and distinguished by dark rosettes on the back and flanks and solid spots on the face. The background colour ranges from off-white to russet. It is a solitary animal, except when a pair come together for mating, or a mother is accompanied by cubs. Hunting mainly at night, the leopard steals up on its prey, then pounces from close range. It is powerful enough to carry an antelope (impala are its favourite food) up a tree to keep it safe from other carnivores.

Spotted hyena *(Crocuta crocuta)*

With its sloping hindquarters, coarse spotted coat, round face and broad black muzzle, the hyena is unmistakable. They are opportunistic scavengers, but also aggressive hunters – of antelope, zebra and even buffalo. Living in "clans" of four to 15 animals, led by a dominant female, they are active mainly at night, when they keep in contact with an eerie whooping call. The **striped hyena** *(Hyaena hyaena)*, slightly smaller, with dark stripes on a grey coat, is much rarer but occasionally seen in northern Tanzania.

Cheetah *(Acinonyx jubatus)*

Much smaller than a leopard, the cheetah is a lithe, long-legged cat with solid dark spots all over its fawn body, a small head and characteristic black "tear-marks" from the corner of each eye. It prefers open savanna, where it uses its impressive speed – up to 100 kph/60 mph over short distances – to run down its prey (typically Thomson's gazelle). Cheetahs are usually seen alone, in pairs or in small family groups consisting of a female and her cubs. They hunt by day, usually during the cooler hours soon after dawn.

Caracal *(Felis caracal)*

Similar in appearance to a lynx, the caracal is a medium-sized cat, anything from pale fawn to chestnut in colour, with long, pointed, tufted ears. It is a solitary hunter, preying on mammals from mice to small antelopes, birds and reptiles. It stalks its prey as close as possible, then relies on a pounce or a short run. Its powerful hind legs enable it to leap vertically 3 metres (10 ft) to swat a bird. Caracal are widespread throughout Tanzania's drier regions, but are mainly nocturnal and rarely seen.

Serval *(Felis serval)*

Another spotted cat, smaller than a cheetah but with a similar build, long legs and a short tail. Its black-on-gold spots give way to black streaks near the head. The serval is usually a solitary animal, but is sometimes seen in pairs or small family groups. It hunts mainly at night, and sometimes in the early morning or late afternoon, preying on small mammals, birds and reptiles. Although it is not uncommon, its favoured habitat of long grass and reedbeds, and its elusive habits, mean it is rarely seen.

African wild cat *(Felis lybica)*

This small carnivore resembles a tabby cat – in fact, it is the ancestor of most domestic cats – but is distinguished by striped legs and ginger fur on the backs of its ears. It is a solitary nocturnal hunter (except when a female is accompanied by kittens), feeding on small mammals up to the size of hares, and birds, including ostrich chicks. The wild cat is found throughout Africa, especially in areas where rodents are plentiful. This often means the outskirts of human settlements, where it may interbreed with domestic cats.

Black-backed jackal *(Canis mesomelas)*

This jackal is a medium-sized canine, mostly tawny-brown, with a black "saddle" flecked with white on its back. Unlike most dogs, jackals are not pack animals, and are usually seen alone or in pairs. They are efficient hunters of small mammals, but also scavenge from other predators' kills. Their characteristic call is a scream followed by three or four short yaps. In areas close to man (such as farmland) black-backed jackals hunt mainly at night, but they are commonly seen in daylight in the national parks.

Side-striped jackal *(Canis adustus)*

Slightly smaller and less common than the black-backed, the side-striped jackal looks uniform grey-brown from a distance, but has a faint pale stripe fringed with black on its flank. The white tip to its bushy tail is perhaps a better identifier. Usually seen alone, but sometimes in pairs or small family groups, it is most active at night and in the early evening. Unlike the black-backed, the side-striped jackal avoids open savanna, and prefers wooded areas. It is omnivorous, eating fruit as well as small prey and carrion.

African wild dog *(Lycaon pictus)*

Unlikely to be mistaken for any other canid, the wild dog (or hunting dog) has long legs, huge ears, a bushy white-tipped tail and a body covered in black, white and tan blotches. No two animals have exactly the same markings. They are superb hunters, traditionally working in packs of 10 to 15 animals, maintaining a chase over several kilometres if necessary, and overwhelming even quite large antelope by sheer weight of numbers. Once common, they are now threatened with extinction and rarely seen.

Giraffe *(Giraffa camelopardalis)*

The subspecies found in Tanzania is the Maasai (or Kenyan) giraffe (*G. c. tippelskirchi*), characterised by ragged edges to its blotchy markings. The world's tallest animal, a male giraffe can grow to 5.5 metres (18 ft); females are somewhat shorter. The giraffe prefers open country to woodland, although its main food is leaves, especially from the tops of acacia trees, which it grasps with its amazing 45-cm (18-in) tongue. Giraffes are non-territorial, roaming around in loose herds of up to 15, of both sexes.

Zebra *(Equus burchellii)*

The plains or Burchell's zebra (the only species found in Tanzania) is an unmistakable striped horse with a long erect mane. A zebra's stripes are as individual as a human fingerprint, and serve to break up the animal's outline and so confuse predators. A typical zebra herd consists of one stallion and half a dozen mares with their foals. Zebras mingle happily with other herbivores, but can eat long, coarse grass that is unpalatable to other grazers, so they are often the first to arrive in grazing areas, followed by wildebeest.

Buffalo *(Syncerus caffer)*

Africa's only species of wild cattle, buffalo are very heavily built (up to 150 cm/5 ft at the shoulder), with relatively short, stocky legs. Large ears fringed with hair hang below massive curved horns which meet in a central boss. They are gregarious, living in herds from a few dozen to several thousand in number, though it is not unusual to encounter lone bulls (which can be dangerous). They most often graze at night, and drink in the early morning and late afternoon, spending the day resting or chewing the cud.

Wildebeest *(Connochaetes taurinus)*

Africa's most abundant antelope, the wildebeest or white-bearded gnu is an ungainly creature, dun-grey with a straggly black mane, black face and buffalo-like horns. Wildebeest generally congregate in herds of around 30, but huge concentrations take part in the annual migration round the Serengeti and north into the Maasai Mara, following the rains and the fresh young short grass that is their sole diet. Breeding is synchronised so that hundreds of thousands of calves are born in the Serengeti in February and March.

Eland *(Taurotragus oryx)*

Africa's largest antelope (up to 180 cm/6 ft at the shoulder), the eland is cattle-like in build, with a large dewlap and relatively short spiral horns. Its fawn coat sometimes has fine white stripes on the sides. Eland are widespread in the Serengeti and other grasslands, in nomadic herds of 20 or more, but are shy and difficult to approach. They are active both diurnally and nocturnally, and spend more time feeding at night in the hottest months. A prodigious jumper, an eland can clear 2 metres (6 ft) from a standing position.

Topi *(Damaliscus lunatus)*

The topi is a distinctive antelope: its shoulders are higher (125 cm/49 in) than its rump, and its glossy reddish coat has dark patches on the upper legs. Both sexes have a dark face and stout ridged horns that curve backwards and upwards. The topi is a grazer, found on open grassy plains all over Tanzania, usually in small herds of five or six individuals controlled by one dominant bull, who defends his territory against other males. It is one of the fastest antelopes, and uses its speed and endurance to outrun predators.

Hartebeest *(Alcelaphus buselaphus)*

Similar in build to the topi, Coke's hartebeest or kongoni *(A. b. cokei)* has a longer, pointed head, narrow ears and a white rump. Both sexes have smallish lyre-shaped horns set very close together at the base. Fleet of foot, hartebeest prefer open grassy plains and are often found in small family groups in the Serengeti and Ngorongoro, where they sometimes post sentinels on termite mounds to watch for predators. A close relative, Jackson's hartebeest *(A. b. jacksoni)*, lives in small numbers in western Tanzania.

Sable antelope *(Hippotragus niger)*

You could never confuse the sexes of this handsome large antelope: both have magnificent curved horns (particularly long and striking in the male) and distinctive black-and-white faces, but the male's body is jet black and the female's chestnut brown. Sable avoid dense woodland and the open plains, preferring to live in dry, open woodland, mainly in the south of Tanzania. A herd of 10–30 individuals will be controlled by one dominant bull. Sable are generally grazers, but sometimes browse in the dry season.

Roan antelope *(Hippotragus equinus)*

The second-largest antelope after the eland (150 cm/ 5 ft at the shoulder), the roan has a stocky, horse-like build, a short neck and a distinct erect mane. Both sexes have backward-curving, ringed horns (shorter in the female) and black-and-white face markings. Roan are grazers, but prefer long grass. They are rare in the Serengeti, and more commonly seen in the reserves of southern Tanzania, in herds of six to 12. Territory is defended by an adult bull, but the herd is actually led by a dominant female who selects feeding areas.

Oryx *(Oryx gazella)*

The oryx or gemsbok is a statuesque antelope with a grey body, a striking black-and-white face and unmistakable long, straight horns (both sexes). Tanzania's only variety is the fringe-eared oryx *(O. g. callotis)*, which has curious long tufts of black hair growing from its ear tips. Oryx can live for months in dry open country without access to water. They are predominantly grazers, but also browse and sometimes eat fruit and acacia seed pods. Oryx are common in Tarangire, in herds of up to 30 led by a territorial bull.

Common waterbuck *(Kobus ellipsiprymnus)*

This large, robust antelope (up to 135 cm/4½ ft at the shoulder) with a shaggy grey-brown coat has a pronounced white ring on its rump, as if it has sat on a freshly painted toilet seat. The males have gently curving, lyre-shaped horns. Its close relative, the **Defassa waterbuck** *(Kobus defassa)*, also has a solid white circle on its behind, and is more common to the west of the Rift Valley. Both waterbuck species are grazers, and generally seen in family groups of five to 10 individuals in grassy areas, always near water.

Greater kudu *(Tragelaphus strepsiceros)*

A large, elegant antelope with slender legs, big ears, a grey-brown coat and six to 10 white stripes on each side of the body. The male has a fringe of hair on his throat and chest, and magnificent spiralling horns. Greater kudu are found all over Tanzania in small herds, usually in woodland or thickets and never far away from cover. They browse on seeds and shoots, but also eat seed pods and occasionally graze. The smaller and rarer **lesser kudu** *(Strepsiceros imberbis)* is found in small groups east of the Rift Valley.

Grant's gazelle *(Gazella granti)*

Grant's gazelle is between the impala and a Thomson's gazelle in size. It has a white belly, a pale side-stripe and a chestnut back, with black lines flanking white buttocks. Both sexes have long, elegant horns, particularly striking in the male. They live in herds of about 30, controlled by an adult ram who will perform elaborate displays when confronted by a rival. Herds are mostly nomadic and can last long periods without water, but when food is plentiful, they stay in a small territory, both browsing and grazing.

Thomson's gazelle *(Gazella thomsoni)*

The most abundant gazelle in East Africa (with numbers approaching 1 million), the dainty "Tommy" is distinguished by a broad black horizontal stripe on its flank, with chestnut above and white below. Both sexes have upright, almost parallel horns, shorter and slimmer on females, and short black tails. Tommies graze on open savanna, preferring short-cropped grass, and often follow the wildebeest herds around the Serengeti. When threatened, they bounce around stiff-legged (known as "pronking").

Impala *(Aepyceros melampus)*

Common throughout Tanzania, this slender, elegant, chestnut-coloured antelope is distinguished by unique black-and-white stripes on the rump and tail. Males have impressive lyre-shaped horns. Impala prefer wooded savanna, where they feed on fruits, seed pods, leaves and sometimes grass. They live in two kinds of groups: "bachelor herds" (all male) and "harems" of females and young. In the breeding season, a ram will take over a harem – and then battle with challenging males to preserve his breeding rights.

Gerenuk *(Litocranius walleri)*

An unusual gazelle, the gerenuk is unmistakable for its long legs, elongated neck and huge ears. Males have fairly short, lyre-shaped horns. Equally distinctive are its feeding habits: the gerenuk is the only antelope habitually to stand on its hind legs to browse on new leaf growth, buds and flowers high up on trees and bushes. Gerenuk are often solitary, but are sometimes seen in small mixed groups with a single ram. They are found in the northeastern regions of Tanzania, in arid areas, where they can live without drinking water.

Bushbuck *(Tragelaphus scriptus)*

A medium-sized antelope that appears in various hues: males are often dark brown and females paler chestnut, but there is much variation. Both sexes may have white spots and/or stripes, but this too is inconsistent. The male has straight, sturdy horns. Bushbuck are both browsers and grazers, preferring woodland and bush, always near water. They are mainly nocturnal, but often feed in the early morning and late afternoon. When they venture into open areas, they stay close to cover and seem nervous, so are often hard to spot.

Reedbuck *(Redunca redunca)*

The bohor reedbuck is a fairly nondescript reddish-brown antelope, identified by bare patches behind the ears and (in the male) smallish horns that turn forward at the point. Reedbuck are mostly active at night, but may be seen during the day, singly or in small groups, grazing in open grassland, always near water. In the south of Tanzania, the bohor's place is taken by a close relative, the **southern reedbuck** *(R. arundinum)*, which is less red in colour and more commonly seen in daylight.

Grey duiker *(Sylvicapra grimmia)*

Also known as the common or bush duiker, this small antelope can be anything from grey to chestnut in colour, with a distinctive tuft of black hair between its ears. Rams have short, pointed horns. It is the most widespread of all the duiker species, found (singly or in pairs) in savanna woodland or open bush, and often close to human habitation. It has a remarkably wide diet, feeding on shoots, leaves, fruits and cultivated crops, digging for tubers and roots with its front hoofs, and even taking termites and other insects.

Kirk's dik-dik *(Rhynchotragus kirkii)*

Also called the damara, this tiny, delicate, grey-brown antelope is easily identified by a crest of dark hair on its head, large eyes and an elongated nose like a small trunk. The ram's short, spiky horns may be hidden by the head crest. Usually seen in pairs or small family groups, dik-diks favour dry bush country and scrub, where they browse on leaves and also feed on flowers and fruit knocked to the ground by larger animals. Pairs mate for life and live in permanent territories, with regular paths between resting and feeding sites.

Oribi *(Ourebia ourebi)*

A graceful, small, reddish-brown antelope with a long, thin neck and a short, black-tipped tail. Rams have short, straight horns. Oribi are usually seen in pairs or small groups of one ram, which is vigorously territorial, and several ewes. They occasionally browse but are mainly grazers, preferring short grassland with longer grass patches to provide cover. When disturbed, they give a sharp whistle or sneeze and run off with stiff-legged jumps. Alternatively (and unusually for antelopes), they lie down and hide in long grass.

Warthog *(Phacochoerus aethiopicus)*

The only African wild pig that's commonly seen by day, the warthog has a grey body sparsely covered with bristly hairs, a dark coarse mane and upward-curving tusks. It is named after the wart-like growths on its face (the male has four, the female two). Warthogs graze on a variety of grasses, and in the dry season also root for bulbs and tubers, kneeling down and digging with their tusks. They live in family groups of females and young with one dominant male, sleeping and hiding from predators in networks of burrows.

Bushpig *(Potamochoerus porcus)*

This hairy pig varies in colour from grey to reddish brown, and has a characteristic crest of hair along its spine, tufted ears and a "beard". Males are larger than females (up to 170 cm/5½ ft long). The bushpig is probably as widespread as the warthog in East Africa, but is seen much less often, as it prefers thick vegetation and is mainly active at night, snuffling around for roots, fruits and fungi. Bushpigs are a favourite prey of leopards and spotted hyenas; they are also hunted by humans for food.

Bat-eared fox *(Otocyon megalotis)*

A small, silver-grey fox with black legs, a bushy tail, pale face, pointed black muzzle and enormous ears – the key to their success as insect-eaters. Their main food is harvester termites, which they pinpoint up to 30 cm (1 ft) underground with acute directional hearing, before digging furiously to unearth them. They live in scrub, grassland and lightly wooded areas, in burrows which they dig themselves, or in other creatures' holes, which they modify. They hide during the heat of the day, emerging to feed in early evening.

White-tailed mongoose *(Ichneumia albicauda)*

A very large mongoose, dark grey-brown with black legs, a rump that is higher than its shoulders, and a distinctive bushy white tail. Like most African mongooses, it is a solitary creature – though pairs are occasionally seen – and hunts mainly at night, feeding on a wide range of invertebrates, small mammals (up to the size of a hare) and wild fruits. By day, it lies in burrows dug by other animals, in rock crevices or amid dense vegetation. It is widespread in Tanzania, mainly in wooded areas and forest margins.

Dwarf mongoose *(Helogale parvula)*

One of the two social species of mongoose, the dwarf is also one of Africa's smallest carnivores, about 32 cm (1 ft) long including its tail, a sleek chestnut-brown creature with short legs and a pointed snout. A family of 10–20, led by a dominant male and female, will have up to 20 dens within its territory, often in old termite mounds. From here, they forage as a troop, hunting insects and other invertebrates, reptiles and birds. Usually only the dominant female breeds, but all the troop members care for the young.

Banded mongoose *(Mungos mungo)*

The most often seen of the mongoose family, and the most social, the banded is dark grey-brown with 10–12 dark stripes on its rump. They live in family groups of between five and 40 individuals, and rarely venture far from the troop. Sleeping at night in burrows, they spend most of the day foraging for food, occasionally pausing to stand upright to look around for danger. They are truly omnivorous, eating insects and other invertebrates, small rodents, lizards, birds, eggs and sometimes fruit and berries.

Large-spotted genet *(Genetta tigrina)*

Genets are long, agile, feline creatures with short legs and a long ringed tail. The large-spotted species, which grows up to 105 cm (41 inches) overall, is creamy-yellow with distinct dark body spots and a black tip to its tail. Normally solitary and nocturnal, it hunts large invertebrates and small mammals, and is an agile climber. Its close relative, the slender **small-spotted genet** *(Genetta genetta),* is greyer with very small spots and a white-tipped tail. Both species are sometimes seen scavenging round camps and lodges.

African civet *(Civettictis civetta)*

The size of a medium-sized dog, the civet is a stocky, powerful omnivore, its pale coat marked with dark blotches which merge into stripes nearer the head. It is a solitary hunter and may be seen at night (occasionally in the early evening) trotting with its head down in search of insects, rodents, reptiles – including venomous snakes – birds or carrion. It also eats fruit and can even digest poisonous plants. It is purely terrestrial, unlike its relative the forest-dwelling **tree civet** *(Nandinia binotata)*, which rarely comes to ground.

Ratel *(Mellivora capensis)*

A powerful, low-slung carnivore, mostly black but with a silver-grey mantle from head to tail, the ratel is the same size as a badger (its other name is honey badger, after its habit of breaking into beehives to eat honeycomb and larvae). Hunting mainly at night, usually unaccompanied, ratels use their massive claws to dig out scorpions, rodents and other burrowing animals. They frequently scavenge round rubbish dumps and camps in parks and reserves, and will attack humans aggressively if they feel threatened.

Chimpanzee *(Pan troglodytes)*

This agile, muscular ape, standing about 120 cm (4 ft) tall, is covered in black hair except for its bare face, hands and backside. Chimps live in woodland areas, in large communities of up to 100 individuals, usually dividing themselves into smaller family groups of six to eight. Their diet is varied, including fruit, leaves, bark, insects, eggs and animals such as bushpigs, guinea fowl and monkeys, which they hunt ferociously through the trees. In Tanzania chimps are found on the northeast shores of Lake Tanganyika.

Baboon *(Papio cynocephalus)*

The baboon is Africa's largest monkey, in varying shades of grey-brown, with a distinctive doglike black muzzle and a permanently kinked tail. Baboons are active during the day and largely terrestrial. They climb trees to gather fruits, to take refuge from predators or to sleep at night; otherwise they are found on the ground in complex social groups of up to 100, foraging, fighting, playing, grooming, nursing or courting. They feed on all kinds of plants, including crops, and also take insects, eggs and small mammals.

Vervet monkey *(Cercopithecus aethiops)*

The vervet or green monkey is small and slender, with a long tail, grey-green fur, a white belly and black face and hands. It is common throughout Tanzania, living mainly in savanna and sparse woodland rather than thick forest, in troops of up to 30. Vervets are agile in trees, where they eat fruits, leaves and flowers, but are equally at home on the ground foraging for seeds and insects. They are very social, communicating with each other by a wide variety of calls, gestures and facial expressions.

Blue monkey *(Cecopithecus mitis)*

This medium-sized primate (also called Sykes' monkey) has a dark blue-grey coat, with darker patches on the crown and limbs, and sometimes a white throat patch. Blue monkeys live in woodland in troops of 10–20, controlled by a single adult male. They are active during the day and spend most of their time in the trees, where they feed on leaves, fruits, seeds, gum and bark, and occasionally insects and birds. They have a wide range of calls, including a very loud, far-carrying bark to warn of danger.

Black-and-white colobus *(Colobus polykomos)*

A distinctive medium-large monkey, entirely black except for a white brow and "beard" round its face, long white frills on its flanks and a bushy white tail. You will rarely see one on the ground: they live high in trees in forest areas, in family troops of 10–20. In the early morning they will often sun themselves in the upper tree canopy. Later you may see them leaping athletically from tree to tree, where they feed almost exclusively on leaves. The colobus family are unique among monkeys in that they have no thumb.

Red colobus *(Procolobus spp.)*

A medium-large monkey with long legs and a small head, a red-brown back and pale underside. Red colobus are less commonly seen than their black-and-white cousins, but there are several species in Tanzania, all tree-dwelling leaf-eaters. **Gordon's red colobus** *(P. gordonorum)*, with a greyish "cape", is fairly conspicuous in the Uzungwa Mountains. Jozani Park in Zanzibar is the last stronghold of the endangered **Kirk's red colobus** *(P. kirkii)*, which has bushy white "eyebrows", black shoulders and a red back.

Spring Hare *(Pedetes capensis)*

Despite its name, this is not a member of the rabbit family; and, despite its appearance, it is not related to the kangaroo. The spring hare is a true rodent, around 80 cm (2½ ft) long, yellowish-fawn above and paler below, with large ears and eyes, a long bushy tail and enormous hind legs. It propels itself with these, in a series of leaps or hops, and uses its tiny forelegs solely for feeding or digging. It is a solitary animal, living alone in a burrow, and largely nocturnal, feeding on roots, grass and other plants.

Greater galago *(Galago crassicaudatus)*

Galagos are small nocturnal primates, distant relatives of the lemurs of Madagascar. The greater or thick-tailed galago is by far the largest (80 cm/2½ ft overall), silver grey-brown with a darker bushy tail and large leathery ears. It is omnivorous but prefers fruit, especially figs. It has a loud screaming call, like a human baby in distress. The **bushbaby** *(G. senegalensis)* is the commonest of the smaller galagos. It has huge eyes and ears, and forages by night, usually alone, feeding on sap and insects.

Rock hyrax *(Procavia capensis)*

Hyraxes look like large rodents, brown, round and short-legged, but are in fact distant relatives of the elephant. Rock hyraxes live in small colonies on rocky hillsides or kopjes, where they are often seen basking in the early morning. They feed on leaves, flowers and fruits, never moving far from the shelter of rock. They often become tame when accustomed to people, for instance around lodges. Their relative the **tree hyrax** *(Dendrohyax arboreus)* is a solitary, nocturnal forest animal with an eerie shrieking call.

Porcupine *(Hystrix spp.)*

Easily recognised by its covering of long, black-and-white-banded quills, the porcupine grows up to a metre (3 ft) in length. Two species are found in Tanzania, both very similar in appearance and both sharing the same habits. They live in burrows (often several animals in the same network) in all types of habitat except thick forest, emerging only at night to forage for roots, bulbs, tubers and tree bark. A porcupine makes use of regular pathways: their quills are easily detached and often found along these trails.

Aardvark *(Orycteropus afer)*

An unmistakable creature, the aardvark is vaguely piglike, but with a long tail, long, tubular snout and huge ears. Digging is its speciality, using its powerful forelegs and massive front claws to excavate extensive burrows where it hides during the day. The aardvark is a solitary animal, and active only at night, when it may wander for several kilometres in search of termites, ants or larvae. When it finds a colony, it digs into it vigorously, lapping up insects with its long, sticky tongue.

The Elephant Clan

African elephants display intriguingly complex social behaviour. Living in a matriarchal society, the herd consists of a core family group, led by the oldest female and her offspring (usually about four members). The family group, including the matriarch's sisters and their young, and ranging to about 10 elephants, in turn then expands to the bond groups of the extended family, with up to 30 elephants or more. Bond groups spend up to 50 percent of their time together. The large herds formed by five to 15 bond groups joining together are called clans, while unrelated elephants using the same area are known as a sub-population.

During the wet season, elephants can gather in herds of up to 500. Great excitement is displayed when two families meet. Trumpeting, growling, rumbling, defecating and urinating accompany the greeting ceremony. Trunks are entwined, with much touching and caressing as the elephants renew their acquaintance. As the water dries up and food resources shrink, the group splits up, but will stay in touch. Elephants can communicate over remarkably long distances using very low frequency infrasound, below the level of human hearing.

It is particularly moving to see the gentleness with which elephants nurture their young. Calves are born at night, weighing about 100 kg (220 lbs), and can fit under their mother's bellies until they are six months old. A mother will use her trunk and feet to guide her baby under her tummy to shelter from the sun, or to her teats between her front legs. When on the move, she'll hold the baby's tail, guiding it forwards, crook her trunk around its rump to help it in steep places, lift it out of a wallow and spray it to keep it cool. As the baby grows, its older sisters help to look after it, preparing themselves for motherhood.

When a baby elephant is in trouble, its core family rallies around immediately, encircling the baby protectively. Similar concern is also seen if an elephant is injured, its companions using their tusks to support or lift it. When an elephant dies, it is mourned by family members, who display evidence of distress and sometimes will even cover the body with branches. Adolescent males are driven from the matriarch's herd when they become too boisterous, and form often rowdy bachelor herds. When bond groups join in the rainy season (also the main breeding season), the matriarchal herds are often joined by a dominant breeding bull in musth, his readiness to mate recognised by a copious, pungent secretion from the temporal gland, the dribbling of urine and bouts of aggressive behaviour. Young bulls come into musth in their late teens for a few days; in a prime breeding bull, it can last four to five months.

Females come into oestrus for two to six days, every three to five years. The bull chases the cow briefly, lays his trunk along her back and rears up on his hind legs. Penetration only lasts 45 seconds. Immediately after mating, the cow will scream, with her family group gathering around and trumpeting loudly, as if sounding their approval.   ❑

RIGHT: elephants need to learn; evidence shows that orphaned teenagers behave like hoodlums.

BIRDS

Birdwatching in Tanzania offers the opportunity to spot over 1,000 species, from ostriches to sunbirds

LEFT: this flamboyant paradise flycatcher works hard to feed his hungry brood.

East Africa is unequalled in the variety and concentration of its birdlife. So far more than 1,388 species have been recorded – around 15 percent of the world's bird species – and scientists believe that many more are yet to be discovered, especially in remote areas. Compare this figure with the 250 or so species recorded in Britain, or the 850 in Canada, Mexico and the United States, and you will understand why Tanzania, with more than 1,000 species, is an ornithologist's delight.

A few birds are so rare that it is many years since they have been positively sighted. Others, such as the Udzungwa partridge and the Pemba green pigeon, are found only in specific small areas. Even so, the birds you are likely to spot on even a short safari holiday are far too numerous to describe in a book like this. *(See Further Reading at the end of Travel Tips for a list of detailed field guides.)*

We have whittled our list down to a few dozen of the commonest or most remarkable species. They include the largest bird on earth, the world's heaviest flying bird, the most abundant species on the planet and the bird that makes the largest nest of all. And, of course, we have included some of the most spectacularly beautiful birds to be seen anywhere.

Ostrich *(Struthio camelus)*

The flightless ostrich is the world's largest and heaviest bird, growing up to 5.5 metres (8 ft) tall and 90 kg (200 lb) in weight. It is also the fastest running bird, reaching speeds of 50 kph (35 mph). Males are jet black with white primary plumes in the wings; females and young are grey or dull brown. They are usually seen in groups of 5–12 adults, sometimes with large numbers of young. Ostriches are polygamous: one male will mate with several females, who all lay their eggs in one nest and care for the young communally.

Secretary bird *(Sagittarius serpentarius)*

This odd terrestrial bird of prey has the body and head of an eagle (grey with black wingtips and a bare orange face), but legs that are three times as long as an eagle's, so that it walks over 1 metre (40 in) tall. It stalks open country, often in pairs, seeking prey, which it kills by stamping with strong feet. Victims include rodents, large insects and reptiles, including poisonous snakes. Although it hunts entirely on the ground, covering up to 20 km (12 miles) a day, it can fly, and roosts at night on the tops of thorn trees.

Crowned crane *(Balearica regulorum)*

This elegant bird is the only crane resident in East Africa, and the national bird of Uganda. It stands just over 1 metre (40 in) tall, and is slate-grey, with black, white and chestnut on the wings, a black-and-white face and a red wattle. But its unmistakable feature is a straw-coloured spiky crest, carried by both sexes. It is the only crane capable of perching, and it roosts and nests in trees, usually near wet places, but generally feeds in open or wooded grasslands, stomping on the ground to scare up insects.

Kori bustard *(Otis kori)*

A male kori weighs up to 18 kg (40 lb) – it is Africa's heaviest flying bird – and stands up to 120 cm (4 ft) tall; the female is somewhat smaller. Both sexes are dark brown above, paler below, with shaggy grey neck feathers, long legs and a large head. Bustards are largely terrestrial, stalking the savanna and dry bush country with a stately walk in search of insects, reptiles and small rodents. The male's remarkable display involves puffing up its neck feathers like a balloon and raising its tail along its back.

Marabou stork *(Leptotilos crumeniferus)*

This large (150-cm/5-ft tall) stork is grey above, white below, and easily identified by a large pink pouch on the front of the neck. It is also the only stork that flies with its head retracted instead of straight-necked. Marabous are gregarious scavengers, often seen congregating with vultures at a kill. They also feed on frogs and locusts. Other large storks found near water include the **saddle-billed** *(Ephippiorhynchus senegalensis),* with its striking black, red and yellow bill, and the self-explanatory **yellow-billed** *(Ibis ibis).*

White-backed vulture *(Gyps africanus)*

The white-backed can be distinguished in flight from other vultures by its white rump and a white band on the front underside of the wings. Its white back is only visible when it lands to scavenge. It is about 90 cm (3 ft) long, with a bare face and black bill. A similar species, **Ruppell's vulture** *(Gyps ruppellii)*, has three narrow, pale bars on the underside of the wings. These are East Africa's commonest vultures, most often seen in areas with high concentrations of predators and prey, such as the Serengeti.

Black kite *(Milvus migrans)*

If you spend a day in the Ngorongoro Crater, your picnic lunch is sure to be attended by black kites, opportunistic birds of prey which seize on anything from road kill to swarms of insects to tourist sandwiches. Black kites are actually dark brown, 58 cm (23 in) long, with a conspicuously forked tail and a yellow bill. They are among the most adaptable of predators, found in savanna, cultivated areas, towns and the coast. The **European black kite**, a common winter visitor, has a pale-brown head and a black bill.

Sacred ibis *(Threskiornis aethiopica)*

The ibis, once worshipped by the ancient Egyptians, is 75 cm (2½ ft) long, mainly white, with purple-black plumes on its lower back, and a naked black head and neck. It is a wading bird, using its long, thin, downward-curving bill to probe the mud for crustaceans and snails, and also foraging on grassland. An adaptable species, it has colonised river banks, marshland, swamps, coastal beaches and even sewage ponds. Sacred ibis nest in colonies, and at dusk can be seen flying to communal roosts in a V-shaped flock.

African spoonbill *(Platalea alba)*

The spoonbill (related to the ibis) is around 90 cm (3 ft) long, with pure white plumage, a bare pink face and legs, and a large, flattened yellow bill, which it sweeps from side to side as it wades, filtering out tiny water creatures. Spoonbills are common, singly or in groups, in shallow, slow-moving waterways, feeding in the company of other waterbirds. They nest colonially in trees, where they build untidy nests of sticks. Spoonbills can be distinguished from white egrets in flight because they fly with their neck outstretched.

African darter *(Anhinga rufa)*

The darter resembles a long-necked, long-tailed cormorant, around 80 cm (2½ ft) overall, dark brown with a yellow eye-stripe and a long yellow bill. It inhabits inland waters, favouring slow-flowing rivers and fresh and alkaline lakes. The darter fishes underwater, pursuing its prey with powerful webbed feet and stabbing fish with its dagger-like bill. It swims almost wholly submerged, with only its head and sinuous neck showing – hence its common name of "snake-bird".

White-necked cormorant *(Phalacrocorax carbo)*

The white-necked is Africa's largest (90 cm/3 ft) and commonest cormorant, dark brown in colour, with white on the cheeks, the front of the neck and upper breast. Unlike the solitary darter, cormorants congregate in large flocks on lakes and slow-flowing rivers. They are expert divers, hunting fish underwater and surfacing to swallow them. They are commonly seen perching with their wings outstretched to dry. The **long-tailed cormorant** *(Phalacrocorax africanus)* is smaller, with a longer tail and no white neck.

Lesser flamingo *(Phoenicopterus minor)*

Flamingos, which gather in their thousands in East Africa's shallow soda lakes, have a unique method of feeding: with their head upside-down and submerged, they sweep their angular bill from side to side, filtering out tiny water creatures and algae. The lesser flamingo stands 90 cm (3 ft) tall, and has pink plumage, red legs and a dark-red bill. The less common **greater flamingo** *(Phoenicopterus ruber)*, at 140 cm (4½ ft) tall, has much paler plumage, with red-and-black wingtips, and a pink, black-tipped bill.

White pelican *(Pelecanus onocrotalus)*

These large waterbirds (up to 180 cm/6 ft long, with an even greater wingspan) are white or off-white, with an unmistakable huge yellow bill and pouch. Unusually for birds, they feed communally: up to 30 pelicans form a straight line or horseshoe and, plunging their bills into the water simultaneously, drive fish into the shallows where they can be easily caught. Pelicans are clumsy on land, but graceful in flight. The smaller **pink-backed pelican** *(Pelecanus rufescens)* is pale grey with a pink rump, and tends to fish alone.

Hamerkop *(Scopus umbretta)*

The hamerkop is a brown waterbird 60 cm (2 ft) long, with a heavy black bill and thick, square crest that earned it the Afrikaans name for "hammerhead". It is usually seen wading in the shallows of lakes or slow-moving rivers, searching for frogs, tadpoles, fish or mussels. For unknown reasons, hamerkops build enormous nests (up to 2 metres/6½ ft in diameter) from twigs, sticks and even bones, usually in the fork of a tree. The brood chamber within is accessible only through a narrow tunnel.

Goliath heron *(Ardea goliath)*

This stately bird, slate-grey with long, black legs and a reddish-brown neck and head, is most easily identified by its size: at 150 cm (5 ft) tall, it is the world's largest heron. It is seen, alone or in pairs, wading in shallow water spearing fish with its long pointed bill. The **purple heron** *(Ardea purpurea)* has similar colouring, except for a black crown and neck markings, but is much smaller (90 cm/3 ft). Another striking large heron, the **great white egret** *(Egretta alba)*, is pure white with a yellow bill and black legs.

Pied kingfisher *(Ceryle rudis)*

East Africa's 15 species of kingfisher all have large heads and long, pointed bills, compact bodies and very short legs. At 25 cm (10 in), the pied is one of the largest, and also the commonest. It has striking black-and-white plumage and a black dagger for a bill. Like all the aquatic kingfishers (some others are woodland creatures), it has remarkable eyes that adapt instantly from air to underwater vision, and allow for depth and refraction. Uniquely, the pied kingfisher also has the ability to hover above the water, spotting prey.

Crowned plover *(Vanellus coronatus)*

Plovers are waders, although some species – including the crowned – are often seen far from water, in savanna and cultivated fields. The crowned plover is about 28 cm (11 in) tall, and is grey-brown with a white underside, long, red legs, an orange bill and a distinctive black cap with a white crown. It feeds mainly on large insects, standing still, running swiftly and then stopping again to look for prey. Crowned plovers tend to stay in pairs, scraping a shallow nest in the ground and defending it against all-comers.

African jacana *(Actophilornis africana)*

The jacana or lily-trotter is a clumsy flier, and an occasional and reluctant diver, but its speciality is apparently walking on water. It has chestnut plumage, a white throat, glossy black on the top of the head, and a blue bill and forehead "shield". Its most striking features are its extremely long toes, which enable it to walk swiftly across water lilies and other floating vegetation in search of insects, crustaceans and molluscs. The **lesser jacana** *(Microparra capensis)* is smaller, lacks the "shield", and is less often seen.

African fish eagle *(Haliaetus vocifer)*

The fish eagle – sometimes called "the voice of Africa", after its loud, high-pitched cry – is commonly seen on rivers and lakes. Closely related to the North American bald eagle, this large (75-cm/2½-ft) predator has a white head, breast and tail, yellow-and-black bill, chestnut belly and shoulders, and black wings. It preys on surface-feeding fish, seizing them in flight with its huge talons and carrying them off to a favourite perch to eat. It is such an efficient fisher that it may spend 90 percent of the day resting or preening.

Verreaux's eagle owl *(Bubo lacteus)*

Like most owls, this is a nocturnal creature, but is more likely than most to be spotted during the day in acacia woodland – not just because of its considerable size (61 cm/2 ft or more), but because it is often mobbed by smaller birds when at rest. It is grey-brown overall with a finely barred underside, a distinctive whitish face with a black bar on either side, and tufted ears. Despite its size, it flies soundlessly, preying on small birds, rodents and lizards, which it seizes with powerful talons and swallows whole.

Lourie *(Corythaixoides leucogaster)*

The white-bellied lourie – also called the go-away bird, after its noisy, bleating call that sounds like "go 'way, go 'way" – is a striking grey bird with a white belly, long tail and conspicuous head crest. It is a woodland dweller, often spotted (follow the call) at the very top of acacias. It is a clumsy flier, flapping for a while then gliding, like a hornbill. In southern Tanzania you are more likely to see its all-grey relative, the **grey lourie** or common go-away bird *(Corythaixoides concolor)*.

White-crowned shrike *(Eurocephalus rueppelli)*

Common birds of acacia bush country, these shrikes are recognisable by a white crown and rump and wide black patch behind the eye. Their flight is also distinctive – a stiff glide between trees on rigid wings. They are highly sociable: groups of 10–20 birds scurry noisily round trunks and branches hunting insects and spiders. They chatter to each other as they fly, and also make a distinctive bill-snapping noise. Unusually, when a pair breeds, other members of the group help with nest-building and feeding the chicks.

Red-billed hornbill *(Tockus erythrorhynchus)*

This hornbill (one of 20 species) is common in dry bush country and acacia woodland, where its long, hoarse rattling cry is a characteristic sound. It measures 45 cm (1½ ft), with mottled black-and-white wings, a white head and chest and a large curved red bill. Red-billed hornbills are omnivorous and feed mainly on the ground, eating insects, small reptiles, fruits and seeds, often mingling with other bird species and squirrels. They nest in holes in trees, often at a considerable height.

Speckled mousebird *(Colius striatus)*

Mousebirds are so named for their soft, fur-like feathers and their way of running along branches like rodents, in search of fruit. Another curious habit they have is to hang from branches or telegraph wires with their feet at "shoulder" height. The common speckled species is mid-brown above, paler below, with white tips to the feathers that give a speckled appearance. Half of its 33-cm (13-in) length is a long, stiff tail. They are gregarious birds, moving in noisy parties of 10–30 birds. Individual birds often preen one another.

Fischer's lovebird *(Agopornis fischeri)*

Lovebirds are small, plump, short-tailed parrots, green in colour with yellow or orange collars, red bills and white fleshy rings round the eyes. The species, named after the 19th-century explorer G.A. Fischer, is endemic to Tanzania, found only in the north of the country, especially in the Serengeti and Ngorongoro Crater. Lovebirds are gregarious seedeaters, seen in large flocks in open grassland and cultivated areas. They use their bills and legs to climb trees, and often fly en masse to water in the afternoon.

Sunbirds *(Nectarinia spp.)*

This is a large family of small birds with slender, curved bills and, in most species, brilliant metallic plumage in the males. They are found in the vicinity of flowering plants, for their main food is nectar, which they extract with their long hollow tongues, sometimes hanging upside-down from stems. Occasionally they will hover to feed, like hummingbirds. As an indication of their vibrant colouring, the Tanzanian species include the scarlet-chested, green-throated, golden-winged, olive-bellied and amethyst sunbirds.

Lilac-breasted roller *(Coracias caudata)*

This bird's rich lilac breast is unmistakable – but so are its vivid ultramarine rump and wing coverts, its blue head with a white brow, and its elongated, pointed outer tail feathers. Lilac-breasted rollers are usually seen, singly or in pairs, perched on a vantage point such as a dead branch or telegraph pole, scanning the ground for the large insects and lizards which form their diet. As with other rollers, the male performs a tumbling aerial routine to impress his mate, which gives the family their name.

Little bee-eater *(Merops pusillus)*

Bee-eaters are small, brightly coloured birds with a black stripe through the eye and long, pointed bills. Little bee-eaters, the smallest of the family and among the commonest, measure only 15 cm (6 ins) to the tip of their squared-off tail, and have brilliant-green plumage, an orange breast and a dark patch beneath the yellow throat. They are found, usually in pairs, in all kinds of habitats where insects fly: despite their name, bee-eaters also feed on dragonflies, cicadas, wasps or hornets, which they deftly catch on the wing.

Red-billed oxpecker *(Buphagus erythrorhyncus)*

Oxpeckers are members of the starling family that specialise in eating ticks and bloodsucking flies from the hides of livestock and larger game animals. (They also rip hair from the animals to line their nests.) They are slim brown birds, 18 cm (7 in) long, with pale undersides. The common red-billed species, as well as a bright red bill, has a vivid yellow ring around its red eye. The much less common **yellow-billed oxpecker** *(Buphagus africanus)* has a red tip to its yellow bill, no yellow around the eye and a pale rump.

Helmeted guinea fowl *(Numida meleagris)*

The size of a well-fed chicken (56 cm/2 ft), this common bird has white spots all over its grey body and wings, a bare blue neck and throat, a red face and a bony yellow casque on top of the head. Guinea fowl are reluctant fliers (though they roost in trees at night) and prefer to run away from danger. They are opportunistic feeders, eating insects and snails, seeds, fruit and berries. Characteristic habits include "bathing" in dust, to condition their plumage, and congregating in large numbers to drink in the late afternoon.

Crested francolin *(Francolinus sephaena)*

East Africa has 16 species of francolin – plump ground-dwelling birds resembling partridges, usually brown streaked with black, grey or white, with short tails, stout bare legs and thick, slightly curved bills. They are seriously terrestrial, even nesting in shallow depressions in the ground, and only taking flight as a last resort. The crested francolin, common in dry bush country, has a characteristic white eye-stripe, white speckled neck and reddish legs. Often seen with its tail cocked, it raises its crest feathers when alarmed.

Paradise flycatcher *(Terpsiphone viridis)*

Flycatchers are smallish birds with broad, flattened bills surrounded by bristles, adapted for catching beetles and caterpillars in foliage and flying insects on the wing. Most species are nondescript grey or blue-grey birds, but the spectacular exception is the paradise flycatcher, which has a blue-black head and crest, a chestnut back and tail, white undersides and a blue eye and bill. For added dramatic effect, in the breeding season the male's tail feathers grow to twice the length of his body (36 cm/14 in overall).

Red-billed firefinch *(Lagonosticta rubricata)*

Waxbills *(Estrildidae)* are a large family of small, ground-feeding, seed-eating birds, with stout, conical bills that are quite often red. The red-billed firefinch is a good example – and hard to miss, both for its overall pinkish-red colouring and because it commonly nests near human habitation. Disregarding people or other birds, it scurries around the ground industriously, like an animated plum. Firefinches are gregarious, generally seen in flocks of 20–40 birds, although pairs leave the flock to breed and raise their young.

Barbets *(Capitonidae)*

Like their relatives the woodpeckers, barbets are usually found in woodland, where they feed on fruit. An exception is the **red and yellow barbet** *(Trachyphonus erythrocephalus)*, which prefers semi-arid bush country. It resembles a gaudy woodpecker – 23 cm (9 in) long with a red, yellow and black head, bright-yellow underparts and white spots all over its black back, wings and tail. This species is often seen on the ground, and does not even nest in trees but on the ground, in banks or in termite mounds.

Black-headed weaver *(Ploceus cucullatus)*

Weavers are oversized finches, with short, stout seed-eating bills. Males are usually yellow, at least in the breeding season, with black, brown or orange highlights; females are more drab and sparrow-like. The males of all species weave intricate hollow nests from grass, with different species favouring different architecture. The black-headed weaver, for instance, constructs an onion-shaped ball suspended from the end of a branch. The male bird is vivid yellow, with a black head and throat, and red eyes.

Superb starling *(Spreo superbus)*

Many of Africa's starlings have brilliant iridescent plumage, in blues, greens and purples. One of the most striking is also one of the most often seen, as it is fearless of man and will even take food from a table. The superb starling is metallic blue-green on top, orange-brown below, with a white breast band and white eyes. Similar species which lack the white band are the **golden-breasted** *(Cosmosparus regius)*, which is golden-yellow below, and **Hildebrandt's starling** *(Spreo hildebrandti)*, which has orange eyes.

Yellow-vented bulbul *(Pycnonotus barbatus)*

Also called the common or dark-capped bulbul, this is one of Africa's commonest birds, found in most kinds of habitat except dense forest, including gardens and around lodges, where it will raid food tables for scraps. It is 18 cm (7 in) long, dark brown above, much paler below, with a pronounced crest on its head and a bright yellow patch beneath the tail. It is a melodious songster, with a range of whistling calls. On alighting, it has a habit of half-raising its wings and uttering a brief warbling song.

Cattle egret *(Ardeola ibis)*

In the breeding season, the cattle egret's crown, back and chest are washed with orange or yellow, but at other times it is pure white, with a yellow bill and yellow or flesh-coloured legs. Like other egrets and herons, it is a wader, catching small fish, frogs or crustaceans. But it is also associated with cattle and game away from water, feeding on the insects that they disturb. A very similar species, the **little egret** *(Egretta garzetta)*, does not display the yellow breeding plumage, and has a black bill and legs.

Red-billed quelea *(Quelea quelea)*

Apart from its red bill and the male's breeding-season black face and pink crown, there is nothing to distinguish this brown-grey sparrow-like little bird – until you see a swarm of them, which can number hundreds of thousands and blot out the sun. The red-billed quelea is the most abundant bird on the planet, and a serious agricultural pest. It is a seed-eater, and a vast flock of quelea destroys crops faster than locusts. Millions are killed at their roost sites every year in a vain attempt to contain their numbers.

White-browed coucal *(Centropus superciliosus)*

Coucals are heavily built, rather clumsy-looking birds, ungainly in flight but sure-footed and vigorous on the ground, where they hunt for insects, reptiles, eggs and small rodents. The white-browed species, the commonest in Tanzania, has chestnut wings and back, pale undersides, a black head and a distinctive white "eyebrow". It is sometimes called the "bottle-bird", after its bubbling call, like water being poured from a bottle. The slightly larger **blue-headed coucal** *(C. monachus)* is found near swamps and marshes.

Pied crow *(Corvus albus)*

Africa's most common crow is 46 cm (1½ ft) long, glossy black with a white breast and collar, and a heavy black bill. Pied crows are omnivorous, taking small mammals and birds, insects, frogs, reptiles, fruits and seeds. They also relish carrion, often arriving at a kill before the vultures, and have learned to scavenge around human habitation, especially on rubbish dumps. Another common member of the crow family is the **white-necked raven** *(Corvus albicollis)*, larger than the pied crow and without the white breast.

Cordon bleu *(Uraeginthus spp.)*

Cordon bleus are pretty little birds of the waxbill family, small seed-eaters with conical bills. The **red-cheeked cordon bleu** *(Uraeginthus bengalus)* is seen ground-feeding in most habitats, including gardens and around camps. It has an azure-blue face and breast, brown back, wings and crown, and the male has a vivid crimson patch on each cheek. The less common **blue-capped cordon bleu** *(U. cyanocephalus)*, a shyer resident of dry bush country, has a pure blue head and no red cheek-patches.

REPTILES AND AMPHIBIANS

*Fascinating but widely feared, reptiles are among the
world's oldest and most extraordinary inhabitants*

Reptiles are not popular among East Africa's local population.
Many people will kill any snake or lizard on sight, as a
matter of principle. There are poisonous snakes, of course,
and some of the more deadly species are listed below. But most are
quite harmless to humans, and even the most venomous varieties
will only attack a person if they see no means of escape. Many
snakes are nocturnal, and night is the best time to spot them. Others
use camouflage to disguise their presence.

Crocodiles, the world's largest reptiles, are undeniably dangerous, and are responsible for hundreds of human deaths every year.
But, provided you keep well away from those fearsome jaws, you
cannot help marvelling at these prehistoric killing machines.

The smaller reptiles are fascinating, too, and many do a great service to humanity by disposing of huge quantities of unpleasant
insects. Amphibians, with their semi-aquatic lifestyle, have evolved
many extraordinary techniques for coping with the region's long
dry spells. Some, for instance, simply disappear underground for
months in suspended animation until the next rains.

LEFT: a
crocodile lurks
underwater
waiting for
unwary prey.

Nile crocodile *(Crocdylus niloticus)*

Larger and scalier than any other reptile, crocs grow
to an average of 5 metres (16 ft), but they can attain
7 metres (23 ft) and weigh 900 kg (2,000 lb). Though
they rarely venture far from water, their muscular legs
can propel them at 45 kph (28 mph) across the
ground. Up to 70 percent of an adult's diet is fish, but
they also take unwary mammals including baboons,
antelope, wildebeest, young hippos – and humans.
Females lay a dozen eggs in a hole dug in the ground,
which they cover with vegetation.

Nile monitor *(Varanus niloticus)*

Africa's largest lizard ranges in colour from grey-
brown to olive-green, with bands of yellow spots. It
grows up to 2 metres (6½ ft) and is an aggressive carnivore, preying on anything from insects and birds to
mammals as large as a mongoose. Eggs are a favourite
food, and monitors will dig up unguarded crocodile
eggs or climb a tree to raid birds' nests. They are
strong swimmers and can remain underwater for an
hour. Females excavate termite mounds and lay their
eggs inside, for protection against predators.

Common agama *(Agama agama)*

Agamas are sometimes called rainbow lizards, because of their variety of colouring. The adult male, which grows to 25 cm (10 in), is dark blue with a yellowish tail and a bright-red head – though this turns dark brown when two males fight over territory or females. Females and young males are smaller and buff-brown, with a darker olive head. Agamas are often seen around human settlements and lodges. They feed mainly on ants, grasshoppers, beetles and termites, which they catch with a long, sticky tongue.

African skink *(Mabuya spp.)*

There are more than 80 species of lizard in the genus *Mabuya*, several of them found in East Africa. They are slender, smooth-skinned creatures, measuring up to 25 cm (10 in) from their pointed head to the tip of a long, tapering tail. Colours range from yellow through green to dark brown. Skinks are agile insect-eaters who spend most of their time on the ground, either chasing food or basking to absorb warmth. The commonest species in Tanzania is the African striped skink *(M. striata)*, found in all kinds of habitat.

Chameleons *(Chamaeleo spp.)*

While it is not true that chameleons change colour to match their background, most species are capable of a variety of hues – usually greens, browns and greys – conditioned by temperature, light, fear or aggression. They are all well adapted for a life hunting insects in trees, with paired toes for clinging to thin twigs, a prehensile tail coiled like a spring, eyes that swivel independently and a sticky, muscular tongue that can shoot out to the length of its body and catch prey. Some species have neck-flaps, crests or horns.

House gecko *(Hemidactylus mabouia)*

Geckos are small lizards found in most subtropical regions. This common species is about 12 cm (5 in) long, pale brown or pinkish, with a round tail, large eyes and big, splayed feet. The toes have specially adapted scales with minute hairs that catch in small cracks and enable the gecko to climb walls or even waddle across a ceiling. They are often found in human habitation, especially at night – and you should be grateful if you see one: an adult can eat half a dozen mosquitoes in a minute.

Great plated lizard *(Gerrhosaurus major)*

A handsome lizard, armoured with bony scales, even on its belly and the soles of its feet. The scales on its back project upwards like small, tough fins, darker-coloured than the yellowish-brown body, which gives a speckled or striped effect. The great plated grows to 70 cm (28 in) long, though two-thirds of that is tail. These shy creatures live in burrows, often sharing with dwarf mongooses or renovating an old termite mound. They are largely fruit-eaters, but will seize insects or mice if they get a chance.

Leopard tortoise *(Geochelone pardalis)*

Not easily confused with a leopard, this large, ponderous tortoise gets its name from its mottled dark-brown-and-yellow shell. A large male may grow to 60 cm (2 ft) long and weigh over 35 kg (80 lb); females are somewhat smaller. It lives in the savanna, where it feeds mainly on grass and flowers. Its only defence mechanism is to spray urine at an attacker, but its heavy shell protects it against most predators – although some large birds swallow young ones whole, or drop adults from a height to crack them open.

Pancake tortoise *(Malachochersus tornieri)*

Uniquely, the pancake tortoise's beautifully patterned shell is not rigid and domed but flat, light and very flexible. Although it can grow up to 17 cm (7 in) long, it is never more than about 3 cm (1½ in) high. Its flatness and flexibility enable it to squeeze into narrow crevices in rocks. When threatened, it will not crouch down and withdraw its head and legs, like most tortoises, but scamper to the nearest rocky outcrop and hide. It leaves its refuge to feed on grass and other vegetation.

Nile soft-shelled turtle *(Trionyx triunguis)*

The Nile soft-shell grows to 90 cm (3 ft) long and weighs up to 45 kg (100 lb). It is dark-green-brown in colour, with a flattened shell and short legs (the species name *triunguis* refers to its three claws on each foot). It is found in large rivers, ponds and lakes – and occasionally ventures out to sea. Though largely aquatic, it is often seen basking on overhanging logs. Unusually for a turtle, it is omnivorous, eating fruits and other vegetable matter, as well as insects, but the bulk of its diet is fish and molluscs.

Green turtle *(Chelonia mydas)*

The largest of the hard-shelled sea turtles, the green grows to 120 cm (4 ft) in length and can weigh up to 90 kg (200 lb). It is dark brown on top and yellow below: its name comes from the greenish cast of its fatty flesh. Females nest roughly every three years, visiting a beach up to six times to lay about 100 eggs each time. Like all marine turtles, the green turtle is on the endangered list, but around Tanzania it has protected nesting sites in Pemba, Mafia Island and the new Mkwaja Saadani National Park.

Black mamba *(Dendroaspis polylepis)*

The only black part of a black mamba is the inside of its mouth. Its body can be any colour from grey to olive brown, with a paler underside: it is more easily identified by its length (up to 240 cm/8 ft), its slenderness, its speed of movement and its coffin-shaped head. It lives in dry bush country, in abandoned termite mounds or among rocks, and feeds on birds and small mammals, which it paralyses with lethal venom. Its keen eyesight and general alertness means you are unlikely to disturb a mamba unnoticed.

Puff adder *(Bitis arietans)*

Puff adders are responsible for more lethal bites than all of Africa's other snakes combined. They are slow-moving, thickset creatures, 1 metre (3 ft) or more in length, over 8 cm (3 in) in diameter, brown or yellow in colour with black chevrons down the back. When disturbed, the snake makes a loud hissing (or puffing) as a warning, then strikes very fast. Its venom quickly disposes of rodents or birds, which make up its diet, and can kill a human. Unusually among snakes, the puff adder gives birth to live young.

Spitting cobra *(Naja nigricollis)*

This, the commonest cobra in Africa, is a slender snake that grows to 180 cm (6 ft) or more, grey in colour with a darker cobra's "hood" at the back of the neck (*nigricollis* means "black-neck"). It is found in grassy plains and sparse woodlands, where it feeds on small mammals, birds and reptiles. When cornered it will defend itself aggressively, either by biting and injecting venom, or by spitting a mist of atomised venom at the face of its attacker. This can cause blindness in humans if the eyes are not washed immediately.

Boomslang *(Dispholidus typus)*

Also known as the green tree snake, the boomslang is anything from bright olive-green through brown to black. Its long (150 cm/5 ft) and slender build make it well adapted for life in trees, where it hunts birds, reptiles and small mammals such as squirrels. Its large eyes aid vision in the shaded treetops. Its powerful venom is injected from fangs set back in the mouth – so far back that a human, in order to be bitten, would have to put a finger into its jaws. It is not usually aggressive and is more likely to flee when approached.

African rock python *(Python sebae natalensis)*

This is by far the largest snake in Africa, often measuring 450 cm (15 ft) and weighing up to 60 kg (130 lb). Its body colour is variable, but usually a shade of brown with black-edged crossbars or blotches. Pythons are found in open grassland and light woodland, usually near water. They are not poisonous, but kill prey by gripping it with their teeth, then coiling around it to crush it and swallowing it whole. Victims include rodents and hares, young warthogs, monkeys and antelope as large as impala.

African bullfrog *(Pyxicephalus adspersus)*

This giant frog – 20 cm (8 in) long – is dark green, with a thick body and a broad, rounded head. During the dry season, bullfrogs burrow and stay underground until the next rains, when they emerge to breed, depositing thousands of eggs in shallow water. During the rainy season, the males' loud booming call can be heard day and night. As well as the usual amphibian diet of insects and worms, bullfrogs are large enough to take small rodents. If they are really hungry, they will also eat their own young.

Grey tree frog *(Chiromantis xerampelina)*

Tree-dwelling frogs have suction pads on their toes to grip branches, and sticky tongues with which they catch insects. Like all amphibians, they depend on fresh water for breeding: some lay eggs in spawn in water, but others, like the 6-cm (2½-in) grey tree frog, deposit eggs in a nest of foam on an overhanging branch. After a week, tadpoles wriggle out and drop into the water below, which may be a mere puddle. Tree frogs are most active at night, but can often be seen basking by day, absorbing the sun's warmth.

INVERTEBRATES

*Small and often irritating, invertebrates can have more
impact on your trip than any other species*

LEFT: home, trap and work of art, the spider's web is a creation of true beauty.

Apart from dazzling butterflies and irritating flies that bite, it is easy not to pay much attention to Tanzania's myriad insects and other creepy-crawlies. But East African invertebrates (animals without backbones) are worthy of study for several reasons. First, there are tens of thousands of species, in an amazing diversity of forms, physical construction and camouflage, with an extraordinary variety of feeding and breeding techniques, all superbly adapted to the environment in which they live.

Some, of course, are best avoided – including poisonous spiders and scorpions, mosquitoes that carry malaria and flies that spread sleeping sickness. But many species, small as they are, have an enormous positive impact on the environment itself.

Many plants large and small owe their continued existence to pollinating insects; the tsetse fly has been an important agent for wildlife conservation, by discouraging cattle ranching in huge areas that are still the domain of game; the largest consumer of grass on the savanna is not an antelope or buffalo but a creature that measures less than 2 cm (¾ in) long; and if it were not for the industrious dung beetle, the landscape would look very different after a herd of wildebeest has passed through.

Stick insect *(Phasmida)*

Masters of camouflage, the many species of stick insect look like twigs (some also have flattened wing-cases that resemble leaves) and usually live on plants that mirror their coloration – yellow, brown or green. Some even lay eggs that look just like seeds. Adults vary in length from 8 to 20 cm (3–8 in), but even the largest are hard to spot in their natural habitat. They feed almost exclusively on leaves, creeping slowly around a plant to avoid detection. Some species have wings, but only the males fly.

Praying mantis *(Heterochaeta reticulata)*

The mantid family – around 2,000 worldwide – all catch smaller insects with their specialised, spiny front legs, which they hold in an attitude of supplication (hence their name). Tanzania's commonest species grows up to 15 cm (6 in) long (the male is longer and thinner than the female), and resembles green twigs and leaves. It adds to the camouflage by remaining motionless until it strikes – amazingly fast. Unlike most insects, the mantis does not have a grub or caterpillar stage: infants are tiny replicas of their parents.

Dung beetle *(Scarabaeinae)*

There are many species of dung beetle, in all shapes and sizes. Most are black or metallic brown-green and between 5 and 40 mm (¼–1½ in) long. They all feed on the droppings of herbivores, which they mould into a sphere (the size of a golf ball or larger) with their shovel-shaped head, and roll away to bury. The dung provides food for the beetle, which can eat its own weight in 24 hours, and also serves as a brood chamber into which the female lays her eggs. The beetle itself is food for mongooses and bat-eared foxes.

Ant lion *(Myrmeleontidae)*

Curious little predators with an unusual method of hunting, ant lions are the larvae of various species of lacewings (flying insects rather like dragonflies). The larva, which grows to about 15 mm (½ in) long, digs a conical pit of up to 6 cm (2½ in) in diameter in soft sand, and lurks in wait just below the apex of the cone. When an ant or other crawling insect stumbles into the pit, it slides helplessly down the funnel into the waiting jaws of the ant lion, which paralyses its victim with poison and sucks out the vital juices.

Giant African land snail *(Achatina fulica)*

An unmistakable huge snail with a conical brown shell streaked with yellow, black or purple. An adult's shell is normally around 10 cm (4 in), although the largest-known specimen measured 30 cm (nearly 1 ft) fully extended, with a 20-cm (8-in) shell. It feeds on all kinds of vegetation, rasping at food with its "tongue" (radula), which carries several hundred teeth. In some areas the giant snail is a major agricultural pest. It can live up to nine years, and lays eggs in batches of 100–400 – up to 1,200 in one year.

Mopane worm *(Imbrasia belina)*

The so-called mopane worm – not a worm at all, but the larva (caterpillar) of the large mopane emperor moth – is spiny, hairless, about 7 cm (2¾ in) long and brightly striped with red, yellow and black. It feeds exclusively on the protein-rich leaves of the mopane tree, and is in turn a rich food source for local people, who eat the "worm" raw, baked, boiled or deep-fried, and even collect it for processing and canning. The adult moth lives only two or three days, during which it must mate and lay eggs.

Golden orb spider *(Nephila spp.)*

These huge yellow and black spiders (the female's body may be 5 cm/2 in, the tiny male's only 6 mm/¼ in) spin amazingly strong golden-yellow webs up to 2 metres (6 ft) across. The silk is the toughest organic fibre known – stronger than steel of equivalent diameter – and the web is so strong that it can catch small birds (which the spider does not eat) and can last for two years. The female spins a sac for her eggs, which she buries in a pit she digs under debris and soil. The spider's bite is venomous but not fatal to humans.

Giant millipede *(Archispirostreptus spp.)*

There are at least 1,000 species of millipede worldwide. The several giant species of East Africa grow up to 30 cm (1 ft) long and thicker than a human thumb. They look like a fat, black worm, but have several hundred short legs, two pairs on each segment of the body. They feed on dead and decaying vegetable matter, which they seek out with their antennae (they have poor eyesight). When threatened, they curl into a spiral, to protect the head and soft underside, and secrete a noxious fluid that can irritate human skin.

Mosquito *(Anopheles spp.)*

There are about 2,700 species of mosquito, many of them found in East Africa. They are slender-bodied insects with fragile legs and an elongated proboscis. Males, and sometimes females, feed on nectar and other plant juices. In most species the female also feeds on blood, often favouring a particular host animal. The genus *Anopheles* prefer human blood, and it is these that carry the parasites which cause malaria. They breed in fresh water – anything from a lake to a puddle – but can fly several kilometres in search of blood.

Harvester termite *(Hodotermes mossambicus)*

Unlike most termites, which are unpigmented, harvester termite workers are uniformly dark brown, and the soldiers have bright-orange heads. Harvesters do not build mounds, but live in underground nests connected over a wide area by a network of tunnels. Workers emerge in their millions to collect dried grass, which they carry back to feed the queen and her brood. So numerous and industrious are they that they devour more grass than all the wildebeest and other large herbivores put together.

Tsetse fly *(Glossina spp.)*

The tsetse can be anything from yellow-brown to dark grey, and looks similar to the housefly, but larger (up to 16 mm/⅝ in long) and with wings that fold flat on its back. It has a long, stiff proboscis that can pierce the skin of mammals to suck blood. Some species of tsetse carry the parasites (trypanosomes) that cause sleeping sickness in humans; others transmit a deadly disease called nagama to domestic cattle and horses. Tsetse live mainly in dense vegetation, especially near water, and are most active during the heat of the day.

Goliath beetle *(Goliathus spp.)*

Two species of this giant beetle are found in Tanzania – *G. goliatus* (rusty brown in colour) and *G. orientalis* (black with white spots). They grow to over 10 cm (4 in) long and weigh up to 100 g (3½ oz). Despite their size, they are vigorous flyers, making a sound like a small helicopter. They feed on anything sugary, particularly fruit and sap. The Y-shaped "horn" on the male's head is used in battles with other males over feeding sites or for mates. Females use their wedge-shaped head to burrow when they lay their eggs.

Monarch butterfly *(Danaus chrysippus)*

One of the most widespread and easily spotted butterflies, the African monarch is also known as the plain tiger and the lesser wanderer – two names that do it less than justice. Its 8-cm (3-in) wings are bright orange-yellow, edged with black-and-white, and far from plain. Its caterpillar has black and yellow stripes – hence the "tiger". As for the "wanderer", monarchs are strong fliers, sometimes soaring high to take advantage of thermals, and often cover great distances during their lifespan, which may be up to eight months.

Red locust *(Nomadacris septemfasciata)*

Locusts are large short-horned grasshoppers, which occasionally swarm in huge numbers, destroying vegetation in their path. The red locust, one of the most destructive, measures 60–80 mm (2½–3 in) and is beige and brown with red hindwings. When food is plentiful, they live as solitary individuals, slow-moving and relatively harmless. But when food is scarce – in a dry year or because a growing locust population has reached a critical point – they come together in swarms numbering hundreds of thousands.

Driver ant *(Dorylus spp.)*

The forest-dwelling drivers are the largest of all ants: workers measure 33 mm (1⅓ in), while the queen grows to a massive 52 mm (2 in). She can lay broods of up to 3 million eggs every 25 days. During egg-laying periods, driver ant colonies lead a quiet, sedentary life. But in between, they become nomadic, moving to a new spot every day in ferocious columns numbering millions. Using their powerful cutting jaws, they attack everything in their path – other insects, spiders, millipedes and even snakes and small mammals.

Cicada *(Cicadidae)*

There are many species of cicada, measuring from 2 to 5 cm (⅘–2in). They are flying insects, usually grey-green or brown in colour, with two pairs of transparent wings. They feed on sap sucked from plants, and are very common wherever there is lush vegetation – yet their camouflage and secretive habits make them difficult to spot. However, you cannot fail to hear them: male cicadas produce a characteristic loud humming, especially in the heat of the day, by vibrating membranes near the base of the abdomen.

Firefly *(Lampyridae)*

Fireflies are soft-bodied beetles ranging from 5–25 mm (up to 1 in) in length, with special light organs on the underside of the abdomen. The flattened, dark-brown or black body is often marked with orange or yellow. Their speciality is producing short, rhythmic flashes of light in a pattern characteristic of the species. The rhythmic flash is part of a signal system that brings the sexes together. It may also warn predators of the fireflies' bitter taste – although some frogs eat so many fireflies that they themselves glow.

Tanzanian long-claw scorpion
(Iomachus politus)

Scorpions tend to strike fear in humans, but the Tanzanian long-claw (also found in Kenya and Ethiopia) is no real threat. Its tail does contain venom, but it is not very powerful and, in any case, this species is not aggressive and does not attempt to sting when provoked. It is glossy black with brown legs, around 8 cm (3 in) long, and characterised by long, slender claws in the male. Both sexes have a flat profile, which enables them to hide (upside-down) beneath rocks.

FISH AND MARINE MAMMALS

If anything, the range of wildlife in Tanzanian waters – both fresh and salt – is wider and more dramatic than on land

East Africa's abundant wildlife is not only to be found stalking the savannas, lurking in the woodlands or soaring in the skies. Tanzania's streams and rivers, lakes and ponds, and the warm waters of the Indian Ocean are all home to a remarkable wealth and diversity of creatures – including more different species of fish than of mammals and birds added together.

Freshwater angling in these parts is far from a sedentary, contemplative pastime, with fast-moving barbels, ferocious tiger fish and the enormous Nile perch among possible catches.

Deep-sea anglers have even more challenging targets, including powerful marlin and the aggressive barracuda, while divers on the offshore coral reefs can encounter huge variety and extraordinary beauty among the fish population. Around Unguja, Pemba and Mafia Island, for instance, a simple snorkel and face mask is all you need to see hoards of colourful creatures with equally colourful names: you can meet parrots and zebras, unicorns and moorish idols, rubberfish and butterflyfish, surgeons and snappers. *(See also Coral Diving on pages 270–71.)*

LEFT: the octopus is well camouflaged by its coral cave.

Nile perch *(Lates niloticus)*

The largest freshwater fish in the world, this monster grows to about 1.8 metres (6 ft) and 140 kg (300 lb). Its back is blue-grey, its sides and belly silver-grey, and its fins and rounded tail are darker. It is a voracious predator, with a protruding lower jaw and many sharp teeth. The Nile perch is prized by anglers, but more for its rare size than its fighting ability or choice eating. It is found in most large rivers and lakes, including Lake Victoria, where it has devastated the cichlid population since its introduction in 1956.

Nile tilapia *(Oreochromis niloticus)*

The tilapia grows to 60 cm (2 ft) in length and up to 2 kg (4½ lb) in weight. Distinguishing features are a long, spiny dorsal fin, broad vertical stripes on its body and thinner ones on the tail. If you are served fish for dinner in your safari lodge or camp, the chances are it will be tilapia. The species is widely farmed throughout East Africa, but also occurs naturally in a variety of freshwater habitats – rivers, lakes, sewage canals and irrigation channels. It can tolerate the high salinity and high temperatures of the Rift's soda lakes.

Tiger fish *(Hydrocynus vittatus)*

This ferocious predator can grow to 75 cm (2½ ft) long and weigh over 18 kg (40 lb). Its body is silvery-white with darker horizontal stripes, while its fins and deep V-shaped tail are orange-red. The 14 long, razor-sharp teeth on each jaw indicate its carnivorous habits: it preys on smaller fish and crustaceans such as shrimp. It is less common than tilapia but found in many rivers and some lakes. Freshwater anglers treat the tiger fish with respect: it is a fierce fighter and those teeth can do damage even when it is landed.

Cichlids *(Cichlidae)*

The huge cichlid family comprises many related freshwater fish – perhaps as many as 1,500 species, of which hundreds are found in the African Great Lakes, especially lakes Tanganyika, Victoria and Malawi. Most are small (10–20 cm/4–8 in long), with a large dorsal fin and faint vertical stripes on the body. But there is huge variation in colouring, habitat and food. Many live on algae and/or zooplankton (eg water fleas). Most cichlids are unusually attentive parents, taking great care of eggs and small fry.

Giant grouper *(Epinephelus lanceolatus)*

One of the largest reef-dwelling fish, the giant grouper can exceed 250 cm (8 ft) in length and weigh up to 400 kg (880 lb). It takes decades to grow to maturity. Brown in colour and stocky in build, this giant is a solitary fish that is often found in shallow water, although larger individuals sometimes make their home in a cave or wreck. They catch their prey by ambush, lurking in dark holes and seizing whatever passes – crustaceans, especially spiny lobsters, fish, small turtles and even small sharks, all swallowed whole.

Black marlin *(Makaira indica)*

Prized by deep-sea anglers for their stamina and dogged fighting, black marlin normally measure around 2.7 metres (9 ft) and weigh in at about 180 kg (400 lb), but giants have been caught that are 4.5 metres (15 ft) long and 700 kg (1,550 lb) in weight. Females tend to be larger than males. The fish is blue-black above, silvery below, with a crescent-shaped tail and a distinctive pointed bill. It is a fast and fierce hunter, pursuing pelagic fishes such as tuna and swordfish, as well as squid and even dolphin.

Barracuda *(Sphyraena barracuda)*

The great barracuda, the largest species of the family, is a slender, graceful fish, up to 180 cm (6 ft) long, silver overall with dark green along the back and variable blotches beneath. The lower jaw protrudes beyond the upper, and both contain many large, sharp teeth. The barracuda is a powerful swimmer and an aggressive hunter, feeding mainly on smaller fish such as mullet, parrot fish and anchovy, which it usually catches near the surface. Horror stories of barracuda attacking human divers are probably exaggerated.

Zebra fish *(Pterois spp.)*

The distinctive saltwater zebra fish (also known as lion fish and turkey fish) has extremely large pectoral fins, numerous extremely poisonous spines, and colourful vertical stripes. When disturbed, they spread their fins and, if further pressed, attack with the dorsal spines. One of the best-known species is *Pterois volitans*, an impressive fish with dramatic spines and bold red, brown and white stripes, which grows to 30 cm (1 ft) long. It uses its long fins to "herd" smaller fish, then attacks them with its venomous spines.

Parrot fish *(Scaridae)*

Several species of the family *Scaridae* inhabit the coral reefs around Pemba, Unguja and Mafia Island. Parrot fish are elongated, usually rather blunt-headed and deep-bodied, and often very brightly coloured. They use their characteristic birdlike beak to scrape algae and the soft parts of coral from the reef. Colours vary, and the male of a species often looks quite different from the female. For instance, the male surf parrot fish *(Callyodon fasciatus)* is green and orange-red, the female blue and yellow.

Bottlenose dolphin *(Tursiops truncatus)*

This large, robust marine mammal can grow to 4 metres (13 ft) in length and weigh up to 650 kg (1,400 lb). It gets its name from its bottle-shaped beak; other distinguishing features are a dark "cape" over its back and a slightly hooked dorsal fin. Bottlenoses feed on fish and squid, usually catching them near the surface. They are very social animals, and are found in pods of between 10 and 100 in the sea around Zanzibar. They are powerful, acrobatic swimmers, often bow-riding and leaping alongside vessels.

PLACES

*A detailed guide to the entire country, with principal sites
clearly cross-referenced by number to the maps*

You are standing at the top of a 600-metre (1,970-ft) cliff, surrounded by dense montane forest. Bejewelled butterflies dance
in the patchy sunlight while monkeys crash through the canopy
above. A rustle in the undergrowth and you freeze – it could be an
elephant or a buffalo; instead it turns out to be a delicately spotted
bushbuck. You relax and turn back to the view. Laid out in front of
you is a vast, almost perfectly circular volcanic caldera, shadows of
the clouds chasing across the short-cropped golden grassland on its
flat floor. Near the centre, a cloud of pink overlaps the shining ice
blue of a small lake; to one side are some splashes of red, and here
and there are dots of white or charcoal-grey. Use the binoculars and
the pink turns into a flock of flamingos; the red into Maasai tribes-
men taking their cattle to water; the white dots are safari vehicles;
the grey, the rocky bulk of black rhinos.

This is the Ngorongoro Crater, one of the most beautiful and out-
standingly rich game sanctuaries in the world. A few hours' drive to
the west and you reach the broad Serengeti plains, home to the great
migration of some 2 million wildebeest, zebra and antelope. A few
hours' drive to the east and you are standing at the foot of Mount
Kilimanjaro, for all the world like a giant Christmas pudding, its
rounded top, iced with streaming glaciers, peering out from a festive
dish of clouds. Head south to Tarangire, where lions loll in the shade
of the trees and giant fleshy baobabs stand like sentinels above the
rolling red dust. Further south still, you pass the rock paintings of
Kondoa, left by bushmen centuries ago, as you head towards the
great Rufiji River that slices through the Selous Game Reserve.

In the west, you reach the great lakes – the clear, deep waters of
Lake Tanganyika, home to hundreds of species of brightly decorative fish, with the snorkelling as enticing as any coral reef. Along the
shoreline, the primeval forests of Gombe Streams and Mahale
Mountains protect some of the world's last thriving colonies of
chimpanzees. By contrast, the steel-grey waters of Lake Victoria,
shrouded in an almost perpetual haze, are less forgiving and more
mysterious – fitting for the source of the Nile.

Perhaps, instead, you choose a short plane ride across to Zanzibar,
the offshore coral paradise with its gleaming, fluoride-brushed
beaches, turquoise seas and fragrant clove forests, its ancient cities
and full-bellied fishing dhows. Whichever direction you take,
Tanzania offers inspiration. It could take a lifetime to explore.

The country has some wonderful places to stay. Details of all the
lodges and hotels mentioned in the following pages can be found in
the Travel Tips, pages 281–96. ❑

PRECEDING PAGES: baobabs at Tarangire National Park; wildebeest graze under a
stormy sky in the Serengeti; women fishing off the east coast.
LEFT: Mawenzi at dawn from Gilman's Point, Mt Kilimanjaro.

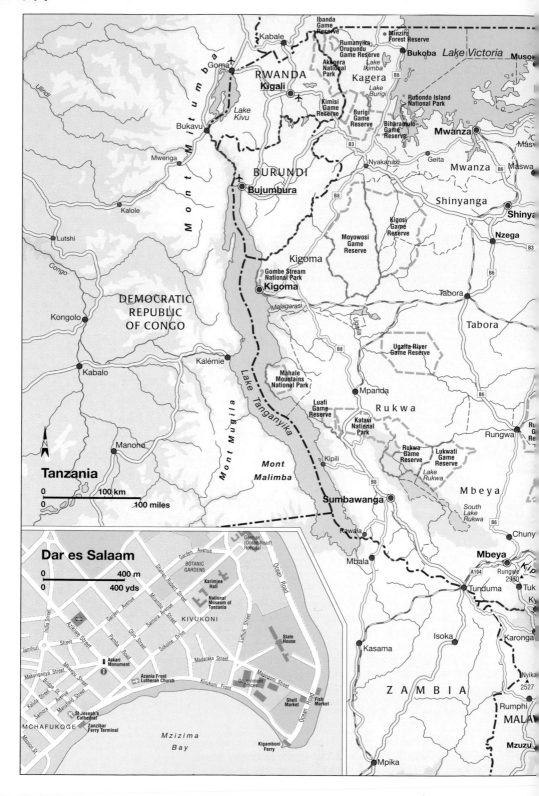

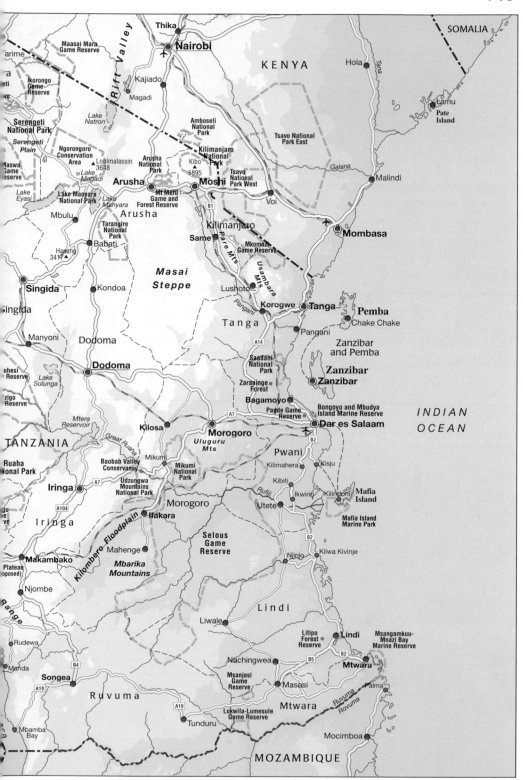

DAR ES SALAAM

*If not technically the capital, Dar is the unchallenged
economic and administrative hub of Tanzania
and a vibrant, entertaining city*

Map
on page
148

Dar es Salaam is like the curate's egg – good in parts. Frederic Elton, who went there in 1873, wrote: "The site is a beautiful one and the surrounding countryside green and well-wooded". Sixty years later, the writer Roald Dahl found it little changed: "A vast rippling blue lagoon and all around the rim of the lagoon there were pale yellow sandy beaches, almost white, and breakers running up onto the sand, and coconut palms with their little green leafy hats were growing on the beaches."

Time has moved on. The rippling blue lagoon is now a sullen mass of water sludgily washing a dirty beach. Dahl's paradise beaches are still there but you need to look for them. Even so, it's worth lingering to discover some of Dar's less obvious charms – its architecture, its people, its markets and its museums.

House of Peace

In 1862 Dar, one of many small fishing villages along the coast, was called Mzizima. Sultan Majid of Zanzibar was so impressed with its natural harbour and scenery that he established a trading centre there. In 1886 he built a two-storey palace of coral which he named *Dari Salaam* (House of Peace).

The Arab settlement developed into a sophisticated town, but Majid died in 1870 after a fall in his palace, and his successor, his half-brother Barghash, had no interest in the town. Dar was forgotten, and Bagamoyo, the end of the slave caravans and an important dhow-building port in the north, gained ascendancy *(see page 155)*.

In the 1880s a station for Christian missionaries was established, followed by a seat for the German colonial government in 1891. The Germans felt that Dar's protected harbour was a safer bet for steamships than Bagamoyo, and Dar es Salaam became Tanzania's undisputed capital until 1973, when the legislature and official government transferred to Dodoma.

By 1914, when the Germans finished building the central railway line, the city was flourishing. Relics of the German architecture and their acacia-lined streets survive today. However, the Germans were forced out in 1916, and the British moved in, staying until Tanganyika gained its independence in 1961.

Under these colonial influences, the city of Dar developed a fine harbour, lovely parklands, tree-lined avenues and a good commercial centre. After independence, however, as local culture once more took its hold and the nationalisation of many industries resulted in economic freefall, the city slid into decline. By the 1980s it was in a sorry state. Since then Dar es Salaam has begun to move forward again.

Today, it is the largest city in Tanzania, covering over 1,350 sq. km (521 sq. miles), with a population

LEFT: street scene.
BELOW: keen
customers at the
market in Dar.

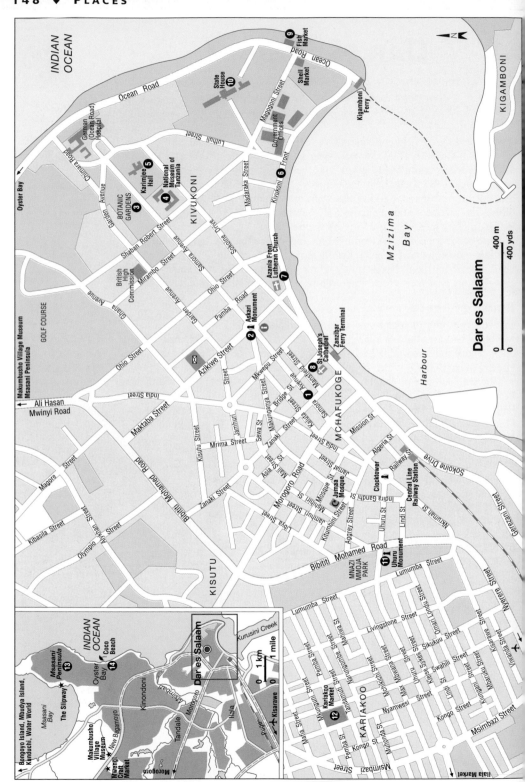

Dar es Salaam

of around 3 million. Although technically no longer the capital of Tanzania, it is still the commercial, political and social heart of the country, as well as its most important port. Even many political offices have "failed" to move to Dodoma, in spite of having 40 years to do it. Dar is still pretty run-down, with all the usual excesses of Africa – deep and dirty poverty, dilapidated buildings and ramshackle roadside shelters alongside shiny Mercedes, gleaming glass towers and business people with lifestyles more akin to the developed world.

Many tourists never visit Dar because it is so easy to get to the main centres by air, but its people and architecture offer an interesting cultural mix of British, German, Asian and Arab influences in a city which is still unmistakably Swahili. Although most live a hard life, crowded on buses and *daladalas* and scratching a living from the streets, the people of Dar are friendly and helpful, and there is little of the hassle factor. They are proud of being Tanzanian and want to welcome visitors and show their country to people from overseas.

Just one word of warning: after the poverty of the Socialist years, Tanzania is embracing capitalism with a vengeance, and for most Tanzanians a tourist's face spells money. You must bargain for everything.

Erected by the British in 1927, the Askari Monument remembers the African soldiers who fought in World War I.

Getting around

Getting about in Dar is easy. The city centre is relatively small and easily explored on foot, during the day. Don't walk anywhere in the city at night. The cheapest way to get around is to catch a *daladala* (ancient minibuses, pick-ups or lorries), but they are dirty and overcrowded (they are only considered full when people start falling off). Watch your luggage carefully. Taxis are not too expensive, but establish a price before you start and be prepared to bargain. Drivers will frequently try to charge three times the going rate for a ride from the airport to Dar, hoping to catch unwary innocents. Local tour operators will provide a seat on a scheduled tour or a car and driver/guide for the day, and take you round all the sights if you want to do things the easy, but more expensive way.

BELOW: a friendly stallholder.

Samora Avenue

The city centre runs along **Samora Avenue ❶** from Morogoro Road – where the intersection is marked by a small and decidedly uninteresting **clocktower**, built in 1961 – to the **Askari Monument ❷**. This small bronze statue at the junction with Azikiwe Street is dedicated to the many Africans who fell during World War I – Tanzania was the site of a whole, if little-known theatre of war *(see page 39),* and many black Africans lost their lives on both sides. Samora Avenue has shops with clothing and electrical goods. Everything from food and newspapers to boots and brightly coloured tie-dye fabrics can be bought from the decrepit street stands lining the road. This is also where you will find most of the city's useful offices and banks.

The names of the surrounding streets are a tour of African nationalist history. Samora Machel was independent Mozambique's first president; Albert Luthuli was the former president of South Africa's

African National Congress; Shaban Robert was one of Tanzania's best-known writers; and Edward Mornge Sokoine was a former prime minister.

To the northeast of the Askari Monument, in a shady, tree-lined area, are the fragmentary remains of the **Botanic Gardens** ❸, first planted in 1893, more recently a run-down and dusty haven in the middle of this very busy, noisy African city, and now the site of the Souther Sun hotel, one of several conspicuously modern buildings, including the huge British High Commission.

The **National Museum of Tanzania** ❹ (between Samora Avenue and Sokoine Drive; tel 022-212 2030; Mon–Fri 9.30am–6pm, Sat 9.30am–12.30pm; entrance charge) is not terribly inspiring by European standards, but is one of the best collections in East Africa. Highlights include some of the Leakeys' key fossil discoveries from Olduvai Gorge *(see pages 19 and 194)*, some interesting old photographs and traditional craft items, plus displays on the Shirazi civilisation of Kilwa, the slave trade and the German and British colonial periods.

On the other side of Samora Avenue, the **Karimjee Hall** ❺, built by the British in 1916, is where Julius Nyerere was sworn in as independent Tanganyika's first president. This was the House of Parliament before the legislature was relocated to Dodoma, and it's now used for parliamentary committee meetings and political functions. You may see or hear the peacocks which live in this part of the city sitting imposingly on the roof.

BELOW: St Joseph's Cathedral, one of Dar's surviving colonial buildings.

Kivukoni waterfront

A block south of Samora Avenue, **Kivukoni Front** ❻ lines the north side of Dar's impressively busy harbour, where dugout canoes, dhows and container

ships jostle for space in a fascinating trip through the history of Indian Ocean shipping. Many of the government offices overlooking the harbour, including the Ministry of Justice and the Bureau of Statistics, are elegant colonial buildings, dating back to the short-lived German era.

One of the most imposing buildings in the city, the **Azania Front Lutheran Church** ❼, was built by German missionaries in 1898 and is still in use. Equally grand, a couple of blocks west, is the Catholic **St Joseph's Cathedral** ❽, which was built between 1897 and 1902 and still contains many of the original German inscriptions and artwork.

Opposite the Lutheran Church is the huge headquarters of the National Bank of Commerce, while opposite the Catholic Cathedral is the **Zanzibar Ferry Terminal**. Several ferries make the journey every day, the faster services taking less than two hours. Further west, the **Central Line Railway Station** stands on the corner of Sokoine Drive and Railway Street (the Tazara Railway Station, where trains leave for Zambia, is out of town).

Ocean Road

The east end of Kivukoni Front joins up with Ocean Road at the **Kigamboni Ferry**, surrounded by a dilapidated waterfront, with an array of ancient boats and sheds with rusty corrugated-iron roofs and open sides lining the rather grey sand. This area is the place to experience local life (including the risk of being mugged, so take care), with a ragged street market offering piles of fruit and snacks such as corn on the cob grilled over an open brazier. Crows with vicious black beaks pick up anything from old fruit skins to fish heads, and here and there are limekilns – burning cairns of coal. The Kigamboni Ferry scurries across the harbour entrance, cutting long kilometres of bumpy driving if heading towards the south coast, and incidentally offering a reasonable harbour tour.

Almost next door is the **Fish Market ❾**, located in hygienic, Japanese-built quarters. The fish is wonderful, fresh from the Indian Ocean. There are huge prawns and lobsters, and masses of colourful local fish.

Across the road, the **Shell Market** sells beautiful, reasonably priced shells brought in by the fishermen. There are huge snail shells, purple troupe shells, and small lambis, spiky and copper-coloured. There's coral, cowrie and big bladdered porcupine fish. Before you are tempted, remember that catching shells for display is deeply ecologicaclly unsound. Behind the shells are the drying and frying vats, an area of leaping flames and bubbling cauldrons, where thousands of tiny kapenta fish are preserved for future use.

Don't buy large shells, turtle shells, or coral from street or beach vendors or markets – they are mostly taken from endangered reefs and marine species.

Keep heading north along Ocean Road and you come to the vast, palatial **State House ❿**, built by the Germans in the 1890s and restored by the British in 1922, after World War I damage. It is now the official home and office of the president. Beyond that is the **German Hospital**, an interesting building combining Arab domes and windows with iron spikes and corrugated-iron roofing, built in 1897. Recently restored, again by the Germans, it is now a specialist cancer treatment centre. General treatment has been taken over by the shiny Aga Khan Hospital, almost next door. The beach along Ocean Road may look inviting from a distance, but is polluted and dirty and not good for swimming. To the north there are the smarter areas of Upanga, Oyster Bay and Msasani.

BELOW: the State House, another colonial relic.

Kariakoo

Northwest of Samora Avenue, around India and Jamhuri Streets, is the Asian quarter, while west of Mnazi Mmoja Park are the colourful areas of Kariakoo and Ilala. This is an essentially African part of Dar, named when African porters of the Carrier Corps were billeted there. The houses are typical Swahili bandas with corrugated-iron roofs, ornately carved front doors and often a small veranda or a stone slab in the front, shaped like a sofa for sitting outside.

In the Kariakoo area, the **Uhuru Monument ⓫** is a white obelisk with a flame called the Freedom Torch, dedicated to Tanzania's independence. **Kariakoo Market ⓬** is the city's biggest and busiest, held daily. It sells everything, with trolleys filled with great pyramids of fruit and vegetables beautifully laid out in the sunshine. There are woven baskets full of maize, spices and lentils. Nothing is genetically engineered; everything is misshapen, blotchy and beautiful. The crowds are huge, and you may well be the only tourist, but it's quite safe as long as you watch your pockets. **Ilala Market** is similar.

The Msasani Peninsula

The **Msasani Peninsula** , 8 km (5 miles) north of the city centre, is the local diplomatic enclave and Millionaire's Row, lined by high-security walls over which peep the tops of lavishly manicured gardens and crisp white villas. It is also the home of several of the city's best hotels. On the western side of the peninsula, Msasani is a delightful fishing village and the site of one of the oldest Arabic settlements along the Swahili coast. **The Slipway** is a waterfront complex with cafés, bars, art shops, Dar es Salaam's best bookshop, and an ATM machine. It also has a lively but distinctly touristy market and wonderful sea views.

You can catch boats out to **Bongoyo Island** from here (every two hours from 9.30am–3.30pm) and you can also charter boats for fishing. The island has good diving and snorkelling, as does **Mbudya Island**, 4 km (2½ miles) further north, which can be reached from the beach hotels north of Dar. Good diving is also available from Dar. There are a couple of good dive centres just south of the Msasani Slipway; other dive centres can be found at the northern beach hotels.

Northern beaches

Oyster Bay 🄔, better known as Coco Beach, is a popular place for expats to hang out on weekend afternoons (avoid it at other times as thieves operate in this area, and always keep a close eye on your belongings here). The prettier beaches to the north of Dar are several kilometres away, which means using public transport or a taxi for the day. There are several interesting stops en route. The **Makumbusho Village Museum** (New Bagamoyo Road, about 10 km/6 miles from the city centre; daily 9.30am–6pm; entrance charge) is a

BELOW: Makonde carvers at work in Mwengi Market.

well-presented open-air museum comprising a collection of 20 different styles of tribal huts from all over Tanzania. There are artists and craftsmen at work producing ebony signs, paintings, postcards, clay figures and games. Souvenir prices are good here, and there are music and dance performances many afternoons (additional entrance charge).

For more concentrated souvenir shopping, the **Mwengi Craft Market**, off the New Bagamoyo Road, about 3 km (2 miles) further along, is one of the best places in Tanzania for shopping. Craftspeople from all over the country sell spears, masks, bush animals – anything from a tiny malachite hippo to a full-sized African lady – some of it in highly polished ebony, some of it purporting to be ebony (spot the tin of black boot polish under the counter). You can watch them at work under the trees. Friendly, leisurely bargaining is expected here.

Kunduchi is 25 km (15 miles) from the city, but you can get there by bus from the New Africa Hotel in the city centre. It has a number of hotels and a variety of excursions to nearby islands, plus windsurfing and snorkelling. Bahari Beach Hotel, which is made of coral with a thatched roof, has a band playing Fri, Sat, Sun and public holidays. Along the new Bagamoyo Road, next to the Beachcomber Hotel on Jamwani Beach, **Wet 'n' Wild** is East Africa's largest water park, with 22 slides and seven pools, shops, restaurants, and a go-karting centre.

Just up the beach from the Kunduchi Beach Hotel are the ruins of a 16th-century mosque and a fine collection of 18th-century pillar tombs, many decorated with Chinese porcelain plates. Further along to the north, 5 km (3 miles) inland from the main road, are more Arab graves at Mbweni.

South of the city

The best beaches are to the south, with white sands, palm trees and clear water. They can be reached by driving round the river inlet or crossing by ferry to Kigamboni, which itself has a reasonable beach. If you have transport, take the road to Mjamema and head further south. Some 7 km (4 miles) along, **Mikadi** is an attractive beach with backpackers' bandas. Seven kilometres further on, **Kipepeo** (Butterfly) is a very basic expats' escape hatch with bandas, a bar and limited food, but the beach is beautiful and you can swim at high and low tide. Both places are extremely cheap.

A further 4 km (2½ miles) south, the crown jewels of the Dar area, **Ras Kutani** and the **Amani Beach Club**, are both very upmarket and very different. Ras Kutani has luxury beach houses made of natural materials which blend with the area, and a superb outdoor restaurant overlooking the beach. Amani Beach Club has plush bungalows and a good swimming pool.

For a quiet retreat, take a trip to **Kisarawe**, 32 km (19 miles) southwest of Dar, which was used as a hill station to escape the heat and is close to a rainforest. It's a good place for an overnighter, with one or two cheap and cheerful hotels. The menu is likely to be *ugali* (maize porridge) and stew, the national dish of the Tanzanians, rather than anything sophisticated.

Some 4 km (2 miles) further on is the **Pugu Kaolin Mine**, and near by are man-made caves housing a massive colony of bats. ❏

Map on page 148

TIP

Ebony is a very hard, dense wood, recognisable by its greyish outer surface and dark inside. It is a scarce material and its export is restricted by the government; prices are therefore high – any dark-wood objects that are cheap will definitely not be the genuine article.

BELOW: catamaran at Ras Kutani.

THE NORTH COAST

Brave the bumps and you will discover a tantalisingly beautiful corner of Tanzania, with fine beaches, a fascinating history, spectacular mountain scenery and superb birdlife

Map on page 156

anzania is one of the few countries where the bush meets the beach, where before breakfast you can safari and then swim in the warm waters of the Indian Ocean. The mainland's north coast is almost entirely undiscovered by tourists, but a significant part of the slave trade and the first Christian mission are to be discovered in dilapidated Bagamoyo, the largest garden in Africa at Amani, and a superb stretch of undeveloped and little-used beach between Dar es Salaam and the Usambara Mountains. In addition, the necklace of the Eastern Arc Mountains offers wonderful walking and what has become known as the Galápagos of the plant world.

Bagamoyo

The journey begins 70 km (43 miles) north of Dar es Salaam, along a fairly decent road which connects Dar es Salaam with **Bagamoyo ❶**. In Swahili, Bagamoyo means "lay down your heart". This was the end of the caravan route, and it was here that captured slaves arrived and often died after an exhausting march, usually well over 1,000 km (620 miles) from their homelands, carrying ivory and rhino horn to the coast. Initially its name applied to the porters; ultimately it became a reminder that this was also the end of the road for the 1½ million East African slaves who were captured and transported from this port to Zanzibar.

The slavers captured their human cargo and kept them in Nchichi near Lake Tanganyika until there was enough ivory for them to carry to the coast. The march to Bagamoyo took three to six months, and slaves too weak to accomplish the journey were killed. Of those who survived, most were sold in Zanzibar and exported to Mauritius, Persia, Arabia and India. In the 19th century, with pressure building to stop the international trade, the Omani sultans introduced spice farms to Zanzibar to mop up the excess labour.

In 1860 a Catholic mission was established in Bagamoyo. The missionaries bought slaves, liberated them and settled them in a Christian Freedom Village which was established as a sanctuary in 1868. Nine hundred liberated slaves lived there at one time, and after 1873, when the trade was officially abolished, British ships patrolled Bagamoyo and Zanzibar to catch smugglers. In an unusual cooperation between the French and German missionaries and the British authorities, it was also here that the Catholics built East Africa's first primary school, secondary school and hospital. Today, the **Catholic Mission** (daily 10am–5pm; entrance charge) houses a museum which tells the story of slavery, graphically illustrated with gruesome artefacts such as slave collars and whips.

Bagamoyo's fortunes, hit by disease and the end of

LEFT: working at the harbour, Bagamoyo. **BELOW:** Holy Ghost Mission, built in 1868, the first Catholic Mission in East Africa.

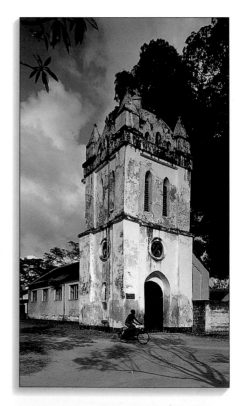

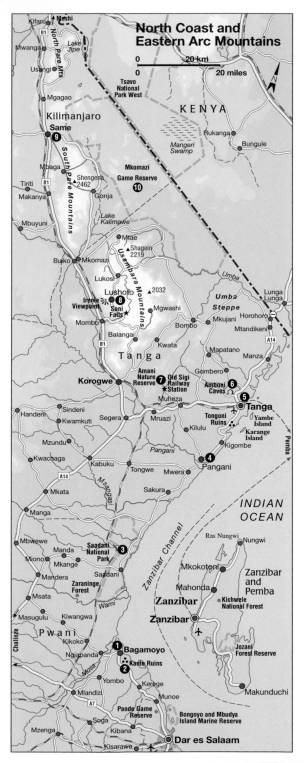

the slave trade, rose again in 1887 when it became the first capital of German East Africa. In 1897, however, the Germans realised that the harbour was too shallow and moved down to Dar. The town's pot-holed streets are flanked by once imposing, now decaying dwellings, but it's worth visiting for its history, its former grandeur, its ancient ruins and beaches, and also for one or two latter-day initiatives aimed at women and children. Although dilapidated, many of the old buildings in Bagamoyo are still lovely; their doorways may be covered in graffiti and falling off their ancient hinges, but they are also magnificent monuments, finely carved with intricate Arab and Swahili decorations.

The oldest building is the **Old Fort**, on the Kaole Road, on the outskirts of the town. It was used as a police post until 1992, but its original function was to hold slaves awaiting shipment to Zanzibar.

Liku House, on India Street, was the German headquarters from 1888; it has a metal-columned awning and a large door. The Germans later moved to the **German Boma**, a crenellated two storey-building which is now used as the District Commissioner's administrative office.

The **Old Bagamoyo Tea House** is an Arabic building with attractive columns, a veranda and arched windows. Further north, the **Jama'at Khana** is the Ismaili mosque, with a veranda and the double-fronted carved doors which once gave the town its air of grand prosperity.

Bagamoyo was, over many years, the most important dhow-building port along the East African coast. Ocean-going dhows are still built here, on a beach 1 km (½ mile) south of the town.

On the Dar es Salaam road, about 500 metres/yards south of town, **Chuo cha Sanaa** arts college has performances of dancing and drumming. Visit **Jimmy's School** on the main road and take pens and paper with you. A few hundred metres up on the right you will see a sign to the excellent **Bagamoyo Women's Project** *(see page 70)*. This centre is run by Marie Cidose, who trains women from all over Tanzania in traditional crafts.

Map on page 156

Kaole

About 4 km (2 miles) south of town, the **Kaole Ruins** ➋ are all that remain of a Shirazi trading centre, founded in the 13th century. Resting in a secluded palm grove are two mosques, some 15th-century gravestones and around 30 tombs. There is also a small room with a selection of artefacts that have been found in the area. Kaole means in Swahili "Go and see for yourself". Many people go there to pray at particular tombs. Some of the Arab traders buried there have fascinating histories, such as Sher Ali, who had eight wives. There are pillars, some of which have collapsed, marking the wives' graves. Sher Ali's pillar is the biggest. Another grave, called the Love Grave, belonged to an Arab travelling from Zanzibar. He fell sick and died, and his wife was so grief stricken that she too died and was buried in the same grave. Other graves have superstitions attached; one tells the story of a young lady who died a virgin. Locals now climb into the grave to pray for something they desire.

The 15th-century well is also a place of pilgrimage where people come to take the water and pray. Politicians also come to Kaole to pray before an election.

Most of the hotels are on a 2-km (1-mile) stretch of road that leads down to the gorgeous beach just north of Bagamoyo. They start at basic backpackers' rates and move up the range to luxurious accommodation. If you don't mind the bumpy 7-km (4-mile) journey, the best place to stay for isolation, location and food is the Kasiki Marine Camp. Near by, **Ann Begani** was built by the Norwegians, who spent millions establishing a fishing village and community but left before they had trained the Tanzanians to take over the fishing business. Now it's a ghost village; the houses are boarded up and nobody lives there but the caretaker.

A half-day boat trip available from most beachside hotels takes visitors round the lagoon, islands and mangrove swamps. There is also the opportunity to swim among the coral reefs. Prices for these excursions vary hugely, so shop around.

"My spirits lift as the drum beats roll, Lay down my heart and calm my soul. At last I'm home in Bagamoyo."

— ANONYMOUS

BELOW: the 13th-century Kaole Ruins include the oldest mosque on the East African mainland.

Saadani

Saadani National Park ➌ is geographically the closest reserve to Dar es Salaam, and a similar journey in terms of time to Mikumi National Park. (Both parks are accessible destinations for weekend mini-safaris.) Saadani is a 200-km (124-mile) drive from Dar, taking around three to five hours on a reasonably good tarmac road. Long-standing plans to build a coastal road from Dar and put in place a ferry crossing over the Wami River have yet to materialise, and the easiest way to get to Saadani is still by air. There is a decent airstrip close to the excellent Saadani Safari Lodge, and a flight from Dar es Salaam takes just 25 minutes. Saadani lies almost directly opposite Zanzibar's Stone Town, just 27 km (17 miles) across the channel. Daily flights with ZanAir from Zanzibar to Saadani take just 15 minutes. Travel by boat from the island is not an option for visitors.

Situated along the coast in the centre of the historic triangle of Bagamoyo, Pangani and Zanzibar, Saadani encompasses over 1,000 sq. km (386 sq. miles) of diverse landscape and is the only national park that borders the sea. For a park that receives so few visi-

Along the shores of the Indian Ocean at Saadani you will see stark pyramids of salt reflected in the man-made lakes, which are built like paddy fields to harvest sea salt. Water trapped in the lakes evaporates in the sun-leaving behind its rich harvest. The lakes are mainly tended by Rwandan refugees who live in a rather less picturesque settlement of dilapidated homes surrounded by litter.

BELOW: sisal plant in bloom.

tors, which is part of its appeal, there is a surprisingly wide variety of safari options available – game drives, boat safaris, fly-camping, walking safaris and birdwatching, all providing a different perspective on this unique area.

The range of different ecosystems sets Saadani apart from all other National Parks in Tanzania. Coastal forests, acacia woodlands, open grasslands and mangroves are host to large numbers of giraffe, zebra and hippo and increasing numbers of lions and elephants. The landscape in Saadani is diverse and constantly changing, from the high grasses and rolling hills hiding lions and elephants in the north to the mangrove forests and acacia plains in the south. The southern areas of Saadani are home to a wide range of plains game, including giraffe, zebra, kudu, wildebeest, eland, waterbuck and warthog, along with reedbuck, hartebeest and baboon. Elephants and lions are quite often seen in these areas.

The highlight of any trip to Saadani is a boat safari along the lush **Wami River**; these can be arranged through Saadani Safari Lodge and A Tent With A View. Beginning in the brackish waters that attract flamingos and pelicans at the mouth of the river, the boat makes its way inland, under the watchful gaze of a spectacular variety of birdlife and the ever-present hippos. Egrets, woolly necked storks and pelicans line the Wami's banks, tiny malachite kingfish peer out from the twisted mangroves, fish eagles soar overhead and beeeaters dart in front of the boat. Large pods of hippo appear around every bend. Nile crocodiles and monitor lizards are also seen on the banks, while blackand-white colobus and blue monkeys play in the trees overhead. The delightful ecology-focused Kisampa Camp is situated along the banks of the Wami River and is the perfect place for keen birders to stay.

The warm waters of the Indian Ocean account for the fantastic food available in Saadani. Prawns and lobster are fished from these waters, and represent some of the freshest, tastiest seafood in Tanzania.

In the park itself there are a multitude of drives to be explored. For the best game viewing it is wise to take an experienced guide with you to assist in locating game and finding your way around. To see the southern areas of the park follow the Mandera–Saadani road west from Saadani village for about 5 km (3 miles) where a track crosses north to south. Turn south and follow this track through dense Acacia stands. In the dry season you are most likely to encounter game in this section of the park, as the game moves south to the Wami River for water. Eventually you will emerge on a bigger road. Follow this to your left (east) to visit the flamingos on the salt pans or take the track past the school to travel back to Saadani village. If on emerging you decide to turn right, the road will take you to **Matipwili** (Wami). You can choose to explore the village (Matipwili has a larger market than Saadani) or cross the railway line before reaching the railway station, identified by huge piles of salt, and continue to the Zaraninge Forest. Stop at the WWF office for advice on where to find the nature trail. You can return to Saadani either by going back past Matipwili or by following the track right around to the road from Mandera to Saadani. Turn right here to return to the park.

Alternatively, drive a loop to the north following the track which crosses the road leading from Saadani village to Mandera to the right. You will cross a sand river and pass by some small waterholes and the Saadani airstrip where water-buck and other game can frequently be observed.

Map on page 156

Pangani

Back on the coast road, it's an 85-km (53-mile) drive from Saadani to Pangani. The journey is an adventure, through river beds, villages and sisal fields. Take it at your peril, but don't attempt it in the rainy season (March–May): you will never get there. Even during the dry season in the essential four-wheel drive, you are likely to end up rearranging the rocks on a river bed in order to drive the vehicle through the water. The safer, but less exciting, alternative around three sides of a rectangle heads away from the coast, back onto the main A14 going north towards Mombo, and then back to the coast again. Either way, you eventually reach Pangani and its rusting ferry which takes you over the estuary.

Pangani ❹ is a small town, once a dhow port, about 290 km (180 miles) from Dar. It enjoyed affluence during the Shiraz era, when the Pangani River became a transport route to the interior, and in the late 19th century when it was the terminus of the caravan route from Lake Tanganyika. From here slaves, ivory, sisal and copra were exported.

Today it still has a strong Arab feel. Relics of its prosperous past can be seen in the carved doorways and colonial buildings, two dilapidated Omani mansions and a German castle (now a coconut market). But it is really a place to seek the sun and relax. It is seen as one of the up-and-coming resorts in Tanzania, with hotels to the north and south of town. To the north, the beach is narrow and

BELOW: net fishing from the beach at Saadani.

Mangrove knees, the strange knobbly roots of the swamp-dwelling mangrove tree, are a vital part of the East African coastal ecology.

BELOW: Soni women traders cluster round any passing vehicle.

tidal, so swimming is limited. The developments in the south have particularly good beaches. As Pangani flanks the Pangani Estuary, access is by ferry. The Tides, an ever popular resort, is located on a glorious cliché of a beach with brightly coloured luxurious bungalows and superb food. There are a number of other developments on this side of the estuary.

Tanga

Tanga 5, 46 km (28 miles) north of Pangani, is Tanzania's second-largest seaport. This quiet town can be reached by road, and there is a daily ZanAir flight from Dar es Salaam. Like Pangani, it was once a springboard for trade caravans to the interior, and was further developed in the late 19th century during the German era, together with the railway line which linked Moshi and Kilimanjaro with the sea. Today, its main industry is exporting sisal from the plantations which stretch from Tanga westwards to the Usambara Mountains. There are regular flights from Dar and Zanzibar with Coastal Aviation (*see Travel Tips, page 277*).

Today, Tanga is a pleasant waterfront town with a population of around 140,000 and a number of attractive if unimportant colonial buildings. The upper- class area of Ras Kazone lies to the east, whilst "on the other side of the track" is the dusty and rather busier Ngamiani quarter. There are no particularly upmarket hotels. One of the most attractive, on the beach, is the cheap and cheerful Inn by the Sea. The Raskazone Hotel inland offers slightly less basic but rather dark rooms at twice the price, and has camping facilities.

The **Amboni Caves 6** are 8 km (5 miles) northwest of Tanga, off the Horohoro–Mombasa road. This is the largest cave system in East Africa, with 10

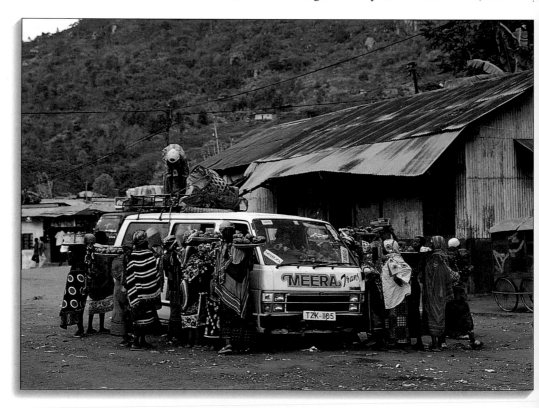

caves leading to a network of limestone tunnels, rumoured to be up to 200 km (120 miles) long. Only about 1 km (1,100 yards) is generally open to the public, but even this is not for the claustrophobic; in parts you have to crawl, sometimes in procession, through to a stalactite-clad cave. Locals believe the main cave is the home of a fertility god and leave their offerings there. There is camping near by.

Primeval forest

The main reason for visiting Tanga is the **Amani Nature Reserve ❼** in the heart of the East Usambaras, 66 km (41 miles) from the town. If driving, you will need a four-wheel drive, and the journey will take about three hours. The road can be impassible in the rainy season. The Botanical Gardens, set up as part of an agricultural research station in 1901, were once the largest in Africa, with almost 1,000 species of plant life. Although neglected, they are still beautiful, and much-needed renovation work is now under way, courtesy of the East Usambara Catchment Forest Project.

In 1997, the gardens were incorporated into a 10,000-hectare (24,700-acre) **nature reserve** that also includes the Nilo Forest Reserve, Nilo Park, and a trek romantically called a Climb into the Clouds (a 1,360-metre/4,460-ft climb up Lutindi Peak). The guided trails through the montane forest offer a wonderful collection of woodland vegetation, black-and-white colobus monkeys and magnificent birdlife, with some 340 species identified, many of them, such as the long-billed tailorbird, the Usambara eagle owl and the Amani sunbird, rare and/or endemic. There is an information centre in the old stationmaster's house (tel: 027-264 6907/0313; email: usambara@twiga.

Map on page 156

Among the many endemic flowers to be found in the East Usambaras, look in damp, shady areas for a very familiar plant. This is the natural home of the Saintpaulia ionantha, better known as the African violet, a resident in many British gardens.

BELOW: the cave complex at Amboni.

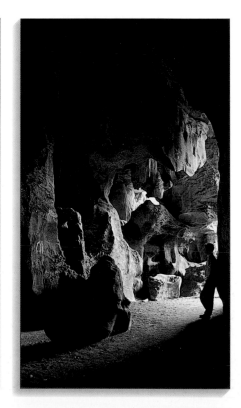

THE EASTERN ARC MOUNTAINS

Although less celebrated than the likes of the Serengeti, the 25 million-year-old Eastern Arc – a series of 13 forested massifs that run in a rough crescent through eastern Tanzania from the Pare and Usambara in the north to Udzungwa and Mahenge in the south – is unquestionably of greater ecological significance.

Listed as one of the world's 20 most important biodiversity hotspots, the forests of the Eastern Arc are the most ancient and stable in Africa, having flourished continuously for some 30 million years due to moisture blown in on winds from the Indian Ocean.

Isolated from other similar habitats by tracts of low-lying savanna, the Eastern Arc ranges possess something akin to an island ecology – they are often referred to as Africa's Galápagos – and harbour an astonishing 16 plant genera, 75 vertebrate species and perhaps 1,000 invertebrates found nowhere else in the world. Over the past century, however, five of the Eastern Arc ranges within Tanzania have lost more than 75 percent of their forest cover due to human activity. Fortunately, none has yet approached the perilous state of the Taita Hills in Kenya, the one Eastern Arc range situated outside Tanzania, where only 2 percent of the original forest remains.

Map
on page
156

com). It is possible to stay there in six-room resthouses; the accommodation is simple and good value.

The Usambaras

The East and West Usambaras, divided by the 4-km (2½-mile) wide Lwengera Valley, are part of an ancient necklace of mountains called the Eastern Arc *(see box, page 161)*; they're known as the Galápagos of the plant world because of the staggering diversity of their endemic species. Other mountains in the range include the North and South Pares, Taira Hills, Ngulus, Ulugurus, Udzungwas and Ukargurus.

The main town, **Lushoto** ❽, is 123 km (76 miles) from Tanga, via Muheza (though this road is often closed in the rainy season) and Segera Junction to the main A14. This becomes the B1 as it heads north, through scattered villages and the small town of **Korogwe**, to **Mombo**, from where it is a 37-km (23-mile) journey through lovely scenery to the valley town of Lushoto. There are a number of hotels in town, and from here you can walk through the arboretum, take hikes in the forest and visit the spectacular **Irente Viewpoint**, which has a 1,000-metre (3,300-ft) drop to the plains below and offers a panoramic view of the Maasai Steppe. There is also a herbarium which houses thousands of plants and interesting birdlife. For those who want to stay out of town there are a number of options. Maweni Farms Mountain Lodge at nearby Soni Falls is a delightful 1920s house set in wonderful gardens and highly recommended.

BELOW: Irente Viewpoint in the Usambara Mountains.

The Pare Mountains

The Pare Mountains, to the north and south of **Same** ❾, on the B1 south of Moshi, are inhabited by the Pare people, although there are also Maasai here.

The **North Pare**, 50 km (31 miles) from Kilimanjaro, is less developed than the other mountains in this area and is best accessed from **Usangi**. There are no hotels or lodges there, but you can stay in the Lomwe Secondary School or with one of the teachers. The local headmaster organises tours in the area. Eleven peaks surround Usangi, and there are excursions through the **Mbale Forest** and to **Goma** to visit caves in which the Pare people hid from the slave traders. The South Pare offers a cultural tourism tour which visits the **Mghimbi Caves** and **Malameni Rock**, where children used to be sacrificed to appease evil spirits. There are also hikes in the rainforest and moorland and to the **Red Reservoir**, plus a three-day hike to **Shengana Forest**. These trips are accessed out of **Mbaga** on the north slopes.

Mkomazi National Park

The **Mkomazi National Park** ❿, a 3,702-sq. km (1,429-sq. mile) park on the northern border, is part of the same migration system as Kenya's massive Tsavo Park. It reputedly has lion, cheetah, elephant, giraffe and other game, but they are shy and keep out of sight. It also has some 400 species of bird. The park is not widely visited and does not offer formal game viewing, though there are walking safaris available. You can drive yourself around, but you are unlikely to see much game or, indeed, many other tourists. ❑

The TAZARA Railway

This must be the cheapest and most comfortable game drive in all of Africa. Snaking through mountains, over rivers and stretching out over the savannas of Tanzania and Zambia, the TAZARA rail line takes in rugged terrain, rural villages and passes through the heart of the Selous Game Reserve. Giraffe run alongside the carriages, hyenas drink from nearby waterholes and elephants wander happily along the track.

First-class passengers are treated to comfy beds, an adequate bar and a waiter who brings breakfast, lunch and dinner to your cabin during the 40-hour trip between Dar es Salaam and New Kapiri Mposhi. The view is fantastic and the ride relaxed, but the roots of this line lay In much higher hopes.

After the Rhodesian Unilateral Declaration of Independence in 1965, landlocked Zambia found itself in a potentially desperate position, totally reliant on getting its copper out to the sea. The only available route was through white-dominated Rhodesia and South Africa. Presidents Kaunda of Zambia and Nyerere of Tanzania, both key players in the nationalist movements, acted quickly and began making plans to construct the TAZARA rail line.

This umbilical cord linking the newly emergent black nations would allow Zambia access to the Indian Ocean, and breathe life into Tanzania's southwest corridor, an area rich in agricultural and mineral potential but isolated from the country's main cities.

Such potential needed heavy funding. China, one of Socialist Tanzania's closest allies, donated US$400 million, as well as expertise and equipment, to assist in building the lines. With over 100 bridges and two dozen tunnels needed, it was no small task.

In 1967 the surveys began along the 1,860-km (1,160-mile) line. Construction started in 1970. The line was inaugurated only six years later, in July 1976.

Though passenger trains were part of the proposed service, its prime purpose was for freight, hauling copper from the mines in northern Zambia and returning to Dar with fuel, fertiliser and goods. Only in 1986 did the line report an operating profit. China has yet to see any return on its original investment, but continues to assist TAZARA with engineers and maintenance.

Unfortunately, the future of this train service is uncertain. There are two scheduled departures from Dar es Salaam every week but the trains do not always run, and there are often long delays en route. Information on the service is also very hard to find. If you wish to travel on it, the best plan is to go to the station in Dar or Kapiri Mposhi and enquire on the spot about services that week. *See also Travel Tips, page 277.*

Let us hope that the railway continues, not least because the communities along the line have become dependent on the train for their livelihoods. Farmers sell their goods at the stations and passengers spend valuable currency. Local tradesmen rely on it to transport their goods to the major cities. But without major investment, this valuable lifeline, and all of its pleasures, may soon vanish. ❏

RIGHT: China, one of Socialist Tanzania's closest allies, helped to fund and engineer the railway.

ARUSHA AND KILIMANJARO

With Africa's highest mountain, the gateway to the great game parks of the north, and the cultural delights of Arusha, this little district packs a big punch

Maps on pages 168 & 171

Dubbed the "Geneva of Africa", due to the United Nations' presence at the International Criminal Tribunal for Rwanda which has been taking place in the Arusha International Conference Centre (AICC) since 1994, Arusha's prime function is as a hub for the buoyant safari industry. Nestling at the foot of the steep slopes of Mount Meru, **Arusha ❶** began as a German garrison in 1900, and subsequently developed as an agricultural market town – coffee, wheat, maize, pyrethrum and horticultural products are grown in the Arusha region. In 1967 it gave its name to Nyerere's momentous Arusha Declaration *(see page 43)*.

For tourists, this is the first stop on the northern safari circuit *(see page 183)*, as well as being close to the parks of Arusha and Kilimanjaro. International flights arrive at **Kilimanjaro International Airport**, 45 km (28 miles) away, but there's also a busy domestic airport on the edge of town, with regular flights to the National Parks, Zanzibar and Dar es Salaam, and a shuttle service to Nairobi.

Arusha town

Bisected by the Naura River Valley, the town's main shopping area, hotels, coffee shops, internet cafés, the tourist office and businesses are east of the river, while the colourful market and industrial area lie to the west. A focal point, centred midway between Cape Town and Cairo, is the **Clocktower ❹** on the Uhuru Road roundabout, sporting a Coca-Cola clock. Maasai women make and sell their beaded jewellery on the pavement near by.

The **Arusha Declaration Monument ❸**, built in 1967, is centred on the roundabout at the junction of Makongoro Road and Swahili Street. Next to it, the **Arusha Declaration Museum ❹** (daily 8.30am–5.30pm; entrance charge) is dedicated to the economic and political history of Tanzania, from pre-colonial times to the present. It contains interesting ethnological paraphernalia and a selection of photographs from the early 20th century – among them a collection of steam engines – and houses the Arusha Cultural Art Association, with artists in residence and work for sale.

The old German fort on Boma Road, north of the clocktower, is now occupied by the **National History Museum ❹** (daily 9am–5pm; entrance charge). It has a small exhibit explaining the evolution of man. Interestingly, at Laetoli, the site of the footprints at Olduvai, there were once giant warthogs as large as rhino.

The AICC Building, north of the clocktower, contains offices in one wing, while the Rwanda Tribunal is conducted in the other. Some proceedings are open to the public.

The headquarters for **Tanzania National Parks** is slightly out of town on the Arusha Airport road. Travelling west of Arusha on the Dodoma road, **Cultural**

PRECEDING PAGES: camping on the Shira Plateau, Kilimanjaro. **LEFT:** Wa-Arusha boy in Ng'iresi village, Mount Meru. **BELOW:** Arusha market.

Heritage has an impressive collection of African arts and crafts, supporting some 12,000 artists. Visitors can also see the artists at work or buy Tanzania's stunning mauve trademark gemstone, tanzanite *(see page 78),* which is mined near Kilimanjaro Airport.

Continuing west to **Kisongo** ⓔ, venue of another large Maasai market every Tuesday, there's a **Maasai Gallery and Cultural Centre**, supporting disabled people and women's groups, a Tingatinga gallery, and the **Meserani Snake Park**. Set in pleasant gardens, with a lively bar, it is a popular stopover point for overlanders. The snakes are well displayed, and knowledgeable guides are on hand. Camel rides and a visit to a cultural Maasai boma are also offered.

Community tourism

Within the Arusha vicinity, a number of cultural tourism programmes have been organised by the Tanzania Tourist Board in association with the Netherlands Development Organisation. Profits from tourist visits to local communities are used to fund educational projects, develop primary schools and provide bursaries. At **Ng'iresi**, **Ilkiding'a** and **Mulala**, on the slopes of Mount Meru, it is possible to experience the local Wa-Arusha culture, visiting homesteads, traditional healers and craftsmen. At **Monduli**, west of Arusha, there are walks with Maasai through the evergreen rainforest on the Monduli mountain range, with panoramic vistas across the Rift Valley to Oldonyo Lengai and Lake Natron, and visits to local herbalists and women making jewellery.

At **Longido**, on the Arusha–Nairobi road, similar activities are offered, together with guided walks on the Maasai plains or climbs up Mount Longido. There is a colourful Maasai cattle market each Wednesday. Trekking and camp-

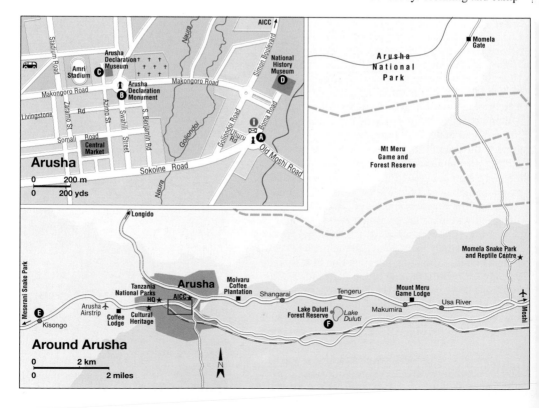

Maps
on pages
168 & 171

ing expeditions, walking through natural forest, can be arranged by safari companies, traversing the length of the Monduli Mountains and scaling the rocky outcrops of Longido.

On the outskirts of Arusha at **Tengeru**, 2 km (1 mile) south of the Moshi road, and a short walk from Serena's Mountain Village Lodge, is **Lake Duluti Forest Reserve F**. A crater lake, Duluti is said to be 300 metres (980 ft) deep and fed by an underground river. It takes an hour to walk around the lake, shaded by tall trees with straggling lianas. There's a good chance of seeing fish eagles and watching fishermen on home-made rafts fishing for black bass and tilapia. Further along the Moshi road, you can go horse-riding through coffee farms and onto the Mount Meru foothills at Usa River. This area also has some delightful places to stay, such as Moivaro Coffee Plantation and the more homely Rivertrees.

Arusha National Park

The turn-off to Arusha National Park is a few kilometres east of Usa River. Near the **Ngurdoto Gate** is another **Snake Park and Reptile Centre**, which breeds chameleons. It, too, has knowledgeable guides, a comprehensive display of snakes and six types of chameleon, including the exquisite, prehistoric-looking giant chameleon, together with tortoises and crocodiles. At Mkuru, 12 km (7 miles) from the **Momela Gate**, at the northern base of Mount Meru, there are camel safaris on offer.

Arusha National Park 2 is small, covering an area of 137 sq. km (53 sq. miles), but has stunning scenery, ranging from the lofty peaks of Mount Meru and its magnificent montane forests, to craters, open glades and the alkaline Momela Lakes – from which both Meru and Kilimanjaro are visible on a clear

BELOW: giraffes in Arusha National Park.

day. Around 570 species of bird have been recorded in the park, along with a wide variety of butterflies and other wildlife. Only an hour's drive from Arusha, the park is often overlooked in the rush to head off on the Serengeti circuit, but it is well worth a visit.

To the left of the park boundary is the area known as little Serengeti – a large, open glade with giraffe, zebra, buffalo, warthogs and the occasional bushbuck on the woodland periphery. From the gate at Ngurdoto, the road winds up through the forest, where troupes of black and white colobus monkeys can be glimpsed in the high canopy, to **Ngurdoto Crater ❸**. From lookout points along the crater rim, one can see herds of buffalo, giraffe and warthog grazing the grasslands on the crater floor, and listen to the less than musical cries of the silvery-cheeked hornbills and woodpeckers.

The road through the park to Momela lakes descends from the Ngurdoto forest to the **Lokie swamp** and two small lakes, **Jembamba** and **Longil**, with hippo, waterbuck and reedbuck, saddlebill storks, heron and Egyptian geese, before reaching the grassland and thornbush around the Momela lakes. A mixture of wildlife, from giraffe to warthog, and a diverse range of birds are commonly seen. Here you can really appreciate the scale of **Mount Meru**, which, when clear of cloud, looms, dark and threatening.

Mount Meru

Known as *Oldonyo Orok* (Back Mountain) by the Maasai, Meru stands at 4,566 metres (14,980 ft), the fifth-highest mountain in Africa. Walks on the lower slopes, climbs to the summit, **Socialist Peak**, and to Little Meru can be arranged with the park headquarters at the Momela Gate. Allow four days for the tough

BELOW: Wa-Arusha woman and child on the slopes of Mount Meru.
RIGHT: vervet monkey.

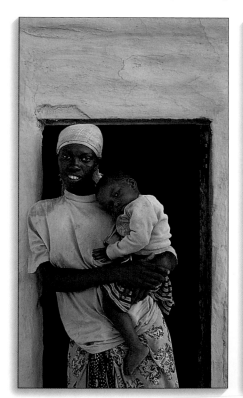

hike to ascend the peak; the best time to go is between July and September. Park guides are well trained and informative. Walking gives a different perspective on viewing the wildlife. Skirting past breeding herds of buffalo, getting to within 50 metres (160 ft) of a giraffe, listening to the raucous sounds of Hautlaub's turacco, and searching for colobus monkeys in the trees, is guaranteed to sharpen the senses. Natural attractions include the giant fig-tree arch, the buttress roots of a strangler fig through which an elephant can pass, and the **Tululusia Waterfall**. Tululusia means sentinel, and the top of Tululusia Hill was used as a lookout point by the Maasai during the intertribal wars with the Wa-Arusha, some 50 years ago. Interestingly, the volcanic rocks give the water a high mineral and fluoride content, staining teeth a dirty brown, as can be seen among the Wa-Arusha living on the slopes of the mountain.

Not much larger than a cocker spaniel (although infinitely more streamlined), the charming little Kirk's dik-dik is a gentle creature which lives in scrubby bush and mates for life.

The route up the mountain

The track up Mount Meru begins at the **Momela Gate**, at 1,500 metres (4,920 ft). There are two routes to the first hut, **Mirakamba**, at 2,600 metres (8,530 ft). The northern route takes three to four hours, and can also be driven. The southern route takes a couple of hours longer, but is more interesting and scenic, crossing streams and open grassland before climbing up through the forest, passing through the fig-tree arch, crossing the Jekukumia River to the Njeku viewpoint, with expansive views to Momela lakes and across the park, before continuing to Mirakamba. On the way there's a good chance of seeing monkeys, bushbucks, duikers, baboons and giraffe.

From Mirakamba it's a four-hour hike to **Saddle Hut**, at 3,600 metres (11,810 ft), passing through glades and forest to **Mgongo wa Tembo** (Elephant Ridge).

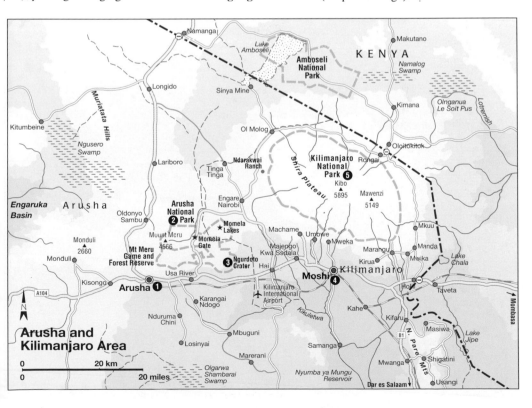

Arusha and Kilimanjaro Area

"Kesho ya manyani" is an old Iraqw proverb literally meaning "tomorrow for the baboons". Every morning, the baboons sit around discussing their plan to build a house, but every day they postpone building it. To this day they have no house, and their bottoms are red from sitting around doing nothing.

From here, it's a pleasant afternoon's excursion to the summit of **Little Meru** (3,820 metres/12,530 ft), from which there are impressive views of the crater, the ash cone and the sheer cliffs of the crater's inner wall towering some 1,500 metres (4,920 ft) high. Look out, along the way, for the agile klipspringer, a small antelope which has adapted to steep and rocky terrain, and the imposing lammergeier vultures soaring on the updrafts.

From Saddle Hut, you can hike to the summit in about six hours, traversing a knife-edge ridge. Start early to watch the sun rising behind Kilimanjaro. Descending from the summit, you can stay at Saddle or Mirakamba Hut before the final descent to Momela Gate.

Bush lodges

Of the lodges and hotels next to the park, the best are Ngurdoto Lodge near the Ngurdoto Gate, and Olare Orok close to the Momela Gate. Hatari Lodge is also a fascinating place to stay, novel for its association with the filming of the 1962 Howard Hawks movie *Hatari!* and its unique interior design.

On the western slopes of Kilimanjaro, a two-hour drive from Arusha, is a private 4,000-hectare (10,000-acre) ranch, called **Ndarakwai**, a pioneer in community conservation work with the Maasai. Dominated by acacia savanna woodland and bisected by riverine forest, there are two resident herds of elephant, and you may see gerenuk and lesser kudu, which are not found in either Arusha or Kilimanjaro national parks. Walking with the Maasai and riding safaris are a speciality of the ranch, and guests stay in a tented camp. Before independence, western Kilimanjaro was the main centre of European farming in the area.

BELOW: volcanic minerals dye the water of Lake Chala a magnificent turquoise.

Map on page 171

Moshi

The small, sprawling town of **Moshi ❹**, due west of Arusha and surrounded by wheat, maize and coffee farms, lies at the foot of Kilimanjaro, dwarfed by the peaks of **Kibo** (5,895 metres/19,340 ft) and **Mawenzi** (5,149 metres/16,893 ft). Founded in 1911 as the terminus of the Tanga railway line, it is now a major staging post for those inspired to conquer Kili. The main gate of **Kilimanjaro National Park** is only 30 km (19 miles) away, a steep climb up through the coffee and banana plantations of the prosperous Chagga tribe.

Within easy reach of Moshi's central clocktower, the main shopping and business area has a useful assortment of safari companies, exchange bureaux, internet cafés, hotels and coffee houses, along with a colourful vegetable market and a few interesting shops. Shah Industries specialises in quality leathercraft, while Our Heritage sells curios. Of architectural interest are the Hindu temple and colonial railway station.

Several worthwhile distractions surround Moshi. Day trips can be arranged to the **Rau Forest**, visiting Rau village and the Materuni waterfalls. At **Mweka**, there's a small wildlife museum attached to the College of Wildlife Management. **Lake Chala** is a small crater lake, about 1 km (1,100 yards) wide, on the Kenyan border. Skirting the eastern slopes of Kilimanjaro, take the road to Taveta, from where a rough road to the lake passes through farmland, west of Holili, with views to Kenya. There's a steep path down the 100-metre (330-ft) crater wall, but crocodiles lurk here so don't be tempted to swim. Less visited is **Lake Jipe**, a shallow alkaline lake some 16 km (10 miles) long. Also sharing a border with Kenya, it is accessible from Kifaru on the Tanga road and offers excellent birdwatching.

LEFT: weighing the porters' loads on Kilimanjaro.
BELOW: trekking through the rainforest zone.

The great mountain

Kilimanjaro National Park ❺ covers an area of 760 sq. km (293 sq. miles). It was gazetted in 1977 to protect the mountain above the 2,700-metre (8,858-ft) contour. Below this is a buffer zone of Forest Reserve to the 1,800-metre (5,905-ft) contour. The summit of Kilimanjaro was first climbed in 1889 by Dr Hans Meyer and Ludwig Purtscheller *(see Climbing Kili, page 179)*. Today, more than 25,000 people a year make a bid for Africa's highest mountain, and Kilimanjaro earns more in park fees than all the other Tanzanian parks put together. Increasing numbers have made a considerable environmental impact on the park's trails. Efforts are being made to counteract the erosion, and the Marangu and Mweka routes have been upgraded.

Climbing Kilimanjaro can be arranged through tour operators in Moshi and Arusha and at the park headquarters at Marangu. The best months to climb the mountain are January, February and September. July and August are also good, but colder. Prices vary, but it pays to go with a reputable tour operator, as scrimping on price usually equates to poor equipment. If you book a tour from the UK or the US, the tour operator will put together a itinerary tailored to your needs. *(For listings, see Travel Tips page 309.)*

Counting the cost

Climbing the mountain is not cheap. Entry fees to the National Park are US$60 per person per day; the money is used to preserve the environment and curb the impact of mass tourism. Expect to pay at least US$1,300 for a budget climb.

Climbing costs differ widely, according to the route taken, the number of days spent on the mountain and the number of people in the party. Camping is

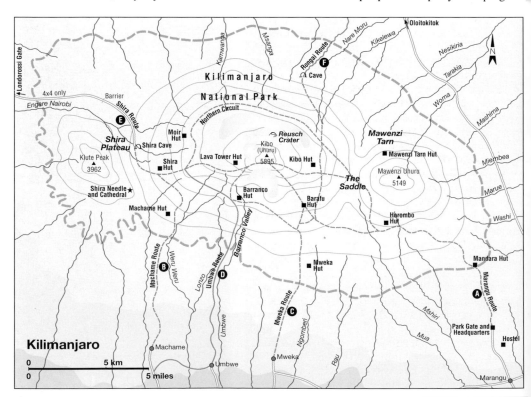

Kilimanjaro

more expensive than staying in huts as more equipment needs to be carried. In addition to the amount paid for the climb itself, it is important to budget for tipping the guides and porters. Approximate figures per day are US$20 for the guide, $15 for the cook and $10 for each porter, but be sure to ascertain the going rate from tour operators before departing.

Climbing Mount Kilimanjaro is marketed as an easy trek to the roof of Africa, attracting many people who have little experience of hill-walking, let alone climbing – and who arrive ill-prepared. Kilimanjaro should not be underestimated: it claims several lives a year. Although walking on the easy routes – Marangu and Rongai – may not be taxing, few take into account the effects of altitude (headaches and nausea), which can be pronounced and debilitating. Being super-fit does not guarantee scaling the summit. You can double your chances of reaching the top by spending several days acclimatising and preferably walking at altitude, before the climb.

Many routes give a number of options for the days taken. It pays to spend an extra day on the mountain if time allows.

Maps
on pages
171 & 174

Everlasting flowers are one of the most charming features of Kili, drying on the bush to turn the slopes into a bouquet.

Which route?

There are six routes up the mountain – Marangu, Mweka, Umbwe, Machame, Shira and Rongai. Research thoroughly before you decide which of these to take. Some are more challenging, more scenic and less well-worn than others. The most popular, the easiest and cheapest (and therefore the most crowded), staying in mountain huts, is the **Marangu route Ⓐ**, commonly called the "Coca-Cola route". About 65 climbers a day can depart on the Marangu trail, which, since the path was renovated, is the best on the mountain. A typical five-day trek is to stay at the Mandara, Horombo and Kibo Huts. The first day is a gentle four-hour climb through the rainforest from the Marangu Gate to **Mandara**, at 2,750 metres (9,020 ft). On the second day, one emerges from the rainforest onto an alpine meadow to **Horombo Hut** (3,820 metres/12,530 ft), with superb views of the peaks and the plains below on a clear day. It's here that the effects of altitude begin to kick in, with a shortness of breath. The third day brings spectacular views of Mawenzi before ascending to The Saddle across a lava desert, and crossing to **Kibo Hut** (4,730 metres/15,520 ft).

BELOW: porters snaking their way up Kilimanjaro.

The quest for the summit begins in the early hours of the morning in the dark, first climbing to Hans Meyer Cave, after which the scree slope becomes extremely steep. It takes six hours to cover 6 km (4 miles), from Kibo Hut to **Gillman's Point** on the crater rim. This is acknowledged to be the top, but if time permits one can continue around the crater rim for two hours to **Uhuru Peak**.

A quotation by Julius Nyerere is engraved on a plaque at the top of Uhuru Peak. He had the idea of the Uhuru Torch in 1959, when he said: "We, the people of Tanganyika, would like to light a candle and put it on top of Mount Kilimanjaro which would shine beyond our borders, giving hope where there was despair, love where there was hate, and dignity where there before was only humiliation."

On 9 December 1961 Tanganyika won its independence, and a symbolic torch, together with the flag of the new nation, was hoisted on the summit of Mount Kilimanjaro.

The descent is equally arduous, returning to Kibo Hut for a short rest and continuing down to Horombo Hut, descending to Marangu on the final day.

In the 1990s the management plan for the Park talked of 16 people a day on Kilimanjaro's other routes, which were considered to be wilderness trails. These days, a maximum of 60 climbers a day are taken on each route.

The whisky route

After Marangu, the **Machame route ❸**, labelled the "whisky route", is the second most popular and one of the most scenic. It's considerably harder going than the Marangu route and involves camping out. From **Machame Gate**, it is a six-hour walk up a well-worn path, crossing tangled tree roots, through rainforest to **Machame Hut**, at 3,000 metres (9,840 ft). On the second day, there's a steady four-hour climb up a steep ridge, like a giant's staircase, before the path flattens out into a gorge, with a gentle two-hour ascent onto the moorland of the Shira plateau to **Shira Hut** (3,840 metres/12,600 ft), which offers dramatic views of mist swirling around the Shira cone and across to Mount Meru.

From here, with the effects of altitude kicking in, you are faced by a long, steady climb, with views of the glaciers on Kibo, before making a steep descent into the Barranco Valley, eventually reaching **Barranco Hut** (3,950 metres/12,960 ft) after about eight hours. The next day begins with a tough two-hour climb in single file up the rock face of the Barranco Wall. Although not technical climbing, at one point you must shuffle around a narrow ledge with

BELOW: the edge of the Shira plateau.

a drop of 600 metres (1,970 ft), before following the southern circuit across scree and ridges to Karanga and **Barafu Hut** at 4,600 metres (15,090 ft).

The slow, final ascent begins at 1am, crossing the Ratzel and Rebmamm glaciers and continuing up to **Uhuru Peak**, in time for sunrise, before descending to Mweka Hut, and continuing down to the Mweka Gate the following day.

An alternative route from Shira Hut is to ascend to Lava Tower Hut (4,600 metres/15,090 ft), climbing up the ridge towards Kibo, which takes about five hours. With an early start, there's a steady nine-hour climb through rocky cliffs – part of the Arrow Glacier – before reaching a ridge-like staircase with a point of no return, and continuing the scramble up to the crater floor. From here it's about an hour and a half to Uhuru Peak. The descent is from Stella Point to Barafu Hut, with the option of continuing to Mweka Hut.

Other alternatives

The **Mweka route** ◉ is the quickest and steepest route to the summit, but is now used for descent. The less steep **Kidia route** (Old Moshi) is used when Mweka is closed for maintenance. From Barafu to the Mweka Hut takes around four hours, and it's another hour's walk along a logging track to the gate.

The **Umbwe route** ◉ runs along a ridge parallel to the Umbwe and Lonzo rivers and starts from the mission near the park boundary. It's a six-hour climb up through the rainforest to the campsite at 2,800 metres (9,190 ft). The next day's climb to **Barranco Hut** is extremely steep, and involves hauling oneself up rock faces via tree roots, with little remission. However, the scenery is beautiful, walking through feathery heather forests with views into steeply wooded valleys, the lobelia forest and moorland of the Barranco Valley. The route is

Map on page 174

BELOW: sunrise over the crater rim at Gillman's Point.

CLIMBING IN COMFORT

It may be exciting, but climbing Kili is rarely easy or comfortable. The biggest danger to watch out for is altitude-related pulmonary oedema, a dangerous illness caused by ascending too rapidly, resulting in fluid build-up in the lungs. Most susceptible are fit young men. Symptoms include laboured breathing, shortness of breath at rest and coughing up frothy spit or blood. This can be fatal. If these symptoms exist it is imperative to descend immediately and get medical attention.

Useful equipment includes:

- two adjustable climbing poles – one for going up and two for the steep descent
- a water pouch with a tube, carried in a daypack
- high-energy snacks
- gloves
- strong sunglasses, a hat and suncream
- layers of clothes
- comfortable and sturdy walking boots
- gaiters
- windproof jacket and trousers
- head-torch
- medication pack with headache and diarrhoea tablets, plasters and rehydration sachets

Map on page 174

little used, as there is no water at the campsite, and is best appreciated if descending the mountain. Walking poles are an invaluable aid.

The **Shira route** starts from the western **Londorossi Gate** (1,800 metres/5,905 ft). It's a steep five-hour ascent through the rainforest to the moorland camp below the Shira plateau. A six-hour hike to Shira Cave, via a detour around a hill on the northern edge of the plateau, gives views to Amboseli in Kenya. The track continues to Shira Cave, with views across the plateau to Kibo.

From here it's a three-hour climb to Shira Hut (3,800 metres/12,470 ft), giving the opportunity to branch off the trail, climb the Shira Needle and Cathedral, look down onto the Machame ridge or visit the cone, the centre of the extinct Shira volcano, looking onto Johnsell Point and Klute Peak, the highest points on the Shira ridge. From Shira Hut, the options to ascend the summit are the same as for other routes.

The **Rongai route** is the least used in Tanzania, with ascents normally made from Loitokitok in Kenya. It's a two-hour drive from Marangu to the **Rongai Gate** (1,800 metres/5,900 ft), from where it's a four-hour walk through the forest to the **Rongai Cave** (3,000 metres/9,840 ft). The next day, it's a steady climb though alpine moorland, with views across the Kenyan plains, to the **Third Cave** (3,800 metres/12,470 ft). The third day gives an interesting climb through the lunar landscape of The Saddle to Kibo Hut, descending via the Mweka Gate.

For those unconcerned about reaching the summit, it's possible to drive up to the Shira plateau and enjoy the superb views of Kibo and the plains below. Alternatively, a three-day trek from Machame to Londorossi Gate, through the rainforest and onto the moorland of the Shira plateau, gives a flavour of the dramatic scenery. Experienced climbers can opt to climb the Western Breach. ❑

BELOW: at the top; triumphant climber at Uhuru Peak, Kibo.

Climbing Kili

A ccording to legend, the first person to ascend Mount Kilimanjaro was King Menelik I, supposedly the son of King Solomon and the Queen of Sheba. He ruled Tigre, the oldest province in Abyssinia (now Ethiopia), in the 10th century BC, and fought battles in the present-day Ethiopia, Somalia, Kenya and Tanzania. As an old man, returning with the spoils of war, he camped between the peaks of Kibo and Mawenzi, at a height of 4,500 metres (14,760 ft). Feeling that death was drawing near, he told his followers that he wished to die as a king. He, his warlords and slaves, laden with jewels and treasure, climbed to the crater, where he died.

The legend relates that one of Menelik's offspring will return to the mountain, climb Kibo and find the king and his jewels. Among these will be the Seal of Solomon, a ring which will empower the wearer with the wisdom of Solomon. The legend was so firmly believed by the Abyssinian Christians that when The Revd Dr Reusch (a missionary who spent many years in the Kilimanjaro area, and who later became president of the Mountain Club of East Africa) reached the summit in 1926, many were deeply sceptical that he had reached the top as he found no trace of the long-dead king.

Although news of a snowcapped mountain was first mentioned in European literature in 1848 by another missionary, John Rebmann, no serious attempts at exploring Kilimanjaro were made until 1861, when it was attempted by Baron von der Decken and Richard Thornton. The first successful ascent of the mountain was eventually made by Hans Meyer and Ludwig Purtscheller, on 5 October 1889.

Since then, many have reached the summit. Africa's highest mountain has attracted the rich and famous, and adventurers, including such unlikely people as the former US president Jimmy Carter and the Australian supermodel Elle Macpherson.

Remarkably, wildlife can survive at this high altitude – John Reader, filming on the mountain in 1983, saw eland, buffalo, jackal and wild dog on the Shira plateau. The explorer Wilfred Thesiger describes being tracked by five wild dogs at a height of 5,750 metres (18,865 ft). Perhaps the most famous was the frozen specimen of a leopard discovered by Dr Donald Latham on his 1926 ascent. This gave its name to Leopard's Point on the crater rim.

In recent years, just climbing Africa's highest mountain hasn't been enough. In 1962, three French parachutists beat the record for the highest parachute drop by landing in the crater. Others have successfully reached the top on a motorbike or bicycle. Several people have paraglided from the summit – on one occasion, a paraglider was blown off course, and was promptly arrested as a spy. Another time a father and son did a dual flight – the son descended safely, but the father and his paraglider disappeared into the forest and were never seen again. Such wacky feats are no longer permitted by the park authorities, but there are now regular expeditions to the summit by wheelchair users and people with various disabilities. ❑

RIGHT: climbing Mount Kilimanjaro the hard way.

THE NORTHERN SAFARI CIRCUIT

Map on page 184

The stuff of legends, this extraordinary area includes the Serengeti, Ngorongoro Crater and Olduvai Gorge, world-class game viewing and much more besides

There is a well-worn tourist track across northern Tanzania. Almost every first-time visitor to the country will, at some point in their trip, visit the region. Some cherry-pick the most famous bits, visiting only the Serengeti and Ngorongoro Crater; others try to cram the whole lot in at breakneck speed. To do the circuit properly, you need three weeks. However you choose to do it, just make sure you do – this is one of the most compelling destinations in Africa, a superb blend of magnificent wildlife, stunning scenery, fascinating, colourful people and outdoor activities.

The jumping-off point for the circuit is **Arusha ❶** *(see page 167)*, with flights coming into Arusha or Kilimanjaro international airports. From then on, you have a choice of driving or chartering a small plane. There are plenty of airstrips in the region, and if you are in a large group, it may not be as expensive as it sounds. Otherwise, it is strongly recommended that you use an Arusha-based safari company to provide a four-wheel drive and driver/guide. This may seem like a luxury, but you need good ground clearance and height for game viewing, four-wheel drive is necessary in some areas, and a driver costs very little more than self-drive hire.

Don't expect to do this without spending money. The area has a variety of lodges, from small tented camps to large hotels. Most are comfortable, some extraordinarily luxurious, but few are cheap. You could bring costs down by taking a camping safari but you still have to pay the National Park fees (see www.tanzaniaparks.com), unless you never enter the parks – which rather defeats the purpose of going.

PRECEDING PAGES: lion up a tree in Tarangire. **LEFT:** Maasai initiate. **BELOW:** olive baboon.

Tarangire National Park

From Arusha, head west on the Dodoma road, through **Makuyuni ❷**, 80 km (50 miles) away. This is part of the Great North Road, the pan-African "highway" that runs from Cairo to Cape Town. The entrance to **Tarangire National Park ❸** is 115 km (71 miles) south of Arusha, with good tarred roads all the way.

Tarangire is a long, thin park covering 1,360 sq. km (525 sq. miles), roughly running north–south along the line of the Tarangire River. It is made up chiefly of low-lying, rolling hills on the Rift floor, its natural vegetation of acacia woodland and giant baobabs only altered by huge areas of swamp which are a magnet for wildlife – including, unfortunately, mosquitoes and tsetse flies. Take precautions. The swamps of black cotton mud produce rich grasslands, while the watercourses are lined by huge trees, including sycamore fig, tamarind and sausage trees. Although it

is relatively small, Tarangire has huge benefits, from its easy access to the fact that it has some of the greatest concentrations of game in Tanzania, second only to the Ngorongoro Crater, but with far fewer tourists. There are several dry-country species that you will be unlikely to see in the bigger parks to the west, including eland, oryx, Grant's gazelle and gerenuk. Sadly, Coke's hartebeest, once a speciality of the area, have long since vanished, as have the rhinos, shot out by poachers in the dark days of the 1970s and 1980s.

Baby boom

The elephants also suffered badly from poaching, but with the ban on ivory trading, they have recovered with a vengeance, and hundreds now roam the hills. As yet, there are few tuskers, but for cute elephant babies, this is definitely the place to be. The park lies at the southern end of a vast migration area which stretches north to Amboseli in Kenya. As the land dries and the smaller rivers cease to flow, the herds head south towards the permanent water in the

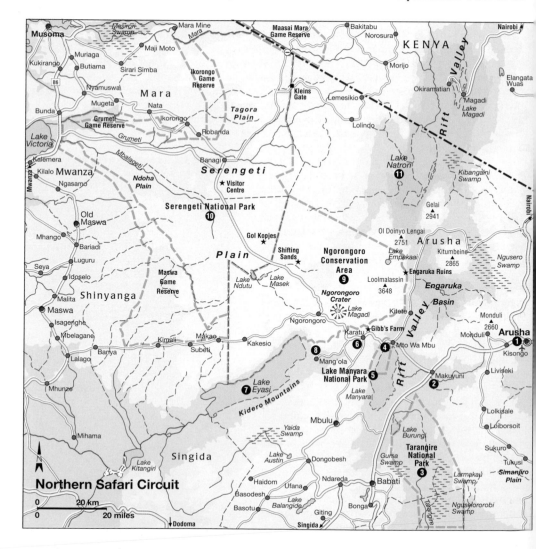

Tarangire River and its surrounding swamps. The first to arrive are the eland and oryx, in June, followed by the elephants, wildebeest and zebra. June to October is the best time to visit. Although the herds remain in the area until March, and it is great to see the thousands of calves born at this time, you will also have to contend with the rain, luxuriant vegetation and the plentiful insect population that make this season less suitable for great game viewing.

The main lodges are all near the gate, overlooking the Tarangire River and baobab-clad hills, although there are a couple of smaller luxury camps in the centre of the park. There is no accommodation in the south, and few visitors ever get there. Do try and make it at least as far as the **Silale Swamp**, the most northerly of several large swamps in the park. Fuelled by natural springs, they are year-round oases of lush green grass. Many of the animals you see near by are coated in black cotton mud, having waded in waist-deep to reach the best shoots. There are also masses of birds, including tawny, steppe and fish eagles, maribou storks, goliath herons, white pelicans, spur-winged geese and sacred ibis. Some 300 species are regularly seen in the park, including a number of European migrants who winter here. It is also near the swamps that you may get to see one of the reserve's party tricks – tree-climbing lions.

Beyond the boundaries

Outside the park, large swathes of the areas to the northeast, crucial to the annual migration, have been turned into conservation zones. A considerable amount of effort is going into educating the local populace on living in harmony with the wildlife, and setting up schemes to ensure they share the financial benefits of having the park on their doorstep. Several of the best lodges are found in this region, reached via a rough track just north of the park entrance.

The **Lemiyon Plain**, north and west of Tarangire, is a huge, flat, dry and desolate area, with the occasional village and small town, way too many cattle and goats and so little grass that dust clouds blow for miles.

Kolo, home of some of the finest of the Kondoa rock paintings, is not far to the south of the park *(see Central Tanzania, page 215)*.

To continue the circuit, head back north to Makuyuni, from where the road turns off to Manyara, Ngorongoro and Serengeti. At the time of writing, the 90-km (56-mile) road to Ngorongoro was still being tarred. Work is estimated to be completed soon. Meantime, expect roadworks and long, dusty, bumpy stretches of poor dirt road.

Mto Wa Mbo

The agricultural and market town of **Mto Wa Mbu ❹** stands next to the entrance of **Lake Manyara National Park**, about 50 km (30 miles) west of Makuyuni, at the foot of the **Gregory Escarpment**, the western wall of the eastern arm of the Great Rift Valley. Named after Scottish geologist John Walter Gregory, the first to map and name the East African Rift, this is one of the most dramatic points along its length, rising almost sheer some 800 metres (2,625 ft) from the valley floor.

Map on page 184

Multicoloured bananas on sale in Mto Wa Mbu, an agricultural oasis in the dry Rift Valley.

BELOW: abseiling down the Rift Escarpment near Lake Manyara.

The phenomenon of tree-climbing lions was first studied at Manyara, but can occasionally be seen across northern Tanzania. It is thought that it began as a way of avoiding the flies, and has been imitated as individuals move across territories. Lions will travel miles to reach a favourite tree.

BELOW: Manyara and Tarangire are famous for their tree-climbing lions.

The enormous amount of groundwater pouring through the rocks of the escarpment has created a lush, green swamp here, and the locals are excellent farmers, growing everything from bananas and maize to citrus fruits, rice and vegetables. The road is lined with produce stalls, and the town has a self-satisfied feeling of wealth – also helped by the estimated 18,000 souvenir salesmen waiting to pounce the moment you leave your car. The downside of all this plenty is that the area is very malarial – Mto Wa Mbu ominously and accurately means "mosquito creek" – so lash on the repellent and take the pills.

The town is a useful stopping point, with several inexpensive lodges, campsites and guesthouses, and a few tour operators, including Serena Active, based in the Manyara Serena Lodge at the top of the escarpment, which offers a wide range of activities from mountain biking, to village walks or abseiling down the escarpment *(see listing in Travel Tips).*

Manyara

Many people pass by **Lake Manyara National Park** ❺ in their rush towards the Serengeti, but although small, this is one of the prettiest, most interesting and game-rich parks in the country. It is only 330 sq. km (127 sq. miles) in size – tiny by Tanzanian standards – and about two-thirds of that is water. The rest is a long thin strip of land sandwiched between the lake and the cliff, served by a very few extremely rough roads. There is only one lodge actually within the park, the exclusive **Lake Manyara Tree Lodge** *(see listing in Travel Tips)* at the far end of the park beyond the reach of most day trippers. Most of the other lodges are built along the rim of the escarpment, with fabulous views across the lake, and safely out of the way of the mosquitoes.

Map
on page
184

The park and lake take their name from the manyara bush *(euphorbia tirucalli)* used by the Maasai to build their stockades. The Maasai actually use the same word, *emanyara*, for a kraal. There is a manyara bush at the park entrance. Once inside, the first part of the park is thick groundwater forest with huge trees, including Cape mahogany, croton, sycamore fig and several sorts of palm. Beneath these soaring canopies, dense undergrowth provides a delightful array of wild flowers and butterflies, but this is not easy country for game viewing.

You should see troops of olive baboons and Sykes monkeys playing beside the road. Bushbuck may emerge from the shade, and as you round a bend, you are quite likely to find an elephant in your path. They frequently choose to use the roads rather than having to struggle through the tangled undergrowth. Remember to keep looking up. As in Tarangire, the local lions sometimes take to the trees, and there are also plenty of leopards, although you need luck to see them. Even if the cats elude you, there are many wonderful birds, including the giant silvery-cheeked hornbill.

The further you reach into the park, the drier it becomes, gradually opening out into forests of umbrella-topped fever trees and baobabs. As the vegetation changes, so does the wildlife, with plains animals such as buffalo, wildebeest, zebra and giraffe making an appearance. Above, martial eagles and bateleurs circle idly on the thermals as they scan for prey. Near the southern end of the park, there are two groups of bubbling, steaming hot springs that have dyed the surrounding ground a rainbow of colours with their chemicals.

Like most other Rift Valley lakes, Manyara is a shallow soda lake, fed by groundwater, and varying hugely in size according to the season. As it shrinks back, a broad floodplain opens up. Many animals choose to graze the new

BELOW: time for a break; elephants wallow to cool off in the heat.

shoots and wallow in the muddy shallows. Amongst them paddle waterbirds such as pelicans, flamingos, cormorants and herons, while a little further out, pods of hippos grunt and puff their way through the heat of the day.

Karatu Highlands

At the top of the Manyara Escarpment, you enter a lush area of richly fertile farmland and superb mountain scenery, with purple hills ringing rich red earth and neatly ordered fields of wheat, sweet potatoes, beans, and coffee, carved up by high green hedges of spiky manyara plants. In the distance are the imposing cones of the great volcanic craters, **Ngorongoro** *(see page 191)* and **Ol Doinyo Lengai** *(see page 199)*.

The roads along the edge of the escarpment lead to most of the Manyara hotels, perfectly positioned for the views. As you head towards Ngorongoro, several signs entice you towards "cultural villages" – of mixed value – and some excellent souvenir shops, including one specialising in jazzy T-shirts. The largest town in the area is **Karatu ❻**, a bustling market and business centre that is a useful stop for travellers, with several campsites, phones and internet cafés.

The lush Karatu Highlands were once a great centre of white farming, colonised by the Germans in the mid-19th century. The plantations have long since been carved up again amongst the Mbulu and Iraqw peoples, Cushitic tribes who moved into the area about 3,000 years ago. The area is heavily populated, with villages scattered across the hillsides, buses groaning past with passengers on the roof and clinging to the fenders. It could not be a greater contrast to the remote, dusty world of Tarangire on the Rift floor.

BELOW: the nomadic Hadza live in family groups of up to 20 people.

Several former plantation homes have been converted into lodges, including **Gibb's Farm**, 4 km (2½ miles) off the main road, which began life as a coffee farm in the 1930s. It is well worth an overnight stop, with magnificent gardens, fine views and superb food, much of it grown on the premises. Staff are only too eager to show you around both the flower gardens and the huge organic vegetable garden. There are also opportunities locally for birdwatching with the resident naturalist, and walking. One of the receptionists runs interesting small-scale Iraqw cultural tours – basically a visit to his home. His English is excellent, his wife hospitable, and he has an amazingly ingenious system of "cow power" to run the gas and lights within the house.

Lake Eyasi

If you have time, spend a day detouring down to **Lake Eyasi ❼**. Look for the turning to the left, 10 km (6 miles) west of Karatu town. The 60-km (37-mile) road is poor almost from the start and gets increasingly bad until, at times, it disappears on the rocks altogether. It is just passable without four-wheel drive in the dry season, as long as you have good ground clearance. As the road drops down from the plateau, the lush farms of the highlands give way to bare earth creviced by erosion canyons, and to acacias and baobabs powdered white by flying dust, and herds of goats and skeletal cows.

Lake Eyasi is a long, skinny soda lake that stretches up to 80 km (50 miles) when the rains are good and virtually dries up at other times. Above it soars the 800-metre (2,625-ft) **Eyasi Escarpment**, one of the more spectacular cliffs in the Tanzanian Rift Valley. At certain times of year, the water can be thick with clattering pink flamingos, while numerous other birds call from the shores. The

Map on page 184

BELOW: the Maasai giraffe uses its height to pick the fresh young shoots from the treetops.

THE HADZA

The Hadza represent a precious link with human prehistory. They are among the last adherents to the hunter-gatherer lifestyle that sustained the world's entire human population for perhaps 99 percent of its existence. Their language belongs to the dying Khiosan linguistic group, distinguished by punctuating clicks that many linguists believe to be a preserved element of the first human language.

The Hadza refuse to adopt a settled lifestyle, so a tract of state land fringing Lake Eyasi has been set aside for their use. Here, small nomadic family bands construct temporary grass shelters, moving according to weather conditions, game movements, or the location of a kill. Anything from sparrows to giraffes is fair game, but the local delicacy is baboon flesh. Meat accounts for only 20 percent of Hadza food intake; the remainder consists of vegetable matter gathered by women.

The Hadza philosophy of living for the moment is encapsulated in their favourite gambling game. A wooden disc, with rough and smooth faces, is thrown down together with one similar disc per participant. This action is repeated until only one person's disc lands same-face-up with the master, deciding the winner.

Bringing home the catch – a Hadza hunter near Lake Eyasi finds a convenient way to carry his supper.

locals fish in the lake, smoking their catch on the foreshore. Hire a local guide at the village of **Mang'ola ❽**, about 10 km (6 miles) from the lake shore. This is also the only place where you can buy basic groceries and cold drinks, so take your own lunch and eat it at the campsite, an idyllic green glade near a hot spring (there are no facilities, other than a basic toilet).

As far as the locals are concerned, the freshwater springs are the real attraction of the area, supporting intensive farming of maize, beans, bananas, rice, wheat and, above all, onions. During the harvest, the whole village reeks of them. More and more people are moving in to rent farmland, putting huge pressure on traditional lifestyles. There is little grazing land left, and the game is all but shot out. Meanwhile, up to 60 tribes now live in the area, and the Maasai are also trying to move in their enormous herds of cattle and goats. The area is a political powder keg, but so far, the lid has stayed on.

Oldest inhabitants

However, the real attraction for tourists lies in the original peoples. The Hadza *(see page 189)* are Tanzania's last remaining tribe of nomadic Bushmen and are thought to have been in the area for at least 10,000 years. There are only around 2,000 of them left, living a nomadic hunter-gatherer lifestyle, using hollowed baobabs for storage and sleeping in the open, with a stockade of thorns or a grass enclosure to protect them from predators. They have few possessions – basic skin aprons, a few beads for decoration, bows, arrows and knives for hunting, and cooking pots, although many now wear T-shirts. Their lifestyle can seem shocking, but they have repeatedly refused attempts to bring them into the modern world. They are used to visitors, will welcome

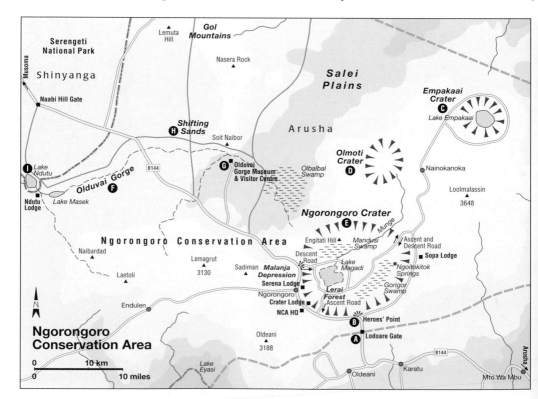

you warmly and will take the hard-of-stomach out hunting with them, if it is arranged ahead of time.

The Datoga are a Nilotic people, closely related to the Barabaig in the Arusha area, who arrived in Tanzania in the 1st millennium AD and, like the Hadza, were chased out of the fertile highlands by the Maasai 200 years ago. They are pastoralists who herd cattle and goats, living in comfortable, thatched rectangular huts, with gaping holes in the walls. The women traditionally wear skin robes with fringes and beadwork, which can take two months to make and last up to five years. Other decorations include huge earrings and holes in their ears, and quantities of brass and copper bangles.

Ngorongoro

The **Ngorongoro Conservation Area** ➒ stretches from the Karatu Highlands to the Serengeti and down to the northern tip of Lake Eyasi, covering some 8,300 sq. km (3,205 sq. miles). **Lodoare Gate** Ⓐ is 29 km (18 miles) west of Karatu. The tarred road ends here; the rest of your circuit will be done on gravel roads that range from bumpy to diabolical.

Be warned – the daily park fee only gets you as far as the rim of the crater. If you wish to drive down into it, you need to pay an additional fee per car. The only road to the Serengeti runs through the conservation area, so you have to pay even if only passing through. Remember that you need to reach the gate before it shuts for the night. From the entrance, the road climbs steeply up through the thick montane forest to a T-junction and **Heroes' Point** Ⓑ, from which you get your first, mind-blowing view of the crater itself. In the parking area is a memorial to rangers killed while protecting the crater from poachers. The right

Maps on pages 184 & 190

BELOW: the play of light across the Ngorongoro Crater provides constant drama.

fork leads to Sopa Lodge, the only hotel on the eastern rim, and beyond that to the **Empakaai Crater** ⊙, a 6-km (4-mile) wide, 300-metre (980-ft) high volcanic crater largely filled by a soda lake. There is a road around the rim and into the crater, but both are rough, and a four-wheel drive is strongly advised. The much shallower **Olmoti Crater** ⊙ can only be reached on foot. Rangers can be hired at the ranger station in the nearby village of Nainokanoka. Back at the crossroads, the left fork leads to all the other hotels, the main access routes to the crater, Olduvai and the Serengeti.

Maasai territory

Formed by the same immense geological upheavals as the Great Rift Valley, Ngorongoro was once a mountain as high as Kilimanjaro. About 3 million years ago, it blew itself to bits, covering the Serengeti in ash while the crater floor sank into the mountain. Today, the rim stands at 2,285 metres (7,497 ft). The **Ngorongoro Crater** ⊙ is the world's largest complete volcanic caldera, with a diameter of about 18 km (11 miles) and an area of 260 sq. km (100 sq. miles). The sheer-sided rim is just over 600 metres (1,969 ft) at its highest point. From the top, it is impossible to see the animals down on the plains without binoculars, but the ever-changing play of light across the flowing grasslands can be hypnotic.

Ngorongoro is a Maasai word; some say it mimics the clatter of cow bells, others that it is a traditional name for a type of bowl, similar in shape to the crater. The Maasai are the traditional owners of the area, although they are relative newcomers, having forced the Mbulu and Datoga out of the area around 200 years ago. Two German brothers farmed the crater floor for a short while in the

BELOW: cheetahs rely on short bursts of tremendous speed to catch their prey.

early 20th century, but when the area was first incorporated into the Serengeti National Park in 1951, around 12,000 Maasai lived in the crater.

A deal was struck that turned Ngorongoro into a Conservation Area, rather than a National Park, allowing them to continue to water their animals on the crater floor, in exchange for moving out and receiving a share of the profits from tourism. Today, with the populations of people, cattle and goats growing geometrically, and water and grazing land short in the surrounding area, some 40,000 Maasai are claiming rights over the crater and demanding a larger slice of the cake. Even though Ngorongoro was declared a World Heritage Site in 1978, there is no room for complacency. To the Maasai the cattle are all-important and the game is there on sufferance.

Into the crater

Perhaps the truest indication of how busy the crater can get is that the access roads operate as a one-way system. The crater is only open between 7am and 6pm, and most people prefer to spend the whole day there. There are two picnic and toilet spots, in the Lerai Forest or at **Ngoitokitok Springs** in the southeast. Watch out for the aggressive tactics of the black kites, who have discovered that chicken sandwiches taste better and are easier to catch than mice.

The main descent road twists down the western wall, near the **Seneto Springs**, used by the Maasai to water their cattle. The crater floor is a true Shangri-La, one of the most densely crowded game areas in the world, home to an estimated 30,000 animals. Because it is enclosed and the flat crater floor is largely made up of open grassland, it is easy to police, with the result that this is a stronghold for endangered species including black rhino and, increasingly,

Map on page 190

The Ngorongoro Crater Lodge has to be the world's most luxurious and unusual safari camp.

BELOW: Maasai women rarely stop working, even when catching up on the gossip.

TIP

Many Maasai boys spend their days hanging around on the roadside dressed in their full tribal finery, waiting for people to take their picture. This is technically illegal in the Conservation Area. If you want to take a photo, negotiate a fee first, or you may find yourself in trouble.

BELOW: Olduvai Gorge, considered by many to be the cradle of mankind.

cheetah. The only downside of the open vistas is that you can see other vehicles – although even they can be a useful way of helping you spot something of interest. The best vantage point is flat-topped **Engitati Hill** in the northeastern corner.

There are no giraffe, topi or impala in the crater – they find it too difficult to negotiate the cliffs, and there is insufficient grazing for large herds of antelope. The usual prey animals are wildebeest, zebra and buffalo. It is easy to spot and track a hunt across the open plain, although in a strange local twist, the local hyenas have become aggressive pack hunters while the resident lions have taken to scavenging hyena kills.

In the southwestern corner, **Lake Magadi** is a large, shallow soda lake, home to large populations of flamingos and other waterbirds as well as hippos, which can also be seen in the central **Mandusi Swamp**. The **Lerai Forest** of fever trees, in the south, is the best place in the park to see elephants, although bizarrely, only bull elephants descend into the crater itself; the breeding herds hang around in the dense forests on the rim. The ascent road is near here.

Olduvai Gorge

From the crater rim, the Serengeti road winds gently down the western flank of the volcano, through rolling grasslands and acacia woodland. It is here that you will find the many giraffe and antelope absent from the crater floor, mingling freely with the Maasai livestock. This is probably also your best opportunity to see the decorative Maasai people; there are several local bomas that offer expensive guided tours of their *manyattas* (homes) that include photo opportunities. Ask your driver to fix the price for you. About 30 km (18 miles) from the crater, a small road on the right leads to the **Olduvai Gorge ❶**.

The **Olduvai Gorge Museum ❷** is 3 km (2 miles) off the road (daily 8.30am–5pm; entrance charge). The area takes its name from the spiky wild sisal plants known to the Maasai as *oldupai*. The gorge, which is about 90 metres (295 ft) deep, lies on the site of an ancient lake, covered by thick layers of volcanic ash which have carefully preserved some of the world's earliest records of mankind. About 100,000 years ago, seismic activity split the earth, creating the gorge and laying bare the rich fossil beds. These were discovered in 1911 by a German professor named Katwinkle while he was out hunting for butterflies. He carried out one small dig in 1913, but little else was done until Louis and Mary Leakey arrived in 1931.

Archaeologists have been working here ever since, and have made many of prehistory's most famous and influential discoveries in the canyon walls (*see The Earliest Inhabitants, page 19*). Standing in the gorge, you are as close as you can get to the cradle of humanity. It is an awe-inspiring thought – especially when you see the cast of footprints made at Laetoli about 3.6 million years ago.

This is just one of the fascinating items on display in the excellent interpretation centre and museum. Although the human exhibits are all copies (the originals are in Nairobi Museum, Kenya), the explanations are fascinating, and there are also plenty of animal remains, many belonging to long-extinct species such as the pygmy giraffe. Guides are on hand to give tours of the gorge and any current excavations, although these generally look very unimpressive to outsiders. The area is also a pleasant place for a walk, picnic and a spot of birdwatching, with a wide variety of small, brightly coloured species such as barbets, rollers and glossy starlings patrolling the grounds.

A few kilometres from the museum, the extraordinary **Shifting Sands** ⊕ are a couple of black volcanic sand dunes, which slowly meander across the plains, according to the winds. The Maasai regard them as a place of meditation.

Ndutu

About 40 km (25 miles) further on, a turning to the left leads down to **Lake Ndutu** ❶, located just inside the southern border of the Serengeti National Park. Like most of the Rift lakes, it is alkaline, although it is still drinkable and is used by a wide array of local wildlife, including many birds. Rather disconcertingly, the black cotton mud around the shores is littered by wildebeest and buffalo skulls belonging to animals trapped as they tried to cross the lake.

The main reason for visiting is to stay at **Ndutu Lodge**, a charming small safari lodge set in acacia woodland, which has the benefits of being within the Serengeti ecosystem but outside the park's boundary. It is used as a base by many wildlife film units. Every evening, a posse of genets invades the lodge, peering down at the dinner tables from the rafters.

The Serengeti

The **Serengeti National Park** ❿ is quite probably the most famous game reserve in the world; it achieved legendary status from the start when Professor Bernard Grzimek wrote *The Serengeti Shall Not Die*, the story of the quest to have it declared a National Park, finally achieved in 1951. It is now also a World Heritage Site.

The National Park covers 14,763 sq. km (5,700 sq. miles), a vast area roughly equal to Northern Ireland. The full Serengeti ecosystem is far larger still, also covering the Maasai Mara in Kenya and the Ngorongoro Conservation Area, totalling a massive 25,000 sq. km (9,653 sq. miles). Animals wander freely throughout the system.

Only about a third of the park is made up of the flat grassy plains which gave the park its name – *Siringit* is Maasai for "the place where the land runs on forever". However it is these plains and their role in the annual migration of some 2 million animals *(see page 196)* which have made the area so special.

About 3 to 4 million years ago, during the massive eruptions of Ngorongoro, Sadiman and Kerimasi volcanoes, a thick rain of ash settled over the plains, creating a rock-hard top coat, known as hard-pan. Although richly fertile, it is too tough to be broken by tree roots, leaving the landscape to the shallow-rooted grasses, packed with nutritious minerals which act as a magnet to grazers such as wildebeest, zebra, impala and Thomson's gazelles. From **Naabi Hill Gate** ❹, the grasslands stretch around you in all

BELOW: the nocturnal genet is shy and well camouflaged, so it's difficult to see.

The Great Migration

I magine a column of wildebeest 40 km (24 miles) long and two or three abreast, patiently plodding across the plain for hour after hour. Now multiply that until you have about 1½ million wildebeest, throw in some 300,000 zebras, another 300,000 Thomson's gazelles, and about 30,000 Grant's gazelles, all on the move in the search for fresh new grass. Imagine it taking over two weeks for the column of animals to pass a single spot, and visualise them all bunching together into protective herds in the evenings or scrambling across each others' backs in their panic to cross the river and stay clear of the snapping jaws of the crocodiles. Imagine the lions and hyenas roaring and cackling as they prowl the outskirts of the herds looking for weakened animals. Now you may just begin to have an idea of the awesome spectacle that is the Serengeti migration.

The various different species that make up the migration live amicably together, part of a carefully balanced cycle that allows them to get the maximum amount of food from any area. The cycle actually begins with the elephants who open up the woodlands, the heavy buffalo and hippo who rip up the coarse, long grass and the antelope such as topi, eland and hartebeest who have their own much smaller migration cycle around the woodland fringes.

The wildebeest are the most dedicated travellers in their quest for the finest shoots. The zebras are less picky, going for quantity rather than quality, so need to travel less far. Behind them come the smaller gazelles, nibbling the delicate new growth. The wildebeest's keen sense of smell, the zebras' fine eyesight and the gazelles' acute hearing together create a formidable early warning system, while the huge herds make it easier to stay alive. These defences are absolutely necessary – such a smorgasbord attracts the predators in droves.

The Serengeti migration is actually a year-round phenomenon, a broad, slow clockwise route march covering a total of around 3,000 km (1,870 miles). The cycle begins in May, when the grass on the southern plains is exhausted and the herds begin to move slowly northwards through the Western Corridor. This is the time of the rut, the bulls working to the point of exhaustion to build and protect their harems.

The migration reaches the Maasai Mara by late June, remaining here until September, when they return south through the Lobo area, following the scent of the small rains. They reach the southern plains by November, remaining there to feed on the nutrient-rich grass during the breeding season. In three weeks from February to March, over 90 percent of the females (around 500,000 animals) give birth. Calves can stand within seven minutes and within two days can outrun a lion, but even so, the predators grow fat. The herds remain in the south, allowing their young time to build strength, before heading north as the grass runs out and the cycle begins again. ❑

LEFT: many migrating wildebeest drown as they pile into the rivers.

directions. There will be animals here at any time of year, but from October to May, the area will be teeming with life, including wildebeest, zebra, warthogs, topi, hartebeest, impala, Thomson's and Grant's gazelles, kori bustards, secretary birds and ostrich. Hyenas and jackals prowl near by, while vultures circling overhead may indicate the position of a kill.

Map on page 198

Lions, almost the exact colour of the grass in the dry season, are more easily visible at some of the rocky kopjes, granite inselbergs scattered across the landscape. The **Moru Kopjes** ❸ are favourites amongst many big cats, including lion, leopard, serval and caracal, and you may even find elephant in the area. Look carefully at the rocks themselves for the faded, centuries-old Maasai paintings. **Simba Kopjes** ❹ are frequently used for sunbathing by the lions after which they are named. You may also see baboon, giraffe and a good variety of birds in the area. **Gol Kopjes** ❺ are popular with cheetah, while the **Maasai Kopjes** ❻ again attract lion and formidably large cobras.

Seronera

At the centre of the park, the **Seronera River Valley** ❻ is one of the richest wildlife habitats in the region, not only providing a valuable water source, but also marking the boundary between the grassy plains and the wooded hills to the north, attracting animals and birds belonging to both environments. In addition to plains animals, the woodlands are favoured by baboons and monkeys, buffalo, giraffe, eland, bushbuck and dik-dik. Waterbuck and reedbuck hang out along the river banks, overlooked by leopards who love to laze away the heat of the day in the shady sausage trees. The river provides a home for hippos and crocodiles, while many of the park's estimated 500 species of bird

BELOW: a lioness brings down a female nyala.

can be found in the area. Seronera is also home to the **Visitor Centre** and **Serengeti Balloon Safaris** *(see Travel Tips page 311).* There can be few experiences more magical than drifting over this endless scenery at dawn, sometimes low enough to skim the trees, at others, soaring to see the true scale of this vast wilderness.

Heading north, the **Lobo area** ⑥ becomes more rugged, with craggy hills covered by scrubby bush and open woodland, favoured by buffalo and elephant. In the gallery forest along the watercourses, look out for rare gingery Patas monkeys and brightly coloured turaccos. Antelope living in the rocky hills include mountain reedbuck, oribi and the grey bush duiker.

The Western Corridor

The **Western Corridor** sticks out like a panhandle, following the line of the **Grumeti River** ⑪ and taking the borders of the Serengeti the whole way to Lake Victoria. A central range of hills is flanked on either side by large areas of

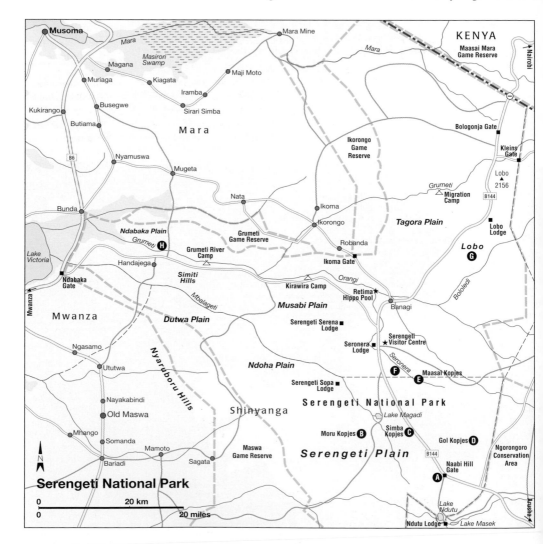

Serengeti National Park

plains, their sticky black cotton soil bursting into flower during the rains. It may look spectacular but is a nightmare for drivers, and the area is best visited in the dry months (June–Oct), when the non-migratory animals cluster along the river. Eland and roan antelope both live in the area, while the wooded river banks are home to black-and-white colobus and some spectacularly large crocodiles (up to 6 metres/20 ft in length), which spring into a feeding frenzy when the wildebeest come through, usually in May to June.

Lake Natron

The road leading back to Arusha from the Serengeti, parallel to the Kenyan border, is almost impassable, and, after a number of security problems in the late 1990s, it is not recommended. To get to **Lake Natron ⓫**, the most northerly of Tanzania's Rift Valley lakes, you need to drive the whole way back around the circuit and then take the road from Arusha. This is an excursion for the rugged traveller, into harsh, dry landscapes virtually uninhabited by people but rich in wildlife. The lake is extremely saline, a fact adored by flamingos which flock here from all over East Africa to breed.

Lake Natron Tented Camp will also organise climbs up **Ol Doinyo Lengai**, an active volcano which last erupted in 1983. It stands at 2,751 metres (9,026 ft) and is sacred to several tribes, including the Maasai, who call it the "Mountain of the Gods" and believe it to be the home of *Engai*, a single deity with both benevolent and vengeful characteristics. The climb to the summit takes a very long day (most operators start at midnight to avoid the baking heat) and you need to be very physically fit: be prepared for sheer, slippery slopes, icy winds near the summit, and an exhausting descent that places huge strain on the knees. ❑

Maps on pages 184 & 198

Weaverbirds live up to their name, building hundreds of carefully constructed nests in apartment trees.

BELOW: they may seem sleepy, but a crocodile can strike with immense force and speed.

LAKE VICTORIA

An inland sea that is the fabled source of the River Nile,
Lake Victoria is a little-known part of Tanzania,
perfect for latter-day explorers

The world's second-largest freshwater body, the 70,000-sq. km (27,027-sq. mile) **Lake Victoria ❶** lies within a shallow elevated basin shared between Tanzania, Uganda and Kenya. Characterised by murky, cloud-toned water and (within Tanzania) a somewhat starkly vegetated shore, this shallow inland sea is perhaps notable more for its dimensions than for any great scenic qualities. Despite its proximity to the Screngeti, Lake Victoria has never featured prominently on tourist itineraries, though the construction of a proper lodge on **Rubondo Island National Park ❷** and the introduction of scheduled flights there from the Serengeti have altered that.

Whether one flies in directly from the Serengeti or boats across from the mainland, 240-sq. km (93-sq. mile) Rubondo Island is a revelation. Jungle-swathed hills tumble down to a shore of lush papyrus swamps and sandy beaches, lapped by the water of the horizonless lake, to create a bewitching and scenically memorable freshwater tropical paradise. This is the least visited of Tanzania's National Parks and the most underrated: a consummate post-safari retreat for those more interested in low-key wildlife viewing than lazing around at an Indian Ocean beach resort.

The island is best explored along a network of walking trails that lead through tangled jungle to rocky bays and rickety stilted hides overlooking the marshy shore. Here, the handsome sitatunga antelope, a localised and elsewhere elusive swamp resident, is exceptionally easy to locate, as are the all-too-similar bushbuck and squabbling troops of vervet monkeys. Alternatively, it can be just as rewarding to hang around the lodge, where exquisite paradise flycatchers flutter their long orange tails through the trees, grey parrots maintain a perpetual mutter and squawk, and pairs of spot-necked otter climb over the offshore rocks. Further afield, the swampy **Mlaga Bay** – inhabited by scores of hippo and waterbirds – can be explored slowly by motorboat.

LEFT: a great white egret, fishing.
BELOW: Rubondo Island Camp.

The floating zoo

Rubondo has an odd history. It was earmarked as a "floating zoo" in 1966, with the idea that the Frankfurt Zoological Society could breed introduced populations of endangered rainforest species such as okapi and bongo. This plan never quite came together, and it was abandoned totally in 1973, but not before troops of chimpanzees and black-and-white colobus monkeys had been settled on the island, together with several non-forest-specific species including elephant, giraffe, suni and roan antelope, and black rhinoceros. All but the last two are still present today.

The chimpanzees of Rubondo, the subject of numerous scientific research projects, are elusive

creatures and chimp-tracking excursions are not always successful, though the scenery and other wildlife seen along the way are ample reward in themselves.

Death of the lake

Lake Victoria's 200 species of cichlid are under severe threat from pollution.

Visited in isolation, Rubondo Island – a forest reserve since German times, its surrounding waters off-limits to commercial fishing – might give a misleading impression of Lake Victoria's ecological state. The Tanzanian littoral has been all but denuded of indigenous vegetation through overgrazing and agriculture. Below the surface, the 200 endemic cichlid species that have evolved since the lake dried up 12,000 years ago are undergoing what one biologist describes as "the greatest vertebrate mass extinction in recorded history", due to the introduction of the predatory Nile perch in the colonial era.

Fifty years ago, cichlids constituted 80 percent of the lake's fish biomass; today they account for a mere 1 percent. This change in the lake's species composition, exacerbated by an inflow of chemical waste, has promoted a fivefold increase in algae levels and a comparable drop in oxygenation since records were first maintained. If present trends continue, ecologists fear that Lake Victoria is destined to die, becoming incapable of sustaining vertebrate life.

Mwanza

Set on a rocky peninsula on the southeastern lake shore, Tanzania's second-largest city, **Mwanza** ❸ (population 350,000), is a pivotal regional transport hub, serviced by a good selection of flights, ferries, trains and buses. More, perhaps, than any other settlement in the Tanzania interior, Mwanza feels like a proper city, reflected in its good selection of hotels and clutch of top-notch

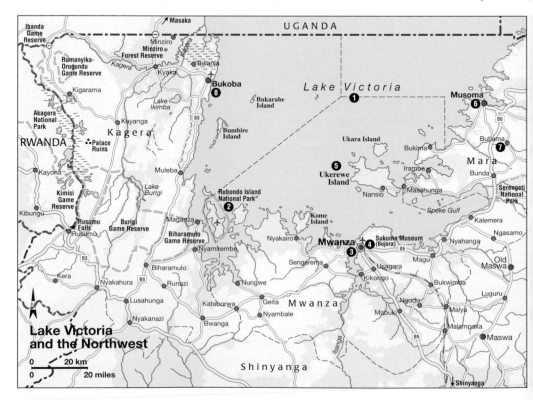

restaurants, whose menus typically reflect the prominent Indian community. The substantial city centre, with its washed-out colonial and Asian façades, has a strong sense of place, too, albeit that of a terminally down-at-heel tropical port. Smooth granite outcrops stud the surrounding peninsula like herds of petrified giant elephants – particularly striking is **Bismarck Rock**, a balancing formation that stands precarious sentinel over the open waters of the ferry harbour.

Map on page 202

The eastern lake shore

A row of cramped cages housing one listless lion, a more visibly disgruntled chimpanzee, and little else, makes a less than compelling case for strolling ten minutes south of central Mwanza to the jetty for **Saa Nane Island** (entrance charge inclusive of boat transfer, two-hourly 11am–5pm). But ignore the feeble and depressing attempt at a zoo if you can, and the island does offer a rare opportunity to observe the natural lake-shore fauna. Rock hyraxes and colourful agama lizards bask on the rocks, monitor lizards stalk the undergrowth like diminutive dinosaurs, and the odd crocodile has been known to stretch out on the beach. Vervet monkeys and introduced impalas range freely on the island, and the birdlife – from the vociferous fish eagle to the localised yellow-throated leaflove – is fabulous.

Situated in Bujora Parish, 20 km (12 miles) east of Mwanza, the **Sukuma Museum ❹** (daily 9am–5pm; entrance charge) preserves the traditions of Tanzania's most populous tribe. Displays include a Sukuma homestead, a blacksmith's house, a traditional healer's workshop and a collection of thrones and crowns. Try to visit on a Saturday afternoon, when the bizarre Sukuma Snake Dance is sometimes performed – complete with live python. The Sukuma are

BELOW: Bismarck Rock, one of the few German names to survive in modern Tanzania.

renowned for their exuberant dance competitions. The main festival days are 7 July and 8 August, public holidays set shortly after the harvest season. For a less institutionalised look at everyday Sukuma culture, a cheap daily ferry connects Mwanza to sleepy **Ukerewe Island** ❺, where fishermen empty their nets onto the pebbly shore, and a network of country roads lead to deserted beaches and rustic Sukuma villages: ideal for hikers and cyclists.

The Serengeti

The road following the eastern lake shore is surfaced for much of its 250-km (155-mile) length to the Kenya border, and it offers regular glimpses across the open water of Speke Gulf. Near Bunda, the road skirts the **western Serengeti**. Wildebeest and zebra graze complacently on the verge, while the lodges in Serengeti's Western Corridor frequently take guests this way for a lakeside lunch. Most tourists visit the Serengeti on an extended northern circuit safari out of Arusha *(see page 195)*, but – worth knowing if you're on a tight budget – it is also easy to visit the National Park from the Lake Victoria side. **Serengeti Stop Over**, situated outside the main western entrance gate, is the best contact for inexpensive day and overnight Serengeti safaris.

Musoma ❻, the largest port on the eastern lake shore, is a very laid-back town, architecturally reminiscent of Mwanza, and set on a narrow green peninsula leading to a rocky outcrop, splattered with the guano of its resident cormorant colony.

Inland of Musoma, **Butiama** ❼, the birth and burial place of former president Julius Nyerere *(see page 47)*, houses an appropriately unpretentious museum (entrance charge) dedicated to the popular leader's memory.

THE RIDDLE OF THE NILE

No geographical enigma was so hotly debated in Victorian times as the elusive source of the White Nile. It was a primary goal of Burton and Speke's 1857–8 expedition, which resulted in the "discovery" of the continent's two largest lakes, but left its protagonists at bitter odds, with Speke citing Lake Victoria and Burton Lake Tanganyika as the most likely candidate. In 1863, Speke returned to Lake Victoria to discover a substantial north-flowing outlet near present-day Jinja.

"The Nile is settled," declared Speke. His detractors sniggered.

Speke died in a hunting accident in 1864, hours before a scheduled public debate with Burton, but the Nile question still had plenty of life in it. It was finally resolved in 1874–7 by Stanley, who tested the various theories by circumnavigating Lakes Tanganyika and Victoria, then following the Lualaba River – Livingstone's favoured candidate – to emerge at the mouth of the Congo.

The Nile did indeed flow out of Lake Victoria at Jinja; the oft-ridiculed Speke had, according to Stanley, "understood the geography of the countries we travelled through far better than any of us who so persistently opposed his hypothesis".

The western lake shore

Roads, of a sort, run west from Mwanza through the booming gold-mining town of **Geita** and the isolated former German administrative centre of **Bihara-mulo** to **Bukoba** near the Ugandan border, but it would require a certain perversity of spirit to elect to drive or bus along them. A far less arduous mode of transport is the overnight ferry (capable of carrying vehicles) between Mwanza and Bukoba – or the daily flights between the ports.

Founded by the Emin Pasha in 1890, **Bukoba ❽** was settled three years later by Catholic missionaries, who built the well-maintained cathedral that stands out from the time-worn colonial buildings that otherwise characterise the town centre. The marshy lake shore below the town hosts large concentrations of waterbirds, while the fishing village of **Nyamukazi**, 2 km (1 mile) northeast of Bukoba, provides an enjoyable glimpse into rural Tanzania life. At **Bwanjai**, 25 km (15 miles) northwest of Bukoba, a mysterious rock art shelter is daubed with ancient geometric patterns and stylised human figures, the sole surviving legacy of some long-forgotten Stone Age artists.

Nestled against the Ugandan border inland of Lake Victoria, the swampy groundwater forest of the little-known **Minziro Forest Reserve** has strong faunal affinities to the West African rainforest. Ornithologists are in for a treat – an incredible 56 Guinea-Congo biome bird species found nowhere else in Tanzania have been recorded at Minziro. High in the canopy, troops of Angola colobus, grey-cheeked mangabey and red-tailed monkey play hide-and-seek with human intruders, while Peter's duiker and bushbuck flit elusively through the undergrowth. Permission to visit and camp in the forest, as well as directions, can be obtained at no charge from the Forestry Office in Bukoba.   ❑

Map on page 202

BELOW: female hippos are devoted and watchful mothers.

LAKE TANGANYIKA

It is a bit of a trek to meet man's genetic cousins, but it is certainly worth the effort when you come face to face with the chimpanzees of Gombe Stream

Map on page 208

Running for a distance of 675 km (419 miles) from Burundi in the north to Zambia in the south, **Lake Tanganyika ❶** is the longest freshwater body in the world, and the second-deepest, plummeting to depths approaching 1,500 metres (4,910 ft). It is also immensely beautiful. Hemmed in by the mountainous western Rift Valley Escarpment, the lake shore is lined by long sandy beaches, rustic fishing villages and patches of ancient forest rattling with birds, monkeys and chimpanzees. The aquamarine water – reputedly the least polluted in the world – is so clear that you can wade in chin deep and still see your toes, and harbours an estimated 1,000 fish species, most endemic to the lake.

Countries have built a thriving tourist industry on less, and yet this lovely part of Tanzania – overshadowed by such big guns as Zanzibar, Kilimanjaro and Serengeti – remains resolutely off the beaten track. What differentiates Lake Tanganyika from most similarly underdeveloped areas, however, is a wealth of world-class tourist attractions. **Gombe Stream** and **Mahale Mountains** offer the best chimpanzee-tracking in Africa, while the little-known **Katavi National Park** supports herds of savanna game that compare favourably with almost any other African sanctuary you care to mention. This, in short, is a region where you can get away from the crowded tourist sights and come back home feeling that you've probably got the better deal.

With the possible exception of Gombe Stream, Lake Tanganyika's major attractions are readily accessible only to those with reasonably deep pockets. There is, however, scope for adventurous budget travel in the region. Heading the list of such possibilities is the historic *MV Liemba*, the weekly ferry that plies from Kigoma south to Mpulungu in Zambia. Originally called the *Graf von Goetzen*, this boat was brought in pieces to Kigoma by the Germans, who assembled it, then – before it had embarked on a maiden voyage – decided to scupper it rather than let it fall into enemy hands. Salvaged by the Belgians in 1924, when it was given its modern name, this handsome old boat has been in non-stop service ever since, providing a vital lifeline to remote parts of the lake – and an offbeat excursion that embodies the romance of African lake travel.

Kigoma

Kigoma ❷ is the largest town on the Tanzanian shore, favoured by the Germans for its deep natural harbour, and since 1914 the lake shore terminus of the central railway line. Historical landmarks include the stately German-era **Railway Station** and **Kaiser House** – linked together, some say, by a World War I escape tunnel. The town is serviced by scheduled flights and trains from Dar es Salaam, as well as

LEFT: the shoreline of Lake Tanganyika.
BELOW: boarding the *MV Liemba*.

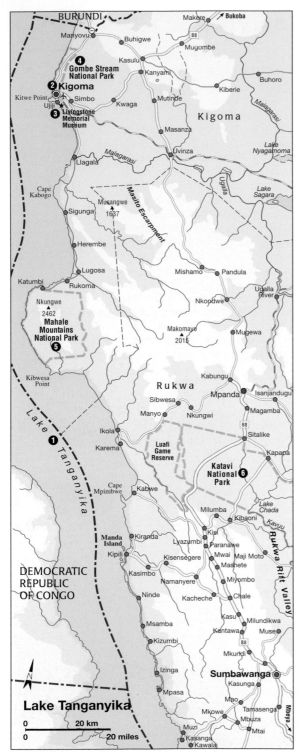

Lake Tanganyika

0   20 km

0   20 miles

ferries to Zambia, Burundi and the Democratic Republic of Congo (DRC), making it a useful springboard for extended travels around the lake.

Kigoma is also an inherently agreeable place to spend a couple of days, its shady avenues leading down to a stretch of lake shore routinely lit up by spectacular sunsets. Since the early 1990s, Kigoma has served as a centre for Western aid organisations and refugee programmes related to the ongoing instability in neighbouring Francophone territories.

Ujiji

Pre-colonial Kigoma was dwarfed in significance by the Arab trading post of **Ujiji ❸**, which lies only 8 km (5 miles) to its southeast and has retained a distinct Muslim atmosphere, epitomised by the coastal-style dhows that billow out from the old fishing harbour. For most travellers, Ujiji's main point of interest is its association with various Victorian explorers. It was here, in 1858, that Burton and Speke became the first Europeans to set eyes on Lake Tanganyika; here, too, that Stanley uttered perhaps the most famous – and most ridiculed – phrase ever spoken on the African continent: "Doctor Livingstone, I presume."

Modest though it looks, the memorial marking the place where Stanley and Livingstone met in 1871 is rather affecting, while the adjacent **Livingstone Museum** houses some whimsically captioned paintings and life-size papier-mâché models of the explorers raising their hats in greeting. The local Washirika dance group performs Waha dances in traditional bark dresses in the museum grounds (Wed, Fri and Sun 5–6pm; donations). The **Kitwe Point Sanctuary** was founded by the Jane Goodall Institute on a headland 5 km (3 miles) south of Kigoma to provide refuge to three orphaned chimpanzees rescued from poachers in 1994. It also protects zebra and antelope, and a variety of birds. The sanctuary was closed to the public in 2001. The village of **Katonga**, outside the perimeter fence, is a good spot to watch local fishermen lay freshly caught shoals of dagaa (a tiny fish) out to dry on the beach, before they are packaged to be sold at the market. Twenty minutes' walk from here, the small but sandy **Zungu Beach** is the place to catch a tan or take a dip in the lake.

Map on page 208

Gombe Stream National Park

Covering a mere 52 sq. km (20 sq. miles), Tanzania's smallest national park, **Gombe Stream National Park ❹**, protects a hilly stretch of lakeshore transected by forest-fringed permanent streams. Gombe Stream's fame derives from its association with Jane Goodall's chimp research project *(see page 211)*. Inevitably, it's the chimp community habituated by Goodall that forms the centre of tourist activities at Gombe, but there are numerous other reasons for visiting. Look up and you'll see red colobus monkeys (which are hunted and eaten by the chimps) crashing about in the canopy. The olive baboons that beachcomb in front of the rest camp are also relatively tame and easy to photograph. Birdlife is prolific, with normally secretive forest birds such as the lovely Peter's twinspot often spotted around the rest camp.

David Livingstone was in Ujiji when he was found, so memorably, by Stanley.

Gombe Stream lies on the eastern lake shore 25 km (16 miles) north of Kigoma. The park is only accessible by boat. The easiest way to visit is with Chimpanzee Safaris (www.chimpanzeesafaris.com), which runs the high-quality Gombe Forest Lodge.

A more affordable option, although you will need two nights, is to use a public boat-taxi from **Kibirizi** (3 km/2 miles north of Kigoma). These leave in the afternoon, returning in the early morning, and take two hours in either direction. Guided forest walks can be arranged on the spot, with a near-certainty of encountering chimps in the morning.

BELOW: grooming is an important part of the daily ritual for chimps.

Map on page 208

TIP

Kigoma and Kasanga have proper jetties. Elsewhere, the *Liemba* is met by a flotilla of rickety fishing boats whose captains jostle aggressively for position. Strategic advice upon disembarking? Jump and hope for the best!

BELOW: disembarking from the *MV Liemba*.

Mahale Mountains National Park

Mahale Mountains National Park ❺ extends for 1,613 sq. km (623 sq. miles) across a bulbous peninsula of forested mountains, roughly 120 km (75 miles) south of Kigoma. In many respects it is more rewarding than Gombe Stream. The scenery alone is magnificent: rugged mountains rise sharply from sandy beaches, through tangled miombo woodland and montane forest and grassland, to the 2,462-metre (8,077-ft) **Nkungwe Peak**.

This diversity of habitats is reflected in the wide variety of birds, butterflies and mammals. Savanna residents such as lions, African hunting dogs, elephants, giraffes and sable antelopes are resident, though seldom observed, as are West African rainforest species such as the brush-tailed porcupine and giant forest squirrel. Aside from the famous – and easily seen – chimpanzees, smaller primates such as red colobus, red-tailed monkey, Syke's monkey, vervet monkey and yellow baboon should be encountered by casual visitors.

There is no road access to Mahale Mountains. The upmarket lodges can be visited by charter flight from Arusha or motorboat from the **Kigoma Hilltop Hotel** *(details in Travel Tips)*, generally as part of an all-inclusive package. Hardy and self-sufficient independent travellers can get as far as the village of **Lugosa** with the *MV Liemba*, then hike – or hire a local boat to cover – the remaining 15 km (9 miles) to the park headquarters. Forest walks are easily organised on the spot. Entrance costs US$80 per 24 hours.

Katavi National Park

Covering about 5,000 sq. km (1,931 sq. miles), **Katavi National Park** ❻ is the most inaccessible and untrammelled of Tanzania's major savanna reserves. It is

also inexplicably underrated, offering an undiluted bush experience that's increasingly precious in these days of package safaris and over-orchestrated private game lodges. During the latter part of the dry season, when the Kavuu River and associated tributaries form the only source of water for miles around, the game viewing can be little short of astounding. Thousand-strong herds of buffalo are a daily sight, the park's notoriously aggressive elephant lurk round every other corner, and concentrations of hundreds of hippo huddle tightly in any suitably deep pool. This is one of the few remaining game reserves anywhere in Africa where you can expect to encounter more lions that you will other visitors. Need more be said?

The only comfortable way to see Katavi – short of driving a private vehicle halfway across Tanzania – is by charter package to the Katavi Bush Lodge, the only accommodation apart from a couple of very basic guest-houses. For genuinely adventurous travellers, there is the option of catching a train from Tabora to Mpanda, then a local bus along the 35-km (22-mile) road to the park headquarters at Sitalike, where modest accommodation can be found, and four-wheel drive vehicles are available at US$100 per day. Katavi is best avoided from November to April, when game disperses, roads are impassable, and the heat and insect activity are insufferable. Game viewing is good in May and June, better still from August to October. ❑

Jane's Chimps

Lake-shore Gombe Stream and Mahale Mountains national parks are undoubtedly the best places in the world to track chimpanzees in their natural environment. Even so, Tanzania cannot be regarded as a major chimpanzee stronghold; its estimated total of 1,500–2,000 chimps – roughly half resident in Mahale, another 100 or so in Gombe – represents less than 1 percent of the global population. This only makes Lake Tanganyika's pre-eminence in almost every aspect of contemporary chimpanzee research and conservation more remarkable.

The reason can be summed up in one name: Jane Goodall. In July 1960, this academically unqualified young Englishwoman arrived at Gombe Stream to initiate what has become the world's longest-running – and arguably most ground-breaking – study of any wild animal population.

Goodall's pioneering research cannot be summarised in a few sentences; her absorbing books are requisite reading for anybody heading to Gombe or Mahale. Perhaps the most significant of her early observations, however, were modes of behaviour thought until then to distinguish *Homo sapiens* from other living creatures – the manipulation of twigs to "fish" termites and ants from their burrows; inter-community warfare; the methodical hunting of other primates; and even an orchestrated campaign of cannibalism.

Goodall's work was enhanced by a parallel project in Mahale Mountains, instigated in 1965 by the Japanese primatologist Junichiro Itani. Comparative studies have revealed the fascinating cultural differences in chimp behaviour. The palm nut, for instance, forms a major part of the diet of the Gombe chimps, but is never eaten at Mahale. Up to 40 percent of plants available in both reserves are eaten by one population but not the other.

Chimpanzees are related more closely to humans than to any other living creature. They live in large territorial communities, within which different individuals move around in smaller sub-groups, which can change on a daily basis. Every community is headed by an alpha male, whose dominance is often achieved by the intelligent manipulation of his fellows rather than through brute strength. Male chimps seldom leave their ancestral community, but females regularly migrate outside them.

There are three communities at Gombe, with the largest being Kasekela, the focus of Goodall's studies. Of the 15 communities in Mahale Mountains, the 100-strong Mimikire community is the most habituated, and the one that tourists will normally encounter.

Chimp-tracking is available all year, but the late dry season – July to October – has several advantages: the steep slopes are less treacherous underfoot, and the chimps tend to stick to lower, more accessible altitudes. Of the two reserves, Mahale has better facilities for upmarket tourists, and offers a more holistic wilderness experience, while Gombe Stream is more accessible and more affordable to budget travellers. Whenever and wherever you go, it is an experience that will last your lifetime. ❑

RIGHT: tourist-watching in the Mahale Mountains National Park.

CENTRAL TANZANIA

*Ancient rock paintings, an unknown capital city and
an entertaining train ride are amongst the
highlights of this hot, dusty region*

Map
on page
214

Tanzania's sparsely populated and drought-prone central plateau, all red dirt plains and mean acacia scrub studded with boulders the size of mountains, does possess a certain austere beauty. Realistically, however, a combination of poor roads, lousy buses, long distances and relatively meagre travel pickings make it difficult to recommend the region wholeheartedly, even to those with an express interest in getting away from the established tourist trails. The only exception to the above is the 500-km (300-mile) road connecting **Dodoma** to Arusha, where the rock art of **Kondoa** and forested slopes of **Mount Hanang** head a list of noteworthy and relatively accessible sites that are unheard of by most local tour operators, let alone travellers.

Otherwise, the tiny proportion of tourists who do travel across central Tanzania are almost without fail putting miles behind them en route from the coast to one of the great western lakes. With this goal in mind, the only land transport worth contemplating is the 1,500-km (930-mile) German-built railway line connecting Dar es Salaam to Kigoma, Mwanza and Mpanda. Moderately comfortable rather than luxurious – even the first-class sleeping carriages have seen better days – this remains one of Africa's great train journeys, a leisurely two-day chug through Tanzania's barren heartland, the open horizons enlivened by sporadic patches of forest and swamp on the approach to Kigoma. It is fascinating, too, to watch how torpid small towns spring into entrepreneurial life as the train pulls in and the hungry passengers spill out, to mill around rows of stalls selling freshly grilled kebabs, hearty chicken stews and the local staples of rice and *ugali* (maize porridge).

LEFT: the Kondoa cave paintings.
BELOW: Maasai warriors waiting for the train at Tabora.

Tabora

If the central railway line offers revealing glimpses into small-town Tanzania, it is equally resonant with history. The journey follows a route pioneered long before the days of steam and diesel, when the first trade caravans from the coast undertook the months-long march to Lake Tanganyika in search of fresh sources of slaves. Burton and Speke followed this ancient trade route on their way to Lake Tanganyika. So, too, did Livingstone, in his misdirected and fatal quest to locate the source of the Nile, and Stanley on the expedition that led to his famous meeting with Livingstone at Ujiji.

The pleasant, workaday town of **Tabora ❶**, strategically located at the junction of the lines to Dar es Salaam, Kigoma, Mwanza and Mpanda, is today, as it was in Livingstone's time, the most important transport hub in western Tanzania. Within the leafy confines of the modern town centre, the only physical evidence of Tabora's antiquity is a German railway

station and fort. Only 6 km (4 miles) outside Tabora, however, the restored house built by the slave trader Tippu Tip provided shelter to both Livingstone and Stanley during their trans-African journeys. Known as **Livingstone's Tembe**, this fine – if strangely misplaced – example of coastal architecture, nestled in a grove of mango trees and complete with original carved Zanzibar doors, now functions as a museum (entrance charge), housing some worthwhile displays on the Victorian explorers. In a field next to the museum, the solitary grave of Stanley's companion, John William Shaw, serves as a poignant reminder of the virulent diseases that felled so many of these brave men.

Dodoma

The other large town along the central railway is **Dodoma ❷**, which possesses some curiosity value as the official – albeit improbable – capital of Tanzania, though you'd be hard pushed to find a reason to spend more time here than transport logistics dictate.

The name Dodoma derives from *Idodomya* ("Place of Sinking"), which some say refers to an elephant that became stuck in a nearby swamp. A more colourful tradition has it that the name commemorates a local clan who ate their neighbours' cattle, then placed the dismembered tails in the swamp to try to convince the owners that their missing beasts had been bogged down.

In common with Tabora, Dodoma was an established stop along the 19th-century caravan route, and it served as a regional administrative centre under the German colonials. It was the Germans who first flirted with the idea of making Dodoma their capital, a plan that was aborted due to a series of devastating local famines, only to be revived in 1973 by President Nyerere. Political status

An odd juxtaposition – Livingstone's Tembe was built by Tippu Tip, Africa's most notorious slaver, but used by Livingstone, foremost amongst the anti-slavery campaigners.

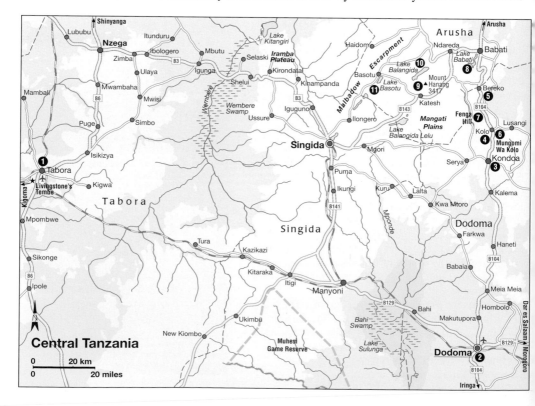

Central Tanzania

0   20 km

0   20 miles

Map
on page
214

aside – and as things stand, most government offices have yet to be relocated from Dar es Salaam – all that really distinguishes Dodoma from other moderately sized upcountry Tanzanian towns is a low-key local wine industry. Sightseeing in the immediate vicinity is limited to a large and climbable rock outcrop – vaguely leonine in outline – which stands over the Arusha road less than 5 km (3 miles) from the town centre.

Aside from the central railway, onward options from Dodoma include a zippy surfaced road running east to Dar es Salaam through Morogoro, a somewhat bumpier dirt road that cuts south to Iringa on the Tanzam Highway, and the equally rough but more interesting Arusha road covered below.

Ancient art

Dusty **Kondoa** ❸, set on the north bank of the synonymous river, lies roughly 160 km (100 miles) north of Dodoma on the road to Arusha and is also easily accessible from Tarangire. It is a convenient town from which to explore the fascinating treasury of prehistoric rock art that decorates the granite faces and overhangs of north-central Tanzania. Although many hundreds of these ancient panels are scattered throughout the Kondoa region, all that is known about the artists is what can be deduced from their fading visual legacy. No credible local tradition relates to the paintings – not surprising when they predate the arrival of Bantu-speakers in East Africa by a thousand-plus years – but they do display inescapable stylistic links with the rock art executed by southern Africa's Khiosan hunter-gatherers into historic times.

The concentration of rock-art sites along the ridges running east of the main road between **Kolo** ❹ and **Bereko** ❺ offers a straightforward introduction for

BELOW: it is worth the effort required to reach some of the Kondoa paintings.

first-time visitors. Starting at the Department of Antiquities office in Kolo, 30 km (19 miles) north of Kondoa, knowledgeable guides will direct visitors along the 12-km (7-mile) back route to the most famous of the region's sites, namely **Mungomi Wa Kolo ❻** (The Dancers of Kolo). Here, three separate panels, easily visited over the space of one or two hours, depict the eponymous dancers, numerous other diagrammatic stick figures with characteristically woolly hairstyles, and a menagerie of wild animals. The final approach (15 minutes on foot) to Mungomi is gaspingly steep, so less fit travellers might prefer to visit a separate cluster of panels at the base of the ridge near **Lusangi** village, a similar distance away from Kolo. Less impressive overall than the finely realised paintings at Mungomi Wa Kolo, Lusangi does display two features not found at that site, namely petroglyphs (engravings) and a number of paintings of the so-called "late white" period. Another good and relatively accessible site is **Fenga Hill ❼**, overlooking the Bubu River 10 km (6 miles) west of Kolo.

Lake Babati

Situated on the outskirts of the small market town of Babati, **Lake Babati ❽** practically laps the western verge of the Arusha road 100 km (60 miles) north of Kondoa. The papyrus-fringed lake shore, encircled by low mountains, attracts a fair variety of waterbirds – orderly flotillas of white pelicans, eagle-eyed herons and egrets, and sweeping spoonbills and yellow-billed storks. Birds are easily seen on foot, but the best way to locate a few of the lake's prodigious hippos is to pay a small fee to be taken out on a boat by one of the local fishermen. This can be arranged informally at the lake shore, or through the offices of Kahembe Enterprises, a Babati-based company that supervises one of Tanzania's

BELOW:
Barabaig girl at her
homestead near
Mount Hanang.

more interesting community tourist projects, designed in collaboration with the national tourist board and a Dutch development agency. Among the excursions organised by this project are overnight cultural trips to the rustic bomas of the various nomadic pastoralists that inhabit this part of the ridge: the Barabaig, the Iraqw, the Bulu and others.

Climbing Hanang

The focal point of the Babati ecotourism project is the 3,417-metre (11,211-ft) high **Mount Hanang ⑨**, an extinct volcanic that towers like a miniature, snow-free Kilimanjaro above the surrounding flat plains, visible from hundreds of kilometres away on a clear day. The third-tallest mountain in Tanzania, Hanang can be climbed over a very long day – fit hikers will need a minimum of 12 hours for the round trip – or, more realistically, as an overnight hike, sleeping in caves or a tent. Experienced and properly equipped independent travellers could arrange a hike from the small town of **Katesh**, which lies at the southern base of the mountain, 50 km (30 miles) from Babati along the Singida road. It is safer, however, to arrange a package through Kahembe Enterprises, whose guides all speak English and have vast experience of the mountain. Either way, because Hanang lies outside the national park system, hikes are light on the pocket in comparison with the Kilimanjaro and Meru climbs.

The Hanang area is also notable for its many lakes. The saline **Lake Balangida ⑩**, set at the base of the Rift Valley Escarpment immediately north of Hanang, less than an hour's drive from Katesh via Giting, attracts large flocks of waders and flamingos when full, and is reduced to a shimmering white salt flat in years of low rainfall. Roughly 60 km (37 miles) northwest of Katesh, reached via a good dirt road, **Lake Basotu ⑪** is an attractive freshwater body where traditionally dressed Barabaig and Bulu pastoralists still bring their cattle to drink. Fringed by the small town of Basuto, this lake harbours large numbers of hippo and a fabulous variety of birds, including vociferous breeding colonies of pink-backed pelican, reed cormorant and various herons.

The Barabaig are Nilotic-speaking pastoralists who arrived in their present homeland at least 500 years ago. In common with most other pastoralist societies, they measure wealth in terms of livestock and children, and shun centralised leadership. The main social unit is the family stockade, inhabited by a patriarch, his harem of wives, and their offspring.

Staunch traditionalists, the Barabaig refused to be co-opted into the colonial migrant labour system, ignored Nyerere's attempts to outlaw their traditional clothing, and have no time for exotic religions (less than 1 percent of the population practises Christianity or Islam). Most Barabaig women still wear a traditional ochre-dyed, bead-studded hide dress, while men drape dyed cotton cloths over their shoulders and waist, and never leave home without a spear to hand.

Where the road from Katesh reaches the southern tip of Lake Basuto, **Lake Gida Monyot** is sunk within a small volcanic crater, invisible from the road, but only two minutes' walk away. ❑

An unusual feature of Barabaig society is that extramarital sex is openly condoned – all children are raised by their mother's husband, irrespective of whether he is their biological father.

BELOW: a tawny eagle quietly waits for action.

SOUTHERN PARKS AND TANZAM HIGHWAY

Tanzania's second circuit is, to aficionados, even better than the north, a magnificent wilderness teeming with game and virtually devoid of tourists

The **Selous Game Reserve ❶** exists on a barely comprehensible scale. Covering 50,000 sq. km (19,305 sq. miles), it is Africa's largest protected area: 50 percent larger than Switzerland, situated at the core of a 155,000-sq. km (59,800-sq. mile) cross-border ecosystem traversed by some of the world's greatest remaining herds of buffalo (150,000), elephant (65,000), hippopotamus (40,000) and sable antelope (8,000). And yet such statistics, thrown about glibly by tour operators, flatter Selous to the point of deceit. The life-sustaining waters of the **Rufiji River** divide this semi-arid wilderness into two wildly disproportionate sectors: an immense and practically impenetrable southern block used exclusively by commercial hunting concerns, and a more compact northern circuit – about 10 percent of the Selous's total area – dedicated to less bloodthirsty forms of tourism. Selous is a fine game reserve. The statistics are so much hyperbole.

PRECEDING PAGES: lesser flamingos in flight.
LEFT: buffalo herd, viewed from the air.
BELOW: sunset on the Rufiji River.

The Rufiji River

The divisive Rufiji, its constantly mutating course spilling into a labyrinth of intimate, lushly vegetated channels and open lakes, defines the Selous experience. Sandbanks lined with outsized crocodiles, menacing mouths agape, erupt into sinuous energy as a motorboat approaches and the prehistoric beasts slither with one loud splash beneath the river's surface.

Yellow-billed storks and spoonbills scoop methodically through the shallows, pied kingfishers hover overhead like fast-forward clockwork toys, African skimmers fly low across the surface dipping their bright-red beaks into the water, and carmine bee-eaters swirl in a crimson cloud around the exposed mud banks in which they breed. Becalmed channels flow northward from the main river, past swampy islets where elephants browse and waterbuck graze. And, as the motorboat returns to the lodge, a light evening breeze wafts across the water to diffuse the still heat of the day, hippos enter into earnest grunting debate, and a red-coal sun sinks behind a neat row of borassus palms – the quintessential African river scene.

A network of game-viewing roads connects the lakes, where congregations of zebra, giraffe and various antelope slake their thirst during the dry season. The odds of seeing a kill here are unusually high: the lions of Selous seem disinclined to follow the time-honoured leonine strategy of stalking their dinner by night, but instead prefer to laze quietly in the lake-

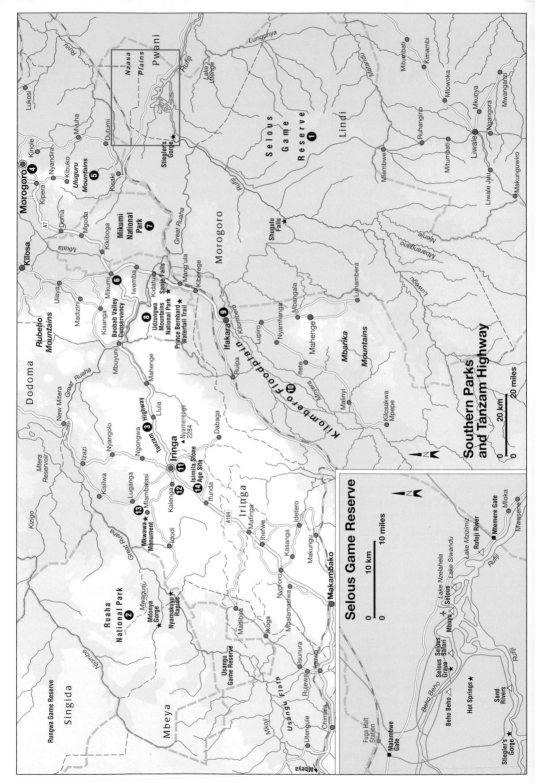

Southern Parks
and Tanzam Highway

Selous Game Reserve

shore woodland waiting for lunch to venture within pouncing distance. Wild dogs snuggle below shady raffia palms in the heat of the day, emerging towards dusk to scamper and frolic at the water's edge. In recent decades, wild dog populations elsewhere in Africa have gone into rapid decline: the estimated 1,300 individuals that roam the Selous account for 20 percent of the free-ranging global population, exceeding that of any other African country.

Offbeat luxury

The Selous (pronounced "Seloo") is named after Captain Frederick Courteney Selous, the legendary game hunter and writer who was killed by German sniper fire near the Rufiji during World War I *(see page 231)*. A year after the war ended, P.H. Lamb trekked to the "wild inhospitable district" where a plain wooden cross marked Selous's grave, and predicted that "the object of most people who have seen it will be to avoid it carefully in the future". Inherently, the Selous remains as wild and inhospitable today as it was in 1919. By comparison to the more famous Serengeti, it is also remarkably free of safari traffic, visited by a mere 1 percent of tourists to Tanzania.

Lamb would doubtless have revised his gloomy prediction had he been hosted by one of the seven exclusive tourist lodges that scatter the Selous today. With their combined bed space less than that of many individual hotels along the northern circuit, these lodges are justifiably known for their luxurious accommodation, personalised service and integrated bush atmosphere. Guided game walks add vivid immediacy to exploring the Selous – the thrill of emerging from a riverine thicket onto a plain where a surprised elephant bull trumpets a warning, or a herd of buffalo stare down the oddly clad intruders.

Map on page 222

Visitors are often shocked to learn that 90 percent of the Selous is leased to commercial hunting concerns. However, they do play an important role in policing more remote parts of the reserve, and the net fees they generate are four times greater than those raised by more passive safaris.

BELOW: young wild dogs tear at a kill.

Roan antelope are among the most handsome and least common antelope in Tanzania.

Not exciting enough? Then take things one step further and arrange to spend a night or two at a private fly-camp, separated from the pristine night sky by a transparent drape of mosquito netting. As hippos and elephants tread gingerly past the makeshift tent, sleep might not come easily, but this primal African nocturnal experience will never be forgotten.

Ruaha

The Selous features prominently in many seasoned African travellers' top ten wilderness areas, but ask a Tanzania-based wildlife lover what their favourite game reserve is, and odds are that the reply will be **Ruaha National Park ❷**. Like the Selous, this rugged 10,300-sq. km (4,000-sq. mile) tract of wilderness forms the core of a much vaster ecosystem, extending into half a dozen other protected areas. Characterised by parched slopes covered in dense brachystegia woodland, and wide open baobab-studded plains, Ruaha fulfils every expectation of untrammelled Africa, no less so because its 400-km (250-mile) road circuit has only two small lodges and a few campsites – even the Selous seems crowded by comparison.

Game-viewing roads follow the perennial Great Ruaha River and seasonal Mwagusi River through thick riparian forest frequented by one of Africa's densest elephant populations. Cheetahs pace the open savanna, which is grazed upon by herds of buffalo stretching to the horizon, as well as the usual cast of ungulates: impala, waterbuck, zebra and Grant's gazelle. The woodland, transitional to the eastern savanna and southern miombo biomes, is the most southerly haunt of the shy striped hyena and delicate lesser kudu, as well as two endemic birds, the black-collared lovebird and ashy starling. Ruaha also harbours a trio of lovely antelope that are rare in northern Tanzania, the imposingly horned greater kudu and sleekly handsome sable and roan antelope. Near the Mwagusi River, prides of 20-plus lions reduce a freshly killed buffalo or zebra to skin and bone in a couple of hours.

Ruaha, like Selous, is an important refuge for the endangered African wild dog, which often makes its dens in the Mwagusi area over June and July. Fine game viewing indeed, and yet if Ruaha leaves one overwhelming impression, it is the sense of solitude associated with driving for hours through untamed Africa without encountering another human soul.

The Tanzam Highway

Selous and Ruaha are linked to each other, and to Dar es Salaam, by a daily scheduled flight, and most tourists who visit one or both reserves fly in from Dar es Salaam. Yet the two reserves also form part of a looser road circuit connected by the **Tanzam Highway ❸** – the endless strip of asphalt that runs southwest from Dar es Salaam, via Morogoro and Iringa, to the Zambian capital of Lusaka (Tanzam being an abbreviation of Tanzania-Zambia). The Selous can be reached from Morogoro along the rough 120-km (75-mile) Matombo Road (named for a buxom pair of peaks known as *Matombo* – "Breasts") while a fair 100-km (60-mile) dirt road runs west from Iringa to the main entrance gate of Ruaha.

Bypassed by the Tanzam Highway, 200 km (120 miles) out of Dar es Salaam, **Morogoro ❹** (popula-

tion 250,000) is a lively town transformed into one of the prettiest cities in Tan-zania by the **Uluguru Mountains ⑤**, which rise to a majestic 2,635 metres (8,645 ft) on the southern horizon. Clear freshwater streams tumble down the forested slopes of the Uluguru to provide generous sustenance to the local agri-cultural community, a vital source of fresh produce for Dar es Salaam. Neat, compact and energetic, Morogoro makes for an agreeable, even relaxing, stopover, and yet it's somehow surprising to learn that this rapidly growing town is Tanzania's largest landlocked urban centre, surpassed in population only by the ports of Dar es Salaam, Zanzibar and Mwanza.

A pretty, whitewashed German boma and mildly pompous railway station stand as isolated reminders of Morogoro's colonial roots, while the packed cen-tral market, stalls laden with succulent papayas, sweet pineapples and cande-labras of bright yellow bananas, reflects its modern agricultural base. An undemanding 30-minute stroll out of town leads to the **Rock Garden Resort**, a botanical garden situated on the lower slopes of the Uluguru.

The Uluguru Mountains

For a more ambitious day walk, **Morningside Camp** is a disused German research station set on the higher slopes, amid patches of natural forest and pretty cascades. Morningside is difficult to locate without a local guide – avail-able from the **Uluguru Mountains Biodiversity and Conservation Project** (UMBCP) office in Pamba House, which also arranges cultural visits to **Nugutu**, famed locally for its skilled Luguru craftsmen and powerful traditional healer.

The UMBCP office is also the best place to enquire about travel deeper into the Uluguru Mountains, a vast Eastern Arc range inhabited by dedicated Luguru

Map on page 222

BELOW: a women's project in Morogoro is promoting fuel-saving stoves.

agriculturists who work their fertile, well-watered smallholdings throughout the year. Between the cultivated fields, approximately 500 sq. km (200 sq. miles) of indigenous forest harbours black-and-white colobus monkey and various small antelope – as well as 40 vascular plant, 10 reptile and amphibian species, and more than 100 invertebrate species found nowhere else in the world. The secretive Uluguru bush shrike, a striking canary-yellow bird with a jet-black cap, is one of three endemics to tantalise ornithologists. At present, the forests of the Uluguru are realistically explored only from **Nyandira**, a humble Luguru village situated 25 km (16 miles) from the Tanzam Highway along a four-wheel-drive-only road that forks to the left, 20 km (12 miles) south of Morogoro.

Mikumi

Unprepared travellers driving southwest along the Tanzam Highway towards the town of **Mikumi 6** (120 km/75 miles from Morogoro) are frequently taken aback at the sight of an elephant emerging from the bush or a herd of buffalo masticating lazily on the verge. This is one of the few trunk routes in Africa to cut through the heart of a major game reserve, and indeed the **Mikumi National Park 7** directly owes its protected status to the construction of the Tanzam Highway, which opened up the formerly remote area to poachers. Gazetted in 1964 and later expanded to share a border with the Selous, Mikumi is the fourth-largest national park in Tanzania, extending over 3,230 sq. km (1,247 sq. miles).

Popular with expatriate weekenders, Mikumi has never caught on among international visitors. It is, nevertheless, delightful. The extensive Mkata Floodplain, crossed by a 60-km (37-mile) road loop running northwest of the Tanzam Highway, feels like a compressed replica of the Serengeti. Its seasonally inundated

BELOW: the tiny suni generally lives alone, in pairs or small family groups in dry country with thick bush.

grassland hosts impressive herds of zebra, wildebeest, buffalo, eland and impala; hippos snort and grunt in the waterholes, and around 400 species of birds have been spotted here. Giraffes lope elegantly through stands of flat-topped acacias, elephants maintain a perpetual presence at the waterholes below Kikoboga Lodge, and the majestic greater kudu and sable antelope skulk in the thick brachystegia woodland. Mikumi has few wild dogs since the resident pack migrated to the Selous in the late 1990s, but lions and hyenas are regularly heard serenading the night sky.

Mikumi town, on the western border of the national park, was founded in 1914 and named after the borassus palms that flourished in the vicinity. Sadly, no palm groves grace Mikumi today: this scruffy little town, whose shape is defined by the highway along which it seems to creep further with each passing year, has all the aesthetic appeal of an overgrown truck stop. However, it is a popular budget base from which to explore the National Park, and it also lies at the junction of the approach road – signposted left – to the marvellous Udzungwa Mountains.

Udzungwa

The road to Udzungwa runs south from Mikumi for a freshly surfaced 37 km (23 miles), before crossing the white-water rush of the Great Ruaha River to enter the lively, small town of **Kidatu**. Humid and low-lying, Kidatu has a naturally torpid atmosphere, overlaid with the heavy scent of molasses emanating from the adjacent Kilombero Sugar Estate – which, along with a hydroelectric scheme on the Great Ruaha, has stimulated rapid local population growth in the last decade. Unfortunately, neither the tropical riverside setting nor the Udzungwa Mountains on the western horizon are sufficient to justify a stop here. Certainly not when another 25 km (16 miles) of rutted road leads south to the overgrown village of **Mang'ula**, at the entrance gate to **Udzungwa Mountains National Park ❽**.

Map on page 222

The 1,900-sq. km (730-sq. mile) Udzungwa Mountains National Park protects the most extensive of the Eastern Arc ranges, a craggy, forest-swathed massif that erupted from the plains more than 100 million years ago. The undemanding self-guided **Prince Bernhard Waterfall Trail**, named after the Dutch royal who opened the park in 1992, provides a lovely introduction to the magic of Udzungwa's forests. Turkey-sized trumpeter hornbills flap heavily through the canopy, the exquisite green-headed oriole betrays its presence with a repetitive song, pairs of forest weaver flit restlessly through the mid-strata, and dozens of different butterfly species flutter above the shadowy forest floor.

Lucky visitors may catch a glimpse of a shy suni crossing the forest path, or a chequered elephant shrew rummaging its elongated nose through the litter. Common around the waterfall, the endangered Uhehe red colobus is distinguished from the ubiquitous blue monkey by its translucent orange fringe.

Primates and partridges

A longer guided hike leads from the entrance gate to **Sanje Falls**, which plunge 300 metres (980 ft) down the escarpment in three discrete stages. It was here,

BELOW: mountain pass in the scenic Udzungwa Mountains National Park.

The pivotal battle of the Maji Maji Rebellion was fought at Mahenge, 80 km (50 miles) south of Ifakara. In 1905, an unarmed local army, doused in the spring waters they believed made them immune to bullets, marched on the German fort to be greeted by a machine-gun barrage that left hundreds dead or wounded.

BELOW: citrus swallowtail butterfly.
RIGHT: the Sanje Waterfalls.

in 1979, that two ecologists heard a whooping call similar to that of a mangabey, a West African monkey not known to occur within a 1,000-km (620-mile) radius of Udzungwa. Initially, the ecologists thought they were victims of a prank, but their guide told them that an orphaned monkey of the type that made the call was being tended at Sanje village on the main road to Mikumi. It turned out to be a new species: the Sanje crested mangabey, which, in 2000, achieved the dubious distinction of being the sole East African species on a list of the world's 25 most threatened primates, compiled by the IUCN Primate Specialist Group.

Udzungwa, a contender for East Africa's most important biodiversity hotspot, yields previously undescribed species with sensational regularity. In 1991, for instance, biologists working in the western Udzungwa noticed a pair of strange feet floating in their "chicken stew". Upon enquiry, they were shown a snared specimen of a wildfowl that more closely resembles the Asian hill partridges than it does any African bird. Subsequently named the Udzungwa partridge, this localised endemic underscores the great antiquity of the Eastern Arc forests – the sole living representative of a lineage dating back 15 million years to when Africa and Asia were linked by a forest belt along the Arabian coastline.

Kilombero

Bisected by the Umena River some 40 km (25 miles) south of Mang'ula, the small town of **Ifakara** ➒ wouldn't win any beauty contests. Continue 5 km (3 miles) south of Ifakara along the Mahenge road, and you'll reach the **Kilombero River**, a wide and muddy tributary of the Rufiji crossed by a regular motor ferry. The 4,000-sq. km (1,544-sq. mile) **Kilombero Floodplain** ➓, an unprotected extension of the Selous ecosystem, is East Africa's largest seasonal wet-

land, home to 50,000 puku antelope (70 percent of the global population) and attracting up to 5,000 elephants in the dry season. The area has thrown up three previously undescribed bird species since 1986. Much of the floodplain is inaccessible to all but self-sufficient four-wheel-drive expeditions, but hippos, and, on occasion, the endemic birds can be observed near the ferry crossing. For a small fee, the dugout-canoe owners who hang around the ferry will carry travellers upstream in search of elephant and buffalo.

Iringa

For 50 km (30 miles) south of Mikumi, the Tanzam Highway runs through undistinguished acacia scrub, before abruptly giving way to a steep valley densely packed with haunted forests of ancient baobabs. This magnificently austere landscape is softened by the Great Ruaha River, which meanders along the valley floor flanked by a ribbon of lush riparian woodland. Within this valley, the private **Baobab Valley Conservancy**, still under development, abuts the western border of Udzungwa Mountains National Park. Situated on a migration route associated with Ruaha National Park, Baobab Valley attracts a significant seasonal elephant population, and there is no better place to see the stately greater kudu, which regularly comes to drink at the river.

There's nothing about **Iringa** ⓫ to set pulses racing, but this substantial town, perched on a small plateau overlooking the Little Ruaha River, is possessed of an architectural and cultural cohesion lacking in many of its peers. The covered central market sells the rugs and basketwork for which the region is famed, while well-preserved German and Asian colonial-era buildings on Majumba Street house a miscellany of small shops. The local Hehe tribe,

Map on page 222

BELOW: kudu and impala come down to drink, relying on safety in numbers.

Map on page 222

The severed head of Mkwawa, a local conquistador, was removed to Germany and only returned to Tanzania in 1954. The skull was displayed in the Kalenga Museum for decades, but in 1998, on the centenary of Mkwawa's suicide, it was finally interred with the rest of his remains.

BELOW: the Isimila Stone Age Site, near Iringa.

probably the most populous in southern Tanzania, arose as a powerful expansionist empire forged under Chief Munyigumba in about 1850 – their name derives from their hee-hee battle cry.

The name Iringa is a corruption of the Hehe word *lilinga* (fort), a reference to **Kalenga ⑫**, the fortified capital of Chief Mkwawa, 15 km (9 miles) from the modern town. Mkwawa, a merciless conquistador who profited greatly from the slave trade, has been transformed by posterity into a folk hero for his resistance to German colonisation. In 1891, Mkwawa's army ambushed a German war party in Hehe territory, killing three-quarters of the troops. German revenge came three years later, when Kalenga was destroyed by a hilltop bombardment. The remains of the fortified walls are still discernible today, and a touching museum houses several of Mkwawa's personal effects. Following the destruction of Kalenga, Mkwawa inflicted a series of successful guerrilla attacks on German positions, but in 1898, his encampment at Mlambalasi surrounded, the chief shot himself rather than face capture. Mkwawa's body was buried where it fell. An 11-km (7-mile) road signposted off the road from Iringa to Ruaha leads to Mkwawa's tomb and centenary memorial at **Mlambalasi ⑬**.

Situated 22 km (14 miles) southwest of Iringa along the Tanzam Highway, the **Isimila Stone Age Site ⑭** (entrance charge) is a dry watercourse incised through sequential layers of sediment deposited by a lake which dried up 60,000 years ago. The site museum displays tools and weapons used by Stone Age hunter-gatherers, as well as the fossilised remains of the creatures they preyed upon: buffalo-sized swine, giraffe-like ungulates with huge antlers, and gargantuan hippos with projecting eyes. Ten minutes' stroll from the museum, a deeper gorge is dotted with tall sandstone pillars carved by an extinct river. ❏

Selous

Born in London in 1851, the son of the chairman of the London Stock Exchange, Frederick Courteney Selous was even as a child an avid naturalist, inspired by David Livingstone and the hunting pursuits of Gordon Cumming and Charles Baldwin.

In 1871, he realised his boyhood dream, emigrating to southern Africa where he led a colourful existence as a hunter-explorer, killing hundreds of elephants and other animals, and acting as a guide for Cecil Rhodes in opening up Zimbabwe to European settlers. Writing about his exploits – *A Hunter's Wanderings in Africa* and *African Nature Notes and Reminiscences* – earned him international fame, and he was hired as a hunting guide for American president Theodore Roosevelt, with whom he became friends, staying at the White House on several occasions.

Selous showed the hunter's passion for his quarry, possessing a remarkable skill for observing the wildlife he shot, and for debating wildlife issues. He also developed a deep respect for the San and Matabele, who taught him bushcraft. His writing gives a valuable insight into the state of African wildlife at the end of the 19th century, and led the way to modern methods of conserving wildlife.

On noticing that black rhinoceros were extinct in many areas where they had previously been plentiful, he suggested that certain species be protected – today there is a major rhino conservation project running in the Selous. He also envisaged National Parks, believing that it would be possible to establish large sanctuaries in uninhabited parts of the country to preserve considerable numbers of wildlife.

After his hunting career, Selous retired to England. At the outbreak of World War I, he volunteered for duty, only to be told that at 63 he was too old. He reapplied, was appointed as an intelligence officer in the 25th Royal Fusiliers and sent back to East Africa. Here he pitched his cunning against the legendary skills of the German commander, Colonel Paul von Lettow-Vorbeck *(see page 39)*.

Climate and disease took their toll on his company – of the original 1,166-strong force, only 60 remained by the time they drove the Germans out of the fortified village of Kisiki in 1916. For his action and bravery in the field, Captain Selous was awarded the DSO.

Remarkably, even during the war, Selous still found time to pursue his interests as a hunter and naturalist. After battle, he took out his butterfly net to collect specimens, and also went out hunting, bagging a kudu trophy. But his glory was to be short-lived.

In January 1917 the company was involved in a series of skirmishes near the Rufiji River, and, while out scouting, Selous was shot dead by a German sniper. His grave can be seen north of the Rufiji River near the Selous Safari Camp, not far from Beho Beho.

A simple concrete slab is marked by a small plaque, which reads: "Captain F.C. Selous, DSO, 25th Royal Fusiliers, Killed in Action 4.1.1917". The Selous Game Reserve was named after him in recognition of his contribution to wildlife as a naturalist and conservationist. ❑

RIGHT: Frederick Selous, greatest of the great white hunters.

MBEYA AND LAKE NYASA

*Virtually unknown, southeastern Tanzania is a glorious
landscape of lakes and mountains, rich in
wildlife, birds and flowers*

Map
on page
234

Tanzania's remote southern highlands climb steeply from the sultry northern shore of Lake Nyasa in a spectacular montane crescent, shaped by the
same ongoing tectonic violence that wrenched open the Rift Valley around
Nyasa many millions of years ago. Studded with dormant volcanic peaks, mysterious crater lakes, wild tracts of indigenous forest, pretty waterfalls and haunt-
ing volcanic rock formations, the southern highlands, seldom visited by tourists,
are rich in offbeat pickings for devoted hikers and keen natural historians.

Mbeya

The urban pulse of this lovely region is **Mbeya ❶**, Tanzania's fifth-largest city,
a neat, bustling, well-equipped and climactically pleasing base from which to
explore the highlands, yet curiously unmemorable in itself. The **Sisi Kwa Sisi
Tourism Office** (corner School Street and Mbalizi Road; tel: 0744-463 471;
email: sisikwasisi@hotmail.com) offers travel advice and inexpensive guided
tours to all accessible sites of interest in the southern highlands. Its services
are virtually essential for hikes on Ngosi, Rungwe and the Kitulo Plateau. Make
all arrangements directly through the office, since several impostors hang around
the bus station and streets of Mbeya.

LEFT: a territorial
hippo roars to ward
off invaders.
BELOW: the fish
eagle perches high
to spot its prey.

The Mbeya mountain range, noted for its wet-sea-
son floral displays of orchids and proteas, rises above
central Mbeya to the 2,656-metre (8,714-ft) **Loleza
Peak**, which can be ascended in two hours along a
footpath starting on Hospital Hill Road. The more
challenging 2,827-metre (9,275-ft) **Mbeya Peak** is
more easily climbed from the out-of-town Utengule
Country Hotel.

Mbeya was founded in 1927 to service a gold rush
centred on **Chunya ❷**, reached by a rough but scenic
72-km (45-mile) road that leaves Mbeya opposite the
Rift Valley Hotel, skirting the eastern slopes of the
Mbeya range. It is part of a circuit that can be
completed over a day in a private four-wheel drive in
the dry season. About 22 km (14 miles) out of Mbeya,
the **World's End Viewpoint** affords expansive views
over the arid Usungu Flats. Chunya is a peculiar
settlement, with most of the grand boomtown buildings
derelict or boarded up, and although the gold was
commercially exhausted long ago, optimistic pro-
spectors still pan the local rivers.

A longer, more southerly road back to Mbeya runs
through Makongolosi and Saza to Mbalizi on the
Tanzam Highway. About 5 km (3 miles) east of this
road, near Kanga, **Lake Magadi** is often rose-tinted
with flamingos between July and October. The **Galula
Mission**, around 8 km (5 miles) past Kanga, has a
curious wooden church built in the 1920s.

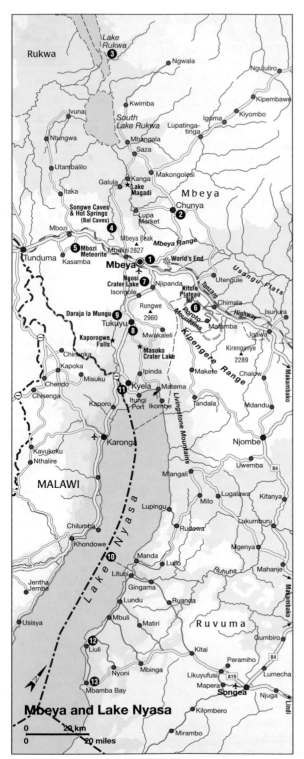

Mbeya and Lake Nyasa

0   20 km
0   20 miles

Lake Rukwa

The roads around Chunya offer views across **Lake Rukwa ❸**, a vast alkaline sump set in an inhospitable arm of the Rift Valley, all but bereft of human habitation. The Rukwa Floodplain supports plentiful game, including the localised puku antelope and high densities of hippos and crocodiles, as well as incredible concentrations of waterbirds.

Rukwa is a genuine wilderness, and any expedition there should be self-sufficient in spare vehicle parts, fuel, food, drinking water and camping equipment. From Chunya, a two-hour drive northwest through Saza and Mbangala leads to the fluctuating lake shore, as does a rough track from Galula Mission to Totoe. A third approach crosses the Ufipa Plateau west of Sumbawanga (on the Tunduma–Mpanda road).

Marble and meteors

From Mbeya, follow the Tanzam Highway west for 25 km (16 miles) to **Songwe** township, then turn left through a limestone quarry dotted with local kilns. After 10 km (6 miles), you will arrive at the pink-marble quarry that houses the **Songwe Caves and Hot Springs ❹**. Eroded into a limestone cliff, the caves harbour a colony of six bat species, which stream spectacularly out of the entrance at dusk.

Further west along the Tanzam Highway, a right turn 30 km (18 miles) past Songwe leads to the **Mbozi Meteorite ❺**, a 12-tonne block of dense nickel-iron alloy listed as the eighth-largest celestial body ever found on the earth's surface.

Kitulo National Park

From Chimala, a small town straddling the Tanzam Highway 78 km (48 miles) east of Mbeya, a thrillingly scenic south-bound dirt road navigates 57 hairpin bends en route to Matamba, gateway town to the 1,300-sq. km (502-sq. mile) **Kitulo National Park ❻**. Locals refer to Kitulo as Bustani ya Mungu (God's Garden), an apt name for what is the first national park in East Africa gazetted primarily for its floral wealth. The plateau is best visited between November and May, when the rains transform the grassland into a dazzling floral kaleidoscope. Bright-orange red-hot pokers reach skyward from the crags above a carpet of multi-hued lilies, asters, geraniums and orchids punctuated by otherworldly giant lobelias and pretty protea shrubs. Large mammals are scarce, but blue swallow, Denham's bustard and mountain marsh widow top a long list of endangered or localised birds. The Kitulo plateau is most easily visited in a four-wheel-drive from Chimala, but a second, rougher approach road from Isongole (in the Poroto Mountains) is possible.

Map on page 234

The Poroto Mountains

A nippy, surfaced 140-km (87-mile) road runs southeast from Mbeya to Kyela (near Lake Nyasa), passing for most of its length through the scenic **Poroto Mountains**. The highlight of the Poroto region is **Ngosi Crater Lake ❼**, brooding at the base of a 300-metre (980-ft) deep volcanic caldera. Ngosi's brackish green waters reputedly provide refuge to an enormous serpentine monster, which is able to change colour to disguise or reveal itself according to mood – disappointingly, it's invariably in camouflage mode when travellers come past. Still, the extensive evergreen and bamboo forests around the lake harbour a wealth of less elusive birds and monkeys, plus an endemic species of three-horned chameleon. The turn-off to Ngosi is signposted from **Isongole** on the main Mbeya–Kyela road. You can drive the first 5 km (3 miles) from the junction, but the final two-hour ascent to the crater rim is on foot only.

The 12-tonne Mbozi Meterorite, made of a nickel-iron alloy called siderite and at least 1,000 years old, was first identified in 1930 by W.H. Nott.

Towering over the northern horizon of Isongole, the 2,960-metre (9,711-ft) **Rungwe Volcano** last erupted around 1800, though a spate of tremors in 2001 suggests that further seismic activity is likely in the near future. Rungwe's uninhabited higher slopes, protected within a forest reserve, are home to troops of acrobatic black-and-white colobus monkeys; they also form an important stronghold for the rare Abbott's duiker, while the moorland above around 2,500 metres (8,202 ft) is dotted with colourful ground orchids and protea scrubs. During the dry season, a reasonably fit person should be able to climb to the peak and back within a day. The easiest ascent is from Kagera Estate Timber Camp, set on the northern footslopes 18 km (11 miles) by road from Isongole.

BELOW: the Kaporogwe Falls.

The Bridge of God

Midway between Mbeya and Kyela, the main surfaced road snakes through **Tukuyu ❽**, an attractive small town founded in the southern foothills of Mount Rungwe during the German colonial era. Tukuyu is a useful base for exploring the region, particularly by public transport.

From here, follow the Mbeya road for 6 km (4 miles) to Kyimo, then turn left. After 10 km (6 miles) you'll reach the remarkable **Daraja la Mungu ❾** (Bridge of God), a solidified lava flow spanning the Kiwira River to form a natural bridge wide enough to walk across. The nearby **Kijungu Boiling Pot** consists of a small waterfall that tumbles into a circular pothole before flowing under another small natural bridge. Further downriver, the 20-metre (66-ft) high **Kaporogwe Falls** plunge over a basalt ledge into the

Kiwira Gorge. To get there, follow the Kyela road south from Tukuyu for 5 km (3 miles), then turn right onto a track signposted for the Lutengano Moravian Centre.

South of Tukuyu, an alternative route to the surfaced Kyela road is the well-maintained dirt road to Ipinda. Both roads wind in a leisurely fashion through fertile green hills dotted with the tidy Nyakyusa homesteads that the 19th-century explorer Joseph Thomson called "perfect Arcadia", the charming views enhanced by tantalising glimpses of Lake Nyasa in the Rift Valley below. Some 19 km (12 miles) out of Tukuyu, the Ipinda road skirts **Masoko**, a pretty market village perched above a deep, green crater lake. This, incongruously enough, was a German military base in World War I. The stone courthouse on the crater rim started life as a garrison, while the occasional old coin that washes up on the shore helps fuel a rumour that a stash of German gold and other valuables was dumped into the lake when defeat became inevitable.

Lake Nyasa

The climatic contrast between the breezy Poroto highlands and **Lake Nyasa** ⓾, set in the Rift Valley floor at an altitude of 437 metres (1,434 ft), could hardly be more dramatic. Nor, for that matter, could Lake Nyasa itself.

Known as Lake Malawi south of the Malawian border, Nyasa runs for 585 km (364 miles) through a stretch of the Rift Valley hemmed in by a sheer escarpment rising sharply from the shore. The lake's trademark sandy beaches, studded with giant baobabs and whispering palms, resonate with the high eerie cry of the fish eagle, while the startlingly clear turquoise water supports the world's greatest diversity of freshwater fish.

BELOW: dugout canoes on Matema Beach, Lake Nyasa.

Many seasoned African travellers regard Nyasa to be the most beautiful lake on the continent, but no such eulogies have ever been directed at **Kyela** ⑪, a substantial but overwhelmingly scruffy town, 10 km (6 miles) from the lake shore at the southern terminus of the surfaced road from Mbeya. From Kyela, a 15-km (9-mile) road leads north to Ipinda, connecting with the back road from Tukuyu via Masoko, then after another 27 km (17 miles) to **Matema Beach** on the northern tip of Nyasa. Matema is the closest thing to a resort on this part of the lake, and yet – serviced only by a pair of church hostels – it retains a refreshingly unspoilt, rustic African character. To bask in the deliciously warm water that laps Matema Beach, gazing up at the Livingstone Mountains rising to 2,500 metres (8,202 ft) within 4 km (2 miles) of the shore, is bliss. And there's plenty in the area to occupy more energetic travellers.

Lyulilo, east of Matema, is the site of a famous Saturday pottery market, while the nearby **Pango Cave** was an important sacrificial site before the missionaries arrived. Thirty minutes from Matema by local canoe, the village of **Ikombe** is the main source of the region's distinctive pale Kisi pottery, sold at Lyulilo for distribution all around the country. A canoe is also the best way to reach the swampy **Lufirio River Mouth**, 3 km (2 miles) west of Matema, which provides excellent viewing for birds, crocodiles and hippos.

The inland navy

A ferry service circumnavigates the Tanzanian portion of Lake Nyasa thrice weekly, departing from **Itungi Port**, near Kyela. Geared primarily towards locals, the Nyasa ferry makes few concessions to luxury, but it does provide a fabulous overview of the scenic northern lake shore, punctuated by regular stops at isolated ports where the ship is greeted by a rapturous fleet of local boats. **Liuli** ⑫, the penultimate stop, is dominated by an impressive rock formation from which its German name of Sphinxhafen was derived. Bizarrely, Liuli was the site of the first naval encounter of World War I. London's *Times* proclaimed "Naval Victory on Lake Nyasa", rather overstating the more farcical reality. Captain Rhoades took the only British ship on the lake to fire on the only German ship while it was in dry dock. The German captain, a long-time drinking buddy of Rhoades, rowed out in a dinghy to leap on board the British ship and berate his old pal, only to find himself a prisoner of war – a war that he was unaware had been declared.

The ferry service terminates at **Mbamba Bay** ⑬, a pleasant lake shore port set on a palm-lined beach near the Mozambique border, and ideally positioned to catch the legendary sunsets over the lake.

Aside from the ferry, the only escape route from Mbamba Bay is a scenic but poor 170-km (106-mile) road that winds treacherously across the rift escarpment to **Songea**. This is a large, prosperous town notable only for its small museum, dedicated to the Maji Maji Rebellion. From Songea, a superb surfaced road runs for 350 km (217 miles) – passing through the pretty but undistinguished highland town of **Njombe** – to the Makambako, at the junction of the Tanzam Highway. ❑

Map on page 234

The Kisi women of Ikombe make their nationally renowned pots by hollowing out a ball of clay, then rotating it manually to smooth the edges, before applying a feldspar finish that gives the product a distinctive creamy hue. Attractive souvenirs, Kisi pots sell locally for a fraction of their price in the cities.

BELOW: Kisi pottery, for sale throughout Tanzania.

THE SOUTH COAST

The journey to the south coast is not easy, but it's worth the effort in order to explore an enchanting area that encapsulates the traditional Swahili lifestyle

Map on page 240

With its sticky tropical ambience and generous quota of postcard-perfect beaches and atmospherically time-worn ports, the 600-km (370-mile) coastline that stretches from Dar es Salaam south to the Mozambican border shares most of the elements that have made Zanzibar such a popular post-safari chill-out destination. What it lacks, however, is any semblance of a conventional tourist infrastructure. The roads, almost without exception, are bumpy dustbowls that transform into impassable quagmires at the height of the rains.

What's more, aside from **Mafia Island** (which has few travel links to the facing mainland), it would be positively actionable to advertise any hostelry more than an hour's drive south of Dar es Salaam as an idyllic beach resort.

Mafia excepted, the south coast is about as well suited to package holidays as it would be to dedicated ski parties, but the region has much to recommend it to travellers seeking genuine insight into Swahili culture past and present. It is not merely that the area's assortment of ruined and living settlements collectively provide a cross-section of coastal trade and history over the past millennium. There is, too, a pervasive aura of cultural continuity hanging over this forgotten corner of Tanzania, the feeling that while its front foot stretches gamely towards the future, the other one remains firmly planted at the cusp of the 19th and 20th centuries.

Kilwa

The south coast has not always been the backwater it is today. Exhibit one for the defence, and un-questionably the region's one "must-see" attraction, is the extensive, ruined medieval port of **Kilwa**, described in 1331 by the insatiable Arab sightseer Ibn Buttata as "one of the most beautiful and well-constructed towns in the world". For three bountiful centuries before the arrival of the Portuguese, Kilwa was the greatest trade emporium on the coast south of Mogadishu, the site of the first coin mint in sub-equatorial Africa, as well as of a clutch of buildings that stand at the pinnacle of Swahili architectural achievement. Every year, at the peak of the monsoon winds, the island's small harbour bustled with commercial activity, as fleets of ocean-going dhows sailed from the sultanates of Arabia and great empires of Asia to purchase or barter for Kilwa's legendary stockpiles of gold, sourced from Great Zimbabwe.

The ruins of Kilwa lie on **Kilwa Kisiwani** ❶ (Kilwa on the Island), divided by a narrow estuarine channel from the rather nondescript mainland port of **Kilwa Masoko** ❷ (Kilwa Market). Connected to Dar es Salaam by occasional flights and a 300-km (180-mile) curate's egg of a road, Kilwa Masoko is dotted with

LEFT: the design of the Swahili dhows is little changed since ancient times.
BELOW: the Gereza, Kilwa Kisiwani.

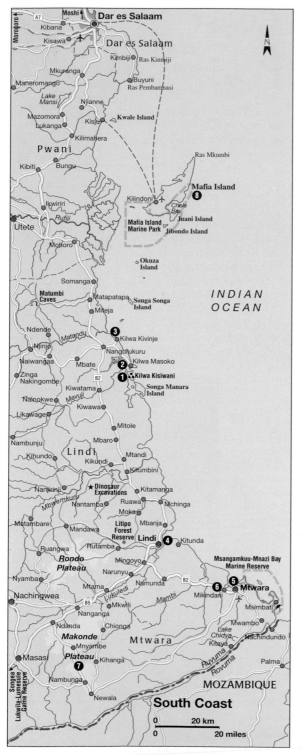

South Coast

0   20 km

0   20 miles

unpretentious local guesthouses. You need to obtain written permission to visit the island from the local cultural office in the administrative buildings. Paperwork completed, for a nominal fee, the dhow trip across the channel can take anything from 10 to 45 minutes, depending on the prevailing winds and currents; allocate at least half a day for the expedition.

The shoreward side of Kilwa Kisiwani is dominated by an imposing, partially collapsed fort known locally as the **Gereza**, built around 1800 during a brief Omani occupation of the island, and entered via imposing wooden Zanzibar doors. A short footpath leads uphill past the fort, through a cheerful fishing village, to the abandoned medieval trading centre, studded by semi-collapsed mosques and palaces, as well as the ornately carved tombs of a succession of powerful sultans.

The singularly lovely **Great Mosque** is the most inspired Swahili building of the medieval period. Its exquisite domed roof, supported by bays of precisely hewn arches, remains largely intact a full seven centuries after it was constructed. Ten minutes' walk east of the main ruins, on a rise overlooking the beach, stands the **Husuni Kubwa**, the isolated and ostentatious palace – complete with sunken audience court and swimming pool – where the Sultan of Kilwa played host to Ibn Buttata in 1311.

Mainland replacement

Kilwa's decline, precipitated by a Portuguese naval bombardment in 1505, was sealed 50 years later when the cannibalistic Zimba raided the island and corralled its 3,000 residents to devour at their leisure. The area enjoyed a revival in the early 19th century, with the arrival of a group of Omani settlers who stayed briefly on the island before founding the mainland port of **Kilwa Kivinje** ❸ (Kilwa beneath the Casuarina Trees); this was the terminus of the slave caravan route to the Lake Nyasa hinterland.

During the 20th century, Kilwa Kivinje degenerated into a fascinating time warp of alleys lined with decaying balconied Omani mansions, leading to a mangrove-lined waterfront dominated by the hulk of a disused German Boma (colonial office). Spend time in Kilwa Kivinje, and its fading architectural grandeur starts to feels curiously anomalous – as if the Omani ghost town had been superimposed on a randomly selected overgrown fishing village. Decidedly strange but satisfyingly authentic, Kilwa Kivinje will reward any traveller who wishes to spend a few days absorbing the slow pace of a traditional Swahili settlement – ruled today, as in medieval times, by the vagaries of the tides and the winds.

Map on page 240

Lindi

Situated some 230 km (140 miles) south of Kilwa, **Lindi** ❹ is the most substantial settlement on the coast between Dar es Salaam and Mtwara. Lindi was founded on the north bank of the Lukuledi River Estuary at about the same time as Kilwa Kivinje, but it was not an especially significant port during the Omani era, and the only major structure dating from this time is a tall stone jail near the seafront. The grid-like layout and architectural style of the run-down town centre speak of a degree of prosperity during the early colonial period, evidently curtailed by the emergence of Mtwara as the main regional harbour in the 1950s.

Immediately north of the centre, a curving, sandy beach runs into a busy, traditional dhow harbour. Regular motorised ferries leave from in front of the defunct Lindi Beach Hotel to the fishing village of **Kitunda**, while local fishing boats can be rented to explore the estuary upstream or to visit the fruit-bat colony on the offshore **Bat Island**. Further afield, some 30 km (19 miles) east of Lindi and accessible by dirt road, the **Litipo Forest Reserve** harbours a rich variety of birds of the coastal forest biome, while a trio of lakes bordering the reserve harbour a few hippos and are sporadically visited by elephants.

The fish catch is strung on poles for smoking round a huge fire.

BELOW: interior of the 14th-century Great Mosque, Kilwa Kisiwani.

Mtwara and surrounds

Linked to Lindi by a blissfully smooth stretch of tarmac, **Mtwara** ❺ is a substantial harbour town of 135,000 residents, situated 20 km (12 miles) north of the Mozambique border. It was founded in 1947, when its deep-water harbour was developed to service the disastrously misconceived post-war Groundnut Scheme *(see page 41)*. As a consequence of this debacle, Mtwara has never really grown to flesh out its ambitious skeleton. The nominal town centre, main market area, residential suburbs and harbour are all divided from each other by open fields. The town is not overly endowed with character, but the lovely beach, friendly atmosphere and adequate facilities ensure that it's an agreeable place to break your journey.

Straddling the Lindi road 10 km (6 miles) north of Mtwara, the tiny village of **Mikindani** ❻ is where David Livingstone set off on his final expedition into the African interior. A plaque commemorating Livingstone's "reputed dwelling place" is nailed to the wall of a balconied two-storey house which, while rather picturesque, has several architectural quirks suggesting it was constructed nearly a century after the explorer's death. However, Mikindani does have several genuinely interesting German- and Omani-era relics, most impressively the fortified 19th-century **German Boma**, immaculately restored to its whitewashed pomp by the British charity Trade Aid in 1998, and now a hotel.

Committed to opening up the far southeast to all levels of tourism, Trade Aid (www.tradeaiduk.org) can also arrange trips to (or advise independent travellers about) several obscure but rewarding local attractions, including the forested **Rondo Plateau**, the superb **Msimbati Beach**, the **Lukwika-Lumesule Game Reserve** and crocodile-infested **Lake Chidya**.

BELOW: sandbar near Mafia Island.

Inland of Mtwara, the **Makonde Plateau ❼** is home to the most celebrated traditional sculptors in East Africa. The Makonde, unusually for this part of Africa, have a strongly matrilineal society, and their carvings, traditionally sculpted and carried by men only, relate to a complex ancestral cult of womanhood.

Makonde sculptures achieved renown in the 1950s after a carving workshop was founded in Dar es Salaam, and outstanding works sell for high prices to international collectors. Dar es Salaam is now entrenched as the main centre of Makonde carving, and it is difficult to visit traditional carvers *in situ* without local contacts.

The main town of the Makonde is **Masasi**, situated at the base of the plateau amongst tall granite outcrops reminiscent of parts of Zimbabwe. The breezy highland town of **Newala** is distinguished by a sweeping view across the Ruvuma River, proclaimed by more than one Tanzanian resident to be the most beautiful in the country.

The Mafia archipelago

Linked to Dar es Salaam by regular flights, Mafia is more realistically viewed as a stand-alone upmarket destination than as an extension of the rough-and-ready travel circuit on the south coast. The archipelago, which lies some 20 km (12 miles) east of the Rufiji River Delta, is comprised of the 50-km (30-mile) long **Mafia Island ❽** as well as a dozen smaller islets and numerous coral outcrops. The only settlement of any substance is **Kilindoni**, the main port on Mafia Island, and site of its only airstrip. Elsewhere, the isles are scattered with rustic fishing villages, while a cluster of top-notch and very exclusive lodges lies along **Chole Bay**, 12 km (7 miles) by road from Kilindoni.

Mafia is East Africa's premier diving, snorkelling and game-fishing venue. The extensive offshore reefs, protected within an 820-sq. km (317-sq. mile) **marine park**, are comprised of 50 genera of coral and harbour some 400 species of fish. Recommended for their colourful coral formations and kaleidoscopic shoals of small reef fish are the **Kinasi Wall** and adjoining **Chole Wall**, near the outlet of Chole Bay, while a 12-metre (40-ft) coral pinnacle within the bay is a reliable place for sighting giant cod and moray eels. Further afield, sharks and giant tuna haunt the **Dindini North Wall** and **Forbes Bay** on the main barrier reef. Snorkellers are also well catered for: the two larger coral islets in Kinasi Pass host a volume and variety of reef fish that compares favourably with any site in East Africa.

Nor does Mafia lack historical interest. A short dhow trip across Chole Bay leads to **Chole Mjini** (Chole Town), where a stand of ancient baobabs houses the disintegrating walls of several 19th-century mansions, built by wealthy Omani merchants who held slave plantations on the main island (then known as Chole Shamba – Chole Farm). Further afield, on **Juani Island**, the ruined city of **Kua** was founded at about the same time as Kilwa, and is one of the few medieval ports in East Africa to have been inhabited continuously into the 19th century. Nearby **Jipondo Island** is an important traditional shipbuilding centre, where dhows are constructed using traditional tools. ❑

A dhow glides elegantly along the coast.

BELOW: bringing home the catch, off Mafia Island.

ZANZIBAR AND PEMBA

*These legendary spice islands still exude an air of mystery
and romance that have made them one of the world's
favourite honeymoon destinations*

Map
on page
250

Mention that you are going to Zanzibar and the response will be one of two things: "Oh, is it a real place, then? Where is it?" or, just as frequently, "You'll love it, I went there for my honeymoon." Go into almost any resort hotel along the east coast and you'll find the lovebirds lined up two by two, arms entwined, around the bar or pool, champagne at the ready. If you have the temerity not to be on your honeymoon, you will probably give up and get married along the way, so relentless are the congratulations. It is funny, but you can see why it is so popular – a perfect blend of African charm, Middle Eastern exoticism, picture-perfect beaches, romantic hotels and a sophisticated range of activities from spice tours to diving. The weather may get slightly warmer or wetter at some times of year, but is basically good all year round. And it is all within easy reach of Kenya and the Tanzanian mainland, should you choose to tack on a safari.

As for the other question: it may be the stuff of legends, even featuring in the tales of Sinbad, but Zanzibar is very definitely real. "Northerners" have been trading along this coast since the days of the Pharaohs, around 3000 BC. The region was certainly known to the Mesopotamians, Phoenicians and Romans, but it was the Greeks who first recorded it as the Island of Menouthesias, in *The Periplus of the Erythraean Sea* (*c.* AD 60) and Ptolemy's *Geography* (*c.* AD 150). Above all, it was the arrival of Islamic Arabs and Shirazi (Persian) settlers from the 8th century onwards that changed the face of the region for ever, with the evolution of the Swahili language and culture (*see Swahili Traders, page 25*). At its apogee in the mid-19th century, Zanzibar was the capital of the entire far-flung Omani Empire and one of the most important cities on the Indian Ocean.

Rise and fall of a city state

Today Zanzibar is actually the name of the province made up of two main islands, **Unguja** (usually just called Zanzibar) and **Pemba**, along with a host of smaller islands, some not much more than coral rocks.

Lying only 40 km (29 miles) off the mainland, Unguja is about 100 km (60 miles) long and 35 km (22 miles) wide, while Pemba, 50 km (30 miles) to the north, is roughly 70 km (45 miles) by 20 km (12 miles). The total provincial population is approximately 1 million, of whom around 200,000 live in **Zanzibar Town ❶** (usually called Stone Town) and about 300,000 live on Pemba. The vast majority are Muslim.

After centuries of being batted backwards and forwards by the Arabs, Portuguese and British, in 1964 the locals revolted. Over 17,000 people died, Sultan Jamshid fled, to live the rest of his life in the UK,

PRECEDING PAGES:
Matemwe Beach;
dhow racing on
Zanzibar.
LEFT: dugout canoe
on Bwejuu Beach.
BELOW: road
maintenance crew,
Stone Town.

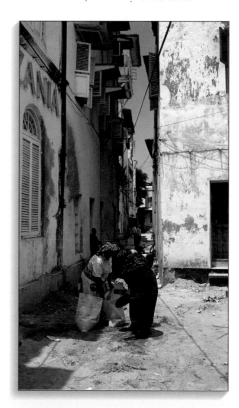

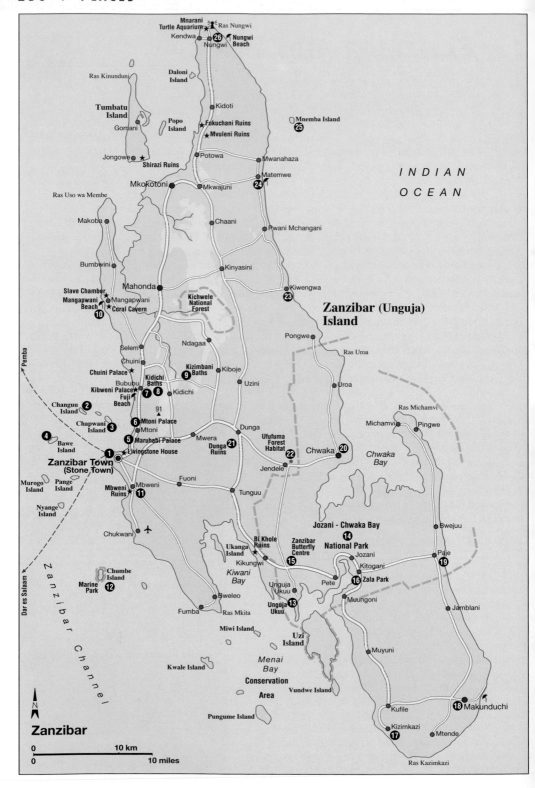

I N D I A N
O C E A N

Mnarani
Turtle Aquarium ★ ⚓ Ras Nungwi
Kendwa ⬤26 ↑Nungwi
Nungwi Beach

Ras Kinunduni
Daloni Island

Kidoti

Tumbatu Island
Gomani
Popo Island
Mnemba Island ⬤25

★ Fukuchani Ruins
★ Mvuleni Ruins

Jongowe ● ★ Shirazi Ruins
Potowa
Mwanahaza ●
Matemwe ●24

Mkokotoni ●
Mkwajuni ●
Ras Uso wa Membe
Makoba ●
Chaani ●
Pwani Mchangani ●

Bumbwini ●
Kinyasini ●

Slave Chamber
Mangapwani Beach ★
Mangapwani ●10 ★Coral Cavern
Mahonda ●
Kichwele National Forest
Kiwengwa ●23

Zanzibar (Unguja) Island

Selem ●
Ndagaa ●
Pongwe ●
Ras Uroa
Chuini ●
Chuini Palace ★
Kizimbani Baths ●9
Kiboje ●
Uroa ●
Bububu ● Kidichi Baths
Kibweni Palace ★ ●7 ●8
Fuji Beach Kidichi ●
Uzini ●
Changuu Island ●2
91 ▲
Chapwani Island ●3
⬤6 Mtoni Palace
Mtoni ●
Dunga ●
Ufufuma Forest Habitat
Michamvi ●
Ras Michamvi
Pingwe ●

Bawe Island ●4
⬤5 Maruhubi Palace
⬤1 ●Livingstone House
Mwera ●
Dunga Ruins ●21
●22
Chwaka ●20

Zanzibar Town (Stone Town)
Fuoni ●
Jendele ●
Chwaka Bay

Murogo Island
Pange Island
Mbweni ● Mbweni Ruins ★ ●11
Tunguu ●

Nyange Island

Chukwani ●
✈

Jozani - Chwaka Bay National Park ⬤14

Bwejuu ●

Dar es Salaam
Chumbe Island
Marine Park ●12

Bi Khole Ruins ★
Ukanga Island
Kikungwi ●
Zanzibar Butterfly Centre ●15
Jozani ●
Kitogani ●
Paje ●19
Zala Park ●16

Zanzibar Channel

Kiwani Bay
Bweleo ●
Fumba ●
Ras Mkita
Unguja Ukuu ●
●13
Pete ●
Muungoni ●
Jamblani ●

Miwi Island

Uzi Island

Menai Bay
Conservation Area

Muyuni ●

Kwale Island

Vundwe Island

Kufile ●
⬤18 Makunduchi

Kizimkazi ●17
Mtende ●
Pungume Island
Ras Kazimkazi

N

Zanzibar

0   10 km
0   10 miles

while many of the Arabs and Indians headed north to Oman, their property confiscated and their businesses nationalised. Claims for restitution continue to this day. The new government, under Sheikh-Abeid Amani Karume, signed an Act of Union with the mainland, creating modern Tanzania.

At best, it is an uneasy alliance. Having ruled the roost for hundreds of years, the Zanzibaris are uncomfortable about coming second to the mainlanders, and many still retain close ties to Oman. Elections are regularly marked by riots, intimidation and allegations of corruption. Many islanders talk longingly of breaking away again as an independent state. It may yet happen.

Stone Town

Stone Town is the most common name for the old heart of Zanzibar Town, a small triangular peninsula first settled by the Portuguese in 1560, although most of the buildings date from the mid-19th century.

Begin your city tour in the **Forodhani (People's) Gardens Ⓐ**, which runs along the seafront near the dhow harbour, beside several of Stone Town's most famous monuments. Make sure you come back here at sunset. As the sea turns to gold and billowing dhows creep back to the shore, people gather to watch the world go by, chat and enjoy the warm night air. Originally laid out in 1936 to celebrate the Silver Jubilee of Sultan Khalifa, the gardens underwent a US$2.2-million facelift in 2008, funded by the Aga Khan Historic Cities Programme.

From the gardens, look across the road. To the right of the fort, the **Bank Building Ⓑ** was once the home of Princess Salme, daughter of Sultan Said. The building next door housed the German trading company. Salme fell in love with a young German, Heinrich Reute, whose balcony almost touched her own,

Maps on pages 250 & 252

TIP

Stone Town covers a very small area and is best explored on foot. The narrow alleys protect you from the sun, but take plenty to drink. If you want to go slowly, do the Creek Road section as a separate walk.

BELOW: busy street in Stone Town.

eloping with him when she became pregnant in 1866. Once in Germany, she renounced Islam, changed her name to Emily and married her lover, remaining in exile even after his tragically young death in 1871. Her lasting legacy was a book, *Memoirs of an Arabian Princess*, one of few real insights into life at court.

Tucked out of sight, about a block inland, is the Catholic **Cathedral of St Joseph ⓒ** (Cathedral Street), built by missionaries in 1898; it was designed by the French architect M. Bérangier, who was also responsible for the Basilique de Notre Dame de la Garde in Marseille. Inside it is decorated with tiles, murals and stained glass – none masterpieces, but the overall effect is colourful.

To the right again, **Kenyatta Road ⓓ** is the town's main shopping street, while the building with the arch on the far right is the **Zanzibar Orphanage**.

The Arab Fort

Back on the seafront, the **Arab Fort ⓔ** (Ngome Kongwe; tel: 0744-278 737; daily 9am–5pm) is the town's oldest surviving building, built by Omani Arabs

"When the flute is played in Zanzibar, all Africa east of the Lakes must dance."
– OLD ARAB PROVERB

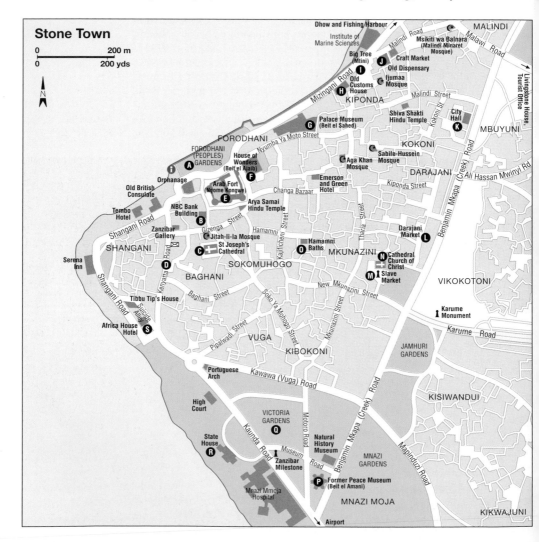

Stone Town

in 1698–1701 around the original Portuguese church (1598–1612). With thick coral rag walls, battlements and arrow slits, it is a formidable fortification, but has rarely been put to the test. Instead, over the years, it has done duty as the local prison, railway station (the gatehouse was demolished to allow trains access), tennis club and, today, a museum and cultural centre. Inside are some nice craft shops and a shady café, as well as an open-air theatre which hosts the ZIFF Festival of the Dhow Countries each July (www.ziff.or.tz). On three evenings a week, there are lively cultural evenings, with dinner and traditional music and dance. There is also a tourist information desk inside the fort, but its opening hours are erratic and it has few resources to give out. The inconveniently located tourist office in Livingtone House *(see page 259)* is not much help either; however, visitors can find plenty of information about what's on offer from advertising or from their hotels.

The royal palaces

Turn right as you leave the fort. Next door, the **House of Wonders** ⑦ (Beit el-Ajaib; daily 10am–6pm; entrance charge) was built in 1883 by a British marine engineer for Sultan Barghash, on the site of a 17th-century palace built by Queen Fatima. Inside this huge four-storey structure, girdled by iron balconies, there are only a few cavernous rooms. It was designed purely for ceremonial purposes and was never intended to be a residence. The decoration is magnificent, from the marble floors to the ornate carving on the doors, but it gained its name from its dazzling technology. Not only was this the tallest building in sub-Saharan Africa, but the first to have electricity or a lift, while caged animals in the courtyard helped add spectacle for the people. The clocktower was

The stench... is quite horrible. At night, it is so gross and crass, one might cut a slice and manure the garden with it. It might be called "Stinkibar" rather than Zanzibar.

– DAVID LIVINGSTONE

BELOW: the House of Wonders, one of Stone Town's most impressive buildings.

The Old Dispensary borrowed its ginger-bread architecture from 19th-century India.

added in 1896. The cannons at the entrance were captured from the Portuguese in 1622. It is now a museum and exhibition space, and well worth a visit, if only for the spectacular view from the magnificent balconies. In the late 19th century, the House of Wonders was one of three adjoining palaces connected by high-level walkways. The next along was the Beit el-Hukm (House of Government), and beyond that was the Beit el-Sahel (House of the Coast), built by Sultan Seyyid in about 1830. In 1896 there was an attempted coup, and both the Beit el-Hukm and Beit el-Sahel were destroyed by a British naval bombardment.

The **Palace Museum** Ⓖ (Beit el-Sahel; Mizingani Road; Tues–Sat 10am–6pm; entrance charge) was built as a replacement, and remained the Sultan's official residence until 1911. It was renamed the "People's Palace" after the revolution. Today it is a museum, with an interesting collection of original furniture and costumes, and a room dedicated to Princess Salme *(see page 252)*, furnished according to her own detailed descriptions. There are plenty of guides in the foyer, if you would like a tour.

Mizingani Road

As you continue along the road, a less than riveting collection of warehouses on your left marks the back of the modern dhow harbour and port, built on reclaimed land in 1925. Before they were built, this was prime real estate with many magnificent mansions and offices, most now sadly decaying. The old **Customs House** Ⓗ shows what can be achieved with some care, having been beautifully restored as a conservation centre by the Stone Town Conservation Authority. It has particularly fine doors with maritime decoration. A little further on is a giant banyan, planted in 1911 by Sultan Khalifa and known simply as the **Big Tree** ❶ (Mtini). It is one of the best-known landmarks of the city and a popular meeting place for locals.

The **Old Dispensary** ❶ (daily 9am– 6pm; free), with its elaborate fretwork gingerbread decoration, rivals the House of Wonders. It was originally built in the 1890s by a local Ismaili Indian trader, Tharia Topan, who donated it to the city to be used as a cottage hospital and dispensary, a role it fulfilled until the 1970s. Restored by the Aga Khan Foundation, it is now grandly but erroneously called the Stone Town Cultural Centre. There is a café and a small exhibition space on the ground floor and a few shops upstairs. Next door is you will find a **Craft Market** where you can watch Tingatinga painters and carvers at work. Prices are reasonable.

There is little more to see along Mizingani Road, so your best bet is to dive into the alleys away from the seafront. You will almost certainly get lost, but it really doesn't matter. Every new corner brings something interesting to look at, and the area is so small that it is impossible not to pop out eventually onto one of the main roads. **Hurumzi Street** and **Gizenga Street** are busy shopping thoroughfares which eventually lead back to Kenyatta Road. **Malindi Street** will take you inland to **Benjamin Mkapa Road**, better known to everyone as Creek Road.

Creek Road

When the Portuguese arrived, the little peninsula was effectively an island, cut off by Darajani Creek. Over the years this silted up, until eventually, in 1957, it was filled in to become Creek Road, a busy, broad road that marks the boundary between the historic and modern cities. Cross the great divide and you'll see a very different town, with housing from shanties to high-rise Socialist blocks, all with a great deal of life and very little charm.

At the north end of Creek Road, the **City Hall Ⓚ** belongs firmly to the British era, a flourish of neo-Gothic grandeur that would feel at home in Manchester. Head a few blocks south and you reach **Darajani Market Ⓛ**, which has long since outgrown the Market Hall, built in 1904, to spread across the surrounding streets. There are few souvenirs on offer, although spices are well to the fore. Instead, take time to enjoy the vibrant colours, salesmen's patter and the extraordinary array of fruit, vegetables and fish on sale. You will be guaranteed to find things you have never seen before, such as Zanzibari apples.

The Slave Market

A block south of the market, twice weekly public auctions (Wed and Sun) are held in the small park. Walk through this and you come to a far more chilling salesground. Only a monument now marks the site of the infamous **Slave Market Ⓜ**, founded in 1811 by Sultan Seyyid and eventually closed in 1873. At the height of the trade in the 1830s–50s, more than 60,000 people a year were sold *(see page 27)* to work on the plantations or for shipping to Oman.

In the basement of St Monica's Hostel next door, guides will take you on a harrowing tour through what are purported to be the slave storage chambers,

BELOW: shopping at Darajani Market.

Swahili Architecture

Stone Town has a collection of around 2,000 historic buildings. Few of them date back further than the mid-19th century, but they represent one of the world's finest collections of Swahili architecture, a fascinating cultural marriage between Arab, African and Indian styles. Sadly, many are in a dire state of repair, although the Aga Khan Trust for Culture (www.akdn.org) and the local conservation association have embarked on some serious restoration.

The narrow alleys, designed for shade in a time when donkeys were the only form of transport, are organised by quarters *(mitaa)*, usually named after a significant local landmark or the family by which they were founded. Each would have its complement of coffee shops, stone benches, mosques and shops to cater for the social, spiritual and physical needs of the community. What can appear to

be scruffy, vacant lots are frequently badly maintained graveyards. Arabs began trading and settling along the coast in the 5th century AD. In Stone Town, however, the real creation of the city began in the 17th century. Some of its earliest settlers were from Hadhramaut in the Yemen, closely followed by other Swahili people from along the coast.

The typical Swahili mansion was plain on the outside, the status of the residents only displayed in the magnificently carved doors. In fact, the door was often bought first and the house built around it. Doors centuries-old have been handed down through the generations. Typical designs included maritime themes, chains (to symbolise security), Quranic inscriptions and Indian-influenced lotus blossoms.

Inside, the entrance porch *(daka)*, where visitors were traditionally greeted and served coffee, led to a much more ornate courtyard, decorated with carved coral or stucco, surrounded by long, thin rooms. Many of the houses were linked by upper-storey galleries to allow the women to socialise in privacy.

Working-class houses were far more African in style, with wattle and daub used and a thatched roof overhanging a broad veranda, which often served as a shop. The courtyard of the more formal houses became a working yard shared by the whole family and their livestock.

The most significant period of building began when the capital of Oman was moved here in 1840. Many Omani houses were semi-fortified, with crenellated walls. The downstairs rooms became servants' quarters, while the family slept in the airier rooms above. A screen surrounded the public areas of the courtyard, shielding the women from public view.

The houses with outside verandas, many of them sporting intricate fretwork designs, were almost all the property of Indian merchants, who added the balconied upper storeys as living space over the simple Swahili shops. The rows of shuttered windows on the upper levels were designed to catch the breeze. ❑

LEFT: doors in Zanzibar are traditionally intricately carved with geometric and delicate floral designs.

Map on page 252

although some maintain that it is far more likely to have been a bathhouse.

Next door is the Anglican **Cathedral Church of Christ**  **N** (daily 8am–6pm; entrance charge), built in 1873 by Bishop Edward Steere, Bishop of Zanzibar from 1874 to 1882 and funded by the Universities' Mission in Central Africa. The altar stands on the same spot as the "whipping tree", to which slaves were probably tied while being sold. The small wooden crucifix to the left of the altar is made from a tree in the village of Chitambo, where David Livingstone died and his heart was buried. There is also a stained-glass window dedicated to Livingstone, whose influence in abolishing the slave trade has earned him a special place in the hearts of the Zanzibari people. Other windows are dedicated to African saints. The mosaics on the altar were donated by Caroline Thackeray *(see page 261)*.

Wriggle down through the alleys behind the cathedral to visit the **Hamamni Baths O**, the city's first public baths, commissioned by Sultan Barghash and designed by Persian architect Haju Ghulamhusain, who was also responsible for the Kidichi Baths *(see page 260)*. Sultan Barghash (1870–88) was a great innovator and builder, responsible for the House of Wonders, for bringing piped clean water to all parts of the city, and for buying Zanzibar its own fleet of steamships, which were used during the Haj to carry the local faithful to Mecca, free of charge. In between, the money rolled in from their cargo routes.

Women's hands and feet are traditionally painted with intricate henna patterns for celebrations.

The British influence

Alternatively, carry on south down Creek Road and turn right onto Museum Road to visit the now defunct **Peace Museum P**, built as a World War I memorial and modelled (in miniature) on the Ayghia Sophia in Istanbul. The architect, John Sinclair, worked in Zanzibar for 27 years and is responsible for many of the civic buildings of the British era.

This interesting but decaying building was once home to an intriguing collection of vintage photographs, documents and other assorted memorabilia, including Livingstone's medical bag. However, these have now been moved to the House of Wonders.

Now walk down Museum Road. At the end, turn right onto Kaunda Road, the main road back to the town centre. On your right, the **Victoria Gardens Q** were created by Sultan Barghash for his harem, but given to the people by Sultan Seyyid Houmoud. Sir John Kirk *(see page 260)* transformed them into a botanical garden. At the centre, **Victoria Hall**, built over the harem baths, was the seat of the pre-independence Legislative Council. Near by, look out for the green octagonal **milestone** showing distances all over the island – and to London (12,978 km/8,064 miles, via the Suez Canal).

Opposite is the **State House R** (no photographs allowed), now the official residence of the President of Zanzibar, but built in 1903 as the British Residency. Both this and the **High Court**, a little further along on the left, were built by John Sinclair. Just at the turning of Kenyatta Road and Shangani Street, an insignificant house on the right was once home to Zanzibar's most famous modern citizen, the late rock

BELOW: Zanzibar is a Muslim society, so dress modestly.

Clove buds on trees are picked by hand – a task involving a dangerous climb of over 6 metres (20 ft) – and dried on mats in the sun, perfuming the air.

BELOW: Maruhabi Palace, built by Sultan Barghash for his harem.

idol Freddie Mercury, lead singer of Queen, who was born here in 1946 as Farouk Bulsara, son of a local accountant. His family came from Persia, via India. Turn down Shangani Street and, two blocks on, the **Africa House** ⓢ was once the British Club. It is now a restaurant and bar, and still has one of the best sea views in the city from its airy balcony. Follow the road round and it passes two mansions, carefully restored into fine hotels, the **Serena Inn** and **Tembo Hotel**. Just before you reach the archway underneath the orphanage *(see page 252)*, is a mansion that served as the **British Consulate** from 1841 to 1874. This was base camp for many of Africa's most famous expeditions, with Speke, Burton, Grant and Stanley all staying here; David Livingstone's body lay here for five days in 1874. After his death in Chitambo, his body was dried and his servants carried it for four months back to the coast and across to Zanzibar, from where it was sent back to England for final burial.

Around Unguja Island

It is possible to reach every part of Unguja Island on a day trip from Stone Town, but few choose to do so, preferring to match the historic charms of the city with the glories of the beaches. However, some excursions are best done before you leave the city. There are few decent roads on the island, and you may well find yourself having to come back into town anyway.

Just offshore are several small islands. **Changuu Island** ❷, also known as Prison Island, was originally used as a lock-up for disobedient slaves by its Arab owner. It was bought in 1873 by General William Lloyd Matthews, a British officer who became Commander-in-Chief of Sultan Barghash's army, and specifically charged with stopping the smuggling of slaves. Matthews

built a house here, but in 1893 it became a real prison, while in the 1920s it was used as a quarantine centre for immigrants from India.

The luxurious Changuu Private Island Paradise Resort (www.eihr.com/changuu) now occupies part of the island, but it is still possible to visit the colony of giant tortoises, imported from the Seychelles in the 18th century. This is one of Zanzibar's most popular excursions. Nearby **Chapwani (Grave) Island ❸** has a British cemetery dating back to 1879 and a pleasant swimming beach. **Bawe Island ❹** is quiet, completely uninhabited and fringed by good swimming and snorkelling spots. Either take a guided tour or hire a boat for the day from the dhow harbour.

The northern suburbs

About 2 km (1 mile) north of Stone Town, look for a run-down mansion on the right. The **Livingstone House** (Bububu Road; tel: 024-223 3485) is now officially, but ineffectively, the city tourist office. However, it has a more illustrious past. Built in 1860 for Sultan Majid, it was used, like the British Consulate, by various explorers as a base camp, including Burton, Speke, Stanley and Livingstone; the latter lived here while preparing for his last big expedition in 1866.

A kilometre on, a small turning on the left leads to the **Maruhabi Palace ❺** (open access; entrance charge), built by Sultan Barghash in 1882 as the home of his one official wife and 99 concubines. The walled complex, supposedly modelled on English country houses seen by the Sultan during his visit to Europe in 1875, was approached by an avenue of stately mango trees leading to a huge lily pond. Inside were several bathhouses, while stairs of black-and-white marble led to a broad balcony supported on giant pillars. Maruhabi was destroyed by fire in 1899, but is still Zanzibar's most charming and atmospheric ruin.

The **Mtoni Palace ❻** is easy to miss. A short way north of Maruhabi, look for the signpost to Mtoni Marine, a laid-back beach bar and pizza place that is popular with expats. The ruins are on the beach near by. This was the first of the Omani royal palaces, built by Seyyid Said, the Sultan who moved the imperial capital from Muscat to Zanzibar in 1840. It was a typical Omani complex, with a number of low, flat-roofed buildings housing up to 1,000 people, surrounding a large pool and courtyard. At one end stood a conical wooden tower, from where the Sultan could survey his fleet. Princess Salme grew up here and describes it in detail in her memoirs (*see page 252*). All that now remain are the main walls and the roof.

The spice tour

So popular it is almost compulsory, the spice tour is a highlight of most trips to Zanzibar, and less overtly touristy than it may seem from the number of options available. Either take one of the many scheduled tours, or hire a private guide if you prefer to do things at your own pace. Don't try to do it without a guide. Much of the island is covered in spices, but unless

Maps on pages 250 & 252

BELOW: outside the city, houses are poor, commonly made of mud or coral rag and thatch.

Sir John Kirk first came to Africa as the medical doctor and botanist attached to David Livingstone's 1858–59 expedition. He created the core collection of flora of East Africa and became a leading opponent of slavery; he was also Surgeon General and British Vice-Consul in Zanzibar, eventually leaving the area in 1877.

BELOW: a Kirk's red colobus monkey, found only in Zanzibar's few remaining forests.

you know what you are looking for, you won't know they are there. The massive clove trees look like indigenous forest, henna like scrubby bush and lemon grass – like grass. Most of the spices are grown around people's houses and not in the sort of serried rows that the word "plantation" might conjure up. Head north from Zanzibar Town for about 10 km (6 miles) to **Bububu** 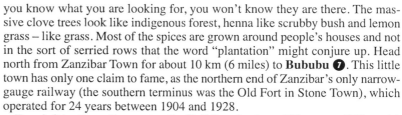. This little town has only one claim to fame, as the northern end of Zanzibar's only narrow-gauge railway (the southern terminus was the Old Fort in Stone Town), which operated for 24 years between 1904 and 1928.

Turn left by the police station for **Fuji Beach**, about 500 metres (550 yards) from the main road and the nearest good swimming beach to Stone Town. Turn right, and after about 2 km (1 mile) you reach the row of spice stalls which mark the first stop on the spice tour. Take plenty of money for shopping; prices are significantly lower than in town, and the variety of spices on sale, from vanilla pods to cinnamon sticks and weird and wonderful blends for use in cooking, will be difficult to resist. Some of the plants, such as pineapple or ginger, are relatively easily recognised, but even the most insignificant-looking bush may prove to be a source of lipstick or the local headache cure. It would be easy to spend the whole day here. However, there are usually a couple of other stops to look at fruit and nut plantations and local sights of interest.

About 3 km (2 miles) from the turn-off, the **Kidichi Baths** (open access; entrance charge) were built in 1850 by Sultan Seyyid Said for his Persian wife, Binte Irich Mirza (also called Sherezade). Each of the royal plantations had baths, so that visitors could refresh themselves after a hot, dusty journey. These are the finest and most complete baths surviving on the island, with much of their elegant Persian-style stucco still intact. About 3 km (2 miles) further on, the **Kizimbani Baths** were built by the 19th-century merchant Saleh bin Haramil, the first man to plant cloves on the island.

Mangapwani Beach is about 11 km (7 miles) north of Bububu, just off the main road. Many of the spice tours choose to make a day of it and bring their clients here for lunch at the open-air restaurant, run as a satellite of the Serena Inn in Stone Town, followed by an afternoon on the beach.

Those who still have the energy for sightseeing should visit the coral cavern, near the sea, and the slave chamber, about 2 km (1 mile) further north. The official abolition of the slave trade in 1873 drove business underground. A local slaver, Mohammed bin Nassor al-Alwi, built these illegal holding pens and auction rooms, away from prying city eyes.

The southern suburbs

About 7 km (4 miles) south of Zanzibar Town, near the airport, **Mbweni** is now the city's most exclusive residential suburb, full of grand mansions and millionaires and home to Zanzibar President Amani Karume. First settled by the Arabs in the 7th century, the Persians arrived in the 12th century and the Portuguese in the 16th and 17th. In 1871, Bishop Tozer bought the large house of a wealthy Arab fam-

ily on behalf of the Universities' Mission to Central Africa, to set up an Anglican Mission and village for freed slaves.

The 60-hectare (150-acre) settlement included schools, houses, workshops, sugar, coconut and maize plantations, and had a population of around 250. The original house, with three additional wings added, was turned into St Mary's School for Girls, with between 60 and 85 pupils at any one time. They were taught a mix of academic, religious and practical skills, while less academic girls were given industrial skills that would ensure their future survival.

Caroline Thackeray (the cousin of William Makepeace Thackeray, author of *Vanity Fair*) arrived in 1877, remaining as headmistress for 25 years. She stayed on the island until she died in 1926 at the age of 83, and is buried in the neighbouring oriental-looking **St John's Church**, built in 1874 by Bishop Tozer's successor, Bishop Steere, who also built the Anglican Cathedral in Stone Town *(see page 255)*.

Although some descendants of the original freed slaves still live in the area, the school eventually closed in 1920 and the buildings sank into ruins, which now stand in the grounds of the Mbweni Ruins Hotel. The owners are gradually restoring them to create a museum, library, conference centre and other hotel facilities.

Meanwhile, they welcome visitors both to the ruins and their fine botanical garden, containing over 150 species of palm and over 500 species of indigenous and exotic plants. It is based on the magnificent botanical garden created by Sir John Kirk on land adjacent to the mission, sadly now overgrown and in private hands, so not open to the public. The wide range of foliage and the adjacent shoreline attract over 60 species of bird.

Map on page 250

BELOW: dhow building is an ancient yet still flourishing craft on the islands.

UNDER THREAT

First identified and catalogued by Sir John Kirk *(see margin opposite)*, the Kirk's red colobus is one of Africa's prettiest primates, with its vivid chestnut coat, white shirtfront, bushy tail and Victorian whiskers. It is also one of the rarest, found only in Zanzibar and isolated from the mainstream of evolution for the past 10–15,000 years. Unlike most other monkeys, Kirk's red colobus has only four elongated fingers and no thumb. Uniquely among primates, it has four stomachs, designed for digesting the tough leaves and unripe fruit on which it lives. It is unable to digest the sugars in ripe fruit.

Colobus are very social creatures, living in forested areas in large troops of 30–50, led by one to four adult males. They live for about 20 years, reaching sexual maturity at around five or six. Gestation takes six months, and females produce only one baby every two years.

Their Swahili name, *"kima punju"*, means "poison monkey", and the monkeys are associated with evil – which doesn't help their chances of survival.

There are currently fewer than 2,500 known to exist, of which about half live in the Jozani Forest. Colobus are susceptible to human diseases, so anyone who has a cold is asked not to visit them.

The world's largest living land crab, the rare Chumbe Island coconut crab, can climb palms and crack a coconut with its claws.

BELOW:
Chumbe Island
resort from the air.

Chumbe Island

The Mbweni Ruins Hotel is also where you catch the boat across to tiny **Chumbe Island** ⓬, about 8 km (5 miles) offshore. Only about 3 km (2 miles) long and 1.3 km (¾ mile) wide, Chumbe is Tanzania's first privately run marine park, guarding a 1.1-km (½-mile) long reef containing an extraordinary 200 species of coral and 400 species of fish. Until the building of the eco-lodge which manages the reserve, the only buildings on the island were a ruined mosque and the lighthouse. The lodge is run on strict ecological principles, and the design of the basket-weave chalets is one of the most fascinating aspects of a visit. Tours include snorkelling, beach and forest walks, all led by trained naturalists. Look out for giant fossil clam shells and, more alarmingly, giant live coconut crabs. The only way to visit is as a guest of the lodge. It is not cheap, but profits go to the upkeep of the reserve and a strong education and research programme, which includes free visits for local schoolchildren.

Jozani Forest

To reach the south and east of the island, take the main road east from Stone Town. About 21 km (13 miles) from town, a small turning on the right signposts **Unguja Ukuu** ⓭, the oldest known settlement on the island, dating to the 8th century AD, and thought to have been founded by Swahili people fleeing from violence on the mainland. It was abandoned again in the 10th century. Only attempt to go there if you have plenty of time. The site is about 6 km (4 miles) from the main road, but it seems far longer. The road winds through the villages, within touching distance of doors, gradually getting smaller until it virtually disappears. Once you get there, all you will find are a few bits of wall.

Back on the main road, the **Jozani-Chwaka Bay National Park** ⓮ (daily 7.30am–5pm; forest paths closed in the rainy season; entrance charge) is a further 11 km (6 miles) on. Although it is usually billed as the last remnant of indigenous forest on the island, once there, you discover that while some of it is original, much of it has actually been replanted – the land was a working timber plantation in the 1930s and 1940s. However, it doesn't really matter; it is a magical place. The replanting has been sympathetic, and it is now a 2,512-hectare (6,207-acre) nature reserve, part of the larger Jozani-Chwaka Conservation Area, under consideration for Unesco World Heritage listing.

There is an excellent interpretation centre next to the car park, from where guides lead forest walks. In addition to the many trees, climbers and other plants, wildlife includes around 50 species of brightly coloured butterflies, over 40 species of bird, including the rare but spectacular Zanzibar Fischer's turacco, Sykes (blue) monkeys, and small antelope such as the endangered Aders' duiker and suni. However, the undoubted stars of the show are the red colobus monkeys, which obligingly hang around in bright sunlight near the car park for maximum photographic impact. On the far side of the road, a 1-km (½-mile) dirt track leads down to a mangrove swamp, laid out with boardwalks.

Just before you reach Jozani-Chwaka Bay National Park, you will find the **Zanzibar Butterfly Centre** ⓯ (ZBC; daily 9am–5pm; entrance charge). The sanctuary includes a butterfly display and guided tours of the botanical garden, and aims to encourage the conservation and proliferation of butterfly species indigenous to the area and also protect the local environment. The ZBC works closely with the national park and NGOs to assist local development projects, particularly those that are involved in conservation and poverty alleviation.

Map on page 250

BELOW: meeting the local children is always a pleasure.

If swimming with the dolphins, enter the water quietly, stay close to the boat and let them approach you. Slapping the water with their tails is a sign of distress and a signal for you to leave them in peace.

BELOW: at low tide, the local women flock to Makunduchi beach to dig out octopus and crabs, harvest seaweed and husk coconuts.

Zala Park

The main road to the south of the island branches off just after Jozani Forest. The BP petrol station at the crossroads is the last you will meet if heading south or east, so take advantage of it. A couple of kilometres south of the crossroads, on the right, look out for the easily missed sign for **Zala Park** ⑯ (daily 8.30am–5pm; donations), a scruffy-looking but fascinating community project started by a local teacher with a passion for science and biology. His main aim is to educate Zanzibari children about the island's wildlife and ecology, and to that end he has gathered a small collection of animals that are either endangered, seen as food, or feared through superstition. Among them are some tiny suni antelope (your best chance to see these shy forest dwellers); tortoises and terrapins; several types of snake; chameleons, thought by locals to presage death if they drop on your head; land crabs, said to bring divorce with them into a house; and the plated lizard, whose bite can supposedly only be cured by sleeping with your sister! There is also a nature trail through the forest to a mangrove pool and a tour of the local village, which now owns the park.

Dolphins

Head south and turn right at the T-junction for **Kizimkazi** ⑰ in the southwestern corner of the island, where children mob the tourists asking for pens, selling shells and trying to look winsome enough for handouts. They are undeniably cute, but it is sad to see them developing the pattern of expectation that is so far refreshingly absent elsewhere on the island. Their efforts are directed at the many tour groups now visiting the village to go **dolphin-watching**. The coast around here has several caves that are favourite dolphin calving grounds,

and some 100 bottlenose and 50 humpback dolphins have taken up permanent residence. Trips run year-round and visitors have an excellent chance of sighting pods of 20–30 animals.

There may be an opportunity to swim with the dolphins before the boats move to a nearby coral reef for snorkelling. These trips are very cheap if you hire your own boat locally; the price is doubled if you go on an organised excursion, although transport to Kizimkazi and lunch at one of the two simple restaurants which flank the bay will be thrown in. Some of these tours have a reputation for harassing the dolphins, so choose carefully. The town is also home to what is technically the oldest mosque on the island still in use. It was originally founded in 1107 by Sheikh Abu Mussa Al-Hassan bin Mohammed, but was virtually rebuilt in 1770. Inscriptions on either side of the mihrab mark the two dates.

Among the surrounding graves are several said to belong to relatives of the Prophet, including the one-handed Sheikh Omar Ali and the one-legged Sayyid Abdallah Said bin Sharif. The mosque is extremely plain, looking more like a barn from the outside. Non-Muslims should only enter if invited.

Return to the T-junction and take the other fork for **Makunduchi** ⓲, in the far southeastern corner of the island. This is one of the few major coastal villages that is virtually untouched by tourism, and a wonderful place to experience true Zanzibari culture, with the women wading the shore, digging for crabs and octopus or using the coral rocks to husk coconuts. Along the roads you will see lines of women with bundles of wood on their heads, while the smaller side roads through the village offer an intimate glimpse of daily life in the small palm-thatched houses, many with surprisingly elegant carved doorways.

In July, during the Shirazi New Year, Makunduchi is the site of Zanzibar's most famous – and strangest – festival, **Mwaka Kogwa**, when the local men challenge past foes with banana leaves. The contestants then flail one another until hopefully they make amends. Meanwhile, the townswomen dance around the banana-beating men singing songs. A house of spirits is constructed and set on fire to burn away the misery of the previous year. The evening sees fewer banana beatings and plenty of drinking and dancing with new-found friends.

The road up the east coast is extremely poor, and it is better to retrace your route back through Jozani.

The southeast coast

As you head across to the eastern half of the island, the landscape changes dramatically from the lush farm- and woodlands of the west to dry, scrubby grassland that clings precariously to the coral rock. However, this is also where you will find all the best beaches – mile upon mile of powder-soft, snow-white sand, the shallow shelving water an almost surreally bright turquoise. Offshore, breaking waves mark the line of the coral reef, beyond which the water changes to a rich indigo. If you are very lucky and have a good pair of binoculars, you can watch the humpback whales spouting and breaching as they migrate.

Only one thing potentially mars the perfection – from mid-November through to mid-February, the

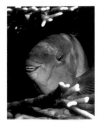

Map on page 250

Thank the humble parrot fish for the magnificent sand. It chews up coral and expels it as a fine white powder.

BELOW: Matemwe Beach is one of the finest on Unguja island.

TIP

While the British think of Zanzibar as a luxury holiday, the Italians regard it as a mass-market destination, and the island has several large, noisy young Italian resorts. If you are after peace and quiet, you need to check not only your own hotel, but also its neighbours.

prevailing winds can wash ashore huge quantities of sludgy brown seaweed, which disappears again with the start of the rainy season. Inevitably, anywhere this idyllic is resort-land, lined for much of its length by hotels to suit a variety of budgets, from small backpacker guesthouses to upmarket hotels. Most offer, or will organise, tours to Stone Town and the spice plantations, snorkelling, diving and a range of watersports. The main road east from Jozani stops at the village of **Paje** ⑲, from where a slow, bumpy, crater-filled dirt road leads north and south along the coast. It is only about 12 km (7 miles) from Paje to the tip of **Ras Michamvi**, but it takes over an hour to drive. Along the way, you pass a wide variety of resorts, including that famous honeymoon hotspot, **Breezes Beach Club**.

The east coast

There are no connecting roads between the southeast coast and the east coast, so once again, head back towards Stone Town, from where a road leads due east as far as **Chwaka** ⑳, a large attractive fishing village and former slaving town, with a lively fish market and one or two small guesthouses. Along the way, look out for the **Dunga Ruins** ㉑ (daily 8am–6pm; entrance charge), signposted off the road near Dunga village, 14 km (9 miles) east of Stone Town. Built by the Swahili *Mwinyi Mkuu*, King Mohammed, in 1846–56, the still imposing walls are persistently rumoured to have had live slaves buried in the foundations, and human blood used to mix the mortar.

About 8 km (5 miles) further on, near Jendele village, is the **Ufufuma Forest Habitat** ㉒ (organise a guide in Jendele; entrance charge), a tiny remnant of indigenous forest with a good variety of birds and small animals, including

BELOW: deserted beach along the east coast.

Sykes and red colobus monkeys. Also ask your guide to take you to the Shetani spirit caves, used by traditional healers.

The so-called road north along the coast from here is nigh on impassable, so return to Stone Town again and head north on the Bububu road. At **Selem**, the main road forks inland through **Mahonda** from where there is a turning east to **Kinyasini** and further on to **Kiwengwa 23**, a tiny village surrounded by a clump of resorts, including the **Bluebay Beach Resort**.

To reach the more northerly resorts, head north at Kinyasini to **Mkwajuni**, where a road to the east connects with the sandy track leading to **Matemwe 24**; this is perhaps the most enchanting of all the beaches on the Unguja coast, its white sand framed by jagged coral rocks, for all the world like mini-Himalayas. Seaweed-drying frames are strung between whispering coconut palms, and children play happily between the blindingly white coral rag houses and the outriggers of the beached canoes. There are several places to stay near by, of which the most charming are the laid-back **Matemwe Bungalows** and the cheaper Matemwe Beach Village.

About 5 km (3 miles) offshore, **Mnemba Island 25**, run as a private marine sanctuary by luxury lodge operators CC Africa, is a picture-perfect tropical island with superb diving and snorkelling *(see page 270)*.

The north coast

At the far northern tip of Zanzibar Island, **Nungwi 26** and **Kendwa** feel like real backpacker destinations, with small guesthouses scattered amongst the villagers' homes. Foreign children play happily alongside the locals, while the beach rings to the sound of sawing and the thunk of hammer on wood as the dhow-builders work in the shade of the coconut palms. To get there, head north

Map on page 250

BELOW: Mkoani town, Pemba, from the air.

In close-up, coral forms a superb range of geometric patterns.

on the main road from Mkwajuni. There are just two large resorts in the area, **Ras Nungwi** and **La Gemma Dell'Est**. The only "sight" is the **Mnarani turtle aquarium**, in Nungwi, with green, loggerhead and leatherbacks on show in a natural lagoon.

Pemba

Pemba, 80 km (50 miles) northeast of Unguja, is the place for those looking to get away from it all. For the moment, the island has only a couple of small upmarket hotels and a handful of guesthouses catering to hard-core dive enthusiasts. Savour it while you can.

Physically, the island is built of rock, not coral, so is far hillier and more densely forested than Unguja, with peaks rising to 1,000 metres (3,280 ft). It is also much poorer: its people survive on a meagre diet of cassava, rice, fish, tomatoes and onions and earn their living almost entirely on farming and fishing. Around 80 percent of Tanzania's cloves are grown here; the roads are lined by drying mats, and the air is heavily scented with their delicious aroma.

Many people work far away, in Dar or even Oman, while back at home society is polarised, with the north largely Arab and the south mainly African. Politically, the island is extremely active – many of the riots surrounding recent elections happened here, and there is a strong movement to disassociate from the mainland. However, within the local community Islam and Christianity live comfortably side by side, also rubbing along astonishingly well with the island's third great tradition. Pemba is reputed to be one of the great witchcraft centres of the world. Few will talk about it, but the tradition lives on, with voodoo practitioners visiting from as far afield as West Africa and South America.

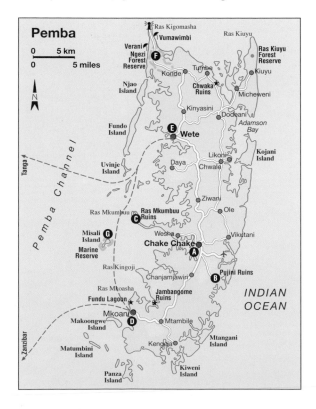

Pemba

0   5 km
0   5 miles

Chake Chake

There really is very little for visitors to see here. The capital and home of the airport is **Chake Chake A**, roughly halfway up the island, on the west coast. It is as old as Stone Town, but remained a backwater under the Omanis and has few historic buildings, other than a less than exciting fort. However, it is a pleasant place, with a lively market, and there are several ruins close to the town.

The **Pujini Ruins B**, 10 km (6 miles) to the southeast, consist of a few scattered remains of a 14th-century town, including part of the ramparts, a few houses and a mosque, purportedly built by a local tyrant, Mohammed bin Abdul Rahman, known as the *Mkame Ndume* (Milker of Men) because of his harsh treatment of his subjects.

At the 11th-century Swahili city of **Ras Mkumbuu C**, 20 km (12 miles) west, most easily reached by boat, are a mosque, some houses and pillar tombs. This was one of the most important towns in East Africa in its heyday.

To the south and north

Mkoani ⓓ, 38 km (24 miles) south of Chake Chake, is the island's main ferry port. Across the bay, reached by boat, the remote and exclusive **Fundu Lagoon** is set on the picture-perfect white sand of Wambaa Beach.

Wete ⓔ, 30 km (19 miles) north of Chake Chake, has some fine colonial architecture, but is most interesting during the clove season, when the local port is busy with big ocean-going dhows.

Head north for a further 20 km (12 miles) to the **Kigomasha Peninsula**, to find Pemba's finest onshore attraction, the **Ngezi Forest Reserve ⓕ** (daily 8am–4pm; entrance charge). There is a network of footpaths across the reserve, a 1,500-hectare (3,700-acre) remnant of primeval rainforest, mangrove swamp and coral scrub, offering the opportunity to see a fascinating variety of endemic species, including the Pemba green pigeon and Pemba flying fox (a large fruit-eating bat). There are also a couple of fine beaches, at **Vumawimbi**, on the east coast and **Verani** on the west coast.

The main reasons people come here are offshore. Much of the coast is lined by mangrove swamps, with relatively few sandy beaches to rival Zanzibar. However, the island is virtually surrounded by magnificent coral reefs which provide some of the finest dive sites in Africa. **Misali Island ⓖ**, off the west coast, easily reached from Chake Chake or Mkoani, is a tiny place (1 km by 500 metres/1,100 by 550 yards), ringed by coral and protected as a marine reserve. It has superb diving and snorkelling *(see page 271)*, while onshore are fine beaches, some set aside as turtle breeding grounds, and forest and mangrove swamps which support a rich array of bird life. Captain Kidd is rumoured to have used it as a hideout in the 17th century. ❑

Map on page 268

BELOW: cloves drying in the sun. In season, Pemba's air smells delicious.

Coral Diving

Before your depth gauge even starts to register, you feel the current pulling you towards the mainland. Descend to 25 metres (82 ft), adjust your buoyancy and you're off, sweeping along the huge reef wall with the deep blue of the open ocean on your left. Navigating video-game style, you steer around the obstacles where the reef juts out, spot the eagle rays and turtles as they glide the other way, take time to inspect the caves and holes with their morays and lion fish, before being spat out into the washing machine which spins you around as you try to take hold for some decompression time. This is Deep Freeze, drift diving at its best, catching the incoming tide through the gap between Uvinje and Fundo Islands on the west coast of Pemba.

On a good day you can see the sandy ocean floor 70 metres (230 ft) below. The Zanzibar archipelago and Mafia Island, to the south, have an excellent combination of shallow water reefs for less experienced divers

and high walls and deep channels for the more adventurous. Both the soft and hard corals are in relatively prime condition, despite El Niño, and the variety of reef fish and larger pelagics is as good as anywhere. You won't encounter as many of the glorious colours of the Red Sea or the Barrier Reef, but you won't find hordes of other dive boats either. In Pemba and Mafia you will have the site to yourselves. You won't find many sharks, but large rays, turtles, whale sharks and whales are wonderful compensations.

Zanzibar Island (Unguja) is the largest of the islands but has the least impressive diving. Two main areas are worth consideration. There are four or five smallish reefs about 30 minutes from Stone Town where the coral is in good condition but marine life is limited. With nothing deeper than 20 metres (66 ft) and often nothing bigger than a parrot fish, they are fine for a warm-up dive. The highlight is a wreck, thought to be the *Pegasus*, which lies 40 metres (131 ft) down, a 15-minute speed-boat ride from town. No coral has developed, but there are huge shoals of barracuda and jacks, and what remains of the deck is littered with lion fish. Another recommended site is the Boribu reef, at 15 metres (49 ft).

Mnemba Island, some 5 km (3 miles) off the northeast coast, near Matemwe, offers enough variety for two to three good days. The reef has a range of good inner and outer wall dives, and some beautiful coral gardens. The best diving is on the south side, where strong currents mean excellent drift dives. The hard corals are in excellent condition, and you will find honeycomb, pillar and brain, clouded with shoals of sergeant fish, fusiliers and wrasse. The island is now a marine sanctuary. Good sites include Kichwani (20 metres/66 ft), Aquarium (20 metres/66 ft) and Big Wall (25 metres/82 ft). The highlight of the year is when the migrating whale sharks stop over in about March. They range in size from 5 to 12 metres (16–39 ft), and there is nothing more graceful or harmless in the oceans.

Pemba has more interesting, more varied and more spectacular diving than anywhere else in East Africa. The coastline is dotted with

LEFT: photographing a giant grouper; **RIGHT:** a red snapper drifts past a coral wall; **FAR RIGHT:** fine coral, rich fish life and warm Indian Ocean water.

tiny, uninhabited islands surrounded by almost unlimited dive sites, while on the far side, the 800-metre (2,620-ft) deep Pemba channel provides world-class deep-sea fishing. There is excellent drift diving along the big walls, and some huge independent bommies teeming with reef fish. **Njao Gap** in the north hosts table-top coral, sea whips and gorgonian sea fans with giant groupers, Napoleon wrasse, titan triggerfish and regular darting pelagics wahoo, jacks and giant trevally. In the south, **Misali Island** is the coral jewel in the crown, with shallow water reefs in pristine condition so even snorkellers can indulge. Recommended sites include Manta Point (30 metres/100 ft), Murray's Wall (35 metres/115 ft), Deep Freeze (40 metres/130 ft), Trigger Corner (25 metres/80 ft) and Chillies Wall (35 metres/115 ft).

Live-aboard enthusiasts should take a trip down the east coast with its strong currents, large pelagics, fantastic soft corals and the likelihood of large shoals of hammerhead sharks. At the right times of year, you can encounter schools of pilot whales and the awesome humpbacks.

Mafia Island, 150 km (90 miles) south of Zanzibar, has some sites that rank alongside those on Pemba. Most of the diving is focused around Chole Bay, and from September to March it is possible to dive the walls outside the reef that protects the bay. There are three types of dive sites here. The sloping reefs (12–25 metres/39–82 ft) are home to small coral bommies, huge moray eels, ribbontail rays, nesting turtles and guitar sharks. The coral walls stretch down 10–25 metres (33–82 ft), with visibility around 30 metres (98 ft), and caves, caverns and gullies to explore. Here you will encounter dolphins, huge groupers defending their caverns, large turtles, reef rays and the occasional bull shark.

The coral gardens, at a maximum of 20 metres (66 ft), provide the best hard corals in East Africa, with brain and stag horn in abundance, and crocodile fish, turtles and stripe barracuda among the colourful reef fish. Recommended sites include Kinasi pass (24 metres/79 ft inside reef), Mlila (23 metres/75 ft outside), Juwani North (28 metres/92 ft outside) and Milimani (18 metres/59 ft inside).❑

INSIGHT GUIDES

TRAVEL TIPS

TRAVEL TIPS

T RANSPORT

GETTING THERE AND GETTING AROUND

GETTING THERE

By Air

Tanzania and Zanzibar are well served by international airlines. The points of entry are Dar es Salaam, Kilimanjaro and Zanzibar international airports.

From Europe: major international airlines flying to Dar es Salaam include KLM (via Amsterdam and Nairobi), Ethiopian Airlines (via Addis Ababa), Swiss (via Zurich), SAA (from Johannesburg) and British Airways (direct from London). Others include Emirates, Kenya Airways, Yemen Airways, Egypt Air and Air India.

Zanzibar is served by Kenya Airlines (from Nairobi), Ethiopian Airlines, South African Airlines and Air Tanzania.

Kilimanjaro International is also served by many airlines, including Air Tanzania, Ethiopian and KLM.

From North America: there are very few direct flights, so it is usually necessary to fly via Europe; the cheapest option is via London.

Airports

Dar es Salaam
Located 15 km (8 miles) west of the city, the airport is well staffed, with a foreign exchange bureau, ATMs, wheelchair facilities, many taxi stands and hotel information. Flight information is more difficult to come by. The best option is to contact the airline directly. Otherwise, contact the airport on 022-284 4324.

Zanzibar
The airport, located 5 km (3 miles) south of Stone Town, has money-changing facilities and is well served by taxis and local buses (dala dalas).

Taxis cost TSh10–12,000, much more than the buses, but are worth the price as Stone Town is very easy to get lost in. If you've prebooked at a reputable hotel or one of the beach resorts, transfers should be provided.

Kilimanjaro
Kilimanjaro International is roughly 40 km (24 miles) east of Arusha, halfway to Moshi. Taxis are available, and some airlines run a hotel shuttle service. Most safari companies organise pick-ups and drop-offs.

International Airline Offices

Dar es Salaam
Air India
Cnr Bibi Titi Street/AH Mwinyi Road
Opposite Peugeot House
Tel: 022-215 2642
www.airindia.com
Air Malawi
Tel: 022-212 7746/2043
www.airmalawi.com
Air Tanzania
ATC House
Ohio Street
Tel: 022-211 7500
www.airtanzania.com
Air Zimbabwe
Raha Towers Building
Maktaba Street
Tel: 022-212 3526
www.airzimbabwe.com
British Airways
Royal Palm Hotel
Ohio Street
Tel: 022-211 3820/2
www.ba.com
Emirates Airlines
Haidery Plaza ,
Ali Hassan Mwinyi Road
Tel: 022-211 6100/2/3
www.emirates.com
Ethiopian Airlines
TDFL Building
Cnr Ohio Street/AH Mwinyi Road

Tel: 022-211 7063–5
www.flyethiopian.com
Kenya Airways
Peugeot House
Cnr Bibi Titi/AH Mwinyi Road
Tel: 022-211 9376–7
www.kenya-airways.com
KLM
Peugeot House
Bibi Titi/AH Mwinyi Road
Tel: 022-211 3336
www.klm.com
Precision Air
NIC Building
Cnr Samora Avenue/Pemba Road
Tel: 022-213 0800
Dar es Salaam International Airport
Tel: 022-284 3547
www.precisionairtz.com
Qatar Airways
Tel: 022-284 2675
www.qatarairways.com
South African Airlines
Raha Towers Building
Maktaba Street
PO Box 5182
Tel: 022-211 7044–7
Fax: 022-211 0205
www.flysaa.com
Swiss
Luther House
Sokoine Drive
Tel: 022-211 8870–2
www.swiss.com

Arusha
Air Excel
Subzali Building, Suite 2
Goliondoi Road
Tel/fax: 027-254 8429/
0732-102 546
www.airexcelonline.com
Air Tanzania
Boma Road
Tel: 027-250 3201
Ethiopian Airlines
Boma Road
Tel: 027-250 6167/4231

KLM
New Safari Hotel Building
Boma Road
Tel: 027-250 6063
Kilimanjaro Airport
Tel: 027-255 4252

Air Charter Companies
Air Charter Services
PO Box 21236
Dar es Salaam
Tel: 022-37013/15/17
Northern Air
PO Box 2782, Arusha
Tel: 027-250 8059
Email: northernair@habari.co.tz
Tanzanair
Royal Palm Hotel
PO Box 364
Dar es Salaam
Tel: 022-284 3131/3
Email: info@tanzanair.com
Coastal, **Precision**, **Regional Airlines**
and **ZanAir** all handle charter
services as well as scheduled flights.
For details, *see pages 277–8*.

By Rail

Though a major shipping centre, the
passenger trade in Zanzibar and
Tanzania consists mainly of internal
ferries. Some cruising companies
have discovered the beauty of a
cruise here, including Hayes
and Jarvis (www.hayesandjarvis.co.uk)
and African Safari Club
(www.africansafariclub.com)

By Rail

The TAZARA rail line, originating in
Zambia, is the only passenger train
that crosses the borders of Tanzania
(see page 163). The train departs
Kapiri Mposhi, north of Lusaka, if all
is going well, on Tuesday and Friday,
taking just over 36 hours to reach
Dar es Salaam.
This is a beautiful journey,
passing through the Selous
Reserve and offering the
opportunity to see many animals
near the tracks. The first-class
sleeper is very reasonably priced.
However, the service is somewhat
erratic and there are often long
delays en route.
   It is best to book in person at
Kapiri Mposhi (New) Station, and
double-check exact departure times
and whether food and drinks will be
available on board the train.
   On a far more luxurious note,
Rovos Rail runs an all-inclusive,
annual rail tour originating in Cape
Town and utilising the same railway
track from Zambia to Dar es
Salaam. See www.rovos.co.za for more
details.

Bus/Coach

It is possible to travel by bus from
neighbouring countries into Tanzania,
and the costs are a fraction of the air
fare. However, be warned that a
journey on bumpy African roads can
mean many hours of discomfort, not
to mention a few days' recovery time.
Once you arrive at Ubungo bus
terminal in Dar es Salaam, you must
keep your wits about you:
pickpockets are rife and you risk
being ripped off by unscrupulous taxi
drivers *(see also page 279)*. For
these reasons we recommend taking
regional flights, but for intrepid
travellers, here is the bus/coach
information.
   From Kenya: the main border town
between Kenya and Tanzania is
Namanga, located about halfway
between Nairobi and Arusha. Regular
shuttle buses connect the two cities
and take 4–6 hours. There is also
the option of going on to Moshi. Daily
coaches also travel between Nairobi
and Mombasa to Arusha and Dar es
Salaam. The safest are Scandinavian
Express. Public buses and *dala dalas*
are also an option from the quieter
border posts of Horoho, Taveta,
Illassit, Bologonya, and Sirari.
   From Malawi: travellers entering
Tanzania from Malawi must pass over
the Songwe River bridge southeast of
Mbeya. Bus services between
Lilongwe and Dar es Salaam, and
Lilongwe, Mzuzu and Mbeya depart
several times each week. Again,
Scandinavian Express is the best bus
service, taking just over 30 hours to
reach Dar from Lilongwe.
   From Mozambique: overland
transport to Tanzania from
Mozambique is fairly limited until the
completion of the bridge over the
Ruvuma River (due in 2010). There is
a ferry at Kilambo (south of Mtwara)
and several other ferry crossings at
larger towns and junctions; however
foreigners must pass through Kitaya
to get their passport stamped.
   From Uganda: you can cross into
Tanzania at Mutukula, northwest of
Bukoba. Buses connect Kampala to
Dar es Salaam several times a week.

GETTING AROUND

By Air

In addition to the three international
airports – Dar, Kilimanjaro and
Zanzibar – there are over 50 local
airports and airstrips. Most national
parks have landing strips. Air travel is
a major form of internal transport

due to the long distances and the
poor quality of most roads. Air
charter companies abound in Dar
and Arusha and offer both scheduled
flights and special services all over
the country.

National Airline
Air Tanzania
PO Box 543
Dar es Salaam
Tel: 022-211 7500
Reservations: 022-211 8411/27
Interline office (24 hours)
Tel: 022-284 4239
Fax: 022-212 4806
www.airtanzania.com
Tanzania's national airline provides
comprehensive coverage of the
country. Though they have a
schedule, flights tend to leave on
"African time".

Air Tanzania offices
Arusha
Boma Road
Tel: 027-250 3201
Dodoma tel: 026-232 4426-9
Kilimanjaro tel: 027-250 4319
Moshi tel: 027-275 5205
Mtwara tel: 023-233 147
Mwanza tel: 028-250 0368
Zanzibar tel: 223 0213

Other Airlines
Coastal Aviation
Upanga Road (Airline District)
PO Box 3052
Tel: 022-211 7959/7960
Fax: 022-211 8647/7985
Mobile: 0754-324 044 (emergency)
www.coastal.cc
Dar es Salaam Airport
Tel: 022-284 3293
Fax: 022-284 3033
Mobile: 0713-325 673 (emergency)
Zanzibar International Airport
Tel/fax: 024-223 3112
Mobile: 0713-670 815
Tanzania's premier flying safari
company, operating a mix of
scheduled services and charters into
the Northern, Southern and Western
parks. Scheduled routes currently
include: Arusha, Dar es Salaam,
Seronera, Grumeti, Mwanza,
Rubondo, Kilwa, Mafia, Selous (Beho
Beho, Kiba, Matambwe, Mbuyu,
Mtemere, Siwandu, Stieglers), Ruaha
(Msembe), Pemba, Pangani, Tanga
and Zanzibar.
Precision Air
Dar es Salaam
NIC Building
Cnr Samora Avenue/Pemba Road
Tel: 022-213 0800/216 8000
Call Centre: 0787-888 408/9
Arusha
New Safari Hotel Building
Boma Road

PO Box 1636
Tel: 027-250 6903
www.precisionairtz.com
Zanzibar
PO Box 961
Mazson's Hotel
Stone Town
Tel: 024-223 4520
Tanzania's premier domestic
airline, with flights to Arusha,
Bukoba, Dar es Salaam,
Grumeti, Kigoma, Kilimanjaro
International, Lake Manyara, Lindi,
Mafia Island, Mtwara, Mwanza,
Pemba, Seronera, Shinyanga, Tabora
and Zanzibar. Precision also operates
regionally to Nairobi and Mombasa in
Kenya.

Regional Air
Tel: 027-250 4477/2541
Email: resvns@regional.co.tz
Reliable scheduled and charter
services throughout Tanzania.

Tanzanair
Royal Palm Hotel
Ohio Street
PO Box 364
Dar es Salaam
Tel: 022-211 3151/2
Dar es Salaam Airport
Tel: 022-284 3131–3
Fax: 022-211 2946
Email: info@tanzanair.com
Tailor-made charter services, used
for medical evacuation, holiday and
business travel.

Twin Wings
PO Box 3397
Tel: 024-223 6783

ZanAir
Malawi Road
PO Box 2113
Zanzibar
Tel: 0713-605 230
Reservations: 024-223 3186
Zanzibar Airport
Tel: 024-223 993
Dar es Salaam Airport
Tel: 0741-605 230
www.zanair.com
Very dependable company with
scheduled and chartered flights to
and from the mainland. Primary
supplier of emergency medical flights
from Zanzibar.

By Boat

There are regular ferries between Dar
es Salaam, Zanzibar and Pemba.
There are currently no commercial
services north to Kenya. Dar es
Salaam Boat Terminal is opposite St
Joseph's Cathedral.

Coastal Ferries

It's easy to book tickets to Zanzibar
on the day of travel – the ferry
companies have ticket offices at the
ferry terminal, off Sokoine Drive.

ABOVE: local buses are cheap but the accident rate is high.

Traveller's cheques are accepted.
The price for visitors is higher than
that advertised for locals. There is a
fast catamaran service to Zanzibar,
but the boat is more pleasant on the
choppy sea.

Azam Marine
Zanzibar
Tel: 024-223 1655
Mobile: 0811-334 884
Dar es Salaam
Livingstone/Max Mbwana Street
PO Box 2517
Tel: 022-212 3324
Mobile: 0811-334 884
www.azam-marine.com
Thrice-weekly services between
Zanzibar and Pemba; daily services
between Dar and Zanzibar.

Flying Horse
Zanzibar
African Shipping Ltd
PO Box 3231
Tel: 024-223 3031
Dar es Salaam
PO Box 775
Tel: 022-212 4507
Daily catamaran service between Dar
and Zanzibar (journey time about
three hours).

Mega Speed Liners
Tel: 0774-447 333
Fast triangular route between
Zanzibar, Pemba and Dar, operating
three times a week. Journey time
between Zanzibar and Pemba three
hours.

Sea Express Services Ltd
Zanzibar
PO Box 4096
Tel: 0777-411 505
Dar es Salaam
Sokoine Drive Marine Port
PO Box 5829
Tel: 022-211 4026
Email: zpd@cats-net.com
The easiest and fastest way to get
between Dar and Zanzibar, with
several hydrofoil services daily
(journey time 70 minutes).

Sea Star Services
Zanzibar
Tel: 0741-411 505
Daily services between Dar and
Zanzibar (journey time two hours).

Lake Ferries

Marine Services Company Ltd
Mwanza
Tel: 028-280 3950
Weekly trip along Lake Tanganyika
from Kigoma to Mpulungu in Zambia,
on the *MV Liemba*, a renovated 1919
German ship. Theoretically, it leaves
Kigoma on Wednesday afternoon and
Mpulungu on Friday morning, arriving
back in Kigoma on Sunday morning.
Foreigners must pay in hard currency.
No advance booking.
There are also regular ferry
services on lakes Victoria and Nyasa.
Services from Mwanza to Bukoba on
Lake Victoria depart on Sunday,
Tuesday and Thursday evenings,
arriving the next morning. Return
journeys embark the following
evening, arriving back at Mwanza the
next morning.

Tanzania Railway Ltd
PO Box 70364
Dar es Salaam
Tel: 022-213 3428
Ferries from Mwanza cross to Port
Bell, Uganda, on the *MV Victoria*
(once a week; journey time 18
hours); Bukoba (three times a week;
journey time 12 hours); Nyamirembe,
via Kome, Kahunda and Maisome
(weekly; journey time 24 hours); and
Ukerewe Island (twice daily; journey
time three hours).

By Bus

The Ubungo bus terminal, located 5
km (3 miles) from the centre on
Morogoro Road, Dar es Salaam, is
the starting point for domestic
services to the Southern Highlands,
the Northern Safari Circuit,

Morogoro, Dodoma, Mwanza, Singida and Shinyanga. It is not the most pleasant place to hang around in: avoid it at night and keep a close eye on your belongings during the day. If you need a taxi you can get a better deal from one of the many drivers outside the gates.

Major Inter-City Bus Companies

There are two grades of buses on the **mainland**. The most common are brightly coloured vehicles run by locals with the furnishings of a small village on top and no room inside. These are the cheapest – foreigners are charged more but are guaranteed a seat, whereas many locals stand, even during eight-hour journeys. A trip on one of these is certainly an experience, but not everyone's idea of a pleasant one.

The other category includes "luxury" buses. They are similar to National Express in the UK (a bit better than Greyhound). These serve all main routes, cost more (but are still reasonable), and – most importantly – are air conditioned.

Dar es Salaam Express
Colonel Middleton Road
Arusha
Scandinavia Express
PO Box 2414
Dar es Salaam
Terminal at the corner of Msimbazi Strcct and Nyerere Road
Tel: 022-286 1947
Fax: 022-286 1950
www.scandinaviagroup.com
Scandinavia Express has cornered the market on tourist travel and is probably your best option.
Arusha terminal
By the bus stand
Tel: 027-250 0153
Iringa ticket office
Tel: 026-270 2308 or 270 2695
Mbeya ticket office
Tel: 025-250 4305

Most country buses on **Zanzibar** start from Creek Road. The No. 9 goes to Jambiani, Paje and Bwejuu;

No. 10 to Makunduchi and Kizimkazi in the south; No. 1 to Matemwe and Pwani Mchangani on the east coast; No. 2 to the slave caves in Mangapwani; No. 16 to Nungwi in the far north of the island; No. 17 to Kiwengwa. From Mwembe Ladu Hospital, the No. 6 goes to Chwaka, Uroa and Pongwe.

A shared minibus is the normal way around the country for tourists. A trip north costs around TSh4,000, and to the east, TSh3,000. You have to arrange this in advance, however, so you can be fitted into the schedule. Talk to any minibus driver (they scout hotels and guesthouses between 8 and 9am) for more information. A taxi will be much more expensive.

By Train

Trains within Tanzania run from Dar to Mwanza on Lake Victoria (Tues, Wed, Fri and Sun) and Kigoma/ Gombe Stream National Park (Tues, Thur, Fri and Sun). The train service from the TAZARA Station in Dar es Salaam to Zambia *(see pages 163 and 277)* stops at Mbeya near the border. Advance information on timetables, etc is hard to find, though you may find some details on www.seat61.com.
Tanzania Railways Ltd
PO Box 70364
Dar es Salaam
Tel: 022-213 3428
www.tazara.co.tz

Dar es Salaam Stations

Central Railway Station
Cnr Railway and Gerezani streets
Tel: 022-211 0600
Domestic services only.
TAZARA Station
Cnr Nelson Mandela Expressway
Nyerere Road
Tel: 0784-771 416

City Transport

You can easily make your way around Arusha or Stone Town on foot, and

both are safe to walk around by day. In the evening, walking is less advisable. In Dar es Salaam, the centre can be negotiated on foot, but many outlying areas are better reached by taxi or shuttle bus.

Buses

In Dar es Salaam, buses operate from the centre to the suburbs from Old Posta Station, at the corner of Sokoine Drive and Azikiwe Street, and the new Post Office on Azikwe Street and Mnazi Mmoja, at the end of Samora Avenue. If you are heading to the hotels north of Dar, you will need to change at Mwenge Station.

Taxis

The larger cities all have a plentiful supply of taxis that come (usually) at a reasonable price. It is safest not to use unmarked cars. Always negotiate the fare before getting in. Expect a town-centre journey to cost around TSh5,000–6,000.

In Arusha, licensed taxis have black serial numbers on the door and should charge between Tsh 4,000–6,000 for journeys in town.

Taxis rarely cruise when empty, so you will need to find a taxi rank or ask someone to call you a cab; most cafés, restaurants, shops and offices are willing to do this. Many cabbies now have mobile phones, so if you got good service, you can take the number and call again.

Reputable hotels usually provide transfers from the nearest airport. If this service isn't available, approximate taxi rates are as follows: from Zanzibar Airport to Stone Town Tsh 6,000–10,000; from Kilimanjaro International Airport to Arusha US$25; from Julius Nyerere International to Dar es Salaam city centre US$15–20.

Daladala

The most common form of local transport is the *daladala* or shared taxi. These often creaky minibuses and vans usually leave from ranks scattered across the city and run on

Bus Travel Times (in hours)

Town	Dar	Morogoro	Iringa	Mbeya	Dodoma	Arusha	Moshi
Dar	—	3.5	7	11	7–9	9	8
Morogoro	3.5	—	3.5	4	5–7	★★★	—
Iringa	7	3.5	—	4	9–12	—	—
Mbeya	11	4	4	—	13–16	—	—
Dodoma	7–9	5–7	9–12	13–16	—	★★★	—
Arusha	9	★★★	—	—	★★★	—	1
Moshi	8	—	—	—	—	1	—

★★★ There are regular services between Arusha and Dodoma/Morogoro, but the road is very poor. Times are unpredictable.

roughly set routes. They wait to leave until full, but can be waved down beside the road. Reluctant to turn anyone away, they are piled high with people inside, and some even cling to the fenders outside. Fares are extremely low, but the accident rate is high, and they are not to be recommended if you have luggage or for any long journey.

Driving

To drive in Tanzania, you need an International Driving Licence, available from motoring organisations before you leave home. Your national licence will not be sufficient.

Drive defensively. Traffic is on the left, as in Britain, and while there are official speed limits, the reality is that people drive as fast as possible. Fortunately, the state of Tanzanian roads often keeps this down to a crawl, but when it does not, beware. Drivers frequently fail to signal, while others signal right to warn following traffic against overtaking due to oncoming traffic, and left when it is safe to overtake. In rural areas watch out for children or animals running out in front of the car. Driving after dusk should be avoided: cars often do not have lights, and there is also more danger of being robbed.

Roadblocks

You will meet frequent police roadblocks. These are money machines for the local cops as much as they are a serious attempt to check papers or get unsafe vehicles off the road, and bribery is the general order of the day. The good news is that as long as your papers are in order and you are polite, tourists are infrequently asked to pay the fine/bribe. If you have a local driver he may need help paying up.

Fuel

Filling stations are usually found on the edge of town or at major route intersections. They are relatively infrequent, so fill up when you can. Fuel is cheaper than in Europe, and more expensive than in the US. It is unlikely that you will be able to pay with plastic and even if you do, there will be a hefty surcharge. Many filling stations are shut on Sundays.

Automobile Association of Tanzania

Dar es Salaam
Azikiwe Street
PO Box 3004
Tel: 022-212 4494
Fax: 022-212 7727
Email: aat@cats-net.com

Arusha
PO Box 361
Golden Rose Hotel
Tel: 027-250 7959/8861/3699 or 0744-287 639
Tanga
PO Box 444
Tel: 053-47230
The AA offers the usual services for members, such as international driving permits, discounted accommodation rates and insurance, travel advice and breakdown cover.

Breakdowns

Mobitel, Vodacom, Celtel, TTCL and Zantel subscribers can call for help on 133.

Car Hire

There are numerous car-hire companies in Tanzania. There are some internationally franchised companies in Dar es Salaam, but the majority are small, local outfits. Prices and the quality of the vehicles can vary, so it is worth shopping around.

In Zanzibar, most car-hire operators are one-man bands with a couple of vehicles. It is best to ask your hotel, tour operator or a local travel agent to sort out your car hire for you.

Some companies offer only chauffeur-driven services, although self-drive is becoming more common. Rates are low, so it may be cost-effective to take the driver as it cuts the insurance cost without, necessarily, costing much more. If you plan to drive yourself, you need an International Driving Licence to rent any vehicle, including a scooter. If you don't have a credit card, you will be asked to leave your passport and a cash deposit with the rental company.

If you are travelling out of the city, it is strongly advised that you use a four-wheel drive with good ground clearance. Make sure your vehicle has insurance and a valid road permit. Also check that it has a spare wheel and basic tool kit. If you are planning to travel long distances, it is worth carrying spare fuel, oil and water, and a basic survival kit, including food, water and a blanket.

In addition to the car-hire companies listed below, most tailor-made tour operators in Tanzania also offer chauffeur-driven car hire *(see page 297)*.

International Car-Hire Firms in Dar
Avis
c/o Executive Car Rentals
Nyere Road and New Africa Hotel
Tel: 022-286 1214

International Reservations Centre
08700-100 287
www.avis.com
Europcar (Inter Rent)
Tel: 022-211 1083
UK Central Booking
Tel: 0870-607 5000
US Central Booking
Tel: 1-877-940 6900
www.europcar.com
Hertz Rentals
Mövenpick Royal Palm Hotel
Ohio Street
Tel: 022-211 2967
Email: hertz@cats-net.com
UK Central Booking
Tel: 0870-848 4848
US Central Booking:
Tel: 1-800-654 3131
www.hertz.com

Local Car-Hire Firms
Dar es Salaam
Evergreen Car Rental
Nkrumah Street
Tel: 022-218 3345
Fax: 022-218 3348
Email: evergreen@raha.com
Hima Tours
Simu Street
Tel: 022-211 1083
Email: hima@raha.com

Arusha
Arusha Naaz Rent a Car
Tel: 027-250 2087 or 0754-282 799/0754-286 660
Fax: 027-250 8893
www.arushanaaz.net
Danavu Car Hire & Tours
Tel: 027-250 7452
Serena Car Hire & Transport
Tel: 027-250 9833
www.serenacarhire.com

BELOW: directing the traffic.

A CCOMMODATION

HOTELS, YOUTH HOSTELS, BED & BREAKFAST

Choice of Accommodation

The Socialist years in Tanzania during the 1970s and 1980s meant that tourism development here is far behind that of neighbouring Kenya – which is, in many ways, an excellent thing.

The mainland: for such a vast area, there are relatively few places to stay, and there is a huge gulf in the centre of the market: superb luxury lodges at one end, dingy, cockroach-infested dives at the other, and little in between. There are also very few well-equipped camp sites – most camping is done with safari companies, which generally operate their own sites.

Zanzibar: there has been a massive expansion in hotel accommodation in the past few years, and there is now a wide choice of wonderful places to stay, and prices to suit any budget. Most

hotels offer a bed-and-breakfast deal. Camping is not allowed on the islands.

Hotel visitors in Tanzania pay 20 percent VAT: check that this is included in the rate quoted when you reserve your room. There are two price brackets for accommodation; residents and non-residents. As a foreign tourist you will have to pay the higher non-resident rates, which are generally quoted in US dollars but payable in Tanzanian shillings. During high season (June to September), room rates are hiked up, so be sure to confirm the price for the time of year you intend to visit.

Most large and medium-sized establishments accept credit cards; cash is required for smaller, budget hotels.

When calling hotels (or any number in Tanzania), mobile (cell) phones are generally more reliable than landlines.

Hotel Chains/ Safari Lodge Operators

CC Africa
P. Bag X27
Benmore 2010
Johannesburg
South Africa
Tel: +27-11-809 4300
Fax: +27-11-809 4400
Europe: +49 211 2297 5440
US: +1-888 882 3742
www.ccafrica.com

Foxes Africa Safaris
Box: 10270
Arusha
Tel: 0784-237422
Fax: 022-286 357
www.tanzaniasafaris.info

Kempinski Hotels
Toll-free reservations lines:
Europe: +800-426 313 55
US: +1-800-426 3135
www.kempinski.com

Moivaro Lodges and Tented Camps
Box: 11297, Arusha
Tel: 027-255 3243
www.moivaro.com

Protea Hotels
PO Box 75
Sea Point 8060
South Africa
Tel: +27-21-430 5000
Fax: +27-21-430 5320
www.proteahotels.com

Serena Lodges and Hotels
PO Box 2551
Arusha
Tel: 027-250 4158/4153
Fax: 027-250 4155/4058
www.serenahotels.com

Sopa Lodges
PO Box 1823
Arusha
Tel: 027-250 0630
Fax: 027-250 8245
US: +1-941-951 6611
www.sopalodges.com

BELOW: relaxing on the beach is an ideal way to follow a safari.

ACCOMMODATION LISTINGS

DAR ES SALAAM

City Centre

African Sky Millennium Towers Hotel
PO Box 7530
Tel: 022-277 4588
Fax: 022-277 4599
www.africanskyhotels.com
Located close to the airport, beach and city centre, the African Millennium Towers Hotel has facilities for all occasions including banquets, conferences and private functions. Amenities include minibar, swimming pool, room service, room safe and bar. **$$$**

Golden Tulip Hotel
PO Box 6300, Toure Drive, Msasani Peninsula
Tel: 022-260 0288
www.goldentuliptanzania.com
Modern hotel, built on a cliff alongside the Indian Ocean, close to the city centre. Luxury hotel with traditional Arabic influences both in the decor and furnishings. All of the 90 rooms have ocean views. Shopping centre, business and conference facilities, swimming pool, gym, hydrotherapy and beauty salon. The hotel is in a quiet position and offers swimming at Oyster Bay beach. **$$$**

Harbour View Suites
PO Box 9163
Tel: 022-212 4040
Fax: 022-212 0333
www.harbourview-suites.com
International-standard accommodation with individualised service situated above a vibrant shopping mall and business centre. All rooms come fitted with a kitchenette for self catering. **$$$**

Heritage Motel
PO Box 786
Tel: 022-211 7471
Fax: 022-212 1509
www.heritagemotel.co.tz
In the heart of the city, this is an ideal bed and breakfast option. Air conditioned with internet connection, electronic safe, television and fridge. Real value for money. **$$**

Kilimanjaro Hotel Kempinski
Kivukoni Street
Tel: 022-213 1111
Fax: 022-212 0777
www.kempinski-daressalaam.com
Flashy, modern hotel with luxurious rooms and facilities. Fantastic bar with views over the city, as well as remarkably good and cheap cocktails. There is also a casino and spa. **$$$–$$$$$**

Mövenpick Royal Palm Hotel
Ohio Street
Tel: 022-211 2416
Fax: 022-211 3981
www.moevenpick.com
Expensive but stylish modern hotel with pool, gym, over 200 rooms, a 24-hour business centre and shopping arcade. Very central, with peaceful gardens leading onto a superb pool. Excellent food. Every night in the main restaurant is themed but try and make the seafood evening – the buffet is unforgettable. A few minutes' walk from the centre. **$$$**

Palm Beach Hotel
PO Box 1520
Tel: 022-213 0985 or 0713-222299
Fax: 022-211 9272
www.pbhtz.com
Set near the beachfront within easy reach of a golf course and a tennis club and within walking distance of the city centre. Recently restored to its Art Deco glory, the hotel offers 32 en-suite bedrooms, a conference room, a pleasant garden restaurant and bar, air-conditioned café and free wireless internet connectivity throughout the hotel. **$$**

ABOVE: modern luxury at the Mövenpick in Dar.

Peacock Hotel
Bibi Titi Mohammed Road
Tel: 022-211 4126/0334
www.peacock-hotel.co.tz
A middle-of-the-road hotel right in the centre of Dar. It can be noisy, but has a good restaurant and bar. The 93 rooms are all en suite, pleasantly furnished and functional. **$$**

Protea Hotel Oysterbay
Theatre Square
Tel: 022-266 6665
Fax: 022-266 7760
www.proteahotels.com
The two-storey whitewashed building with its balconied rooms provides 48 comfortable apartments set round a central swimming pool. Rooms have TV and air conditioning. There's a gym, laundry, shop, barbecue area and email access. A peaceful haven just 17 km (9 miles) from the airport. **$$$**

Protea Hotel Courtyard
Sea View,
Ocean Road
Tel: 022-213 0130/0560
Fax: 022-213 0100
www.proteahotels.com
This attractive hotel is set around a lush courtyard. It has a swimming pool, 52 rooms and suites, all with TV, air conditioning and Wi-fi. It's not far from the city centre but is in a quiet part of town, 12 km (7 miles) from the airport. This is a tranquil, good-value introduction to Dar. **$$**

Q Bar & Guest House
Msasani
Just off Haile Selassie Road
Tel: 022-260 2150
Fax: 022-211 4033
Email: qbar@hotmail.com
This is backpacker land. It has one six-bed room with a bathroom and other single/double rooms with TV, fridges, en-suite bathrooms and mosquito nets. It is cheap, relatively clean and has its own bar and a restaurant where the food is surprisingly good. Basic, comfortable and an easy stopover 18 km (10 miles) from the airport. **$**

Southern Sun
Garden Avenue
Tel: 022-213 7575
Fax: 022-213 9070
www.southernsun.com/daressalaam
Formerly the Holiday Inn, this is one of Dar's all-singing, all-dancing city-centre hotels, in the Botanical Gardens. It has 152 rooms, some non-smoking, a business centre

with conference facilities, a pool, gym and all the usual facilities. Breakfast is served in the Kivulini Room overlooking the pool and gardens, and the decor is up-market African, with a host of traditional Zanzibar carved doors. Rooms on the upper floors have stunning views over the city and ocean. **$$$**

Starlight Hotel
Bibi Titi Mohammed Street
Tel: 022-211 9387
Fax: 022-211 9389
The seven-storey concrete facade is not very welcoming, but the accommodation is acceptable at this basic medium-to-low-priced hotel in the city centre. There are 150 rooms, all with hot and cold water and showers, TV and fridges. It's clean, reasonably comfortable and functional but, because it is so central, it is likely to be a bit noisy at night. **$**

Travertine Hotel
PO Box 6550
Tel: 022-217 1005–6
Fax: 022-217 1007
www.hotel-travertine.com
Impeccable service, calm environment, scrumptious meals and tastefully appointed rooms. **$**

North of Dar

The Beachcomber
PO Box 4868, Dar es Salaam
Tel: 022-264 7772–4
Fax: 022-264 7050
www.beachcomber.co.tz
Slightly concretey in appearance, but extremely comfortable, well-run and friendly, this is one of the most popular hotels along the coast, 30 minutes' drive north of Dar. It has a large pool, fine beach, gym, sauna and steam room, internet café, restaurant and bar. Diving and airport transfers offered. **$$**

Jangwani Seabreeze Lodge
PO Box 934, African Road
Tel: 022-264 7215/7067 or 0784-944977
Fax: 022-264 7069
www.jangwani.org
Smart, efficiently run German hotel on Mbezi Beach. Good food, an excellent beach and pool, and a range of water sports including waterskiing, paragliding, boat trips and a dive school. Children's pool and activities. **$$**

Silversands Hotel
PO Box 60097
Tel: 022-265 0567 or 0754-850001

Fax: 022-265 0428
www.silversandshotel.co.tz
The best of the cheaper hotels along this stretch, the Silversands is laid-back, has a reasonable pool and bar, good, if not exciting food, and a nice beach front location. Air-conditioned en-suite rooms and a 22-bed dormitory offer accommodation at a variety of prices. Snorkelling and diving on offer; children's play area. **$**

South of Dar

Amani Beach
Amani-Gomvu Beach
Mjimwema–Kimbiji road
Tel: 0754-410 033 or 0755-775566
www.amanibeach.com
This luxury hotel has beautifully appointed, modern cottages set in grounds by the Indian Ocean. It is 45 minutes by road south of Dar city. Facilities include phones and TVs in all the rooms, an excellent restaurant, swimming pool, tennis courts, water sports and a open-air bar area with wonderful sea views. **$$$$**

Kipepeo Beach Campsite
Tel: 022-212 2931 or 0754-276178
Fax: 022-211 9272
www.kipepeocamp.com
Remote backpacker hang-out on a stunning stretch of beach 7 km (4 miles) south of the ferry. There is a range of accommodation, including beach *bandas* (simple huts or bungalows), dormitory rooms and camping, with good, cheap food and a bar. **$**

Ras Kutani
Amani-Gomvu Beach,
Mjimwema–Kimbiji road
PO Box 1192, Dar es Salaam
Tel: 022-211 4802/3220
Fax: 022-211 2794
www.selous.com
This wonderful hideaway is one of the finest hotels in Tanzania. It is in a fabulous location, with 12 luxury cottages built from local materials, set on the edge of the Indian Ocean and a palm-draped lagoon. The food, served in a restaurant overlooking the sea, is local and superb. The staff are friendly and welcoming. Activities include sailing, fishing, island trips and riding. Some 45 minutes by road from Dar, or you can fly in. **$$$$**

THE NORTH COAST

Bagamoyo

Bagamoyo Beach Resort
PO Box 250
Tel: 023-244 0083
Fax: 023-244 0254
Email: bbr@baganet.com
This is a charming backpackers' haven, set right by the beach with 18 air-conditioned rooms with basic bathrooms and toilets. Four of the huts are actually on the beach (no air-con but naturally ventilated with ocean air). There is a restaurant which serves seafood and international dishes, and a friendly owner. Facilities include table tennis, darts, ball games, and trips to the swamps. **$**

Kasiki Marine Camp
Kasiki

Tel: 0744-278 590
Fax: 0741-322 4707
www.bagamoyo.org
If you don't mind the bumpy 7-km (4-mile) journey out of Bagamoyo, this is the best place to stay for food, location and value for money. It is run on an old pineapple plantation overlooking the Indian Ocean by two Italian women. It consists of a few basic but comfortable bungalows, a large *banda* (beach-side) restaurant, lounge and bar and fabulous Italian cooking. Activities include speed- and sailing-boat excursions, fishing, diving and birdwatching. **$**

Lazy Lagoon
Tel: 023-244 0194
Fax: 0741-327 706

www.tanzaniasafaris.info
Isolated and beautiful luxury lodge on a sand spit beside the Mbegani Lagoon, 7 km (4 miles) south of Bagamoyo. There are 10 attractively decorated thatched beach chalets, excellent seafood, a pool, fine beach and good snorkelling on the nearby coral reef. **$$$**

Livingstone Club
Tel: 023-244 0059/0080
Fax: 023-244 0104
www.livingtone.ws
Like most Bagamoyo hotels, this is on the 2-km (1-mile) stretch of road leading down to the beach, north of the main town. It is sited at the end of a string of backpacker hostels. The accommodation comprises

40 rooms in 10 brick bungalows; each has a fridge, hot water and telephone. There is a pool, outdoor seating and eating area, and sport facilities. **$$**

Millennium Sea Breeze Resort
PO Box 155
Tel: 023-244 0201/3
Fax: 023-244 0204
www.millennium.co.tz
A state-of-the-art conference hotel situated

in beautiful gardens, close to a fantastic beach; 28 air-conditioned rooms with sea view. Excellent conference facilities and business centre with a swimming pool and restaurant serving seafood and international cuisine. **$$$$**

Paradise Holiday Resort
PO Box 119
Tel: 023-244 000/244 0111
Fax: 023-244 0142
www.paradiseresort.net
Comfortable beach-front resort with 95 rooms, several restaurants and bars, swimming pool, tennis courts, kids' club and live music. Snorkelling and diving available. **$$**

Pangani

There are several camps on the northern side of Pangani, all of a similar standard, offering limited sea swimming but reasonable rates. Newer, more up-market developments can be found on the south side of Pangani River.

Emayani Beach Lodge
PO Box 111, Pangani
Tel/fax: 027-264 0755
www.emayanilodge.com
Twelve thatched beach-front bungalows with shady verandas, to the north of Pangani. All have en-suite bathrooms with solar-heated showers. There is a bar and a restaurant which serves freshly caught seafood. The lodge has an airstrip (flights by arrangement). Activities include snorkelling, game fishing, birdwatching, sailing and windsurfing. **$$**

Mkoma Bay Tented Lodge
Tel: 027-263 000/0786-434001
www.mkomabay.com
Clean and cheerful property, 2 km (1 mile) north of Pangani, providing *bandas*, bungalows and tents at varying prices, reasonable food and a pool and small beach. There are opportunities to visit Maziwe Island for diving and snorkelling. In the evenings the lodge offers a river trip up the Pangani to see the birdlife.

Kayaks and mountains bikes are also available to guests. **$$–$$$**

The Tides Lodge
Tel: 0784-225 812
www.thetideslodge.com
Nestled among coconut palms in a secluded and idyllic stretch of coast to the south of Pangani, this is a small and intimate beach lodge built and run by a German couple, Stephanie and Uli. The seven lodges are luxurious, with rustic *makuti*-thatched roofs and many traditional artefacts to personalise them. Externally, each is painted a different primary colour. There is an enclosed, lamplit restaurant with superb food, including a daily catch from the Indian Ocean. Visitors can sail in from Zanzibar or arrive by car. Activities include snorkelling and a Pangani River safari. **$$**

Pare Mountains

Mbaga-Same
About 30 km (18 miles) southeast of Same, this small village is right by the Mkomazi Game Reserve. It's great for hikes around the southern Pare villages and is a good starting point for the three-day hike to the top of Shengena Peak. En route, camping is the only option unless you can find a villager to take you in.

Hill-Top Tona Lodge
PO Box 32, Mbaga-Same
PO Box 1592, Dar es Salaam
Tel: 027-275 8176
Simple but good accommodation in self-contained cottages, set in the bush with views over the Mkomazi Plains. You can swim in the river and have lunch or dinner if arranged in advance. You can camp here, or in other areas of the South Pare by arrangement with the lodge, but take water-purification tablets. **$**

Mwanga
About 50 km (30 miles) north of Same on the Dar es Salaam–Arusha highway, Mwanga is a good place to

start exploring the undeveloped North Pare.

Rhino Hotel
Mwanga
Very basic and simple hotel, 2 km (1 mile) out of Mwanga on the road to Usangi. **$**

Usangi
Another good base for exploring the North Pare, some 25 km (15 miles) from Mwanga on the B1. There is no public accommodation, but several families offer accommodation through a cultural tourism programme. Visitors can also stay in the three-bedroom rest house at Lomwe Secondary School or with one of the teachers. Local food is inexpensive and can be arranged on request. **$**

Same
Same is a small, dusty town on the Moshi road standing as the gateway to the South Pare Mountains. It is made up of a street of concrete huts, with a colourful fruit market, but there is not much to choose from in the way of accommodation.

Amani Lutheran Centre
Tel: 027-275 8107
Situated near the market, this is a clean, very basic hotel, generally recognised as the best place to stay in Same. It has a restaurant with acceptable food. **$**

Elephant Motel
PO Box 192
Tel: 027-275 8193
Salaam–Arusha highway, 1 km (½ mile) southeast of Same
www.elephantmotel.com
This is the most up-market of a limited selection. The rooms are comfortable and basic, and there is a TV in the main dining room. **$**

Usambara Mountains

Maweni Farm Mountain Lodge
Soni Falls
Tel: 0784-279 371
www.maweni.com
Delightful hotel, conference and media centre in the Usumbara Mountains.

Beautiful 1920s design, roaring log fires and excellent food. Great atmosphere and lovely hosts. Interesting range of activities on offer. **$–$$**

Tanga

Tanga does not have any up-market hotels, but there are some basic and acceptable places to stay on the waterside and in town.

Mkonge Hotel
Hospital Road
Tel: 027-264 3440
Fax:028-264 4444
Email: mkongehotel@.kaributanga.com
Probably the best accommodation you'll find in Tanga. Overlooks the sea. **$$**

Inn by the Sea
Hospital Road
PO Box 2188
Tel: 027-264 4614
This is a very basic but good-value hotel with rooms overlooking the sea. Ask for one with air conditioning: it's effective, if noisy, and infinitely preferable to those rooms with a fan. The rooms are fairly clean and the view out over the ocean makes up for much. There's also a restaurant and a bar selling drinks. **$**

Hotel Panori
Off Hospital Road, near the Raskatone
Tel: 027-264 6044
Fax: 027-264 7425
Email: panori@ yahooafricaonline.co.tz
This hotel has two levels of accommodation – an old, rather run-down wing and a pleasant newer wing which is better value. There is also reasonable food – this is one of the few hotels in Tanga with a restaurant . **$**

Raskazone Hotel
Off Hospital Road
Tel/fax: 027-264 3897 or 0741-670790
Email: raskazone@hotmail.com
This hotel is about five minutes' walk from the sea. The rooms all have a fridge, telephone, hot shower and mosquito nets; you pay extra for a fan or air conditioning. There are special rates for

TRANSPORT

ACCOMMODATION

EATING OUT

ACTIVITIES

A – Z

LANGUAGE

backpackers, and camping is available. This hotel is good value and provides breakfast. **$**

Saadani National Park

This is the only national park in Tanzania where the bush meets the sea. The wildlife isn't as prolific as in other parks, but this is improving. Boat safaris down the Wami River offer spectacular scenery and hippo viewing. The local industry is prawn fishing, which accounts for the delicious food found in the three lodges in the area.

Kisampa Camp
Sanctuary Tanzania,
PO Box 23000, Oyster Bay
Tel: 0754-927 694 or 0753-005442
www.sanctuary-tz.com
Kisampa Camp is wonderfully situated along the banks of the Wami River, near the park. Set in a private conservation area within 40 sq. km (15 sq. miles) of pristine and varied bush, Kisampa Camp is rustic, secluded and comfortable, with an emphasis on cultural tourism. Their unique "stargazer" tents allow you to sleep under the stars, while being protected from

insects and the elements.
$$–$$$
A Tent with a View
PO Box 40525
Tel: 022-211 0507
Fax: 022-215 1106
www.saadani.com
Located on the Mkwaja coastline, just outside the northeast boundary of Saadani National Park, A Tent with a View Safari Lodge consists of eight delightful *bandas* perched on stilts and individually spaced out along the beach. Foot safaris combining the bush and the beach, birdwatching by canoe on the Mafue River and game drives are all

available from the lodge. Boat safaris on the Wami River can be organised as part of a full-day game drive. **$$$**
Saadani Safari Lodge
PO Box 105854,
Dar es Salaam
Tel: 022-277 3294
Fax: 022-277 3294
www.saadanilodge.com
The only lodge situated within the national park. Luxurious tents opening out onto the beach, delicious food, fantastic staff and beautifully landscaped swimming pool. Activities include game drives, boat safaris, fly-camping and bird walks. **$$$**

ARUSHA AND KILIMANJARO

Arusha

Arusha Coffee Lodge
Dodoma Road
Tel: +27-11-803 0557
Fax: +27-11-803 7044
www.elewana.com
Set in a coffee plantation near Arusha Airport, this is the newest of Arusha's luxury lodges, with 21 spacious, colonial-style chalets. The furnishings and service are impeccable, the welcome warm and meals are taken at Redds restaurant, part of the same complex. **$$$**
The Arusha Hotel
PO Box 88
Tel: 027-250 7777
www.thearushahotel.com
Overlooked by Mount Meru, this hotel lies in beautiful gardens full of exotic birdlife and plants. Its 86 elegant executive rooms overlook the gardens, swimming pool and the awesome mountain beyond. Facilities include a gym, Wi-fi, conference rooms and business centre. **$$$**
Ilboru Safari Lodge
PO Box 8012
Tel: 0754-270 357
www.ilborusafarilodge.com
About 2 km (1 mile) north of Arusha town centre. This is an efficiently run and friendly establishment, with a

good restaurant and pool. There are 10 *bandas* neatly laid out in a small compound, in a lush tropical garden which attracts numerous birds. All rooms are en suite and decorated in traditional Maasai materials of bright red checks. **$**
The Impala Hotel
PO Box 7302
Tel: 027-250 8448
Fax: 027-250 8220
www.impalahotel.com
A popular businessman's hotel in central Arusha, the Impala has spacious rooms with en-suite bathrooms. Outdoor swimming pool. **$**
Lake Natron Tented Camp
Moivaro
PO Box 11297
Tel/fax: 027-250 6315
www.moivaro.com
Modern and clean 'A'-frame safari tents with en suites, comfortable beds and incredible views. Owners will organise hikes up Ol Dihyo Lengai. **$$$**
Moivaro Coffee Plantation
PO Box 11297
Tel/fax: 027-255 3242–3
www.moivaro.com
Attractive, colonial-style hotel with thatched cottages scattered across brightly coloured gardens at the foot of Mount Meru, 7 km (4 miles) from the town centre. The hotel has a

pool, its own 16-hectare (40-acre) coffee plantation, and a children's playground. It also offers internet facilities and massage. **$$**
Mount Meru Hotel
PO Box 877
Tel: 027-250 2711–2
Fax: 027-250 8221
A large, impersonal, international-style hotel overlooking a golf course. Popular with conference and UN clientele, but overpriced when compared with other hotels and lodges in Arusha. There are 168 rooms, all en suite with TV, and 12 suites. Facilities include free access to a fitness centre and a big swimming pool, together with a couple of grill restaurants. It's ideal if you're taking the early-morning shuttle bus to Nairobi. **$$**
Serena Mountain Village
PO Box 2551
Tel: 027-255 3313
Fax: 027-255 3163
www.serenahotels.com
Ten minutes from central Arusha, 40 minutes from Kilimanjaro Airport. Set in beautiful mature gardens, designed to resemble an African village, and surrounded by a coffee estate, with views to Mount Kilimanjaro and Mount Meru and

overlooking the small crater lake of Diluti. Spacious en-suite rooms in creeper-clad *bandas* thatched with banana stems. In addition to the usual hotel facilities, on offer are massage and nature walks around Lake Diluti. **$$$**

Arusha National Park

Hatari Lodge
PO Box 3171,
Arusha
Tel: 027-255 3456
www.hatarilodge.com
Wonderful "safari-retro" design, named after the Hollywood film. Beautiful setting; highly recommended. **$$$**
Momella Wildlife Lodge
PO Box 999,
Arusha
Tel: 027-250 6423
Fax: 057-250 8264
www.lions-safari-intl.com/momella.html
Near the Momella Gate to Arusha National Park. A shadow of its former glory,

PRICE CATEGORIES

Price codes (based on double occupancy in high season)
$ = under US$50
$$ = US$50–150
$$$ = US$150–300
$$$$ = US$300–500
$$$$$ = over US$500

ABOVE: dinner in a safari lodge.

the lodge's Hollywood association and large swimming pool are now its main draw. Harry Kruger and John Wayne stayed here when filming *Hatari!* in 1960. Rooms are in bandas or cottages, with en suite bathrooms. **$**

Mount Meru

Dik Dik
PO Box 1499,
Arusha
Tel: 027-255 3499
Fax: 027-255 3498
www.dikdik.ch
On the slopes of Mt Meru, with views of Kilimanjaro, about 25 km (14 miles) from Arusha. A smart, Swiss-run establishment with nine bungalows, each with two double rooms facing onto the garden. There's an outside bar and swimming pool, and the restaurant is renowned for its excellent, freshly prepared food. **$$$**

Keys Hotel
Uru Road, Meru,
PO Box 933, Moshi
Tel: 027-275 2250
Fax: 027-275 0073
www.keys-hotel-tours.com

A friendly, family-run hotel with a lively bar and music in the evenings, and a good swimming pool. There are spacious, airy en-suite rooms with TV inside the hotel, together with *bandas* (also with en-suite facilities, no TV) on the compound. It's a good base for climbing Kilimanjaro. The restaurant has a mixture of African and European cuisine. **$**

Mount Meru Game Lodge & Sanctuary
PO Box 2747,
Arusha
Tel: 027-255 3643
Fax: 027-255 3885
www.mountmerugamelodge.com
Located 20 minutes from central Arusha, half an hour from Kilimanjaro Airport. This former hunting lodge has been given a stylish modern makeover. There are also two suites in small cabins in the garden. Adjacent to the Mt Meru Game Sanctuary, the hotel was started by a Hungarian family in the 1960s as a sanctuary for old and injured animals – some of them are kept in cages. **$$$**

Ngare Sero Mountain Lodge
PO Box 425,
Arusha
Tel: 0787-560055
Tel/fax: 027-255 3638
www.ngare-sero-lodge.com
Located 20 km (12 miles) from Arusha, 30 km (18 miles) from Kilimanjaro Airport. Ngare Sero means "sweet water", and this farmhouse dating from the 1900s is set in lush gardens and forest, with magnificent birdlife and colobus monkeys, next to a spring which leads into a lake full of tropical plants. There are eight suites in the garden and two in the main house. It's a perfect place to relax, with views of Kilimanjaro from the balcony. Horse riding, hiking and trout fishing are available. **$$–$$$**

River Trees Country Inn
PO Box 235,
Arusha
Tel: 027-255 3894 or 0741-339873
Email: rivertrees@habari.co.tz
Near the Usa River, opposite the Mt Meru Game Sanctuary, 20 minutes' drive from Arusha and 30 minutes to Kilimanjaro Airport. A delightful, peaceful setting, near the river, on a farm growing flowers for seed. There's a friendly, informal atmosphere, and the six guest rooms are comfortably furnished and located in the main farmhouse or in the garden, while delicious meals are provided by arrangement. Guests can relax in the garden or on the veranda, or go walking on the farm. There's also a sitting room and a small satellite TV lounge. **$$**

Safari Spa Polo
c/o African Encounters
www.africanencounters.com
More like a private guesthouse than a hotel, set in the foothills of Mt Meru, about 40 minutes' drive from Arusha. Exclusive and private, it has a fully equipped fitness centre, sauna, steam room, jacuzzi, aromatherapy massage,

tennis court and tropical pool. The cottages, decorated in an *Out of Africa* style, overlook the pool. Polo and horse riding are offered to experienced riders. **$$$**

Kilimanjaro

Hotel Capricorn
PO Box 938, Marangu
Tel: 027-275 1309 or 0794-0138571
Fax: 027-275 2442
www.capricornhotel.com
Located 3 km (1½ miles) from the Marangu Gate to Kilimanjaro National Park. A medium-sized hotel (24 rooms and suites) with friendly staff and well-furnished public areas and rooms. Suitable for disabled visitors. A peaceful setting in tropical gardens. International cuisine with local produce. Walks can be arranged through the surrounding coffee plantations. **$$**

Marangu Hotel Kilimanjaro
PO Box 40,
Moshi
Tel: 027-275 6594/6362
Fax: 027-275 6591
www.maranguhotel.com
This hotel on the slopes of Kilimanjaro stands in 5 hectares (12 acres) of gardens, with views up to the towering mountain. The central building, a former farmhouse, was built in old-world style at the turn of the last century, and the guest accommodation is provided in cottages. There is a swimming pool, a croquet lawn and some excellent walking, but the thrust of the hotel is to get its guests up Kilimanjaro. The staff are friendly and helpful, the food good and the enthusiasm for Kili enormous. **$$**

PRICE CATEGORIES

Price codes (based on double occupancy in high season)
$ = under US$50
$$ = US$50–150
$$$ = US$150–300
$$$$ = US$300–500
$$$$$ = over US$500

THE NORTHERN SAFARI CIRCUIT

Tarangire

Oliver's Camp
PO Box 425,
Arusha
Tel: 027-250 8548/0744-465 473
www.oliverscamp.com
Paul Oliver's small luxury camp in the eastern section of the park, overlooking the swamps, has just eight beautifully furnished tents. The camp has an excellent wildlife library, knowledgeable guides and permission to run walking tours within the park (also available to those staying elsewhere). $$$$

Tamarind Camp
PO Box 2047, India Street,
Arusha
Tel: 027-250 7011
Fax: 027-254 8226
www.kirurumu.com
Looking as if it is ready to pack up and leave at a moment's notice, Tamarind is probably the closest you will come to the 1900s safari experience. About 6 km (4 miles) off the main road, just outside the western boundary of the park, it is set in flat, dry, sandy acacia scrubland. Accommodation is in 10 tents, with bucket showers and chemical toilets. Even the dining room is a tent. There is no electricity. Best used as a base for visiting the park. $$

Tarangire Safari Lodge
Serengeti Select Safaris,
PO Box 2703, Arusha
Tel: 027-254 4222
or 0784-202777
www.serengetisafaris.com
Stretched out along a ridge, with a fabulous view of the Tarangire River in the northwest corner of the park, only 15 minutes' drive from the main gate. Accommodation is in five small thatched chalets and 35 tents with thatched-roof covers, permanent bathrooms behind and a small veranda area in front. The tents are rather too close together for privacy; furnishings are simple but adequate. The communal areas include a large bar and terrace, pool and dining room. Solar power is available 6am–3pm, and 6–11pm. It is possible to book game drives through reception. $$

Tarangire Sopa Lodge
PO Box 1823,
Arusha
Tel: 027-250 0630
Fax: 027-250 8245
www.sopalodges.com
Large but attractive hotel with 75 rooms (four with facilities for the disabled) in the central area of the national park. The rooms are all in double-storey *bandas* (village Africa theme), while the central area, with bar, restaurant, sitting room, conference and TV room, is supposed to resemble an elephant. The views are superb, and lunch is a buffet beside a magnificent swimming pool set among rocks and baobab trees. $$

Tarangire Treetops
Elewana Africa
About 20 km (12 miles) off the main road, Tarangire
Tel: 027-250 0630–9
www.elewana.com
A delightful small lodge in the Lolkisala Conservation Area, east of the national park. There are 20 tree-house suites with showers and private balconies. Other facilities include a bar, dining room and plunge pool. Walks, mountain biking (only for the fit), night drives, bush dinners and village visits are available at an additional cost. The food is wonderful, the atmosphere relaxed. Elephants are frequent visitors. $$$$

Lake Manyara

Kirurumu Tented Lodge
PO Box 2047, India Street,
Arusha
Tel: 027-250 7011
Fax: 027-254 8226
www.kirurumu.com
Luxury lodge, with 22 large, well-furnished en suite tented rooms scattered through the bush, although the feeling of remote wilderness is marred somewhat by the village football pitch next door. The location, at the top of the escarpment, offers superb views, with the bar perfectly situated for spectacular sunsets. The food is good, the lodge well run and friendly. $$$

Lake Manyara Serena Lodge
PO Box 2551,
Arusha
Tel: 027-253 9161–3
Fax: 027-253 9164
www.serenahotels.com
The best of the Serena lodges, with 67 en-suite rooms in thatched *bandas* and a swimming pool, on the edge of the Rift Valley Escarpment, looking down into the park and across the lake. $$$

Lake Manyara Tree Lodge
CC Africa, P. Bag X27,
Benmore 2010, Johannesburg,
South Africa
Tel: +27-11-809 4300
Fax: +27-11-809 4400
www.ccafrica.com
Set deep in the southwestern part of the national park, CC Africa has created an idyllic lodge, its 10 simply but beautifully furnished timber and thatch rooms cradled in the boughs of a mahogany forest. Other facilities include an open-air living room, bar, dining room and excellent game viewing. Activities (such as game drives and canoeing) are included in the price). Closed Apr–May. $$$$

Twiga Campsite and Lodge
Mto wa Mbu
www.zara.co.tz
Right in the town, at the foot of the escarpment, near the park gate, this is the best of the budget accommodation on offer in the Manyara area, with basic en-suite double rooms, a camp site and restaurant. $

Karatu

Gibb's Farm
PO Box 280,
Karatu
Tel: 027-253 4397
Fax: 027-253 4418
www.gibbsfarm.net
This charming coffee farm near Karatu has become a local legend. Situated on the edge of the Ngorongoro cloud forest, it has 20 twin-roomed, prettily furnished cottages, set in an idyllic garden. The gardeners are only too happy to show you around the flower garden, the vast organic vegetable garden and the coffee plantation. The resident naturalist is on hand for forest and bird walks, while one of the receptionists runs an excellent Iraqw cultural tour. The food is excellent. $$$

Ngorongoro Safari Resort
Tel: 025-253 4287
Fax: 025-253 4288
Email: safariresort@yahoo.com
Right in the centre of Karatu, this offers relatively cheap, clean rooms in an unexciting motel block that is the nearest thing in Tanzania to a motorway service station, with a garage, cheap and cheerful restaurant and internet café, plus a small, well-kept camp site. A good compromise if you can't afford the nearby lodges. $

Octagon Safari Lodge
PO Box 129
Tel: 027-253 4525
www.octagonlodge.com
This is a delightful country lodge close to Ngorongoro Crater and Lake Manyara. Set amidst 2.8 hectares (7 acres) of beautiful old-style gardens, it provides a perfect spot to relax on safari. The lodge has an excellent reputation for organic food grown in their own garden. Lively Irish bar serves whiskey and Guinness. $$$$

Plantation Lodge
Tel: 027-253 4364/5
c/o Tanzania Odessey
UK: +44-20-7471 8780
US: +1-866-356 4691
www.tanzaniaodyssey.com
Slightly cheaper version of the Gibb's Farm experience, staying in an attractive old thatched farmstead not far from Karatu, at the edge of the forest. $$

Ngorongoro

Ngorongoro Crater Lodge
CC Africa, P. Bag X27,
Benmore 2010, Johannesburg,
South Africa
Tel: +27-11-809 4300
Fax: +27-11-809 4400
www.ccafrica.com
A unique experience, this
extraordinary hotel brings
high-camp Baroque design
to the African bush, with
spectacular views across
the crater. The sumptuous
accommodation, which
comes complete with
chandeliers, raw silk, log
fires, rose-strewn bubble
baths and a personal
butler, is divided into two
camps with 12 suites each
and a tree camp with six
suites. Must be seen to be
believed. Take out a
mortgage, if necessary,
but go – it's worth it.
$$$$$

Ngorongoro Serena Lodge
PO Box 2551,
Arusha
Tel: 027-253 7050/52/53/55
Fax: 027-253 7056
www.serenahotels.com
In a very 1970s version of
eco-friendly unobtrusive
design, this 75-room lodge
is built long and low along
the crater rim. It isn't
visible from a distance, and
once inside, the lack of
charm isn't evident, leaving
a comfortable chain-style
hotel with superb views
from all rooms. **$$$**

Ngorongoro Sopa Lodge
PO Box 1823,

Arusha
Tel: 027-250 0630
Fax: 027-250 8245
www.sopalodges.com
The only lodge on the
eastern rim, with its own
access route to the crater
floor, this is the most
traditional of the three
lodges. It has 100
attractive, centrally heated
suites, a swimming pool for
the hardy, and like the
others, superb views, with
the added benefit of
sunsets over the crater. **$$**

Serengeti

Grumeti
CC Africa, P. Bag X27,
Benmore 2010, Johannesburg,
South Africa
Tel: +27-11-809 4300
Fax: +27-11-809 4400
www.ccafrica.com
This wonderfully luxurious
small bush camp in the
Western Corridor has ten
tents, protected by
banana-leaf thatch,
overlooking a hippo pool
on a tributary of the
Grumeti River, with year-
round wildlife and front-
row seats for the
migration. The furnishings
are stylish and
comfortable, the service
and food flawless, and
wildlife from buffaloes to
birds regularly visit. One
to save up for. **$$$$$**

Kirawira Camp
PO Box 2551,
Arusha
Tel: 028-262 1518

Fax: 028-262 1517
www.serenahotels.com
Unlike the other Serena
properties, which are all
large lodges, this luxury
tented lodge deep in the
Western Corridor,
overlooking the Grumeti
River, is pure Hollywood
safari fantasy, with
Edwardian decor and 25
spacious en-suite tents.
There's a large swimming
pool and fine food. **$$$$$**

Klein's Camp
CC Africa, P. Bag X27,
Benmore 2010, Johannesburg,
South Africa
Tel: +27-11-809 4300
Fax: +27-11-809 4400
www.ccafrica.com
Set on a 10,000-hectare
(25,000-acre) private
concession in the Kuka
Hills on the northeastern
edge of the Serengeti, this
delightful lodge has the
best of all worlds, slap
bang on the migration
route, but with game walks
and the possibility of
driving off-road at night.
There are 10 beautifully
decorated, twin-bedded en-
suite cottages, a lounge
and pool. **$$$$$**

Hemingway's Camp
PO Box 2047
Tel: 027-250 7011/7541
Fax: 027-254 8226
www.kirurumu.com
A luxury tented camp in a
remote and stunningly
beautiful location. The
camp is a day's drive from
Ngorongoro, in a private
concession on a game-

controlled area, right on
the edge of the Serengeti,
with no boundary fences
and high game densities.
Unparalleled opportunities
for walking safaris and fly-
camping. The camp works
in partnership with the
local Maasai community.
Price fully inclusive of
drinks and activities.
$$$$

Ndutu Safari Lodge
PO Box 6084,
Arusha
Tel: 027-250 6702/2829
Fax: 027-250 8310
www.ndutu.com
This friendly, laid-back bush
lodge is technically still in
the Ngorongoro
Conservation Area, on the
southern border of the
Serengeti. It has 32 simply
furnished double rooms,
excellent food, wonderfully
friendly staff, and is
popular with visiting film
crews and naturalists, so
you can guarantee
interesting conversations
round the campfire. The
local genets arrive every
evening to watch the
diners. **$$$**

Serengeti Migration Camp
PO Box 1823,
Elewana Africa
Tel: 027-250 0630–9
www.elewana.com
Perched on a rocky kopje
overlooking the Grumeti
River, in the park's
northern sector, this
exclusive camp has 16
luxurious en-suite tents,
while the pool, library,

BELOW: game viewing in the Ngorongoro Crater.

dining room and viewing platforms are linked by timber walkways. The staff are friendly and helpful and the food good. **$$$$**
Serengeti Serena Lodge
PO Box 2551, Arusha
Tel: 028-262 1519/262 1507
Fax: 028-621 520
www.serenahotels.com
This large hotel is built in the style of an African village, complete with 66 beehive-thatched *bandas*. About 20 km (12 miles) west of Seronera, its hilltop location offers wonderful views and an excellent base for exploring the central Serengeti, although the immediate area is a little overgrown for really good game viewing. Pool. **$$$**

Serengeti Sopa Lodge
PO Box 1823,
Arusha
Tel: 027-250 0630
Fax: 027-250 8245
www.sopalodges.com
Located in the park's best game-viewing area, between the Moru Kopjes and the Seronera Valley, all 100 spacious en-suite rooms at this large, unwieldy lodge have a private balcony. The local game viewing is excellent and the food good. Swimming pool. **$$**

For cheaper accommodation near the western gates of the Serengeti, see the section below on Lake Victoria, between Mwanza and Musoma.

LAKE VICTORIA

In addition to the hotels listed below, basic guesthouses proliferate in the larger towns and also operate in Nansio, Bunda and Geita.

Rubondo Island National Park

National Park Campsite & Bandas
1 km (½ mile) north of Rubondo Island Camp.
Booking is seldom required at this beach-side campsite, which has simple *bandas* using communal showers ($) and smart self-contained chalets ($$). The staff shop sells basic food-stuffs, beers and sodas, and there is a cook, but it's best to bring food with you.
Tanzania Photographic Safaris
PO Box 284, Arusha
Tel: 027-250 8790
www.tzphotosafaris.com
Swiss contact
Tel: +41-31-392 5450
Exclusive tented camp magnificently set on a secluded sandy beach punctuated by rocky outcrops and hemmed in by tall gallery forest. Tranquil, relaxed mood and good home cooking. Swimming pool and bar/restaurant built into a natural rock outcrop. Guided walks, boat trips and game fishing available. **$$$$**

Mwanza

Hotel Tilapia
PO Box 82, Station Road, 1 km (½ mile) from town centre, adjacent to Saa Nane jetty
Tel: 028-250 0517/0617 or 0784-700500
Fax: 028-250 0141
www.hoteltilapia.com
Attractive, efficient mid-range hotel with pretty lake-shore location, swimming pool, car hire, business centre, and popular Thai and Indian restaurants. En-suite double chalets have air conditioning and satellite television. **$$**
New Mwanza Hotel
PO Box 25, Post Road, city centre
Tel: 028-250 1070–1
Fax: 028-250 3202
www.newmwanzahotel.com
Renovated former government hotel steeped in a bland, quasi-international atmosphere, more likely to win over business travellers than tourists. Business centre, coffee shop, good restaurant, casino and shopping arcade on site. En-suite rooms with air conditioning and satellite television. Standard rooms **$$**. Suites **$$$$**
Tunza Lodge
off Airport Rd
10 km (6 miles) from city centre and 3 km (1½ miles) from airport
Tel: 028-256 2215
www.renair.com
Clean and unpretentious en-suite chalets with fan but no airconditioning. The lodge has neat gardens on a private swimming beach. Windsurfing and water-skiing are available, and fishing trips can be arranged – this almost qualifies as Lake Victoria's one and only beach resort. Decent grills and fish served in the thatched restaurant. Lively bar at weekends. **$$**

Between Mwanza and Musoma

Serengeti Stop Over
Alongside main road 1 km (½ mile) south of Serengeti's Ndaraka Gate, 18 km (11 miles) south of Bunda
Tel: 028-262 2273
www.serengetistopover.com
Presentable, friendly and clued-up budget lodge, ideally positioned for self-drive forays into the Serengeti; also able to arrange day and overnight safaris for those without a vehicle. En-suite chalets **$$**. Camping **$**
Speke Bay Lodge
PO Box 953, Close to main road, 125 km (74 miles) from Mwanza and 15 km (9 miles) south of Serengeti's Ndaraka Gate
Tel: 028-262 1236
Fax: 028-262 1237
www.spekebay.com
This attractive lake-shore lodge has eight thatched en-suite bungalows and 10 standing safari tents (communal showers only). Birdwatching and game fishing can be arranged. The highly rated restaurant is regularly visited for lunch by day-trippers from western Serengeti lodges. **$–$$**

Musoma

Afrilux Hotel
PO Box 519, town centre, 500 metres/yards from the bus station
Tel: 028-262 0031
www.afriluxhotel.net
Acceptable multi-storey block of clean en-suite rooms with satellite television, fan and hot water. Good Indian restaurant. **$**
Peninsula Hotel
PO Box 440, lake shore about 500 metres/yards west of the town centre
Tel: 028-262 0119
Nicely refurbished hotel with good restaurant serving Indian and European food. Very reasonably priced en-suite doubles with satellite television, air conditioning, fridge and hot bath **$**. Suites **$$**

Biharamulo

Robert Hotel
Facing the bus stop on the main road into town
Good food, air-conditioning and en-suite rooms. **$**

Bukoba

Lake Hotel
Lake-shore end of Jamhuri Avenue
Tel: 028-222 0237
Scenically located and, despite recent renovations, somewhat faded old colonial hotel with gardens and a not unattractive period feel. En-suite rooms have fans, nets and (intermittent) hot water. Unexciting but thoroughly edible food. Camping permitted. **$**

PRICE CATEGORIES
Price codes (based on double occupancy in high season)
$ = under US$50
$$ = US$50–150
$$$ = US$150–300
$$$$ = US$300–500
$$$$$ = over US$500

LAKE TANGANYIKA

Outside Kigoma, Mahale Mountains and the Katavi National Park, accommodation in western Tanzania is very basic. Simple local guesthouses operate in Mpanda, Ujiji, Ikola, Kasanga and Sumbawanga.

Kigoma

Kigoma Hilltop Hotel
Chimpanzee Safaris, 2 km (1 mile) south of the town centre
Tel: 028-280 4435–7
Fax: 028-280 4434
www.kigoma.com
This well managed, attractively laid-out hotel has a great cliff-top location overlooking Kigoma Bay. Facilities include a pool, water sports, various indoor games, a gym, secretarial services, a generator and private beach. Fishing, snorkelling and chimp-tracking excursions can be arranged. En-suite chalet accommodation with air-conditioning, satellite TV and a fridge. Good Indian restaurant (no alcohol). Standard rooms **$$**. Suites **$$$**
Lake Tanganyika Beach Hotel
Lake shore, 500 metres/yards from the town centre
Tel: 028-280 2694
Former government hotel with shabby en-suite rooms and an erratic water supply, the dinginess is partially redeemed by the lovely location. The (mostly Indian) food is pretty good, and it's a great sundowner spot – beers chilled or warm depending on whether anybody remembered to bung a few in the fridge. **$**

Gombe Stream National Park

Gombe Forest Lodge
Chimpanzee Safaris, PO Box 1160, Kigoma
Tel: 022-213 0553 or 0713-620154
Fax: 022-213 0487
www.chimpanzeesafaris.com
This luxury-tented camp is

operated by Chimpanzee Safaris. Beautifully situated alongside the Mitumba Stream. **$$$$**
Kasekela Rest Camp
Attached to the lake-shore research station
Bookings can be radioed from the Kigoma Hilltop Hotel, but are rarely necessary. This rest house has two scruffy twin rooms, nets, no fan, and a screened porch. There is an even cheaper hostel with smaller, even scruffier rooms, and no nets. Camping is permitted, but costs more than the hostel rooms. Very basic food can be arranged, and warm beers are available, but it is advisable to stock up in Kigoma before you get there. **$**

Mahale Mountain National Park

Bilenge Resthouse
At the park headquarters 10 km (6 miles) north of Kasiha Tourist Centre
Bookings (seldom necessary) can be radioed from the Kigoma Hilltop Hotel or *MV Liemba*. Predictably run-down but fabulously positioned two-bedroom rest house on the lake shore, 300 metres/yards from the main headquarters buildings. Drinks and basic meals are available – along with satellite television – at the staff canteen. **$**
Mango Tree Rest Camp/Kasiha Guest House
Part of the Kasiha Tourist Centre. Set in a mango glade a short walk inland of the lake shore, the run-down old rooms here have been supplemented by six unexpectedly smart semi-detached en-suite chalets. All rooms have nets and, bizarrely, they cost the same, irrespective of whether they're new or old, en suite or not. No food is available. Bookings (seldom necessary) can be radioed from the Kigoma Hilltop Hotel or *MV Liemba*. **$**
Kungwe Beach Lodge
Tel: 022-213 0553 or

0713-620154
Email: nfo@mbalimbali.com
An excellent, beautifully located retreat. Chimp tracking, snorkelling, swimming and other activities are available. Luxurious en-suite standing tents with large double beds, flush toilet and shower. **$$$$$**
The Original Mahale Camp/Greystoke Mahale
3 km (2 miles) south of Kasiha Tourist Centre
www.greystoke-mahale.com
Wonderful safari lodge, established in 1990, and set on a sandy private beach. Consists of six rustic but very comfortable double tents verging on the beach, not quite en suite, but each with a private shower. The chic, two-storey dining area is made entirely of organic material and canvas, and has a good reference library. Chimp tracking, snorkelling and other activities arranged. Open May–Nov only. **$$$$$**

Katavi National Park

Katavi Bush Lodge
Tel: 022-213 0553 or 0713-620154
Email: info@mbalimbaili.com
Situated in the centre of the park overlooking the vast plains of Katisunga. Spacious luxury tents amid fantastic scenery. **$$$**
Lake Katavi Rest House
15 km (8 miles) south of Sitalike, 1 km (½ mile) west of the

Mpanda–Sumbawanga road
Africa's most beautifully located concrete bunker, this unfurnished rest house overlooks the game-rich Katavi Floodplain. Bring everything you need, including water, food, bedding – and a tent, perhaps? Booking by radio only. **$**
National Park Resthouse
500 metres/yards from the main Mpanda–Sumbawanga road, 1 km (½ mile) south of Sitalike
Catering to national park officials but also to tourists, this modern rest house at the park headquarters has comfortable rooms, satellite television, basic meals and a bar. Booking by radio only. **$**
The Original Katavi Camp
www.chada-katavi.com
Set among acacia trees overlooking the Chada Floodplain, a favoured haunt of elephant and lion. It sounds rather basic on paper: no permanent structures or manicured lawns, just half a dozen comfortable but uncluttered double tents with private open-air hot shower and long-drop toilets, dotted around the pristine bush. But more perhaps than any other lodge in East Africa, this offers an immediate and exclusive bush experience reminiscent of the days before package safaris – with superb food and chilled drinks on tap. In a word: fantastic. **$$$$$**

BELOW: the "Out of Africa" style on safari.

CENTRAL TANZANIA

Accommodation in this region, with only two exceptions, is restricted to basic local guesthouses charging less than US$10. Superior guesthouses, with en suite rooms, are listed where they exist.

Dodoma

Dodoma Hotel
Opposite the railway station
Tel: 026-232 1641
Fax: 026-232 4911
Email: dodomahotel@kicheko.com
Dodoma's finest is identifiably a former government institution, despite having been privatised in the late 1990s. Attractively set around a green courtyard, the en-suite rooms are adequate and very reasonably priced. The culinary mediocrity of the restaurant is sometimes alleviated by live local music at weekends. $

Tabora

Orion Tabora Hotel
200 metres/yards from the railway station
Tel: 026-260 6670 ext 2378
Email: oriontbrhotel@spidersat.net
The languid, shady verandas and whitewashed exterior of this low-key but attractive hotel reflect its origin as a colonial-era hunting lodge. Owned by the Tanzania Railway Corporation, it's easily the best hotel in town, though lack of custom has twice in recent memory forced its closure for a substantial duration. The en-suite rooms are clean and have nets, and the food isn't bad. $

Wilca Hotel
Boma Road, east of the town centre
Tel: 026-260 4106
This good-value and popular hotel consists of a dozen no-frills en-suite rooms (hot water, net and fan), set around a green courtyard. Decent meals are served in the garden bar, which also has a pool table, table tennis and satellite television. $

Kondoa

New Planet Hotel
200 metres/yards from the bus station
Tel: Kondoa 180 or 0748-669322
Pleasant, well managed but relatively basic local guesthouse; en suite rooms with net, fan and running water – more than can be said for any other lodge in town. Greasy meat with chips is about the extent of the menu but even this is a cut above par for Kondoa. $

Kolo

Department of Antiquities Campsite
3 km (2 miles) east of town, along the road to Mungomi wa Kolo
In lieu of any roofed accommodation, visitors can camp at this pretty site on the banks of the seasonal Kolo River. Water and toilet facilities are available, but little else. $

Babati

Kahambe's Guesthouse
PO Box 366, 500 metres/yards from the bus station
Tel: 027-253 1088
Email: fidebabati@hotmail.com
Most visitors stay at this basic but clean guesthouse, if only because it's run by the Babati and Hanang Cultural Tourism Programme. Rooms are not en suite. $

Katesh

Colt Guesthouse
Situated opposite the town's main market, this basic local guesthouse has clean, spacious en-suite double rooms with hot running water. $
Mtei Guesthouse
Close to the bus station. This guesthouse is similar in standard and price to the Colt. $

Lake Basuto

Saria Guesthouse
The only accommodation in Basuto town: great lake-shore location, dismal rooms with bucket showers only. $

SOUTHERN PARKS AND TANZAM HIGHWAY

Ruaha National Park

Jongomero Camp
The Selous Safari Company
PO Box 1192, Dar es Salaam
Tel: 022-212 8485/213 4802
Fax: 022-211 2794
www.selous.com
A luxury safari camp set under shady acacia trees on the banks of the Jongomero Sand River in the remote southwestern sector of Ruaha. Jongomero is the only camp situated in this area of the park, ensuring unmatched privacy. The eight large, well appointed tents under enormous thatched roofs each have a spacious private veranda overlooking the river. $$$$
Mwagusi Safari Camp
c/o TropicAfrica
Tel: +44-752-517 0940
www.ruaha.org
Personalised service, fine attention to detail, and a tangible empathy with the bush are hallmarks of this exclusive owner-managed tented camp, set in riparian woodland alongside the seasonal Mwagusi River. The walk-in tents – seriously spacious – are enclosed in wood, thatch and reed shelters leading to a vast private bathroom. Weather permitting, dinner is held in the river bed, below the stars, surrounded by the sounds of the African night. Game viewing is excellent in the surrounding area and other vehicles are scarce. Exciting game walks are offered. $$$$–$$$$$
Ruaha River Lodge
Foxes African Safaris
Tel: +44-1452-862 288
www.tanzaniasafaris.info
Long-serving and highly regarded lodge situated on a rocky hill side overlooking the Ruaha River 10 km (6 miles) from the entrance gate. Game viewing can be very good from the thatched bar and restaurant, as well as on the surrounding roads. The simply furnished stone cottages and standing tents are all en suite. $$$$–$$$$$

Selous Game Reserve

Beho Beho Camp
PO Box 2261
Tel: 022-260 0352–4
Fax: 022-260 0347
www.behobeho.com
This exclusive lodge is set some distance from the river on a hill overlooking a vast extent of open bush. The smart en-suite stone cottages have a fan, a good view, and fun outdoor showers. The dining area, shaded by a high *makuti* roof, is a winner. The remoteness from other lodges is apparent on game drives, when it's unusual to see another vehicle. $$$$$
Rufiji River Camp
PO Box 13284, Ohio Street, Dar es Salaam
Tel: 022-212 8663
Fax: 022-212 8661
www.hippotours.com
Popular and (by Selous's standards) affordable owner-managed lodge in a

PRICE CATEGORIES

Price codes (based on double occupancy in high season)
$ = under US$50
$$ = US$50–150
$$$ = US$150–300
$$$$ = US$300–500
$$$$$ = over US$500

prime location overlooking an action-packed stretch of the Rufiji River. The 20 en-suite tents have fans and are spaced comfortably apart. Informal and inclusive atmosphere enhanced by good Italian home-style cooking and a flexible attitude to activities. An excellent range of boat and foot safaris, as well as half-day game drives (encompassing three nearby lakes) and fly-camping. **$$$$$**

Sable Mountain Lodge
1 km (½ mile) outside the Western Park boundary near the Matembwe Gate
A Tent with a View Safaris, PO Box 40525, Dar es Salaam
Tel: 022-211 0507 or 0741-323318
Fax: 022-212 3812
www.selouslodge.com
Mid-range lodge with eight en-suite double cottages scattered on a wooded hill side overlooking a waterhole frequented by elephants and other large mammals. Guided walks lead through dense local woodland harbouring forest birds and mammals not normally associated with the Selous. Game drives head out to more open areas with the usual array of savanna game. Fly-camping excursions and river trips are available. Budget visits using the TAZARA Railway (when it's running) are a unique feature of this lodge. **$$$$**

Sand Rivers Selous
PO Box 681
Tel: 027-2553 819/20/29/30
www.sand-rivers-selous.com
The most luxurious of the Selous lodges, Sand Rivers consists of 16 airy and elegant en-suite stone cottages overlooking a wide bend in the Rufiji River. The air of exclusivity is enhanced by its end-of-the-road location in an area seldom visited by vehicles from other lodges. Known for its high standard of guiding, Sand Rivers has a good reputation for game walks and fly-camping, while game drives to the lakes and boat trips through Stiegler's Gorge (leopard territory) are also offered. Excellent European food in the restaurant; swimming pool. **$$$$$**

Selous Impala Camp
Adventure Camps
PO Box 40569
Tel: 022-245 2005–6
Fax:022-245 2004
www.adventurecamps.co.tz
This is exclusive luxury, with just eight comfortable tents complete with en-suite bathrooms set on wooden platforms on the banks of the Rufiji River. There is an excellent restaurant and bar with swimming pool. Game drives and boat safaris are included. **$$$$**

Selous Safari Camp
Tel: 022-213 4794
www.selous.com
UK Contact: Tel: +44-1367-253 810
Classic luxury bush camp consisting of 12 standing tents with fans and en-suite open-air showers spaced widely along the waterfront. Excellent food is eaten in a wonderful gas-lit stilted treehouse. Game drives, boat trips, guided walks and fly-camping are all offered. **$$$$$**

Mikumi National Park

Fox's Safari Camp
Tel: 0744-237 422 or 0741-237422
Fax: 0741-327 706
www.tanzaniasafaris.info
UK Contact
Tel/fax: +44-1452-862 288
Established in 2001 by the owners of Ruaha River Lodge, this small, tranquil tented camp is set on a rocky slope offering panoramic views over the Mkata Floodplain and excellent game viewing. It's the only lodge in Mikumi sufficiently far from the Tanzam Highway that you don't hear the trucks.
$$$$–$$$$$

Genesis Motel
Mikumi Town
Tel: 023-262 0461
Fax: 023-262 0443
www.genesismotel.com
Modest town hotel often used by budget tour groups and researchers. En-suite bungalows with satellite television, well-stocked bar and good restaurant. Moderately interesting snake park attached. **$–$$**

Kikoboga Lodge
PO Box 2261
Tel: 022-260 0352–4
Fax: 022-260 0347
Email: oysterbay-hotel@twiga.com
Affordable, under-utilised and good-value lodge consisting of 12 large en-suite stone chalets, each with a private veranda, spaced out in front of two waterholes frequented daily by elephant, giraffe, zebra and other large mammals. Excellent location for game drives, though the night chorus of hyenas and lions is spoilt by rumbling vehicles on the nearby Tanzam Highway. **$$$**

Vuma Hills Tented Camp
www.tanzaniasafaris.com
A dozen classy en-suite tents on stilted wood platforms with verandas offering great views over the bushy hills south of the Tanzam Highway. Justifiably popular weekend retreat for Dar es Salaam residents. Quality Italian cuisine, swimming pool, game drives and guided walks available. **$$$–$$$$**

Morogoro

Hotel Oasis
PO Box 624, 200 metres/yards from railway station
Tel: 023-260 4178/3535 or 0744-377602–4
Fax: 023-260 4830
www.hoteloasistz.com
Smart and well run multi-storey business hotel. En-suite rooms have air conditioning, nets, satellite television and fridge. Good internet café, business centre and Indian restaurant. **$**

New Acropol Hotel
Old Dar es Salaam Road, PO Box 78, Morogoro
Tel: 0754-309 410 or 0715-309410
www.newacropolhotel.biz
This stylish, Canadian-owned hotel somehow brings to mind a misplaced Mediterranean pension, which distinguishes it from the town's blander alternatives. Bright en-suite rooms have a sofa, fridge, satellite television and air conditioning. The attached restaurant serves good pizzas and grills. **$**

UMADEP Guesthouse
Nyandira
NGO-operated guesthouse offering decent no-frills accommodation within easy striking distance of the Uluguru forests. **$**

Udzungwa Mountains National Park

Udzungwa Mountain View Hotel
In Mang'ula, 1 km (½ mile) from

BELOW: sunset cruise on the Rufiji River.

TRANSPORT

ACCOMMODATION

EATING OUT

ACTIVITIES

A – Z

LANGUAGE

the national park entrance gate
Tel: 023-262 0466
Fax: 023-262 0443
www.genesismotel.com
An offshoot of Mikumi's
Genesis Motel, this small,
no-frills hotel and camp site
is used by most tour
groups visiting Udzungwa.
Decent food. **$**

Iringa

Kisolanza Farm
Alongside the Tanzam Highway, 50
km (30 miles) southwest of Iringa
Tel: 0754-306 144
www.kisolanza.com
Family-owned farm offering
cosy, old-world chalets in
the gardens of the colonial
farmhouse, as well as
separate camping and basic
backpacker huts. Great
walking, birdwatching, and a
convenient stopover en
route to Mbeya. Chalets **$$**.
Huts and camping **$**
MR Hotel
PO Box 431, Mkwawa Road
Tel: 026-270 2006

Fax: 026-170 2661
www.mrhotels.co.tz
Iringa's smartest hotel is
clean, tightly managed, well-
regarded and thoroughly
unmemorable. En-suite
rooms have satellite
television and a fan. The
restaurant serves decent
international cuisine. **$**

MBEYA AND LAKE NYASA

In addition to the hotels
listed below, simple
guesthouses are available at
Songwe, Tunduru, Chunya,
Chimala, Matunda, Mbamba
Bay, Songea and Njombe.

Mbeya

Mount Livingstone Hotel
Town centre
Tel: 0741-323 906
www.twiga.ch/TZ/mtlivingstone.htm
The only hotel in central
Mbeya with up-market
aspirations: blandly
comfortable, not bad value
– but not madly inspiring.
En-suite rooms have hot
water and satellite TV. **$$**
Mufindi Highland Lodge
Foxes African Safaris
PO Box 10270, Dar es Salaam
Tel: 0784-237 422
Fax: 022-286 2357
www.tanzaniasafaris.info
Relax in the cool mountain
air, overlooking the 600-
metre (2,000-ft) Rift Valley
in the Southern Highlands
of Tanzania. Fly fish for
rainbow trout or watch the

sun set over rolling hills.
This working 800-hectare
(2,000-acre) farm is all
about the freedom to roam
where you please by horse,
foot or mountain bike in
rainforests, tea estates,
stunning scenery and
villages to discover another
side of Africa. **$$$$**
Utengule Country Hotel
PO Box 138, Mbeya, Tanzania
12 km (7 miles) south of Mbeya on
the Tanzam Highway to Mbalizi,
then 8 km (5 miles) along a side
road to the right
Tel: 0753-020 901 or 0786-481902
www.riftvalley-zanzibar.com
This established, cosy and
welcoming lodge, set on a
200-hectare (500-acre)
coffee estate in the forested
foothills of Mbeya Peak, is
the best – indeed, only –
up-market base from which
to explore the Southern
Highlands. Swimming pool,
tennis and squash courts,
mini golf, pool table,
mountain bike and
motorbike hire, knowledgeable owner-manager,

excellent restaurant and en-
suite chalets with all mod
cons. **$$**

Tukuyu

Langboss Hotel
1 km (½ mile) out of town along
the Masoko road
Adequate local guesthouse
offering en-suite rooms
with hot shower. **$**
Lutengano Moravian Centre
12 km (7 miles) from Tukuyu along
Kaporogwe Waterfall road
Clean hostel with gardens;
meals by advance order.
Single/double/triple rooms
have communal showers.
Camping permitted. **$**

Kyela

Oberoi Park
PO Box 322, 200 metres/yards
from market and bus station
Tel: 025-254 0395
Spotless local guesthouse
offering en-suite rooms
with fan and running water.
Bring your own mosquito
nets. **$**

Matema Beach

**Matema Beach
Evangelical Church Hostel**
Beach-front hostel
consisting of a row of
bright, comfortable
double-storey en-suite
chalets with private
verandas. Fair restaurant,
chilled soft drinks (no
alcohol). **$**
**Matema Lutheran
Conference Centre and
Retreat**
Cheaper and more run-
down hostel with cramped,
stuffy cottages littered
untidily above the beach.
Dour canteen serves barely
adequate meals by
advance order. Camping
permitted; alcohol not. **$**

Songea

White House Hotel
2 km (1 mile) out of town on the
Njombe Road
Fair en-suite doubles with
hot water. Reasonable
garden restaurant. **$**

THE SOUTH COAST

With the exception of
Mafia, accommodation on
the south coast is generally
restricted to basic
guesthouses.
    The Old Boma in
Mikindani, though not
resort-like, is the only
established tourist-class
accommodation in the
region, but new
developments in Mtwara
and Kilwa Masoko have
potential.
    In addition to the hotels
listed below, basic
accommodation can be

found in Kilwa Kivinje,
Masasi and Newala.

Kilwa Masoko

Kilwa Ruins Fishing Hotel
PO Box 44, Kilwa Masoko
Tel: 0748-637 026 or 0787-
712004
www.kilwaruinslodge.com
This unpretentious,
fabulous lodge consists of
air-conditioned *bandas* and
chalets on the seafront and
surrounding a swimming
pool. Open-air dining and
seating area with lovely sea

views. Excursions to Kilwa
Kisiwani and Songo Mnara;
game fishing, snorkelling
and water sports can be
arranged. **$$**
**Mjaka Family Guesthouse
& Village**
Kilwa Masoko
Dependable, friendly,
family-run guesthouse, with
rooms and basic en-suite
chalets. **$**

Lindi

Malaika Hotel
Market Avenue, 200 metres/yards

from the bus station
Tel: 0744-057 736
Easily the best hotel (and
restaurant) in Lindi,
essentially a reflection of
the dismal competition
rather than of any great

PRICE CATEGORIES

Price codes (based on double
occupancy in high season)
$ = under US$50
$$ = US$50–150
$$$ = US$150–300
$$$$ = US$300–500
$$$$$ = over US$500

inherent merit. Clean, spacious en-suite rooms with fan and nets. Acceptable local food. **$**

Mikindani

The Old Boma
Conspicuous hill-top position in town centre
Tel: 0748-360 110
UK Contact
Tel: +44-1425-657 774
Fax: +44-1425-656 684
www.mikindani.com
A certified gem; this lovingly restored 1895 German boma has eight airy en-suite rooms containing net, fan, hot bath and atmospheric Swahili furnishings. Excellent food, swimming pool in lovely wooded grounds, a variety of offbeat excursions arranged, all profits pumped back into community projects. Great value, too. **$$**

Ten Degrees South
Main road through town
Tel: 023-233 4053
www.eco2.com
English-run lodge aimed at the backpacker market. Rooms have Zanzibar-style bed and netting, and communal shower. Outdoor

restaurant serves great Thai, Indian and Portuguese dishes. Satellite television in the bar. **$–$$$**

Mtwara

Mtwara Peninsula Hotel
Town centre
Tel: 023-233 3638
The only established hostelry of any quality in Mtwara, this adequate local business traveller's hotel is on a scruffy back road behind the football stadium. All rooms en suite with air conditioning and satellite TV. **$**

Southern Cross Hotel
Shangani Beach, 2 km (1 mile) from town centre
Tel: 023-233 3206 or 0741-506047
www.msemo.com
Reasonable hotel on beach front with a restaurant that's open daily. All rooms have sea view; camping is also available. Fishing and safari trips can be arranged. **$**

Mafia Island

Kinasi Lodge
Chole Beach
PO Box 18033

Tel: 0713-242977
www.mafiaisland.com
This luxurious lodge caters less to sun-worshippers than to divers and nature-lovers, though the palm-studded gardens rising from the swimming pool and small beach are still the stuff of beach idyll fantasies. There are 14 en-suite coral bungalows with *makuti* roofs and tasteful Swahili furnishing. Spacious bar and dining area with excellent reference library and book exchange. The dive centre arranges numerous and varied dives plus snorkelling, windsurfing and game fishing. Two-hour bird trail; mountain bikes available. Closed April and May. **$$$$**

Pole Pole Bungalow Resort
Chole Beach
Tel: 022-260 1530
Fax: 022-260 0140
www.polepole.com
Italian-managed lodge consisting of seven luxurious bungalows built of natural materials, with nice en-suite bathrooms – arguably a touch overpriced for what they are. Dive school and

snorkelling available to guests. **$$$$$**

Chole Mjini Lodge
Chole Island
Tel: 0787-712 427
www.intotanzania.com
This laudably idiosyncratic and eco-friendly owner-managed lodge consists of six atmospheric tree houses set high in a stand of baobabs rising from the 19th-century ruins of Chole Mjini. It's not billed as a beach resort (mangrove-lined shore, no electricity, no fan, no gift shop) but is arguably the most aesthetically pleasing lodge on East Africa's coast. Diving, snorkelling, village visits. Community fee included in rates. First-class seafood. Not for everybody, but if you like the sound of it, you'll be smitten with the reality. **$$$$**

Mafia Island Lodge
Chole Beach
Tel: Mafia 76 or 022-260 1530
www.mafialodge.com
Great beach location, 40 cheerfully decorated rooms (including two family rooms) with sea view, air conditioning and en-suite bathrooms. Dive centre. **$$–$$$** (April and May **$$**)

ZANZIBAR AND PEMBA

This is by no means a definitive list of the many hotels on Unguja Island, but it does include a cross-section of the best, in various categories and price ranges. There are many others, from huge Italian mass-market resorts to tiny backstreet local hotels.

Stone Town

236 Hurumzi
236 Hurumzi Street, PO Box 3417

Tel: 0777-423 266
Fax: 0777-429 266
www.emerson-green.com
People drool at the mere mention of this charming small hotel in a traditional town-centre Swahili house. Beautifully furnished with antiques, every one of the 10 beautifully decorated rooms is different, some with balconies, sea or rooftop views. Book early to avoid disappointment. **$$$**

Al Johari
116 Shangani,
PO Box 3234
Tel: 024-223 6779
Fax: 024-223 6199
www.al-johari.com
Stylish modern hotel with 15 rooms, each beautifully furnished with marble floors, Persian rugs and intricately carved wooden

Zanzibar beds, LCD flat-screen TVs with 24 hour cable, minibar, climate control and free Wi-fi. All bathrooms have massage showers and are stocked with Kama Ayurveda beauty products. Suites are bright, spacious living areas with their own jacuzzi. **$$$$**

Beyt Al Chai
PO Box 4236
Tel: 0774-444 111
www.stonetowninn.com
Character-filled, traditional Stone Town house, converted into wonderful guest rooms. **$$**

Chavda Hotel
PO Box 540, Bahani Street
Tel: 024-223 2115
Fax: 024-223 1931
Email: chavda@zanzinet.com
Town-centre hotel in an old Swahili house. Comfortable,

very convenient and reasonably priced, with air conditioning, phone, minibar and television in all rooms. Rooftop restaurant and bar and some antiques. **$–$$**

Dhow Palace
Just off Kenyatta Road
Tel: 024-223 3012
Fax: 024-223 3008
www.tembohotel.com/dhowpalace.html
Attractive old restored house in the city centre, with a fountain courtyard, sympathetically furnished en-suite rooms and a rooftop restaurant. **$**

Jambo Guest House
Tel: 024-223 3779 or 0777-496571
Fax: 024-223-8696
Email: jamboguest@hotmail.com
A Stone Town institution, Jambo Guest House offers guests clean, intimate

quarters at reasonable rates. There are eight rooms at the hotel, all containing Zanzibar beds, mosquito nets and ceiling fans, sharing a common bathroom. Single, double and triple rooms are available. All room rates include breakfast. Other services include internet, telephone and fax facilities. Experience the best of Zanzibar on a shoestring. **$**

Malindi Guest House
PO Box 609
Tel: 024-223 0165
Email: malindi@zanzinet.com
Popular with backpackers; clean, comfortable and friendly with good interiors. **$**

Mazson's Hotel
Kenyatta Road, Shangani,
PO Box 3367
Tel: 024-223 3694
Fax: 024-223 3695
www.mazsonshotel.net
This comfortable town-centre hotel, in a restored 19th-century mansion, could not be more convenient. It has 35 en-suite rooms, all with air conditioning, fridge, telephone and TV, a business and conference centre, rooftop restaurant and attractive garden. The decor is a weird and rather kitsch combination of traditional Swahili and 1970s suburban. **$$**

St Monica's Hostel
Next to the Anglican Cathedral
Tel: 0744-223073
Email: actzanzibar@zanzinet.com
If you can ignore the ghostly presence of the slave chambers in the basement, this church-run hostel is the best of the backpacker accommodation, with cool, clean rooms, some en suite, all with balconies and nets. **$**

Tembo Inn House Hotel
Shangani Road
Tel: 024-223 3005
Fax: 024-223 3777
www.tembohotel.com
Once an Omani seafront mansion, smartly restored and now a sophisticated and atmospheric hotel, with a fine pool and restaurant. Its wonderful sea views and central position make this highly popular. **$$**

Zanzibar Serena Inn
Shangani

Tel: 024-223 3587
Fax: 024-223 3019
Central Reservations
PO Box 2551, Arusha
Tel: 027-250 4155/4058
Fax: 027-250 8282
www.serenahotels.com
Sympathetically restored from two historic buildings on the Shangani waterfront – one the former home of the British Consul. The rooms are thoughtfully furnished and come with all the trimmings, including air conditioning and sea views. There are two excellent restaurants, a pool, bar, business centre and shop. The concierge will arrange any excursions. **$$$–$$$$**

Elsewhere on the Island

Bluebay Beach Resort
Kiwengwa, PO Box 3276, Zanzibar
Tel: 024-224 0241–4
Fax: 024-224 0245
www.bluebayzanzibar.com
One of the best large resorts on the island, set on the northeast coast, with a grand Arab-style lobby and 102 rooms and suites, in double-storey thatched cottages, all with balconies. Completely refurbished in 2008. Facilities include tennis courts, a fitness centre, business centre, shop, dive shop, water sports and the usual range of excursions. **$$$**

Breezes Beach Club
PO Box 1361, Zanzibar
Tel: 0774-440883
Fax: 024-224 0450
www.breezes-zanzibar.com
This is the best and most famous of the resort hotels on the east coast, and geared towards honeymooners. The decor is tasteful and the staff are dedicated to your well-being, although the quality of the food can let down the overall effect at times. Great pool, beach, fitness centre, tennis, aerobics and massage, a variety of water sports, a good shop and a disco. **$$$$**

Chumbe Island
8 km (5 miles) off the west coast of Zanzibar, south of Stone Town
PO Box 3203, Zanzibar
Tel/fax: 024-223 1040

UK fax: +44-870-134 1284
www.chumbeisland.com
An enchanting island with virgin forest surrounded by some of East Africa's finest coral reefs. There are only seven award-winning eco-friendly wood and thatch cabins. Lighting and hot water are solar-powered. The water is all carefully stored rainwater. Your rates pay for the maintenance and policing of Tanzania's first marine park and an active educational programme with local schools. Snorkelling and forest walks with trained rangers. Highly recommended. **$$$$**

Flame Tree Cottages
PO Box 1752
Tel: 024-224 0100 or 0777-479429
www.flametreecottages.com
Small beach-front hotel situated on the beautiful north coast of Zanzibar. Rooms are set amongst private gardens with sitting room, bathroom, fans and air conditioning. Self-catering facilities are also available. Snorkelling trips, sunset sails, fishing trips and excursions to Stone Town or Jozani Forest can be easily arranged. **$$$**

Hakuna Matata Beach Lodge & Spa
PO Box 4747

Tel: 0777-454 892
www.hakuna-matata-beach-lodge.com
Located in the ruins of Chuini Palace 12 km (7½ miles) from Stone Town, Hakuna Matata is one of the most beautiful spots in Zanzibar. The restaurant offers a great selection of cuisine with seafood specialities. Weddings and candlelit dinners in the ruins can be arranged. Spectacular sundowners are an evening highlight over tropical cocktails. **$$$**

Kichanga Lodge
Tel: 0773-175124
Email: bookingkichanga@athomehotels.com
Skype: bookingkichanga
A small resort with a private beach on the northern tip of the southeast peninsula, with 18 charming cottages set in perfect harmony with the natural environment. All bungalows have large wooden verandas, some with interconnecting doors suitable for families. Facilities include swimming pool, bar, PADI dive centre, massage, sports, tours, internet connection and a fine restaurant serving seafood and international cuisine. **$$–$$$**

La Gemma Dell'Est
Nungwi Road
Tel: 024-224 0087

BELOW: relax in style at 236 Hurumzi.

ABOVE: lunch at Ras Michamvi Beach Resort.

Fax: 024-224 0089
www.planhotel.com
Situated on the north-western shores of Zanzibar, just out of Nungwi, this enchanting, luxurious and environmentally friendly resort development was designed and constructed to blend in with its magnificent surroundings and the contours of the landscape. Set in the midst of exotic tropical gardens and waterfalls with magnificent views of the Indian Ocean.
$$$$–$$$$$

Matemwe Bungalows
Asilia Lodges and Camps
PO Box 3275, Zanzibar
Tel: 0777-425 788
Fax: 0777-429 788
www.asilialodges.com
Charmingly laid-back small resort, with 12 simple but beautifully furnished, comfortable coral-rag cottages along the cliff top, all with verandas and fine sea views. One of Zanzibar's finest small beaches is next door, and it's a short walk to the local village. Popular with a young crowd and divers. The excellent set meals use local produce and seafood, solar power is used for lighting and hot water, and diving is from a sailing dhow. Closed April and May.
$$–$$$

Mbweni Ruins Hotel
On the west coast, 7 km (4 miles) south of Stone Town
PO Box 2542, Zanzibar
Tel: 024-223 5478
Fax: 024-223 0536
www.mbweni.com
This small hotel is a good mid-range option for those

who want peace and quiet but to stay within easy reach of Stone Town. It is also very convenient for the airport. There are 13 spacious but simple suites, all with air conditioning, Zanzibari-style four-poster beds and private verandas with sea views (no phone or TV in rooms). The hotel has a pool, beach and wonderful botanic gardens with nature trails and birdwatching, a cliff-top bar and restaurant, and the ruins of an old mission station. **$$–$$$**

Mtoni Marine
4 km (2½ miles) north of Stone Town
Tel: 024-225 0140
Fax: 024-225 0496
www.mtoni.com
The nearest resort to Stone Town, this is a popular expat and local hang-out, with people attracted by the beach, pool, beer and snack meals, but it also has a range of comfortable en suite motel-style rooms and bungalows that make an excellent base for families. Dhow sailing trips set out from here. **$$**

Neptune Pwani Beach Resort and Spa
PO Box 1300
Tel: 024-224 0296/97/98/300/301
Fax: 024-224 0302
www.neptunehotels.com
This resort consists of 174 chalets with balconies overlooking tropical gardens and the ocean, covering 12 hectares (30 acres) of prime Zanzibar northeast coast beach front. All rooms have air conditioning, satellite TV, safe, minibar and modern bathroom. Three swimming pools, several restaurants,

spa, and conference centre for up to 150 delegates.
$$$$

Ras Michamvi Beach Resort
Tel: 024-223 1081 or 0774-319319
Fax: 024-223 8696
www.rasmichamvi.com
Harmoniously set amongst powder-white beaches, gardens and tropical forests on the east of the island, all 15 self-contained rooms have sea views; some are suitable for disabled guests. The restaurant offers international and local cuisine and the resort includes a pool, dive centre, shops, fitness centre, spa and conference facilities. **$$$**

Ras Nungwi Beach Hotel
PO Box 1784, Zanzibar
Tel: 024-223 3767/2512
Fax: 024-223 3098
www.rasnungwi.com
Resort hotel in the far north of the island, a few kilometres from Nungwi village. This is an extremely pleasant place to stay, with friendly staff, excellent food, and *makuti*-thatched coral-rag cottages in lush gardens alongside a white-sand beach. You can walk to the reef at low tide, snorkel, dive or go game fishing. Other activities include dhow cruises, waterskiing, windsurfing and kayaking. **$$$**

Robinson's Place
Bwejuu
Tel: 0777-413 479
www.robinsonsplace.net
Absolutely delightful, simple and meticulously clean rooms beautifully situated on Bwejuu Beach. Friendly Zanzibari/German owners/managers. Charming and highly recommended budget accommodation, which is eco-friendly – using no electricity. **$–$$**

Shooting Star
PO Box 3076
Tel: 0777-414 166
www.shootingstarlodge.com
A small, family-run lodge offering ornately decorated suites with private pools, and sea-view cottages with verandas and comfortable garden rooms. The open-air

restaurant has a reputation for fine food, a cosy atmosphere and friendly service. The stunning infinity pool has spectacular views of the Indian Ocean. **$$$**

Sunset Bungalows
Kendwa
Tel: 0777-411 887
Best of a bit of a rough bunch of cheap accommodation on Kendwa Beach. Dark, dampish rooms on one of the best beaches in Zanzibar – worth staying here for this alone. Kendwa is one of the only beaches on the island that is still easily swimable during low tide. **$–$$**

Unguja Resort
PO Box 675
Tel: 0774-477 477
www.ungujaresort.com
Unguja Resort in the south of Zanzibar overlooks the Menai Bay Conservation Area. The hotel consists of 10 private, spacious villas with ocean views, superb restaurant, bar, swimming pool and a PADI dive centre in stunning natural surroundings. **$$$$**

Zamani Zanzibar Kempinski
PO Box 3140, Kilwengwa
Tel: 0774-444 477
Fax: 024-224 0066
www.kempinski-zanzibar.com
Luxurious five-star mega-resort on fantastic stretch of coast. **$$$$$**

Pemba

Fundu Lagoon
Tel: 0763-592820
Fax: 0774-419906
www.fundulagoon.com
Enchanting hideaway retreat across the bay from Mkoani, reached only by boat. There are 20 luxurious tents, all with verandas and beach access (and some with private plunge pool), connected by boardwalks through the coastal forest. There are a couple of bars, a picture-perfect beach, a fine restaurant and friendly staff. Water sports include snorkelling, sailing, waterskiing and kayaking, and there is a PADI-certificate dive school on site. **$$$$$**

TRANSPORT

E ATING OUT

RECOMMENDED RESTAURANTS, CAFÉS & BARS

ACCOMMODATION

EATING OUT

What to Eat

The only towns with good independent restaurants are Dar, Arusha and Stone Town. Elsewhere, the best (sometimes only) food is served by the hotels *(see the hotel listings, pages 282–96)*. The menu will usually include a mix of Western and local dishes. Many of the small towns may also have at least one reasonable Indian restaurant. The food on the coast is heavily influenced by Indian and Arabic cuisine: typical Zanzibari dishes are based on seafood cooked in coconut milk. Try the milky Zanzibar spiced tea.

Maize is a staple (called *ugali*), as are cooked plantains and rice. You can get chips (French fries) in most places. Also popular is grilled meat *(nyama choma)*. Near Lake Victoria, you will find a fresh yoghurt-like milk product called *mtindi*.

Safari, a locally produced lager, is very good and very strong. Kenya's famous Tusker beer is readily available; beers imported from South Africa and Germany are more expensive. Local brews made from bananas *(mbege* – a speciality in the Kilimanjaro area), cashew nuts

(uraka) and pawpaw are also common. Konyagi, a popular gin, feels lethal, much like a train hitting your head, and that's before the hangover. A tasty liqueur is Afrikoko, a chocolate and coconut blend.

Traditional Swahili or Indian restaurants may not serve alcohol.

Where to Eat

The listings follow the order of the main text (there are no listings for the Northern Safari Circuit as virtually all visitors to this area take meals in their lodges).

RESTAURANT LISTINGS

DAR ES SALAAM

Addis in Dar
Ursino Street, Regent Estate
Tel: 0713-266 299
Excellent and atmospheric Ethiopian restaurant, rated by local expats as one of Dar's best restaurants. Closed Sun. **$$**
Baraza Bar & Grill
Holiday Inn
Tel: 022-213 7575
This is one of the trendiest – and best – restaurants in Dar, serving excellent steaks, seafood and traditional Tanzanian dishes. **$$$**
Barbecue Village
Off Kimwere Street, Msasani Area
Tel: 022-266 7927 or 7188
Almost anything you want is available at this relaxed but unashamedly commercial

Indian-run place, which offers Indian, Chinese and European menus as well as a buffet and barbecue. **$$**
La Trattoria (Jan Pizzeria)
Kimweri Avenue
Tel: 0754-282 969
Known by both names, this is a cheerful Italian restaurant with good pizzas, pasta and grills. **$$**
L'Oliveto Restaurant
Mövenpick Royal Palm Hotel
Ohio Street
Tel: 022-211 2416
www.moevenpick-hotels.com
The hotel's excellent Italian restaurant serves authentic cuisine. Stylish decor. **$$–$$$**
Mediterraneo Hotel and Restaurant
Off Kawe Beach Road, Kawe Beach

Tel: 022-261 8350
www.mediterraneotanzania.com
Open-air restaurant with sea views in a beautiful garden setting. Specialising in Mediterranean cuisine including pizza, seafood and home-made pasta. **$$**
Sawasdee Restaurant
New Africa Hotel, Sokoine Drive
Tel: 022-211 7050
Ninth-floor restaurant with wonderful views over the harbour, elegant furnishings and delicious Thai food. **$$$**
The Slipway
Msasani Peninsula
Tel: 022-260 0893
This shopping mall and food hall has several excellent restaurants and cafés (some with sea view),

including **The Terrace** (pasta, seafood and steak), the **Mashua Waterfront** (pizza and barbecue), **The Pub** (European), **Azuma** (Japanese and Indonesian) and **Fairy Delights** (ice cream and coffee). **$–$$$**
Sweet Eazy
Oyster Bay Shopping Centre
Guba Road
Tel: 0755-754074
African and Thai cuisine. Live music and bar. **$–$$**

PRICE CATEGORIES
The price range is based on a three-course meal for one, without alcohol.
$ = US$5–8
$$ = US$8–15
$$$ = US$15–30

ACTIVITIES

A – Z

LANGUAGE

THE NORTH COAST

Bagamoyo

Bagamoyo Beach Resort
Tel: 023-244 0083
A good selection of international and Tanzanian cuisine, along with seafood specials. **$$**

Millennium Sea Breeze
Tel: 023-244 0201
Great Indian favourites and traditional Swahili fare. **$$$**

Palm Tree Village Beach Resort
Tel: 023-244 0245

This resort does an excellent breakfast and has a decent international lunch and dinner menu. **$**

Paradise Holiday Resort
Tel: 023-244 0000
The Resort's Bahari restaurant serves highly recommended themed buffet lunches including Mediterranean, Asian, Italian, African, spicy and barbecue. Relaxed setting overlooking the swimming pool. A la carte menu also available. **$$–$$$**

Livingstone Club
Tel: 023-244 0059
Well known for its great cappuccino, pasta and lobster. An additional three-course set menu is available. **$$**

Travellers Lodge
Tel: 023-244 0077
Tropical open-air restaurant with great seafood (try the Fisherman's platter) and both international and local cuisine. Buffet and à la carte menu. **$–$$$**

Tanga

Mkonge Hotel
Bombo Hospital Road
Tel: 027-264 3440
A la carte menu which includes fish and prawns, pork, Tanzanian dishes and vegetarian options. **$$**

Pangani
Mkoma Bay Tented Lodge
45 km (28 miles) south of Tanga
Tel: 0784 434001
Relaxing poolside bar/restaurant with sea views. **$$**

ARUSHA AND KILIMANJARO

Arusha

AICC Complex
Off Afrika Mashariki Road
Tel: 027-250 8008
The café in the Serengeti Wing offers lunch-time buffets, plus there are . another three snack bars serving burgers, pies, cakes and brownies. **$**

Arusha Crown Hotel
Tel: 027-254 4161
Indian dishes, grills, pizza, lamb chops, steak and seafood. **$**

Arusha Hotel
Facing the Clocktower
Tel: 027-250 7777
Popular buffet lunch with a good à la carte menu including light meals and snacks. Delicious desserts. **$–$$$**

Arusha Naaz Hotel
Sokoine Road
Tel: 027-250 2087
Decent and well priced Indian food with snacks and barbecue. **$–$$**

Jambo's Coffee House, Makuti Bar and Restaurant
Boma Street,
next to TTB
Mobile: 0754-305 430
Email: jambocoffee@habari.co.tz
A lively and popular coffee shop with delicious home-made cakes and fresh juices. At the back there's a shady courtyard restaurant. The friendly proprietors will be glad to offer you books on Arusha or guided tours. **$**

L'Oasis Lodge and Restaurant
Tel: 027-250 7089 or 0745-749934
Seafood specialities served in lush gardens. **$–$$**

Mambo Café
Old Moshi Road,
near the Clocktower
Tel: 027-250 6995
This café has excellent Italian-influenced cuisine and the best ice cream in town. A popular haunt with the locals. Closed Sun. **$$**

Mezza Luna
Moshi Road
Tel: 027-254 4381
A popular Italian restaurant, with a good menu and great atmosphere. **$$**

PizzArusha
Beside Egina's, opposite Mashele guesthouse
Email: pizzarusha@hotmail.com
One of the nicest places to eat in Arusha. Very good-quality food and service in a cosy candlelit restaurant. Highly recommended. **$$**

Redds African Grill House
Dodoma Road,
near the airport
Tel: 027-254 4521
This smart restaurant has a congenial atmosphere and delicious food. Traditional Tanzanian cuisine is a speciality, and there's an à la carte menu for the less adventurous. There's a separate bar area, water garden and pool. In a peaceful setting, it's a handy stopover if

taking an internal flight. **$$–$$$**

Spices & Herbs Ethiopian Restaurant
Moshi Road
Tel: 027-250 2279
A wonderful restaurant with delicious spicy African cuisine, plus European specialities and a barbecue. **$$**

Stiggy's Restaurant and Bar
Old Moshi Road
Tel: 0713-651 129
A lively watering hole popular with the UN fraternity and local expats. A good range of food from pizzas to an à la carte Thai menu. Also has satellite TV and a pool table. **$$**

Moshi

China Garden
Taifa Road,
CCM complex
Tel: 027-53469
Chinese and Thai food in a pleasant garden. **$**

The Coffee Shop
Hill Street
Tel: 027-52707
A popular meeting place, selling a variety of Tanzanian coffees, sandwiches and cakes. Closed Sun and Sat from 4.30pm. **$**

El Rancho
Off Lema Road
Tel: 027-55115
Indian restaurant with excellent vegetarian

choices, and international dishes. Closed Mon. **$**

Golden Shower
Dar es Salaam Road, on the outskirts of Moshi
Tel: 027-51990
This intriguingly named restaurant serves a good variety of food in a garden setting. **$**

Keys Hotel
Tel: 027-275 2250
Offers a selection of Tanzanian dishes. **$$**

Kilimanjaro Impala Hotel
Tel: 027-250 2962
Indian, Chinese and European options. **$$**

Kindoroko Hotel
Mawenzi Road
Tel: 027-275 4054
Italian, Chinese and Swahili cuisine in an atmospheric setting.

M' Cafe
Arusha Road, next to the mosque
Tel: 0748-582464
A good selection of Indian snacks. Closed Sun from 5.30pm. **$**

Moshi Leopard Hotel
Market Street
Tel: 027-275 0884
www.leopardhotel.com
Good-value tasty food, particularly the curried prawns, grilled goat and chicken. Occasional buffets. **$**

Salzburg Steak House
Kenyatta Street
Tel: 027-50681
Steaks, burgers and salads, with Volkswagen memorabilia and a record-player for old '78s. **$**

LAKE VICTORIA

Mwanza

Deluxe Hotel
Kishamapanda Street
Excellent traditional
Tanzanian cuisine. Busy
lunch-time service. **$**

Kuleana Pizzeria
Next to New Mwanza Hotel
This popular restaurant,
open 9am–5pm, funds a
charity supporting street
children. Good pizzas,
snacks and sandwiches,
and fresh brown bread
to take home. **$**

New Mwanza Hotel
Posta Road
Tel: 255-285 010
www.newmwanzahotel.com
Specialises in authentic
Indian food cooked by the
expatriate chefs from
India. A variety of
continental and Chinese
cuisine is also available.
The Coffee Shop is open
24 hours a day and
serves pizza, snacks and
a variety of grills. Both
are open for lunch and
dinner and carry imported
and locally produced
wine and beer. **$–$$**

Ramadd Hotel
Rwagasore Road
Pleasant first-floor
restaurant and bar
serving reasonable food;
satellite TV. **$**

**Rock Beach Garden
Hotel**
Five minutes from town centre
overlooking Bismarck Rock
Slick, lively outdoor bar
and restaurant, perfect
sundowner spot, serving
decent Italian food and
grills. **$$**

Rumours Pub & Grill
Opposite New Mwanza Hotel
Trendy MTV-booming
bar serving draught
beer, a good range
of cocktails and bar
grub. **$$**

Sizzler Restaurant
Opposite the New Mwanza
Hotel
Tel: 0741-341 118
Very good-value Indian
restaurant, with
wonderful evening
barbecue where
delicious chicken
tikka served with
fresh chapatis and roti
bread are on offer. **$**

ABOVE: breakfast on safari.

**Szechwan Mahal
Restaurant**
Next to Sizzler Restaurant
Tel: 0741-530 786
This authentic Indian
and Chinese restaurant
serves some of the best
food in town: deliciously
spicy and piquant
sauces and massive
portions. Good for
vegetarians and utterly
addictive. **$$**

Tilapia Hotel
Capri Point
Tel: 028-250 0141
www.hoteltilapia.com
Enjoy a variety of locations
while dining; by the
lakeside, the pool or on
the terrace. Serves
Italian, Chinese, Indian
and wonderful Thai
cuisine. Not surprisingly,
this is a very popular
place. **$–$$**

LAKE TANGANYIKA

Kigoma

Kigoma Hilltop Hotel
2 km (1 mile) south of town
centre
Tel: 028-280 4435–7
Good Indian restaurant
in the town's most up-

market hotel. No alcohol.
$$

**Lake Tanganyika
Beach Hotel**
Off Bangwe Road
Tel: 028-280 2694
Excellent location with
gardens right on the

banks of Lake Tanganyika.
Fine selection of Indian,
Chinese and European
food. Good spot for a
sundowner. **$**

Mwanga Lodge
Ujiji Road
Tel: 028-280 4643

Budget hotel serving
reasonble food. **$**

New Stanley Restaurant
Main Road
Outdoor restaurant serving
grills, curries and other
tasty dishes. Disco
attached. **$**

CENTRAL TANZANIA

Dodoma

Climax Club
2 km (1 mile) from town centre
on Hospital Road
Popular place to meet
expats, watch TV, down a
cold beer, eat reasonably
priced grills, or swim
in the large pool. **$$**

New Dodoma Hotel
Railway Street
Tel: 026-232 1641
The café offers a
selection of fruit

juices, ice cream, light
meals and panini. Choose
from a mix of Chinese
and light Indian dishes,
salads, steak and
prawns in the main
restaurant. Good value.
$

Nureen Restaurant
Dar es Salaam Avenue
Tel: 026-232 2030
Local Indian cuisine –
great curries. Open
lunchtime only and closed
Sun. **$**

Tabora

**Mayor Hotel &
Ice Cream**
Lamumba Street, 100
metres/yards from the
bus station
Indian snacks, freshly
barbecued chicken and
chips, excellent ice cream
and pineapple juice. No
alcohol. Serves good
breakfasts. **$**

Orion Tabora Hotel
corner of Boma and Station Road

Tel: 026-260 4369
Originally built as a hunting
lodge. The restaurant
serves local dishes as well
as a selection of Chinese
and Indian cuisine. **$**

PRICE CATEGORIES

The price range is based on
a three-course meal for
one, without alcohol.
$ = US$5–8
$$ = US$8–15
$$$ = US$15–30

TRANSPORT

ACCOMMODATION

EATING OUT

ACTIVITIES

A – Z

LANGUAGE

SOUTHERN PARKS AND TANZAM HIGHWAY

Iringa

Annex Staff Inn Lodge
Uhuru Avenue
Tel: 026-270 1344
Tanzanian cuisine served on a pleasant seaside terrace. The liver stew is highly recommended. No smoking or alcohol. $
Bottoms-Up Bar & Cuisine
Store Road
First-floor bar with satellite TV, pool table, and attached restaurant serving Indian, Chinese and European dishes. $

Huruma Baptist Conference Centre
2.5km (1½ miles) out of town
Tel: 026-270 0184
Indian, Mexican, Chinese and Tanzanian cuisine. The pork dishes and tortillas are great. $
Isimila Hotel
Uhuhu Avenue
Tel: 026-270 1194
Good simple menu in a quiet setting. $
Lulu's Café & Restaurant
200 metres/yards off Uhuru Road, past Iringa Hotel
Tel: 026-270 0293

Homely café. Snacks, light meals and ice cream.
Mon–Sat 8.30am–9pm and Sun 9am–3.30pm. $
New Continental Lodge
Tel: 025-250 2511
Traditional Tanzanian cuisine. $

Morogoro

Hotel Oasis
Tel: 023-260 4178
Indian cuisine. $
Mikumi Genesis Motel
Tel: 023-262 0461
A good selection of

Tanzanian favourites. $
Morogoro Hotel
Rwagasore Street
Tel: 023-260 3270
Authentic Indian and Chinese as well as Tanzanian favourites. $
New Green Restaurant
On the main circle opposite the bus station
Long-standing favourite, serving good Indian and Portuguese dishes. $–$$
Tan Swiss
Tel: 0754-878 752
Serves pasta, pizza and fish dishes. $

MBEYA AND LAKE NYASA

Mbeya

Chinese Dragon Restaurant
1 km (½ mile) from town centre on the main road between the Rift Valley Hotel and Tanzam Highway

Excellent Chinese cuisine served here. $
Holiday Lodge
Jamatikhana Road
Tel: 025-250 2821
Specialises in Indian cuisine at reasonable

prices. No alcohol. $
Octopus Restaurant
50 metres/yards from Market Square
The best dedicated restaurant in Mbeya, serving up good steak,

poultry and curry dishes in pleasant surrounds. $
Sombrero Restaurant
Next to Post Office, Market Square
Copious selection of grills, curries and Italian dishes. $

THE SOUTH COAST

Kilwa Masoko

Kilwa Lodge
Hamjambo Road
Tel: 0784-637 026
Terrific location on the beach-front, with seafood dishes at reasonable prices. Order in advance if you are

not staying overnight. $$
Kilwa Sea View Resort
Lumumba Street
Tel: 0784-613 335
Locally run establishment specialising in seafood. Offers hearty meals overlooking Jimbiza beach. $–$$

Mikindani

Old Boma at Mikindani
Tel: 0784-360 110
www.mikindani.com
Fantastic food at great prices. Menu changes daily depending on what is in season and growing in

their own garden at the time, including fresh soups and salads. Vegetarian options are available and often a buffet option in the evening. Enjoy your meal under the trees by the pool. $–$$

ZANZIBAR AND PEMBA

Zanzibar (Unguja)

Stone Town

Africa House
Shangani Road
Tel: 0777-432 340
People come here for the breezy veranda bar, where you can get burgers and cold beer. Food and service patchy at best. This is the old British Club. $
Ahlan Palace
Baghani
Tel: 024-223 1435
A la carte menu with continental, seafood and Swahili selections. $–$$
Amore Mio
Near the Serena Inn, Shangani
Tel: 024-223 3666
Email: e_walzl@yahoo.it

Italian-run ice-cream parlour on the seafront serving light meals and coffee. $
Archipelago Café and Restaurant
Kenyatta Road, opposite NBC Bank
Tel: 0777-462 311
The best coffee in Zanzibar. Great views over Stone Town harbour, friendly staff and delicious food. Highly recommended. $
Asmin Palace
Kiponda (near Kiponda Hotel)
Tel: 0777-276 464
Offers a continental menu in the heart of old Stone Town. $$–$$$
Bahari Restaurant
Inside Tembo Hotel
Tel: 024-223 3005
Zanzibar cuisine. $–$$

Baharia Restaurant/Ndole Coffee Shop
Inside Serena Inn
Tel: 024-223 1015
Cosy yet classy atmosphere overlooking the pool and the Indian Ocean beyond. Enjoy international cuisine, cakes and excellent coffee. $$–$$$
Beyt al Chai
Kelele Square, opposite Serena Inn
Tel: 0774-444 111
One of the best dining experiences in Stone Town, offering fine international and local cuisine in a sophisticated and stylish setting. Live taarab music on weekends. $$$
Camlurs
Shangani

Tel: 024-223 1919
Continental and Goan cuisine. $
Chavda Hotel
Baghani Street
Tel: 024-232 115
An evening at this rooftop restaurant is highly recommended: the menu tempts diners with a good selection of Zanzibari and Indian cuisine, while they enjoy one of the best views in Stone Town. $$–$$$
La Fenice
Seafront Terrace, Shangani Street
Tel: 0777-411 868
Email: fenice@zanzinet.com
Pleasant restaurant, with a breezy seaview veranda, serving good Italian and

Swahili food. Cocktail bar and delicious ice cream. **$$**

Kiponda Hotel
Kiponda
Tel: 024-223 3052
Zanzibar cuisine with Tanzanian favourites. **$–$$**

Le Spice Rendezvous
Kenyata Road
Tel: 0777-410707
Indian and Zanzibari cuisine. **$–$$**

Livingstone Restaurant
Forodhani
Tel: 0773-164939
Ideally located on the beach next to Tembo House Hotel, this is a favourite of expats and tourists alike. Lively atmosphere with regular happy hours. Seafood and international cuisine. **$$–$$$**

Mercury's
Harbour front, near the House of Wonders
Tel: 024-223 3076
Popular, laid-back seafront bar/restaurant, named after Freddie Mercury, who was born in Zanzibar. Good for sunset cocktails, pizza and burgers. **$$**

Monsoon Restaurant
Shangani Street,
near Forodhani Gardens
Tel: 0777-410 410
Email: monsoon@zanzinet.com
Attractive Swahili restaurant, where you can lounge on cushions around brass tables while nibbling on local delicacies. Live music Wed and Sat. **$$**

Mzuri Sana Restaurant
Malindi, opposite Passing Show restaurant
Tanzanian and Zanzibari cuisine. **$**

Old Fort Restaurant
Ngome Kongwe, Forodhani Street
Opposite Forodhani Gardens
This casual bar/restaurant offers a selection of international and Thai cuisine. Live entertainment and pool table. **$–$$**

Pagoda Restaurant
Shangani
Opposite Africa House Hotel
Tel: 024-223 31758
Authentic Chinese cuisine in a convenient location. Good selection of meat, seafood and vegetarian dishes, and a bar. **$–$$**

Passing Show
Malindi
A Zanzibari favourite serving some of the best local cuisine in town. **$**

Radha Food House
Behind NBC Bank
Tel: 024-223 4808
Tasty vegetarian curries. The daily *thalis* are recommended and good value for money, as are the cold beers. **$–$$**

Sambusa Two Tables
Off Victoria Street,
near Kaunda Road
Tel: 024-223 1979
Ask for directions on how to reach this extraordinary little restaurant when you book (essential), or you will never find it. Literally the back room of a private flat, with the family watching TV next door, it has two tables, each seating up to eight people. The Swahili food is delicious and as authentic as you can get. Guaranteed to be one of the most memorable evenings you spend on the island. **$$**

Silk Route
Forodhani
This restaurant has one of the best locations in the area, with fantastic views over the entire Forodhani beachfront and a stylish yet simple setting. Authentic tandoori dishes and south Indian curries. **$–$$**

Stone Town Café
Kenyatta Road
Fantastic sandwiches, excellent coffee. **$**

Tower Top Restaurant 236 Hurumzi
236 Hurumzi Street
Tel: 0777-423 266
Tower-top restaurant where tourists flock to feel the atmosphere of old Zanzibar, with dinner in the open air, seated on cushions, and a view over the minarets and spires of Stone Town. Music and dancing some nights. Book well ahead. **$$$**

Zanzibar Fusion
Inside Al Johari Hotel
Tel: 024-223 6779
www.al-johari.com
Serves an extensive range of continental cuisine with some specials rarely found on the island. Set on the fourth floor of the exclusive Al Johari in one of Stone Town's most fashionable areas. **$$–$$$**

Out of Town

Hakuna Matata
Chuini Ruins/Bububu
Tel: 0777-454 892
www.hakuna-matata-beach-lodge.com
The only fine dining option outside Stone Town or the expensive five stars on the coast. Fantastic seafood with limited continental options and a terrific wine selection. Great views of the ocean and Chuini Ruins over the inlet. **$$–$$$**

Mangwapani Seafood Grill
On the west coast, about 21 km (13 miles) north of Stone Town
Tel: 024-223 3587
Run as their beach resort by the Serena Inn *(see page 295)*, this seafood grill is a popular lunch spot after the spice tour. Free *daladala* transport from the Serena Inn in Stone Town. Gorgeous beach. Recommended. **$$–$$$**

Maruhubi Beach Villa and Restaurant
Maruhubi
Tel: 0777-451 188
Set in a massive *banda* with *makuti* thatched roof, this restaurant has a real island atmosphere. It offers Zanzibari and continental cuisine and a fully stocked bar, all overlooking the water. **$–$$**

Mbweni Ruins
Mbweni
Tel: 024-223 5478
www.mbweni.com
Exquisite location in botanical gardens with the atmospheric Mbweni Ruins in the background. The restaurant and bar overlook the beach front, with Chumbe Island in the distance. Free shuttle bus from the Old Fort in Stone Town. **$$–$$$**

Mtoni Marine
6 km (3½ miles) north of Stone Town
Tel: 024-225 0117
The nearest beach-front restaurant to the city. The daytime offerings are in the line of pizza and beer; at night, you can have candlelit seafood dinners. On Tuesday evenings there is a Taarab orchestra and Zanzibari buffet. On Wednesday and Friday, there is African jazz. On Saturday, try the seafood beach barbecue. **$$**

Spices Restaurant
Zanzibar Beach Resort, Mazizini
Tel: 024-223 6044
Continental and Indian cuisine in a tropical resort atmosphere. Reserve at weekends. **$$–$$$**

Pemba

Swahili Divers
Chake Chake
Tel: 024-245 2786
Range of options including light lunches, dinners with vegetarian options, and seafood buffets offered a couple of times a week. Beer available. **$$–$$$**

Times Restaurant
Chake Chake
Tel: 024-245 4580
International cuisine at a reasonable price. **$**

PRICE CATEGORIES

The price range is based on a three-course meal for one, without alcohol.
$ = US$5–8
$$ = US$8–15
$$$ = US$15–30

BELOW: soak up the atmosphere in the Tower Top restaurant.

TRANSPORT

ACCOMMODATION

EATING OUT

ACTIVITIES

A – Z

LANGUAGE

ACTIVITIES

THE ARTS, FESTIVALS, NIGHTLIFE, SHOPPING, SPORTS AND OUTDOOR ACTIVITIES

THE ARTS

Music and Dance

The Bagamoyo College of the Arts (BCA; Chua Cha Sanaa)
Kaole Road, Bagamoyo
900metres/yards south of the Boma
PO Box 32
Tel: 023-244 0032
www.sanaabagamoyo.com
Open Mon–Sat 8am–3pm.
Dhow Countries Music Academy (DCMA)
Top Floor, Old Customs House
Stone Town, Zanzibar
PO Box 4055
Tel: 024-223 4050/0777-416529
www.zanzibarmusic.org
The DCMA is a non-profit, cultural and educational organisation that provides music lessons and instruments at minimal cost to anyone interested in learning traditional Zanzibar music styles, such as taarab, beni and kidumbak.
MS-Noma Troup
Arusha
The MS Training Centre for Development and Co-operation aims to raise political awareness through the forum of folk music, plays and traditional dances.
Music Mayday presents B-Connected, 5 Countries
Bongo flava, traditional, fusion, reggae and open-mic performances live on stage at Mnazi Mmoja Grounds. http://babkubwa.com/?p=19

Libraries and Cultural Centres

Dar es Salaam
Alliance Française
PO Box 2566
AH Mwinyi Road, behind Las Vegas
Tel: 022-213 1406
Email: infoinso@afdar.com
Gallery exhibition area; library for use by local members only; promotes cultural events.
British Council
PO Box 9100, Cnr Samora Avenue/Ohio Street
Tel: 022-211 6574–7
Fax: 022-211 2669
Email: info@britishcouncil.cr.tz
Library open Tues–Fri 10am–6pm, Sat 9.30am–1pm
Offices Mon–Fri 7.30am–3.30pm
Public access to international newspapers and the BBC World Service. Films shown on Wednesday evenings.
The National Arts Council
Shariff Shamba Ilala Road
Tel: 022-286 3248
Russian-Tanzanian Cultural Centre
2043/3 Seaview Road

Sources of Information

There are three free listings magazines distributed in Dar, the bi-monthly *Dar es Salaam Guide* and the *Swahili Coast*, and the monthly *What's Happening in Dar*.
All are English-language and give details of what's on as well as up-to-date addresses and telephone numbers of venues. Available from most hotels.
An additional publication is available through the Zanzibar Commission for Tourism called *Karibu Zanzibar*. This quarterly magazine showcases the best examples of responsible tourism in the Zanzibar Archipelago and offers an insight into the cultural and environmental heritage of the islands.

PO Box 7722
Dar es Salaam
Tel: 022-213 6577
Email: rtcc@raha.com
All manner of cultural events, such as exhibitions, theatre and opera.
Tanzania Information Services Library
PO Box 9142
Dar es Salaam
Email: maelezo@raha.com
Has reference books on Tanzania, journalism and photography, among other things, plus various newspapers and periodicals.
University of Dar es Salaam Library
PO Box 35092
Email: libdirec@udsm.ac.tz
Strong East African collection, plus 8,000 periodicals

Zanzibar
Nyumba ya Sanaa
PO Box 772
Mwanakwerekwe
Tel/fax: 024-223 2321
Workshop, gallery and art institute.
Stone Town Cultural Centre
The Old Dispensary
PO Box 3716
Zanzibar
Tel/fax: 024-223 3378
Email: stcc@zitec.org
Frequent exhibitions, crafts fairs and cultural shows.
A Night at the Fort
Three times a week from 7pm–10pm at the Old Fort. African dance and drums.

Mwanza
Ladha Meghji Indian Public Library
PO Box 70
Email: lakesecondary@sutrumanet.com
6,000 volumes, and classes in English, French and Asian languages.

Arusha

Cultural Tourism Programme
PO Box 10455
TTB Information Centre
Boma Road
Tel: 027-250 3842
Email: tourinfo@habari.co.tz
An award-winning tourism programme run by locals to benefit locals. Tours to over a dozen local villages nestled around Arusha vary from short visits to weekend stays.
Arusha Cultural Tours
Starting from Jambo's coffee house, this walking tour shows you 12 important sights of the city famous for being halfway between Cairo and the Cape.

Museums and Art Galleries

The museums in Dar es Salaam, Arusha and Zanzibar are all covered in full in the relevant sightseeing chapters. For commercial art galleries, see below, or look at the Shopping section on pages 304–6.

Dar es Salaam

Art n' Frame
Between Q-Bar and CCBRT Hospital
Tel: 022-260 2700
Mandawa Studio
Salvation Army
Tel: 0755-806 742
Raza Art Gallery
Mwcngc
New Bagamoyo Road
Tel: 022-277 5169

Cinema

Apart from the International Film Festival now incorporated into Zanzibar's excellent Festival of the Dhow Countries, there is a dearth of places to watch cinema in Tanzania.

BELOW: the Busara Music Festival.

Cultural Festivals

Zanzibar International Film Festival
Festival of the Dhow Countries, PO Box 3032, Zanzibar
Tel: 0747-411 499 or 0777-411 499
www.ziff.or.tz
The largest cultural festival in East Africa, showcasing world film, music, art and theatre from Africa, India, the Middle East and beyond. Held July.
Saba Saba Fair
Dar International Trade Fair, exhibiting various products in a festive atmosphere at the Saba Saba grounds (Kilwa Road) – including everything from cars to electrical goods to handicrafts, with gypsy tents and refreshments.
The Village Museum
Dar es Salaam
Tel: 022-270 0437
Holds several cultural festivals celebrating different tribal groups in Tanzania, and other cultural groups such as the Tanzanians of Indian origin.

Most films shown are Bollywood, rather than African or Western fare.

Arusha

L'Alliance Franco-Tanzanienne d'Arusha
Tel: 0744-382 117
Email: alliance.arusha@tz2000.com
Occasional film shows.

Dar es Salaam

British Council
Samora Avenue
Tel: 022-211 6574-7
Wednesday evening showings.

Makunduchi New Year Festival
Entertaining festival celebrating the Shirazi New Year (in July). Men challenge foes of the year past with banana leaves. The contestants then flail one another and hopefully make amends. Meanwhile the town's women dance around the banana-beating men singing songs. A house of spirits is constructed and then set on fire as villagers run around the burning misery of last year. Activities are accompanied by much drinking and dancing.
Sauti za Busara
PO Box 3635
Tel: 024-233 2423 or 0777-428 478
www.busaramusic.com
This is a leading musical festival in the Tanzanian calendar. Held in the Old Fort along Stone Town's waterfront in Zanzibar during the first week of February, Sauti za Busara is a celebration of Tanzanian music in all its diversity and attracts international acts and audiences.

New World Cinima
New Bagamoyo Road
Tel: 022-277 1409/277 2178
Western and Bollywood new releases. Very modern multiplex.
Kunduchi Wet 'n' Wild Water Park
PO Box 361
Tel: 022-265 0413
Email: wetnwild@raha.com
Saturday and Sunday showings of British and Indian films (6pm).

NIGHTLIFE

In Dar es Salaam there are many nightclubs and cabarets; Stone Town in Zanzibar has a couple. That is about the extent of the nightlife, unless you head for the large resort hotels. However, even here, you may find yourself dancing the early evening away to hits of the 1970s with two 15-year-olds and their grandmother. Tanzania is not the place to come for rocking nightlife. The adventurous would do better to head away from the white enclaves to the cheaper local bars where you can find Tanzanian bands and plenty of people willing to make music and dance. Don't take any valuables with you, but do take enough, carefully stashed, for a taxi back to your hotel. In Zanzibar, Forodhani Gardens are a good place to go in the evening for a bit of local colour. Sizzling local

Hotel Bars in Dar

Bottleneck Bar
New Africa Hotel
Azikiwe Street
In the city centre, cocktails and snacks, Saturday and Sunday weekend jazz lunch; live band every evening at the Bandari Grill (7.30pm onwards).

Karambezi Café
Hotel Sea Cliff complex
Afro-Mediterranean restaurant and bar; live music on Tuesday, Thursday and Sunday; barbecue Thursday–Sunday. Open 24 hours.

Kibo Bar
Moevenpick Royal Palm Hotel
Live band on Thursday, Friday and Saturday.

Kilimanjaro Kempinski Roof Bar
Kilimanjaro Kempinski Hotel
Highly recommended bar: cheap, fabulous cocktails, superb service in beautiful surroundings.

Maasai Bar
The Golden Tulip Hotel
On the ocean front, perfect place to relax with friends. Great daily specials. Live music on Fridays and Saturdays.

Oyster Pool Bar
Hotel Karibu
11am–11pm

specialities are cooked on open grills and lots of locals watch the sun go down. Remember that many clubs and bars double as pick-up joints and there is an extremely high incidence of HIV among their working population – male and female.

Bars and Clubs

Dar es Salaam

Club Bilicanas
Tel: 022-212 0605
In the city centre, a "wild place for entertainment". African Night on Wednesday.

4Twenty Bar and Restaurant
Toure Drive
Near Sea Cliff Hotel
Just down from the Sea Cliff Hotel complex. A friendly, relaxed open-air bar. Try the dawa cocktail. Only leave here at night with a taxi; even those walking short distances back to their hotel have been mugged near here.

Irish Pub
Msasani
Tel: 022-601 273
Lively pub with karaoke, quizzes and theme nights.

Jahazi Bar
The Courtyard Hotel
Ocean Road
Tel: 022-213 0130

The Q Bar
Off Haile Selassie Road, behind Morogoro Stores
Oyster Bay
Tel: 0754-282 474
Open daily from 5pm to late. Happy hour 5–7pm. Pool tables. Live music on Fridays.

The Slipway
Msasani Peninsula
Tel: 022-260 0893
Nightly music on the terrace under the stars; pleasant atmosphere on the waterfront.

Storm
Above Azam's
Tel: 0754-831 258
Cnr Jamhuri Street/AH Mwinyi Road
Dance club.

Studi Bakers Disco
Kimweri Avenue
Namanga
Open 6pm until late. Dance music from around the world.

Stone Town

Dharma Lounge
Culture Musical Club
Vuga Road, Stone Town
Tel: 0777-413 031 or
024-223 5910
Best tourist bar in Stone Town. Later in the evening, turns into a club.

Komba Discoteque
Bwawani Hotel
Tel: 024-223 0200
Very popular with locals, and the place to go for a true Zanzibar club experience. Open until dawn.

Mercury's
Harbour Front
Near the House of Wonders
Tel: 024-223 3076
Live bands throughout the week, barbecues on the beach. Music ranges from bongo flavour to taarab to cheesy dance. Reasonably priced drinks and good food; bar stays open until 1 or 2am.

Arusha

Colobus Club
Jacaranda Street
Disco on Friday and Saturday. Pool table and casino.

Crystal Club
St Benjamin Street
Disco on Friday and Saturday nights. Not as trendy as it once was, but friendly.

Rick's Club
Off the Moshi–Nairobi road
Opposite Phillips
Tel: 0741-308 521
Live band every Wednesday, Thursday, Saturday and Sunday. Friday night disco. Food available.

Roaster's Garden
Old Moshi Road
Near the Clocktower

Tel: 027-254 4118
Pleasant garden bar with cheap food and plentiful cold beer.

Casino Listings

Casinos are popular with local businessmen and are often the most "happening" nightlife in town.

Arushu

Safari Casino
The Arusha Hotel
Tel: 027-250 4229
Fax: 027-250 8889
Offers American roulette, blackjack, poker and slot machines.

Dar

Las Vegas Casino
AH Mwinyi Road
Between the city centre and the Salender Bridge
Upanga
Tel: 022-211 6512
Open 12.30pm–5am. Roulette, blackjack, pontoon, poker and slot machines. French staff (it has shared parking with the Alliance Française). Two bars offering everything from cocktails to coffee. The complex also has a large pool hall.

Kilimanjaro Casino
Kilimanjaro Hotel Kempinski
Kivukoni Street
Tel: 022-213 1111
Slots open from noon, tables open Mon–Fri 5pm, Sat–Sun 2pm.

New Africa Casino
New Africa Hotel
Azikiwe Street
Tel: 022-2119752
Fax: 022-2118018
Email: nacasino@raha.com
Open daily from noon to early morning. Slots and gaming machines.

Sea Cliff Casino
Hotel Sea Cliff
Tel: 022-2600 380/7
Fax: 022-2600 476
Offers roulette, blackjack, pontoon, poker and slot machines.

SHOPPING

What to Buy

The city and town centres usually have markets which sell curios such as African drums, jewellery, Makonde carvings and an endless supply of colourful *kangas* (wraparound dresses) at very reasonable prices. Tingatinga paintings, batik prints and *bao* board games are also very popular. In Zanzibar, local spices are added to this and well worth the price, especially the saffron which is very cheap. Beware the teas and coffees. There is an endless assortment with multiple names. All, sadly, taste very similarly bland once at home. Another popular item is the embroidered *kofia* (traditional Muslim head covering), seen on nearly all Zanzibari men.

Be aware that many of the items sold here are not from Tanzania, but come from all parts of Africa – the ethnic jewellery is likely to be Ethiopian, the pink-and-cream soapstone is from Kenya, most other stone, along with much of the batik and beadwork, from South Africa and Zimbabwe, the embroidered textiles from West Africa. However – if its exact provenance doesn't matter to you, it is still beautiful, cheap and well worth buying.

Where to Shop
Dar
Arts, crafts and souvenirs
Cotton Club
Shoppers Plaza
Old Bagamoyo Road
Tel: 022-266 6459
Good range of casual clothes and T-shirts.
Haidery Plaza Shopping Mall
AH Mwinyi Road
Corner of Kisutu Street
Karibu Arts and Crafts
Samora Avenue
Tel: 022-264 7587
A good selection of game skins, batiks, African drums, oil paintings and ebony carvings. Willing to ship all over the world.
Morogoro Stores
Msasani Peninsula
Famous for its Tingatinga paintings.
Mwenge Market
Sam Nujoma Road
Towards the university
Take any *daladala* going to Mwenge and then ask locals for directions. It's only a 5-minute walk from the stop. This is probably the best place to shop in Tanzania, with dozens of small stalls. In the centre of the courtyard local carvers work their magic on rough wood. Mwenge is best known for its ebony carvings.
Nyumba Ya Sanaa
Beside the Mövenpick Royal Palm Hotel
Ohio Street
Dar es Salaam
Tel: 0754-264 461
A variety of artistic styles on canvas as well as clothes and crafts are all on sale here, made by artists who have a workshop on site. Food is available by the fountain (Bustani Restaurant).

The Slipway
Facing Msasani Bay
Tel: 022-260 0893/260 0908
Email: slipway@twiga.com
An elegant, Western-style shopping centre, half of it on a boardwalk above the sea. Selection of clothing, art, jewellery and carving shops. Outdoor crafts market.

Books
The Dar es Salaam Printers Ltd
Jamhuri Street
Open Mon–Fri 8.30am–noon, 2.30–5.30pm; Sat 8.30am–1pm
Reasonable range of books in English and Swahili. Don't expect to be overwhelmed.
Mini Newsagent
Royal Palm Hotel
Good for international newspapers and some books.
A Novel Idea
At the Slipway, Steers-Ohio Street and Sea Cliff
Tel/fax: 022-260 1088
www.anovelidea-africa.com
Excellent bookshop, offering a large variety of books, including luxurious coffee-table books on Africa.

Essentials
Shoppers Plaza
Old Bagamoyo Road
Shopping centre with a supermarket, open seven days a week.
Supermarket sells local and Western goods at high prices. Open 8.30am–8.30pm, Sundays and public holidays 10am–4pm.
Shoprite
Nyerere Road
Large, well-stocked supermarket.
Woolworths
PPF Tower
Garden Avenue
Tel: 022-211 2333

Hotel shops
The Southern Sun, Golden Tulip and Mövenpick Royal Palm all have shops with a good variety of quality souvenirs, clothes and jewellery, including tanzanite. *See hotel listings page 282.*

Arusha
Cultural Heritage
3 km (2 miles) from centre on Serengeti Road
Probably the finest crafts shop in Tanzania, with a superb range, from affordable souvenirs to fine art and dazzling tanzanite. Prices are quite high, but the quality is assured. Will ship worldwide. Credit cards accepted.
KASE Bookstore
Joel Maeda Street
Tel: 027-250 2441

A good selection of regional literature in English. Prices affordable but not cheap. Many foreign books.
Lookmanji Curio Shop
Joel Maeda Street
Tel: 027-250 6807
Has work that is more expensive, but chosen with a little more care for craftsmanship – and you can look at it in peace, without having to ward off enthusiastic hagglers. Sells wood and soapstone carvings, batiks and paintings.
Street sellers
Alleyway between the Makongoro/Simon Boulevard/Goliondoi roundabout and Joel Maeda Street
Has an endless array of carvings, and you can watch the carvers at work, on site. Also along Joel Maeda, you can buy Maasai jewellery and fruit.

Bagamoyo
Bagamoyo Living Art and Handicraft Design Centre
Tel: 0744-834430 or 0744-463585
www.jamani.nl/site/blacc.html
Women's crafts training centre offering a high-quality range of pots, tie-dye, batik, printed fabrics and woven baskets. You can meet the women, watch them work, learn about the project and feel good about shopping for a worthy cause. Open daily 9am–4.30pm.

Zanzibar
By far the most enjoyable way to shop here is to wander the backstreets near the Old Fort and haggle with the locals. For *kikois*, the women's stall near the House of Wonders has an excellent range and will bargain. There are a couple of good second-hand bookstalls along Gizenga Street. The Craft Market near the Old Dispensary is a good place for Tingatinga paintings; while

Striking a Deal
Haggling is expected and necessary in most shops and markets. Bars and established shops will have fixed prices as in the West. Obviously, it's a matter of choice how far you want to take it, but it's a good idea to check out a few asking prices before you start – you can expect prices to come down significantly. The interaction need not be intimidating; it's a good opportunity to meet artists and other locals. This is a culture where things take time, and it is considered polite to pause and make conversation.

souvenirs are on sale in the main market on Creek Road.

The following shops in Stone Town are recommended, as they offer a range several cuts above the rest:

The Gallery Bookshop
48 Gizenga Street
Tel: 0773-150 180
Email: gallery@swahilicoast.com
Quality bookshop with a huge range of titles, both fiction and nonfiction. Atmospheric interior with seating and complimentary spiced coffee. Well worth a visit.

La Opala
236 Hurumzi
Hurumzi Street
A small and very exclusive shop with an assortment of beautiful textiles, silver jewellery, antiques, watercolour paintings, local music and books.

Kanga Kabisa
Shangani
Next to Africa House
www.kangakabisa.com
Swedish designs using exclusively locally produced materials. The Kanga Kabisa range is also available at Zawadi Chest and Ras Nungwi Beach Hotel in Zanzibar and the Dar es Salaam Holiday Inn.

Kibiriti
Gizenga Street
Tel: 024-223 6911 or 0744-824445
One of the best of the many galleries and souvenir shops along this busy road, with a fine selection of traditional textiles.

Memories of Zanzibar
Kenyatta Road
Opposite Shangani Post Office
Tel: 024-223 9377
Email: memories@zanzinet.com
Large, all-encompassing souvenir shop, ideal for those looking for easy shopping at fixed prices.

Moto
Changa Bazaar (follows on from Gizenga Street)
www.solarafrica.net/moto
Colourful woven bags, mats, baskets and more by a women's collective based near Paje Beach. Items may be more expensive than elsewhere, but the quality is normally far superior and the money is going to a very good cause.

Mrembo Traditional Spa and Music Shop
Past the Catholic Church (Minara Miwili), close to Abeid Curio Shop; also at the Mtoni Marine Centre, Bububu Road, Mtoni
Tel: 0777-430 117
Email: mrembozanzibar@yahoo.co.uk
Atmospheric and welcoming, Mrembo offers an eclectic range of goods and services, including Swahili beauty, therapeutic and herbal treatments, and Zanzibar gifts, music and *kanga*

fashion. Taarab music workshops and private lessons are also available.

Saifa
Kelele Square, close to Serena Inn Hotel
Email: saifashop@hotmail.com
Produces handicrafts made of *kanga*, *vitenge* and batik from Tanzania and hand screen-printed T-shirts. Also supports other community-based groups selling their products such as jewellery, books and handcrafted souvenirs.

Sasik
Gizenga Street
Cushion covers, duvets and wall hangings by a local women's collective.

Surti & Sons Handmade Sandals
Gizenga Street
Opposite Bureau de Change
Email: pravinsurti@hotmail.com
Tel: 0777-472742
These handmade leather sandals crafted by a third-generation shoemaker are truly the best sandals you will find anywhere. Choose from a large variety of designs and colours. A small range of handbags and laptop cases is also available.

Upendo Means Love
Shangani
Behind National Bank of Commerce
Tel: 0784-300 812
www.upendomeanslove.com
Upendo Means Love is an empowerment project that trains local women to produce high-quality garments using the best of local materials. The shop showcases the designer range of Upendo Means Love children's clothing, which is also available in Memories of Zanzibar and the Cotton Club and Sea Cliff Village in Dar.

Zanzibar Gallery
Mercury House
Kenyatta Road
Tel: 024-223 2721
Email: gallery@swahilicoast.com
Probably the best shop in Zanzibar. In addition to the normal range of souvenirs and spices, there are lots of books on local history and outstanding photographic books by local photographer, Javed Jafferji. This is also the site of the publication of the informative *Swahili Coast* magazine.

Zawadi Chest
Opposite Livingstone Beach Restaurant
Forodhani, Zanzibar
Tel: 024-223 1390
Email: zawadichest@zanlink.com
A good assortment of gifts and souvenirs including clothing, swimwear, books, CDs, spices, postcards and more.

Best of the rest
Abeid Curio
Cathedral Street
Amazing shop in which to lose a few hours. Ask to look upstairs, where you will be led through the owner's house to another two rooms crammed full of voodoo dolls, *ao* games, old toys, antique furniture, clocks and coins. Completely random selection of fascinating artefacts.

Adis Carving and Tailoring
Gizengi Street
Sells exactly what the name proclaims.

Angi Boutique
Malindi
Boutique clothes.

Asante Arts and Crafts
Hurumuzi Street
Woodcarvings, old clothes and paintings.

Gold Souk
Mkunazini Street
Precious stones, gold and silver jewellery.

Imani Antiques and Furniture
Baghani Street
Antiques, including coins, tables and old clocks; also woodcarvings.

One Way
Kenyatta Road
Tel: 0753-285 446/0754-433975/0777-414737
Email: oneway@zanlink.com
Wide variety of T-shirts and safari clothing.

Books
The Gallery Bookshop, Zanzibar Gallery and Memories of Zanzibar have a great selection of books. For light reading, your best bet is to head for the second-hand bookstalls on Gizenga Street.

Essentials
Western brands will cost more than they do at home, but local products are cheaper.

Shamshuddin Cash and Carry
Near the former Empire Cinema
Tel: 0713-326 411 or 0777-411480
Shamshuddin sells stationery, toiletries and Western food at inflated prices.

SPORTS

Participant Sports

Indoor Sports Facilities

Dar
Fitness Centre
Chole Road
Msasani
Tel: 022-260 0786

Ocean Fitness Ltd
Gymkhana Club
Tel: 022-212 0519
FitZone Tel: 022-260 1953

Arusha
Arusha Gymkhana Club
PO Box 59
Arusha
Tel: 027-250 5134
Email: arushgym@bol.co.tz
Body Tech Health Club
PO Box 14190
Corridor Area
Serengeti Road
Tel: 027-254 4638
Noble Fitness Centre
Wapare Street
Tel: 027-250 2418

Zanzibar
Most east-coast resorts have some
indoor facilities.
Zanzibar Beach Resort
Near the airport, has some gym
facilities.

Golf

Golfing is not the biggest tourism
draw in Tanzania, though it is
available in Dar and Arusha. In Dar,
the Gymkhana Club on Ghana
Avenue, behind the Royal Palm Hotel,
is the biggest course in Tanzania,
though the greens are made of
tarmac. In Arusha, there is a golf
course near the Novotel, while Le
Jacaranda has minigolf.

Tennis and Squash

Some of the top resort hotels have
tennis courts. In Dar, you can play
tennis and squash at the Gymkhana
Club on Ghana Avenue, or squash at
the Upanga Sports Club, Upanga
Road.

Cycling

The Bike Racing Association arranges
competitions. Contact the
Department of Sports at the
children's amusement park,
Kinyangwani area, for details.
There are bicycles for hire in
Arusha and Zanzibar for those who
want a less gruelling day out.

Spectator Sports

Football (soccer) is by far the most
popular sport in Africa. Other sports
such as canoe racing and bullfighting
have a following in certain regions.
The two most popular football
teams in Tanzania are Simba and the
Young Africans. In Dar matches are
held at the Dar National Stadium on
the outskirts of the city; in Arusha at
the Sheik Amat Stadium; in Mwanza
at a stadium 3 km (2 miles) out of

ABOVE: Zanzibar's peaceful waters.

town; Zanzibar's Karume Stadium is
outside Stone Town on the road to
the main post office.
Cricket is very popular with the
Asian community, and is played at
the Gymkhana sports grounds (near
the Royal Palm).

Bullfighting in Pemba

Contact the Tourism Commission for
more information. They have a sub-
office in Chaka Chaka.

Dar es Salaam Annual Charity Goat Races

Inspired by the Ugandan goat races,
the Dar es Salaam Annual Goat
Races, held in August, are the
largest event of their kind in East
Africa. Goats gallop around a
specially designed track and punters
can enjoy a flutter on the favourites.
This is a great family day out, with
fancy dress, live music, arts and
crafts and fabulous food; and
millions of shillings raised for charity.
Go to www.goatraces.com for more
information.

Marathon

The annual Mount Meru marathon is
held in Arusha during the month of
August.

Watersports

It is always welcome to have a pool
in the heat of the day, but serious
waterbabies should head for the
coast and islands, where the sea
offers a multitude of entertainments,
from snorkelling or fishing to
windsurfing and sailing.

Diving

Scuba diving and snorkelling are
particularly good around the islands

of Zanzibar and Mafia, which have a
high reputation amongst divers.
There are also many secluded
beaches around the islands, making
for an idyllic setting in or out of the
water.
Diving can be arranged from the
beach hotels or tour operators.
Sharks can be a danger along Dar's
coast, so check out local conditions
before booking.
The best time for snorkelling is in
the morning around 9–10am, and the
visibility is better in summer.
*See Coral Diving feature on page
270, and Tour Operator listings on
page 310.*

Swimming

Most large hotels in Tanzania have
pools, and some are open to the
public for a small fee, although on
the coast and the islands, the sea is
a much more tempting option.
In Arusha, the Mount Meru
Novotel and the Impala Hotel will
allow non-residents to swim; in Stone
Town, you can swim at the Tembo
Hotel and Serena Inn; in Dar, try the
Mission for Seamen, Bandari Road.
Swimming in fresh natural water is
not recommended, due to the risk of
bilharzia and crocodiles. At the big
lakes (Tanganyika and Nyasa), you
should be safe to swim or snorkel off
a boat in deep water, away from any
reed beds.
Swimming and sunbathing on the
beaches immediately in and around
Stone Town and Dar are not
recommended, as there is no
security, and mugging is a risk, as is
polluted water. Once away from the
towns, the water is clear and often
full of colourful fish, even in shallow
water, for most of the year. From mid-
November to mid-February, the
prevailing winds can wash a forest of
sludgy brown seaweed up onto the
pristine beaches of Zanzibar's east
coast, marring its otherwise
impossible perfection.

Fishing

Bagamoyo, Zanzibar and Mafia are all
renowned for excellent deep-sea
fishing. There are numerous resorts
and operators here and in Dar
offering diving and fishing
excursions. July to November is
yellowfin tuna and billfish season;
December to March/April is best for
broadbill, sailfish and spearfish.
Most fish are caught, tagged,
weighed and released these days.
The Pemba Channel Fishing Club
(PCFC) and Sea Adventures Ltd have
been operating from Kenya for the
past 25 years. Visit
www.pembachannel.com for details.

TRANSPORT

ACCOMMODATION

EATING OUT

ACTIVITIES

A – Z

LANGUAGE

Freshwater fishing is available in Mwanza (Lake Victoria) and Lake Tanganyika (contact Kigoma Hill Hotel), and in the Selous Game Reserve on the Rufiji River. Contact **Hippotours & Safaris** c/o Nyumba ya Sanaa, Ohio Street, Dar es Salaam.

For more details of other outdoor actvities, *see Specialist Tour Operators, pages 310–11.*

OUTDOOR ACTITIVIES

Hiking

Most people go on organised tours due to the difficulty of transport, the high national park fees for vehicles and a lack of knowledge of the terrain.

There is excellent hiking in the Ngorongoro Conservation Area *(see page 191)*, the Mahale Mountains *(see page 210)*, Mount Hanang *(see page 217)*, the Uluguru Mountains, *(see page 225)* and the Udzungwa Mountains National Park *(see page 227)*. In Zanzibar, the Jozani Forest *(see page 263)* offers a pleasant, easy day walk, while in Dar, the Wildlife Conservation Society organises weekly bird walks.

Wildlife Conservation Society

Garden Avenue
PO Box 70919
Dar
Tel: 022-211 2518
Fax: 022-212 4572
Email: west@africaonline.co.tz
Bird walks every Friday from the office, monthly talks on wildlife, and a tiny library open to the public

8.30am–4.30pm (closed for lunch 1–1.30pm).

Mountaineering

Many tourists come to Tanzania simply to climb Africa's highest point, Mount Kilimanjaro. Though this is a relatively easy peak to climb, requiring no special skills or experience for the gradual ascent, it is essential to be reasonably fit and have the right equipment. You must take a guide even on the lower peaks, and it is sensible to join an organised climb with food and staff. It is advisable to book well in advance. Visitors should be aware of the dangers of high-altitude sickness which, in extreme cases, can be fatal.

For more details, *see the Kilimanjaro chapter, page 174, and Tour Operator listings, pages 309–11.*

National Parks

Less busy than those in neighbouring Kenya, Tanzania's national parks and game reserves provide some of the world's best destinations for viewing wildlife in their natural habitat. Numerous tour operators can organise tailor-made safaris, either by vehicle, on foot, on horseback or by balloon. Accommodation is either in luxury lodges or designated camping sites – there is little middle ground.

Timing your trip and careful planning are important. The Serengeti is at its best when the migration is around *(see page 196)*. Parts of the Selous are inaccessible during the rainy season (from March

to May) owing to floods. Some areas, such as the Mahale Mountains National Park, are only accessible by plane or boat. In some parks, such as the Arusha National Park, it is possible to drive around without a guide, but those on foot must take an armed guide or ranger. Night-game drives are possible in Ruaha or in private game reserves, but are not allowed within the parks on the Northern Safari Circuit.

Tanzania National Parks (TANAPA) is a government parastatal organisation with headquarters in Arusha. It gazettes, manages and protects the country's national parks *(see box on page 288)*.

TANAPA (Tanzania National Parks)
PO Box 3134
Arusha
Tel: 027-250 3471/4082
Fax: 027-250 8216
www.tanzaniaparks.com
Fees for foreigners to enter Tanzania's national parks are quite high, in the region of US$35–80 per adult per day. The fees generate money to support the infrastructure and to distribute in the local community, but they will eat up a large portion of your travel budget.

Not all the main game reserves are full national parks, for a variety of reasons. Ngorongoro is owned and run by a separate local authority. Parts of the Selous allow hunting, so cannot follow park rules. However, you will be expected to obey the same rules and guidelines, both for the good of the animals and your own safety.

In many national parks, you will not be allowed through the gates without a guide/ranger to protect you

BELOW: a Serengeti leopard, an elusive creature.

against predators (and protect the animals from you).

National Park Rules
Do not disturb any animals or birds.
Do not cause any noise or create a disturbance likely to offend or annoy other visitors.
Do not pick any flowers or cut or destroy any vegetation.
Do not discard any litter, burning cigarettes or matches.
Do not bring a pet into the park.
Do not bring a firearm into the park.
Do not feed the animals.
Some parks require a guide before entering.
Some parks do not accept children under seven years old (check before travelling).
If walking in a park, stay strictly on the main trails.

Safety in the Bush
Tourists are reminded to maintain a safe distance from animals and to remain in vehicles or other protected enclosures when venturing into game parks. Always follow the advice of the guide, who will know the area and the animals inside out.

Tour Operators

UK
Expert Africa
9/10 Upper Square
Old Isleworth
Middlesex
TW7 7BJ
Tel: 020-8232 9777
Fax: 020-8758 4718
www.expertafrica.com
Highly regarded Africa specialists with an expertly designed Tanzania programme concentrating on smaller, more remote parks and lodges – Selous, Ruaha, Mahale, Katavi, Udzungwa and Mikumi – and Zanzibar and Mafia archipelagos. Good value and hands-on knowledge.
Rainbow Tours
Canon Collins House
305 Upper Street
London N1 2TU
Tel: 020-7226 1004
Fax: 020-7226 2621
www.rainbowtours.co.uk
Specialist in Africa and the Indian Ocean, offering tailor-made tours to Tanzania and Zanzibar.
Tribes
12 The Business Centre
Earl Soham
Woodbridge
Suffolk IP13 7SA
Tel: 01728-685971
www.tribes.co.uk or (US)
www.tribestravel.com
Tribes, the award-winning Fair Trade

National Parks Info

Name	sq. km
Arusha	137
Gombe Stream	52
Katavi	4,471
Kilimanjaro	755
Lake Manyara	330
Mahale Mountains	1,613
Mikumi	3,230
Ruaha	10,300
Rubondo Island	240
Saadani	1,000
Serengeti	14,673
Tarangire	2,600
Udzungwa Mountains	1,990

Reserves

Biharamulo	1,300
Burigi	1,300
Ibanda	200
Kilimanjaro	900
Kizigbo	4,000
Maswa	2,200
Mkomazi	1,000
Mount Meru	300
Moyowosi	6,000
Ngorongoro Crater	2,288
Rumanyika-Orungundu	800
Rungwa	9,000
Saa Nane Island	0.5
Selous	55,000
Ugalla	5,000
Umba River	1,500
Uwanda	5,000

Travel company, offers tailor-made and small group holidays throughout Tanzania. From classic safaris to walking safaris guided by Maasai, Kilimanjaro climbs and relaxing breaks on Zanzibar or Mafia.

South Africa
CC Africa
P. Bag X27
Benmore 2010
Johannesburg
Tel: +27-11-809 4300
Fax: +27-11-809 4400
www.ccafrica.com
Owners of some of Tanzania's most exclusive lodges, including Mnemba Island in Zanzibar and the extraordinary Ngorongoro Crater Lodge, CC Africa operates superb lodges and personalised fly or drive safaris.
Wild Frontiers
PO Box 844
Halfway House
Gauteng 1685
Tel: +27-11-702 2035
Fax: +27-11-468 1655
www.wildfrontiers.com
An excellent, competitively priced Johannesburg-based tour operator with more than a decade of experience arranging general and

specialist safaris to all corners of Tanzania, as well as island beach stays and Kilimanjaro climbs.

Tanzania
Bushbuck Safaris
PO Box 1700
Arusha
Tel: 027-250 7779/254 4308/8939
Fax: 027-254 8293
www.bushbuckltd.com
Bushbuck organises customised, tailor-made safaris throughout Tanzania (including Zanzibar). All accommodation is in lodges, resorts or luxury permanent camps.
Coastal Travel
Upanga Road (Airline District)
PO Box 3052
Tel: 022-211 7959/7955
Fax: 022-211 8647
www.coastal.cc
Coastal Travel offers flying safaris to the Selous Game Reserve, Ruaha, Ngorongoro and Serengeti. They also do scheduled flights (see page 277).
Fourways Travel
Main roundabout, Station Road
Mwanza
Tel: 028-250 2273/1853
www.fourwaystravel.net
Mwanza's leading travel agent for the Lake Victoria area: hotel bookings, local and international flights, Serengeti safaris, car hire, local excursions.
Gibb's Farm Safaris
PO Box 2
Karatu
Tel: 027-253 4397
Fax: 027-253 4418
www.gibbsfarm.net
Private luxury camping safaris with experienced guides in Serengeti, Ngorongoro and Tarangire.
Greystoke Safaris
Mahale
Tel: 027-255 3819/ 254 8050
Experts in Mahale and Katavi national parks, where it has operated exclusive lodges for a decade, Greystoke Safaris arranges fly-in charter and other safaris to these parks. Exclusive and expensive.
Nyika Treks and Safaris Ltd
PO Box 13077
Arusha
Tel/fax: 027-250 1956
Mobile: 0754-393331
www.nyikatreks.com
In Zanzibar
Shangani Street
Stone Town
Nyika means wilderness, and that's exactly what this (mainly) budget company offers. Specialises in camping and lodge safaris via truck or camel, hiking (with donkeys carrying packs), night drives in the southern circuit (which are not

allowed in the northern circuit). Also offers five-day camel safaris (budget) on Maasai land near Mount Meru, and trekking at the Ngorongoro Crater. Links with tour operator in Zanzibar and companies offering tours to Selous etc, in the south. Also offers some cultural tourism programmes in Arusha.

Roy Safaris
PO Box 50
Arusha
Tel: 027-250 8010/2115
Fax: 027-254 8892
www.roysafaris.com
This is a family-run company offering tours throughout Tanzania. It specialises in tailor-made photographic safaris, cultural tours, mountain trekking and beach holidays.

Takims Holidays, Tours and Safaris
PO Box 20350
Dar es Salaam
Tel: 022-211 0346/0347
Fax: 022-211 6660
www.takimsholidays.com
Tried and true holiday organisers, from safaris to climbing Kilimanjaro to beach holidays in Zanzibar and Mafia.

Zanzibar

Most tour operators on Zanzibar offer the full range of local options, including the Stone Town city tour, the Spice Tour, swimming with dolphins and visiting the Jozani Forest. The following are some of the more reputable companies.

Eco & Culture Tours
Opposite 236 Hurumzi
Hurumzi Street
Tel: 024-223 0366/0777 410873
www.ecoculture-zanzibar.org

Fernandes Tours and Safaris
PO Box 647
Tel: 024-223 0666
Email: fts@zanlink.com

Gallery Tours & Safaris
PO Box 3181
Stone Town
Tel: 024-223 2088
Fax: 024-223 6583
www.gallerytours.net
Specialising in high-end, personalised tours around Zanzibar. Services include weddings and honeymoons, conferences, and special-interest tours.

Safari Blue
Tel: 0777-423 162
www.safariblue.net
Highly recommended day tours of the stunning Menai Bay Conservation area. Sail by traditional dhow to sandbanks, snorkel coral reefs, watch dolphins, eat a gourmet seafood lunch and sail on traditional outrigger canoe before returning to shore by lantern sail.

Zan Tours
PO Box 2560
Zanzibar
Tel: 024-223 3116
Fax: 024-233 3042
www.zantours.com
One-stop travel resource for Zanzibar.

Specialist Tour Operators

Birdwatching

Masumbo Tours
Iringa
Tel: 026-272 5280
Email: masumbo@masumbo.co.tz
Run by a vastly experienced ornithologist and ecologist born and bred in southern Tanzania, this specialist company arranges birdwatching trips into the seldom-visited western Udzungwa (better than the national park for endemics and near-endemics) and other key birding sites in the Eastern Arc and elsewhere in Tanzania.

Canoeing

Bushbuck Safaris
PO Box 1700
Arusha
Tel: 027-250 7779 or
254 4186/8924/4308/8939
Fax: 027-254 8293/4860
www.bushbuckltd.com
Scenic guided canoeing safaris on the Momella Lake in Arusha National Park, the only place in Tanzania where you can see buffalo, giraffe, bushbuck, waterbuck, 600 species of birds and views of Meru and Kilimanjaro from the water.

Climbing Kilimanjaro

The following specialise in climbing trips up Kili:

African Environments
PO Box 16080
Arusha
Tel/fax: 027-250 8625
www.africanenvironments.com

Keys Hotel
PO Box 933
Moshi
Tel: 027-275 2250
Fax: 027-275 0073
www.keys-hotel.com

Marangu Hotel
PO Box 40
Moshi
Tel: 027-275 6594
Tel/fax: 027-275 6591
Email: info@maranguhotel.com

Dhow Safaris

The Original Dhow Safaris
PO Box 3181
Zanzibar
Tel: 024-223 2088
Fax: 024-223 6583
Hotline: 0777-223932

www.dhowsafaris.net
Original Dhow Safaris offers scheduled and private charter dhow cruises every day. Scheduled cruises include a guide, refreshments and entertainment. Private charters can be arranged for small or large groups, for any occasion.

Diving

While Unguja has some fine reefs, Pemba is spectacular, with world-class diving. Dolphins are more likely to be seen around Zanzibar Island, whereas around Pemba, turtles are abundant. *See also Coral Diving on page 270.*

Zanzibar
One Ocean
PO Box 608
Kenyatta Road
Tel: 024-223 8374
Fax 024-234 877
www.zanzibaroneocean.com
Australian-run expert operation with branches in Stone Town, Matemwe and Kiwengwa. PADI five-star courses available up to Dive Master.

Pemba
Swahili Divers
The Old Mission Lodge
Chake Chake
Tel: 024-245 2786
www.swahilidivers.com
Full PADI accreditation and courses available up to Dive Master. The owner and chief instructor, Raf, is highly entertaining.

Mafia
Jean de Villiers
Tel: radio link only
www.cholemjini.com
Operating out of Chole Mjini on Chole Island, Jean knows the sites better than anyone. Diving is from a dhow, the sites are 15 minutes away, and the pace of the operation fits the surroundings perfectly – you can even return to the lodge for lunch and a nap between dives. Full PADI accreditation and courses available up to Dive Master.

Fishing

Fisherman Tours and Travel
Zanzibar
PO Box 3537
Tel: 024-223 8791/2
Fax: 024-223 8791
Email: reservation@fishermantours.com
www.fishermantours.com
Specialist tours for fishing enthusiasts.

FishingZanzibar.com
Tel: 0773-387 5231/0756-442203
www.fishingzanzibar.com

Located in Nungwi, on the north coast of Unguja Island, FishingZanzibar.com specialises in deep-sea fishing charters around the Zanzibar Archipelago. A member of the International Game Fishing Association

Zanzibar Big Game Fishing
PO Box 1784
Zanzibar
Tel: 024-223 3615
Fax: 024-223 3039
www.zanzibarfishing.com
Zanzibar Big Game Fishing has a fleet of three professional deep-sea fishing boats. Also a member of the International Game Fishing Association.

Horse Riding

Equestrian Safaris
PO Box 429
Arusha
Tel: 0754-595 517
www.safaririding.com
Remote horseback expeditions for experienced riders around Kilimanjaro and Lake Natron.

Makoa Farm
PO Box 203
Moshi
Tel: 0754-312 896/7
www.makoa-farm.com
Makoa Farm offers horse-riding safaris around Kilimanjaro and other areas for riders of all abilities.

Hot-Air Balloon Safaris

Serengeti Balloon Safaris Ltd
PO Box 12116
Arusha
Tel: 027-250 8578
Fax: 027-254 8997
www.balloonsafaris.com
UK contact
Tel: 01225-873 756
Magical hour-long dawn flights daily over the Serengeti followed by champagne breakfast. Pick-ups arranged from all central Serengeti lodges. You should book through main tour operators, as it works out cheaper, although it remains very expensive. June–August are extremely busy, so it's best to book early.

Hunting

Tanzania Game Trackers Safaris
Legendary Adventures
10777 Westheimer Road
Suite 1060
Houston TX 77042
USA
Tel: +1-713-580 7100
www.legendaryadventures.com
One of the largest and most reputable of the hunting outfits, operating in six locations throughout Tanzania.

Kitesurfing

Afrikite
Zanzibar
Tel: 0773-114 976
Email: afrikite@gmail.com
Kitesurfing lessons and hire, on the east coast of Zanzibar.

Thorsten Schmidt
Dar es Salaam
Tel: 0787-158 932
Kitesurfing (sometimes known as kiteboarding) lessons and hire.

Paragliding

AXN Adventure
52-16 94 Street
Elmhurst, NY 11373
USA
www.axn-travel.com
Organises adventure travel to variouis destinations. There are some fabulous areas to paraglide in Tanzania, which is still a relatively new activity in East Africa.

Cultural Tourism

Arusha

Cultural Tourism Programme
AICC Ngorongoro Wing, Room 432
PO Box 10455
Arusha
Tel/fax: 027-250 7515
www.infojep.com/culturaltours
Arusha has begun to develop its potential for cultural tourism, and it is now possible to visit local people, including Maasai, experience their way of life, share food and stories. These projects are locally owned and run, so your money is going directly to the people you meet; you can learn about local culture while contributing to its survival.

Central Tanzania

Babati and Hanang Cultural Tourism Programme
Babati
Office next to Kahembe Guesthouse
Tel: 027-253 1088
www.infojep.com/culturaltours
Exemplary grass-roots ecotourism set-up, arranges a wide variety of trips, from one day to two weeks, plus game walks around Lake Burungi and eastern Manyara, and other cultural visits. Fees include local transport, accommodation and meals, guide and village fees. The trips are not luxurious by any means, but they are totally authentic – perfect for those who want to get off the beaten track affordably, and in competent hands.

North Coast

SNV (Netherlands Development Organisation) Cultural Tourism Programme
AICC Serengeti Wing, Room 643

PO Box 10455
Arusha
Tel/fax: 027-250 2515
Email: tourinfo@habari.co.tz
The Pare Mountains are divided into the north and south regions – neither is very accessible or developed for tourism. SNV offers great days out hiking and birdwatching from Same, Usangi or Mbanga or more extended stays at some of the remoter villages.

Northern Safari Circuit

Momoya Muhindoi
PO Box 120
Karatu
Email: momoyaeyasi@yahoo.com
An enthusiastic and knowledgeable local who speaks excellent English will guide you around the Lake Eyasi area, including visits to the Hadza and Datoga people.

South Coast

The Old Boma
Tel: 0784-360 110
www.mikindani.com
UK contact
Tel: 01425-657774
Fax: 01425-656684
The only company promoting tourism to the south coast, with a strong emphasis on community development and ecotourism. The local headquarters at the Old Boma in Mikindani acts as an information centre and tour operator. Affordable day and overnight excursions include dhow trips, Lake Chidya and the Rovuma River, snorkelling in Mnazi Bay Marine Reserve, Rondo Plateau and the Lukwika Lumesule Game Reserve.

Southern Highlands

Sisi Kwa Sisi Tourism Office
Cnr School Street and Mbalizi Road
Mbeya
Tel: 0744-463 471
Email: sisikwasisi@hotmail.com
Cultural Tourism Programme and Netherlands Development Organisation (SNV) affiliated ecotourism project offering inexpensive guided trips to most sites of interest in the region: Ngosi Crater, Kitulo Plateau, Mbeya Range, Mount Rungwe, etc. A proportion of the fees is pumped into community conservation and development projects. A lot of touts hang around Mbeya bus station claiming to be from Sisi Kwa Sisi, so make arrangements at the office, loosely open Mon–Sat 8am–3pm.

A – Z

A HANDY SUMMARY OF PRACTICAL INFORMATION, ARRANGED ALPHABETICALLY

A irport Taxes

There is a standard departure tax of US$30 for all international passengers leaving Tanzania, which is payable in hard currency at your airport of departure. This may be included in your ticket purchase price, but not necessarily, so it is important to check beforehand. Domestic passengers pay US$1 aviation safety fee and US$5 airport tax at the counter during check-in.

Admission Charges

Admission charges into museums and galleries are usually minimal (under Tsh5,000) and payable in local currency. Many locally run establishments ask for a donation, and what the average tourist would consider a small contribution is often very much appreciated.

B udgeting for your Trip

Budgeting for your visit to Tanzania

very much depends on the sort of experience you are looking to have. Whether you are a backpacker or a luxury client, Africa is certainly cheap by European standards, but does not offer the shoestring prices of Asia. The key in regard to budgeting is thorough research: find out as much as you can about all the options. Tour operators can book your entire trip right down to the last detail and this makes budgeting a whole lot easier.

It is imperative that you put aside extra funds in case of emergencies. Communication, technology and health-care facilities are nowhere near Western standards in most parts of Tanzania. The best cover you can have in any sticky situation is the means to pay your way out. This, coupled with good travel insurance, should allow you the peace of mind to enjoy your trip no matter what happens.

There are two price brackets for almost all accommodation; resident rates (includes Tanzanians and expatriates) and non-resident rates

(everyone else). Non-resident rates are generally quoted in US dollars but payable in Tanzanian shillings. Resident rates are quoted in local currency and always lower. Many establishments increase their prices during high season (June to September), so be sure to confirm the price for the time of year you intend to visit.

Prices for accommodation cover the whole gamut. Budget hotels and guesthouses with basic amenities start at around US$10 per person, per night. Luxury five-star lodgings range from several hundred to sometimes thousands of dollars per night. Lower to mid-range hotels fall somewhere in between, depending on facilities and level of comfort. Generally, accommodation in Zanzibar is pricier than on the mainland.

If you are willing to do as the locals do, you can eat heartily for a pittance. African staples such as *ugali* (maize) with fish or meat stew, *chipsi mayai* (chip omelette) or even the more lavish pilau rice can be purchased for a couple of bucks. International cuisine, served at most high-end hotels, is substantially more expensive than local food.

It is never advisable to drink the tap water anywhere in Africa, so include bottled water as part of the budget for your entire trip. A 1.5-litre bottle of purified water retails at around Tsh700.

Transport comes in a variety of forms; the cheapest option is to travel by local bus (daladala); price depends on the distance you are travelling. This can be anything from Tsh300 for a few stops (sometimes up to 10 km/6 miles), to several thousand shillings for much longer distances.

Scandinavia Express offers a fairly safe, reliable service for long-haul road travel at reasonable prices. This includes internal routes within Tanzania and to the capital cities of several neighbouring countries. Information on all current fares and routes is available on www.scandinaviagroup.com. (There are other bus companies but they are of dubious quality and on the whole considered unsafe to travel with.)

Prices for private hire cars with a driver and taxis are negotiable and depend on the distance you are travelling and the level of your bartering skills. Self-drive is a good option if you are a confident driver. Prices in high season from local hirers start at around US$30 a day plus insurance. Going through a more recognised hirer such as Hertz comes with a higher price tag (usually starting at around US$120 per day for a 4x4 or $80 for a saloon), but offers better quality assurance in terms of safety and cover.

Business Hours

Business hours are becoming much more varied, as more of Tanzania's economy becomes privatised. Here is a rough guide to hours practised.
Offices: Mon–Fri 8am–noon, 2–5pm, Sat 8am–1pm, if open.
Government: Mon–Fri 8am–4pm.
Garages/shops: Mon–Fri 8.30am–noon, 2–6pm, Sat 8.30am–12.30pm.
Banks: Mon–Fri 8.30am–4pm, Sat 8am–1pm.
Post offices: Mon–Fri 8am–4.30pm, Sat 9am–noon.

Business Travellers

For general enquiries on business, trade and investment in Tanzania, contact the following:

Tanzania Chamber of Commerce, Industry and Agriculture
PO Box 9713, Dar es Salaam
Tel: 022-211 9436/7
Fax: 022-2119 437
Zanzibar Chamber of Commerce
PO Box 1407, Zanzibar
Tel: 255-24-223 4713
Fax: 255-24-223 1710
Mobile: 0742-740 298
Email: znocia@zanzinet.com
In the UK, contact the
Tanzania Trade Centre
3 Stratford Place
London W1C 1AS
Tel: 020-7758 8070
Fax: 020-7758 8073
www.tanzatrade.co.uk

Conference Centres

Even small lodges will often have some conference facilities, so if you want to have your meeting in a bush camp, it may well be possible. For full hotel listings, see page 281.

Dar es Salaam
New Africa Hotel
Cnr Azikiwe/Sokoine Drives
Tel: 022-211 7050
Email: banquets@newafricahotel.com
Conference facilities for up to 100.
Golden Tulip
Toure Drive
Tel: 022-260 0288
Email: enquiries@goldentuliptanzania.com
Conference facilities for up to 100.
Royal Palm Hotel
Mövenpick, Ohio Street
Tel: 022-211 2416
The best facilities in town; conference rooms of various sizes (suitable for up to 440 people), with audiovisual equipment.
Sea Cliff Hotel
Msasani Peninsula
Tel: 022-260 0380

Email: operations@hotelseacliff.com
"Executive Floor", with eight executive rooms and four executive suites, plus private lounge and reception area. Conference rooms holding up to 110 delegates.
White Sands Hotel
Janwana Beach
Tel: 022-264 7620
Email: fom@hotelwhitesands.com
Fully equipped conference facilities for up to 300 people, plus accommodation for seminars and workshops.
Paradise Holiday Resort
Bagamoyo
Tel: 023-244 0000
Email: reservations@paradiseresort.net
Accommodates up to 200 people.

Arusha
Arusha International Conference Centre
PO Box 3081
Tel: 027-250 8008/2593/2595
Fax: 027-250 6630
www.aicc.co.tz
The biggest room holds up to 1,000 people.
Novotel Mount Meru
Arusha–Moshi Road
Tel: 027-250 2711
Email: tahifin@yako.habari.co.tz
Two conference rooms holding 200.
New Safari Hotel
Boma Road
Tel: 027-250 3261
Email: newsafarihotel@habari.co.tz
Holds up to 150 people.

Translation and Business Services

Dar es Salaam International Conference Centre (DICC)
Regus Instant Offices
Tel: 022-212 2833
Fax: 022-212 2835
www.regus.com

BELOW: the cost of a safari can be tailored to your budget.

Regus operates a business centre in Dar, offering premises and facilities for any length of time – from a day to a year.

The **Mövenpick Royal Palm**, **Golden Tulip** and **Southern Sun** hotels all have business centres with full secretarial services.

Zanzibar
IBS Zanzibar
(International Business Services)
PO Box 4213, Kenyatta Street, first floor, Shangani Post Office
Tel: 024-223 6761
Fax: 024-223 1962
Email: ibs@zitec.org
Premises for rent, office equipment, legal services, computerised secretarial services.
Zamani Zanzibar Kempinski
PO Box 3140, Kiwengwa
Tel: 0777-444 477
Fax: 0777-444 488
www.kempinski-zanzibar.com
Full business facilities in luxury surroundings of a five-star resort.
Zanzibar Beach Resort
PO Box 2586, Mazazini
Tel: 024-223 0208
Fax: 024-223 0556
www.zanzibarbeachresort.com
Dedicated conference facilities, secretarial services, business centre.
Zanzibar Serena Inn
PO Box 4151, Shangani
Tel: 024-223 3587
Fax: 024-223 3019
www.serenahotels.com
Services provided include internet, photocopying and postal services.

C hildren

Many Westerners are too timid to take their children to any developing country. This is a great shame: not only will they have a brilliant time, but it is a massive learning experience, and Zanzibar also has some of the world's best beaches. Give children a project for the trip, such as a travel diary, to keep them interested and involved. Most Africans adore children, and will help you keep an eye on them; having kids with you can open doors of communication, and local children will immediately involve them in their games and activities. All you need to take are some common-sense precautions.

Babies

Taking small babies into this environment may simply be more trouble than it's worth. They won't like the heat, you may find it difficult to get baby food and supplies, once out of the major towns, and they won't remember it anyway. It is unsafe to have babies on safari (most operators will not accept them). Their cries are said to resemble those of wounded animals and may attract predators.

Health

From the age of four or five onwards, things become far easier, but there are specific health considerations to watch out for.

Children are more susceptible to illness than adults. They also get dehydrated more quickly, so be sure to give them plenty to drink.

Be extra careful of children's delicate skin in the African sun. Large quantities of sunblock and a good hat are essential equipment.

The other main risk is malaria: seek advice before travelling on what anti-malarial medication is suitable for your children; *see page 318* for further information.

There are lurking dangers not found back home. Make sure children wear shoes whenever they are out of the house, and that they wash their hands frequently, do not scramble over rocks without checking where they put their hands, or start playing with any strange insects or wildlife they might meet before it is checked out by someone in the know. If they are scratched, take it seriously and use antiseptic, as bacteria can breed fast in the heat. If they are bitten or stung, get expert advice immediately.

Food for Children

Food on offer in Tanzania tends to be quite plain and frequently involves chips, so there shouldn't be any problems finding something suitable. Tourist hotels usually provide special children's menus (some also have kids' clubs). Bottled water and sodas are available everywhere.

Travelling

One of the biggest problems in travelling with children is simply the many long hours spent en route – even the charms of a Land Rover can pall quickly. Take plenty of drinks, sweets to suck or chewing gum, and emergency food rations. A supply of music, audio books and computer games is essential. Try not to schedule long journeys on consecutive days.

Safaris with Children

Older children on the whole enjoy safaris. Most safari companies advise against taking children under six years on safari, and some luxury

BELOW: Tanzania's children will be delighted to share a game with your kids.

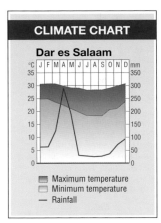

CLIMATE CHART

Dar es Salaam

- ▨ Maximum temperature
- ▢ Minimum temperature
- — Rainfall

lodges ban under-12s. It is considered that they will be bored, and cannot sustain the quiet concentration needed for game viewing. Other lodges accept younger children but insist on the family having a private vehicle to view game. A few enlightened operators offer special child-friendly safaris.

On trekking safaris, children need to be at least 14 years old to keep up with the rest of the group. Younger kids just don't have the stamina.

Climate

Tanzania's hottest months are from October to February, and the main rainy season from mid-March to late May. Heavy downpours during April and May are often accompanied by violent thunderstorms, particularly in the highlands. There is also a short rainy season in November and December. The coolest months, June to September, are also the most pleasant.

Tanzania's varied geography creates drastic climatic differences within the country. Coastal areas are hot and humid, with an average daytime temperature of 30°C (86°F). The central plateau has hot days and cool nights. The hilly area between the coast and the northern highlands averages a pleasant 20°C (68°F) from January to September, while mountainous areas (including Kilimanjaro, the Usambara Mountains and the northern and southern highlands) register lows of 12°C (54°F) in May–August. Mount Kilimanjaro is snowcapped year-round, although climate change means more ice is melting each year.

Crime and Safety

Before Leaving Home

For travel advice, log onto www.fco.gov.

uk for official UK Foreign Office advice. If in the US, go to www.travel.state.gov/travel_warnings.html. Make photocopies of all important documents, including your passport, visas, traveller's cheques, insurance documents and vaccination certificates – this will ensure speedy replacement should they be stolen. Also, leave a copy of everything at home, with someone you can contact if you get into difficulties.

Theft

Tanzania is a very poor country, so it is no surprise that tourists can be the target of crime. Be alert and cautious.

Street crime is fairly common in larger cities. The main threats are pickpockets and muggers. It is asking for trouble to wear expensive jewellery or watches – if there is anything that you could not bear to lose, leave it at home. Leave your passport, tickets and excess money in the hotel safe (not in your room) unless you have to take them.

If you need them or are in transit, consider wearing a concealed money belt and keep a little "giveaway money" separately. Most opportunist thieves will probably be content with that and won't look any further.

Only use credit cards in reputable tourist hotels, as credit card fraud is rife. Don't walk the streets or on the beach after dark – take a taxi.

On the Road

Do not drive at night, and follow local advice. Carjackings are a hazard on rural trips. Do not stop for hitchhikers, and if you see or are involved in an accident, drive on to the nearest town and report it, rather than stopping to help.

Touts and Guides

In Zanzibar, use only guides authorised by the Commission for Tourism – they will have an identity badge.

Although sometimes annoying, most touts who approach you are honest – if persistent – salesmen for safari companies. Beware, however, of the few who aren't. Several scams are on the go, so don't give money upfront until you have checked out the situation. Ignore anyone who approaches you on the street offering to change money. There is no black market in Tanzania, and these guys are looking to cheat you.

Drugs

There is a drug problem in Zanzibar. Beware of touts who approach you off the ferry – many are just looking

for money for their next hit. There are tough penalties if you are caught partaking.

Political Tensions

Political tensions can run high at times in Tanzania. Travellers should avoid political gatherings as they can turn violent.

If you are travelling near the border areas of Rwanda or Burundi, exercise extra caution. The area experiences minor military clashes and has a flow of refugees.

Inevitably, the ominous shadow of Al-Qaeda has fallen over Tanzania, since the American Embassy bombing in 1998. You should be safe, but be aware that in such a large Muslim population there will be some anti-Western sentiment.

Customs Regulations

Duty-free limits for those over the age of 16 are: 1 litre of spirits; 250 ml of perfume; 200 cigarettes; 50 cigars or 250 grams of tobacco.

Disabled Travellers

Disabled travellers to Tanzania face many practical difficulties and a frustrating lack of facilities, but find they are amazed at the help and understanding that they get from local people. At the airport, everything is done manually – ie, you are physically lifted on and off the plane; wheelchairs are available once you are on the ground. On the beaches there are no planks for wheelchair users. Many streets in Stone Town are cobbled. Accessible hotels are few and far between, although in Dar most of the up-market hotels have limited facilities.

Safaris can be a good option for disabled travellers, as you spend so long in vehicles. However, they do tend to be more expensive for disabled travellers because they have to be booked from abroad – and the cheaper companies don't tend to advertise internationally. Many smaller lodges have scattered rooms in inaccessible places, but the larger lodges, such as the Serena and Sopa chains, can usually accommodate people in wheelchairs if given advance warning. Abercrombie and Kent (www.akdmc.com) offer a (pricey) flying safari.

The tourist office should be able to provide a list of local tour operators who accommodate disabled travellers; they include the following:
Dar es Salaam
Takims Holidays and Safaris

TRANSPORT • ACCOMMODATION • EATING OUT • ACTIVITIES • A – Z • LANGUAGE

www.takimsholidays.com
Kearsley Tours and Travel
Email: kearsley@raha.com
Arusha
Ranger Safaris www.rangersafaris.com
Bobby Tours and Safaris
www.bobbytours.com

Zanzibar Association for the Disabled
At the roundabout, Creek Road,
PO Box 2043
Tel: 024-223 1730
Email: uwz@zanzinet.com

In the UK
RADAR (Royal Association for Disability and Rehabilitation)
12 City Forum, 250 City Road,
London EC1V 8AF
Tel: 020-7250 3222
Fax: 020-7250 0212
www.radar.org.uk

In the US
SATH (Society for the Advancement of Travel for the Handicapped)
347 Fifth Avenue, Suite 605,
New York, NY10016
Tel: 212-447 7284
Fax: 212-447 1928
www.sath.org

E mbassies and Consulates

Tanzanian Embassies
Burundi
Patrice Lumuba Avenue, BP 1653,
Bujumbura
Tel: 257-24634
Democratic Republic of Congo
142 Boulevard du 30 Jin B, BP 1612,
Kinshasa
Tel: 242-34364
Kenya
Continental House, Corner of Uhuru
Highway and Harambee Avenue,
PO Box 47790, Nairobi
Tel: 254-233 1056
Email: tanzania@user.africaonline.co.ke
Mozambique
Ujamaa House, Avenida Marites Da
Machava 852, PO Box 4515, Maputo
Tel: 258-490 110
Email: safina@zebra.uem.mz
Rwanda
Avenue Paul IV, BP 669, Kigali
Tel: 250-756 567
Email: tanmose@wm.west-call.com
South Africa
PO Box 56572, Arcadia 0007,
Pretoria
Tel: +27-12-342 4371
Fax: +27-12-4304 383
Email: tanzania@cis.co.za
Uganda
6 Kagera Road, PO Box 5750,
Kampala
Tel: 41-256 272
Email: tzrepkla@imul.com

Electricity

230V, 50Hz, square three-pin
plugs (UK-style). Some round
three-pin plugs remain.

UK
Tanzania High Commission,
3 Stratford Place, London W1C 1AS
Tel: 020-7569 1470
Fax: 020-7499 9321
www.tanzania-online.gov.uk
US
2139 R Street NW,
Washington DC 20008
Tel: 202-939 6125
Fax: 202-797 7408
www.tanzaniaembassy-us.org
Zambia
Ujamaa House,
5200 United Nations Avenue,
PO Box 31219, Lusaka
Tel: 260-227 698
Fax: 260-254 861
Email: tzreplks@zamnet.zm

Foreign Embassies & Consulates
If you are going far off the beaten
track, it is a good idea to register
with your embassy when you arrive in
Dar es Salaam.

Dar es Salaam
Australia
Australians should contact the
Canadian embassy.
Canada
38 Mirambo Street (Cnr Garden
Avenue), PO Box 1022
Tel: 022-211 2831
Fax: 022-211 6897
Email: dslam@dfait-maeci.gc.ca
Ireland
1131 Msasani Road,
Off Haile Selassie Road,
(near the International School),
Oyster Bay, PO Box 9612
Tel: 022-260 2355/6
Fax: 022-266 7852
Kenya
14th floor, NIC Investment House,
PO Box 5321
Cnr Samora Avenue/Mirambo Street
Tel: 022-211 2955
Fax: 022-211 3098
Malawi
38 AH Mwinyi Road, Oyster Bay,
PO Box 7616
Tel: 022-266 6284
Fax: 022-211 3360
Mozambique
25 Garden Avenue, PO Box 9370
Tel/fax: 022-211 6502
Rwanda
32 Upanga Road, PO Box 2918
Tel: 022-211 7631/5889
Fax: 022-211 5888
South Africa
Mwaya Road, Msasani,

PO Box 10723
Tel: 022-260 1800
Fax: 022-260 0684
Uganda
25 Msasani Road, Oyster Bay
PO Box 6237
Tel: 022-266 7391/7009
Fax: 022-266 7224
UK
Umoja House, Garden Avenue,
PO Box 9200
Tel: 022-211 0101
www.britishhighcommission.gov.uk/tanzania
US
686 Old Bagamoyo Road
PO Box 9123
Tel: 022-266 8001
Fax: 022-266 8238
http://tanzania.usembassy.gov
Zambia
Zambia House, Cnr Ohio Street/
Sokoine Drive, PO Box 2525
Tel: 022-211 8481-2
Fax: 022-211 2977

Zanzibar
Diplomatic representation for UK
citizens is available through the
ZanAir office on Malawi Road in
Zanzibar *(see page 278)*.

Entry Regulations

All travellers to Tanzania must
possess a passport valid for at least
six months after intended date of
travel plus a return ticket. If travelling
on business you will be required to
present a letter indicating the nature
of the trip and your business contact
in Tanzania. It is possible to obtain a
visa on entry at any land border but it
is preferable to apply in advance.
 Citizens of Australia, New Zealand,
Canada, the US and of EU member
states require visas to enter
Tanzania. Single-entry tourist visas
are valid for three months; multiple-
entry visas for six months. Visas may
be extended at the immigration office
in any town in Tanzania free of
charge. Visa prices, which vary
according to citizenship, do not
include additional charges for
working or business permits. A
special pass is required for those
wishing to work in Tanzania. Visas
usually take less than a week to

Emergency Numbers

Ambulance/fire/police:
(mainland) 112
Ambulance/fire/police: (Zanzibar)
999
Police (Dar): 0741-322 112
Anti-corruption: 113
Flying doctors (Tanzania): 022-
211 6610, Email: info@amreftz.org

come through and may even be processed within 24 hours.

As information on visas changes frequently, it is advisable to contact your nearest Tanzanian embassy before you travel.

Vaccination certificates for yellow fever are needed to enter Tanzania from certain infected countries in Africa and Latin America (check www.tanzania-online.gov.uk for the latest list).

Finally, keep all receipts for visas and ensure all entries are clearly stamped in your passport. Any smudges may be seen as an opportunity for a fine (bribe).

In Dar es Salaam, the Immigration Service is located at:
Ohio Street/Ghana Avenue
Fax: 022-211 1909
Email: uhamiaji@intafrica.com.
Open Mon–Fri 7.30am–3.30pm.

Etiquette

In Tanzania, greetings are very important, and not to be rushed. Africans often spend minutes holding hands after first greeting each other. It is considered bad manners to rush abruptly into a query without first observing the social niceties.

As in Asia, people eat and shake hands with their right hand. Using the left is considered dirty, as this is normally used for toilet purposes. Putting your feet up on a table or stool is considered rude. Physical displays of affection between sexes are frowned upon, as are open displays of anger and impatience. Realise that things often take longer in Africa, and be philosophical and always polite if you want to get a favourable response from officials. Part of the African experience is to slow down to African time – you'll wonder what all the stress and rushing about are for when you get home.

Elderly people are shown a great deal of respect, particularly when being greeted.

Despite the nation's poverty, Tanzanians place a high premium on being clean and neatly presented. Tourists who dress scruffily will receive less respect than those who are well groomed. You can wear shorts in tourist areas, but they are considered childish. Jacket and tie are recommended for meeting senior officials – if in doubt, dress conservatively.

Remember that a large part of the coast and the islands of Zanzibar are Muslim. In these and other areas, it is appropriate for women to wear discreet, long, loose-fitting clothes.

Local women are often uncomfortable in the company of men. Modest clothes and bare feet are required for entry to mosques. Most mosques are not open to non-Muslims, so never enter unless specifically invited.

G ay and Lesbian Travellers

Tanzania and Zanzibar are culturally conservative. Open displays of affection are frowned upon even between straight couples. Don't assume, if you see men holding hands, that they are gay. It is safe to say that gay relationships are taboo. It is against the law and carries a 14-year prison sentence. However, for the discreet gay couple there should be no problem. Although it has no "scene" (straight or gay), Zanzibar is actually a popular gay destination.

H ealth Precautions

Since health risks are higher in Africa and medical care often inadequate, it is vital that your travel insurance policy is comprehensive and includes emergency evacuation and repatriation. Have a dental check-up before you go and get a spare pair of prescription glasses if you wear them. If you are on medication, make sure you carry enough to last you, plus a prescription and letter from your doctor, to show to border officials who may suspect you of smuggling drugs.

Health Advice

In the UK, detailed health advice, tailored to individual needs, is available from the MASTA (Medical Advice for Travellers Abroad) online at www.masta-travel-health.com. Traveller advice is also available the NHS website, www.fitfortravel.nhs.uk, or check with your doctor.

Two other important medical contacts are **AMREF** (African Medical and Research Foundation; www.amref.org) and **IAMAT** (International Association for Medical Assistance to Travellers). The former offers emergency regional evacuation by the Flying Doctors Society of Africa. A two-month membership costs US$25. Email them via their website or contact the office in Nairobi (254-20-699 4409), Dar (022-211 6610/212 7187) or New York (212-768 2440). IAMAT (www.iamat.org) provides members (membership is free) with health information and a list of approved doctors all over the world, including Tanzania.

Inoculations

Consult your doctor about inoculations at least two months before you leave. A **yellow fever** inoculation is no longer required unless you are travelling from an infected area, but there is a risk on the Tanzanian mainland, so it is sensible to have one. **Diphtheria** and **tetanus** vaccinations are also a good idea. Boosters are required every 10 years after a trio of injections while young. **Typhoid** is recommended for stays over two weeks.

A series of inoculations exists for **hepatitis A** and **B**. For hepatitis A, long-term protection (10 years) is available by an initial injection followed by a booster at 6–12 months. For short-term protection, an injection of gamma globulin will protect you immediately for up to six months, depending on dosage.

Meningitis inoculations are recommended and will protect you against the major forms of the disease. **Polio** inoculations are strongly recommended.

Protection against **tuberculosis** is recommended for those living in the area for over three months, though the risk to tourists is low.

Rabies vaccinations are usually only given if you are likely to be in close contact with animals during your stay (eg, working in a game farm or reserve). A full course of three injections takes several weeks to administer.

Guard your vaccination record as carefully as your passport.

First-Aid Kit

The following items should be in your first-aid kit: strong mosquito repellent; malaria prophylactics; sting-relief cream; antihistamine pills; plasters, antiseptic wipes and spray for blisters and cuts; syringes; Imodium for diarrhoea. Also, take your own condoms and tampons (if required).

Hygiene

Many areas in Tanzania are subject to regular outbreaks of cholera and dysentery due to poor sanitation and hygiene. Be conscientious about washing your hands regularly with soap and water. Good hotels will ensure your water supply is safe. Elsewhere, use bottled, boiled or otherwise purified water for drinking and brushing your teeth. Avoid ice and take care with juices as their water sources may be suspect. Milk should be avoided as it is often unpasteurised. You may also be better off avoiding uncooked vegetables, salads, unpeeled fruit or frozen products unless properly prepared. Wash all fresh food thoroughly in boiled or bottled water before you eat it.

Sun Protection

The African sun is strong: sunblock and a head covering are essential – a wide-brimmed hat is ideal. If your skin is fair, use sunscreen whenever you are going to be out in the sun. Even if you have dark skin, you are still at risk if out all day – particularly if you are going to be swimming or snorkelling. The water reflects the sun's rays, multiplying the effect, and the coolness of the water is deceptive.

Most first-time visitors experience a degree of heat exhaustion and dehydration that can be avoided by drinking lots of water and slightly increasing the amount of salt in the diet. Dehydration is more serious in children, so monitor their intake of liquids carefully.

Health Risks

Aids

Aids is a major problem in Tanzania, with around 6 percent of adults HIV positive; the rate of infection is falling thanks to government programmes such as Aids awareness campaigns and screening of blood donors. Avoid high-risk activities such as unprotected sex. Make sure your first-aid kit includes syringes and avoid receiving blood transfusions, except in case of dire emergency and preferably only after consulting your consulate or embassy.

Altitude Sickness

This is likely to be encountered only by those who are trekking up Mount Kilimanjaro or Mount Meru. It is impossible to predict who will be affected and how severely – it takes little consideration of fitness. Mild altitude sickness will bring headaches, lethargy, dizziness, difficulty sleeping and loss of appetite. Further ascent should be avoided at this stage as the sickness may become more severe without notice and include symptoms of breathlessness, coughing that may produce frothy pink sputum, vomiting and unconsciousness. In this case immediate descent is necessary or it may lead to fatal pulmonary oedema. The good news is that a rapid descent to a lower altitude will cure the symptoms as rapidly as they came on.

Some tips to avoid acute mountain sickness:
Ascend the mountain slowly, giving

your system time to adjust. Unfortunately, many treks on Mount Kilimanjaro and Mount Meru, especially the budget ones, are geared for getting you up and down quickly. Take the longest route possible if this is your first high-altitude experience and don't hesitate to ask your guide to go more slowly. Try sleeping at a lower height than your maximum height that day. Not only does this give you a nice downhill trot at the end of the day, but it allows your body to adjust more easily.

Drink lots of fluid and avoid heavy foods. Avoid alcohol and sedatives, as these further reduce the blood's ability to absorb oxygen.

Bilharzia

Avoid swimming in fresh water: even large lakes such as Lake Malawi/Nyasa are known to harbour bilharzia parasites which live in snails that like reedy, still water. Fast-flowing, very cold or clear water should be safe. If in doubt, rub yourself dry thoroughly with a rough towel and ask for a test on returning home. There is a relatively straightforward treatment to this disease if it is caught in time.

Remember that fresh water may also harbour crocodiles and hippos.

Diarrhoea

This curse of the long-distance traveller usually clears itself up within a few days. If there is no sign of improvement within 48 hours, it could be caused by a parasite or infection, and you should go and see a doctor.

The best way to avoid tummy bugs is by being fastidious about using purified or bottled water to drink and brush your teeth with. Watch out for ice in drinks. If you are felled, stop eating anything but dry toast or biscuits (preferably salty), but carry on drinking plenty of water and fruit juice. Coca Cola and ginger ale are both a good way to inject calories and help settle the stomach. Avoid alcohol, coffee, tea and any dairy products other than yoghurt. Dehydration is the biggest risk, particularly with chronic diarrhoea, which is most dangerous to children, who become dehydrated more quickly than adults. Rehydration requires salt and sugar as well as liquid.

Malaria

Malaria is one of the most serious health risks in East Africa. Seek advice from your doctor or a tropical institute two months before your departure on the most suitable medication for you and your family.

In the UK, the **Health Protection**

Agency publishes a document on malaria prevention, which can be downloaded at www.hpa.org.uk. In the US, the **Center for Disease Control** (CDC) in Atlanta (tel: 404-498 1515/800-311 3435; www.cdc.gov) issues health advice to travellers.

The most commonly recommended prophylactics are Larium (which can have unpleasant, and in rare cases dangerous, side effects); the antibiotic doxycycline (which can cause photosensitivity in some people); and Malarone (which has few side effects and is effective, but is unsuitable for children).

None of these offers 100 percent protection, so it is wisest to avoid getting bitten in the first place. The malaria-carrying female anopheles mosquito is only active between dusk and dawn. At these times, avoid perfumes and aftershave; make liberal use of insect repellent containing DEET; and wear light-coloured clothing that covers arms and legs. Sleep in mosquito-proof quarters (ie, rooms with mosquito screens on the windows and under a mosquito net impregnated with permethrin).

It is important to remember that the most dangerous form of malaria often appears disguised as a heavy cold. If you start displaying flu-like symptoms at any stage within six months of your return home, you should consult a doctor immediately – be sure to tell them where you have been travelling.

It is also important not to panic unduly. Millions of people visit and live in Africa without getting malaria. Furthermore, providing you seek medical assistance quickly, it is easy to treat.

Automobile Accidents

Car crashes are a leading cause of injury among travellers in East Africa, so walk and drive defensively, wear a seat belt and avoid travelling at night.

Bugs and Beasties

Many **snakes** in Africa are poisonous, though most will leave you alone and are as anxious to avoid you as you are to avoid them. If walking in thick grasses or undergrowth, wear sturdy shoes and thick socks, and always walk heavily – most snakes will feel the vibrations and get out of your way. The black mamba is the only snake that is aggressive enough to attack, while the puff adder relies on camouflage and is easy to step on inadvertently. If you are bitten, keep the affected part as immobile as possible and seek immediate help.

Many of the huge **spiders** that

freak out visitors are harmless – some are even mosquito-munching friends. However, it is best to keep a safe distance unless you are certain. Be aware of children's curiosity overcoming common sense. Check the bed and the toilet seat before sitting down, shake out your shoes before putting them on, and never put your hands on a rock or into a crevice without checking it for occupants first.

Tsetse flies can be a terrible annoyance, and some carry trypanosomiasis (sleeping sickness). With an appearance and a painful, extremely itchy bite similar to a horsefly's, they tend to swarm and are attracted to the heat of a car and the colours black and blue. If infected by sleeping sickness, symptoms include swelling five days after the bite and a fever two or three weeks later. Treatment should be sought immediately, as it can be fatal.

Sea Creatures

Sharks can be a hazard along the coast. Make sure you know the local situation before you go swimming or diving.

Although not deadly, the **jellyfish** around Zanzibar can give a nasty sting, so keep an eye out when gazing at the wonders of the deep. Use beach shoes when wading off the shore, not only to guard against rough coral rock or shells, but in case you step on a **sea urchin**. If you get stung, bitten or cut by anything in the shallows, try and identify what caused it and seek medical help.

Health Care
Air Ambulance Services
If someone is seriously injured or has a life-threatening disease, the closest hospital with reliable staff and equipment up to Western standards is in Nairobi, an hour and a half's flying time from Dar/Zanzibar. The bureaucracy of insurance claims takes time, so if you think a condition is serious, sort it out as early as possible.

Dentists
We do not recommend seeking dental treatment in Tanzania or Zanzibar. Visit your dentist before your trip if you have reason for concern.

Doctors
Arusha
Marie Stopes Tanzania
Mererani Marie Stopes International
PO Box 14147
Tel: 0754 273 556

ABOVE: protect yourself against sun and rain.

Zanzibar
Zanzibar Medical Group
Kenyatta Road, near Vuga Road
Tel: 024-223 3134
24-hour emergency number: 0777-410 954

Flying Doctors
Nairobi (emergency), tel: +254-20-315454 or +254-733-628422. Tanzania office for information on membership, tel: 022-211 6610.

Hospitals
Try to avoid a stay in any Tanzanian hospital if possible. Away from urban centres, medical care diminishes rapidly in quality, although some mission hospitals manage to maintain good standards of care. Even in the main areas, patients with severe injury or illness are often flown by air ambulance straight to Nairobi. For less serious conditions, the following are suitable:

Dar es Salaam
Aga Khan Hospital. Ocean Road, Ufulconi.
Tel: 022-211 4096/5151
Nordic Clinic
Valhalla, Msasani
Tel: 022-260 1650/260 0274
Mobile: 0/13-325 569 (24 hours)
Half-private, half-sponsored by Scandinavian governments. Run by Dutch doctors.

Moshi
Kilimanjaro Christian Medical Centre (KCMC)
Tel: 027-275 4377
A clnic in the foothills of Mount Kilimanjaro (about 40km/25 miles east of Arusha) with a good reputation.

Pharmacies
Pharmacies in the major towns of Tanzania and Zanzibar are generally well stocked with Western-brand medicines. Medication in villages is limited. Be sure to check the expiry dates before purchasing medicines. Keep receipts on hand for any purchases, as your travel insurance should reimburse you.

Dar es Salaam
Moona's Pharmacy Ltd
Cnr Samora and Mkwepu streets,
Tel: 022-212 9983

Arusha
Moona's Pharmacy Ltd
Sokoine Road
Tel: after hours 0744-309 052
Mobile: 0754-334567

Zanzibar
Shamsu
Creek Road
Open until midnight.
Darjani Pharmacy
Creek Road
Tel: 024-223 9255
Open 8am–10pm daily.

nternet
There are numerous cafés and bureaux where you can access the internet, which is by far the most reliable form of communication in Tanzania. Below are a few suggestions, but a walk down most streets will land you at an equally good café. Rates are similar in most establishments, although hotels and facilities at up-market shopping centres will charge at least double for a service that's no better.

Arusha

The Patisserie
Sokoine Road
Near the Clocktower
Open Mon–Sat 7am–6pm.
The shop is also a nice place for breakfast or lunch, with hot bread, fresh juice, catering and lunchboxes available. It also sells books and DVDs, magazines and newspapers. Cheap rates for students and Peace Corps workers.
Cybersport
Jacaranda Street

Zanzibar

There is an abundance of internet cafés in Stone Town along Kenyatta Road, Gizenga Street and Shangani Road – they all charge approximately TSh 1,000 an hour.

Maps

Most travellers will be adequately supplied by the maps in this book describing the hubs of Tanzania and Zanzibar. If you would like something more detailed, the best whole-country maps on offer include one by German publisher Harms IC Verlag, who also do detailed regional maps of popular areas (available in the UK at Stanfords, www.stanfords.co.uk), In North America, the Canadian *International Travel Maps Tanzania* is widely available. Local publishers Maco Editions have created an excellent series of detailed maps of Zanzibar and the national parks, complete with entertaining drawings (also available at Stanfords), or you can get simpler sketch maps of the road systems within the parks from national parks offices. Zanzibar Gallery produces and stocks decent maps of Zanzibar.

Media

Television

Most luxury hotels in Tanzania have satellite television. Local stations often broadcast only in Swahili and seem to have a fondness for subtitled Chinese dramas and films. Another channel is STAR TV, broadcasting in English and Swahili from Mwanza, receivable in Arusha and Dar es Salaam. Broadcasting since 1994, ITV is the main station. There is a flourishing DVD market that far exceeds the cinema scene. Quality is bad, however, as most discs are pirated.

Radio

Radio is the primary source of news and entertainment for most Tanzanians. The sounds of Swahili broadcasts can be heard in public transport, shops and offices. The government-run station is **Radio Tanzania** 1442 MW. This station broadcasts in both English and Swahili, whereas its Zanzibari affiliate, **Radio Tanzania Zanzibar**, is predominantly Swahili. **Radio One** 89.5 FM (English/Swahili) is very popular and competes with a medley of other stations, most notably **KISS FM** (English). **Radio Free Africa** (English/Swahili) has a programme typical of "Radio Free" stations. The frequencies are 88.7MHz in Mwanza, 89.0/98.6MHz in Dar, and 89.9MHz in Arusha. Other stations broadcasting in Tanzania are 101.4 (local programmes and BBC news), 103.1 (Classic FM music and more), 98.7/88.4 (Clouds FM) and 98.8/87.8 (East Africa FM). It is not unusual to pick up local or church-run stations in more remote areas.

Newspapers and Magazines

A wide range of newspapers is available in Tanzania, especially in cosmopolitan Dar es Salaam. Foreign editions of UK papers are on sale at luxury-hotel newsstands and occasionally on the street. In Stone Town, you can buy international newspapers and weeklies at **Masomo Bookshop**, behind the markets on Creek Road (open 8am–4pm).

Local English-language newspapers include the *Business Times*, *The Express*, *The Financial Times* and the Kenya-based *East African*. National dailies include the *Guardian*, *Daily News* and the *Family Mirror*.

Highly recommended free magazines while on the road include the bi-monthly *Dar es Salaam Guide* (www.whatsondar.co.tz) and the *Swahili Coast* magazine. Both provide up-to-the-minute activity listings and travel information for their respective areas. Copies are found at hotels, restaurants and shops throughout Dar es Salaam, Arusha and Zanzibar.

Money

Currency

The Tanzanian shilling (TSh; often written /=) is the national unit of currency. It is divided into 100 cents, which are rarely used. Notes come in 200, 500, 1,000, 5,000 and 10,000 notes. Coins are 50, 100 and 200. There are smaller coins, but these are seldom used.

Exchange

You should have no problem changing cash or traveller's cheques in major towns. There is no black market, and the people who approach you offering to exchange money are simply trying to rob you. As a general rule banks offer a better rate, especially on traveller's cheques, than bureaux de change. The National Bank of Commerce (NBC) seems to offer the best rates.

Traveller's Cheques

In major towns, traveller's cheques are easily cashed, but if you travel into the villages of Tanzania, they could quickly haunt you. They are accepted at national parks for fees, etc, and though rates are always lower than cash, if you exchange at an NBC, the difference is minuscule. Many banks and bureaux de change will not cash them without the receipt, normally kept separate for security purposes.

Banks and ATMs

All the larger towns have banks; in smaller towns, opening hours and

BELOW: banking facilities are available in most towns.

services may be limited. Barclays is the only international banking presence, with several offices in Dar and branches in the main towns.

ATMs are popping up all over Tanzania and Zanzibar but they often go down for hours at a time because of power cuts. This being so, it is sensible to bring some traveller's cheques. The most reliable institution for electronic banking services is Barclays Bank, which has several branches in Dar es Salaam and Zanzibar Town. Most of the larger towns on the mainland also have branches. Regional and remote areas of Tanzania, however, do not have facilities like this so if you plan to spend time off the beaten track, it is wise to bring a combination of cash and traveller's cheques.

Dar es Salaam
Barclays Bank
There are branches throughout Dar, including:
Barclays House, Ohio Street, opposite Royal Palm Hotel. ATM
Tel: 022-213 6970
www.africa.barclays.com
Open Mon–Fri 8.30am–4pm,
Sat 10am–1pm.
Slipway branch: Msasani Peninsula. ATM.
Tel: 022-260 2642
Standard Chartered
NIC Life House, Cnr Sokoine Drive/ Ohio Street, PO Box 9011. ATM
Tel: 022-211 3774
International House, Garden Avenue/ Shabaan Robert, PO Box 9011. ATM
Tel: 022-212 2160
Shoppers Plaza Shopping Centre
Old Bagamoyo Road, PO Box 9011.
No ATM
Tel: 022-277 5174
National Bank of Commerce
Cnr Azikiwe Street/Sokoine Drive
Tel: 022-211 1970 or 211 2887
Open Mon–Fri 8.30am–3pm,
Sat 8.30am–noon.
CRDB Bank
Azikiwe Street, opposite Post Office. ATM
Tel: 022-211 7441–7
Good rate for traveller's cheques.

Arusha
Barclays Bank
Sopa Plaza Building, Serengeti Road
Tel: 027-250 9320
National Bank of Commerce (NBC)
Sokoine Road
Tel: 027-254 8662/250 9320
Much better traveller's cheque rate than in the bureaux de change.
Standard Chartered Bank
Sykes Building, Gonliondoi Road. ATM.
Tel: 027-254 4703/5

Stanbic Bank
Sokoine Road
Tel: 027-250 9713
National Microfinance Bank
Sokoine Road
Tanzania Postal Bank
Sokoine Road

Zanzibar
Barclays Bank
Zanzibar State Trading Corporation Building, Malawi Road. ATM.
Tel: 024-223 5796/73
NBC
PO Box 157, Kenyatta Road, Shangani. ATM.
Tel: 024-223 3590
People's Bank of Zanzibar
PO Box 1173, beside Old Fort Shangani
Tel: 024-223 1118
Fax: 024-223 1121

Other
Standard Chartered Bank
CCM Building, Makongoro Road, PO Box 1343, Mwanza
Tel: 028-250 0923
Rindi Lane, Next to Mobitel office, PO Box 3082, Moshi
Tel: 027-275 4491/3

Bureaux de Change
Dar es Salaam
Crown Bureau de Change
Cnr India/Zanaki streets, PO Box 2211
Tel: 022-211 0250
Fax: 022-211 0251
Galaxy Bureau de Change
Cnr Samora Avenue/Bridge Street PO Box 21219
Tel: 022-211 8776
Fax: 022-211 3069
MGM Bureau de Change
Morogoro Road, PO Box 816
Tel/fax: 022-211 6882

Arusha
Northern Bureau de Change
Joel Maeda Street
Tel: 027-250 7119
Open standard hours and offers a fair exchange rate.
Exchange Centre
Joel Maeda Street

Zanzibar
Suma Bureau de Change
Tel: 024-223 4349

Money Transfers
Western Union has offices in Dar and Zanzibar, located in branches of the Tanzania Postal Bank.
Zanzibar
c/o Tanzania Postal Bank, Malawi Road
Tel: 024-223 1798
Open Mon–Sat 8.30am–6pm.

Taxes
Ensure that VAT (20 percent) is included in prices. *For airport departure tax see page 312.*

Photography

Regardless of your ambitions as a photographer, you will find an unlimited number of subjects to shoot: the beaches of Zanzibar, old charms of Dar and Stone Town, Mount Kilimanjaro, the animals and most importantly the people.

Bear in mind the differences in light. Midday can produce harsh shadows; the narrow alleys in the old towns are always in deep shade; and you may spot that elusive leopard only at dawn or dusk.

The most important piece of equipment is a zoom lens. When you are out on safari, the animals seem close enough to touch, but photograph them with a wide angle lens and they look miles away. A good zoom (up to 250–300 mm) will really bring your photos to life.

Avoid photographing anything that may be considered strategic such as bridges, police stations, etc. If in doubt, ask.

Photographing People
Be sensitive when taking photos of local people. You would have to get far off the beaten track to find anyone shocked to see a Mzungu (white person) with a camera. Some will want to pose, while others will run for cover; the more entrepreneurial will want money. The Maasai will make it extremely clear that unless they get money, anyone attempting a sneaky shot will be in trouble.

There is no doubt that the best option is to get to know the people around you. While this may seem too big a task, Tanzanians are very friendly and generous and much easier to get to know than busy city-dwellers back home. However, there may not be time when blowing through a small village, in which case you must decide: photograph and ask or ask and then photograph.

Few Tanzanians are neutral about the camera's eye. If you take a picture without asking, you may get more natural images, but may face the subject's wrath. Some Muslims, particularly women, may be genuinely upset. However, you'll probably be presented with the invoice of an open hand. If you ask first, it will prevent any possible insult and will mean you have some control over the price. However, if people say no, you must be prepared to accept their decision.

If they say yes, you will lose the spontaneity that first caught your eye. Often people will simply ask for a copy. If you agree and take their address, make sure you send them one. It will be a valued present.

Photographic supplies

Dar es Salaam
Shepherd's Plaza
Msasani Peninsula.
No. 1 Color Lab
Haidery Plaza Shopping Centre,
Tel: 022-211 9625
Email: tanzania@jackys.com
Official Kodak distributor. Also provides photocopying service.

Arusha
Burhani Photographic Services
Next to Hotel Impala, PO Box 2457
Email: chomoko@cybernet.co.tz
1-hour processing at Kwik
Sokoine Road, By BP petrol station
Naaz Photo Studio
India Street, PO Box 1014

Zanzibar
Zanzibar Gallery
Mercury House, Kenyatta Road
Tel: 024-223 2721
Email: gallery@swahilicoast.com

Postal Services

The postal service is generally reliable but slow. At best, airmail to European destinations takes five days. It takes mail a couple of weeks to reach Dar es Salaam from Europe/North America, and much longer if going to a smaller village.

Poste restante services are available for a nominal charge. Make sure your correspondents write your name clearly and underline the surname or the letter could languish,

BELOW: take a zoom lens on safari.

Public Holidays

New Year 1 January
Zanzibar Revolution Day
12 January
CCM Foundation Day 5 February
Good Friday and **Easter Monday**
Variable
Union Day 26 April
Workers' Day 1 May
Saba Saba (Peasants' Day) 7 July
Nane Nane (Farmers' Day)
8 August
Prophet's birthday 10 September
Independence Day 9 December
Christmas Day 25 December
Boxing Day 26 December

Islamic Festivals

The dates of these festivals vary from year to year:
Eid El Fitr End of Ramadan
Eid El Haji celebrates sacrifice of Ismail with pilgrimages to Mecca
Maulid/Maulidi Day Prophet Mohammed's birthday.

misfiled, in a backroom for evermore.

Do not send valuable items or money through the post. Courier services (in larger cities only) take less than 24 hours to reach European destinations.

Dar

The main post office is on Azikiwe Street.

Arusha

The main post office is on Boma Road, near the Clocktower. The Meru branch is on Sokoine Road.

Zanzibar

The main post office in Stone Town is outside the city centre in the direction of Amani Stadium. The most convenient post office is on Kenyatta Road.

Couriers

Dar es Salaam
DHL
Pugu Road
Tel: 022-2861 000
www.dhl.com
EMS
Azikiwe Street
PO Box 9551
Tel: 022-212 3112
UPS
Haidery Plaza, Ali Hassan Mwinyi Road, Kisutu Street, PO Box 70603,
Tel: 022-212 2403

Arusha
DHL
Fedha House, Sokoine Road,
Adjacent to NBC Bank

Tel: 022-2861 000
Open Mon–Fri 8am–6pm, Sat 8am–4pm, Sun and holidays noon–2pm.
Sub office, AICC Building, Kilmanjaro Wing

Zanzibar
DHL
Opposite Serena Inn, Shangani
Tel: 024-223 3642/8281
EMS
PO Box 2360, In the post office
Tel: 024-223 0889
Fax: 024-223 3701

R eligious Services

Tanzania has places of worship for all the main religions as well as a wide range of lesser-known faiths and denominations.

Dar es Salaam

Anglican
Cathedral of St Joseph
Sokoine Drive.
Hindu
Hindu Temple
Kisutu Street.
Islamic
Al Jumaa Mosque
Cnr Indira Ghandi and Kitumbini streets.
Lutheran
Azanian Front Lutheran Church
Cnr Sokoine Drive and Maktaba Road.

Arusha

Anglican
St James Church
North of Uhuru Monument
Tel: 027-250 3448
Email: saintjamesanglican@email.com
English service: 1–2.30pm.
Hindu
Maharaj Temple
Morning 7.30–8am; evening 6–6.30pm.
Lutheran
Lutheran Church
Goliondoi Road
English service: 7.30–9am, 9–10.30am, 10.30–noon on Sunday.

Zanzibar

Anglican
Cathedral Church of Christ
Off Creek Road.
Catholic
Cathedral of St Joseph
Cathedral Street.

S tudent Travellers

If you are a student it's a good idea when travelling to carry an International Student Identity Card (ISIC), which offers discounts and

benefits in over 100 countries including Tanzania. To apply go to http://www.istc.org
STA Travel is a travel company that caters to students and young people. Their Tanzania branch is;
STA Travel/Escape – Student & Adventure Travel
Peugeot House
Inside tunnel next to Citibank
Ali Hassan Mwinyi Road
Dar es Salaam
Tel: 022-212 5189/90/91
Fax: 022-212 5189
www.escape-tanzania.com

T elecommunications

Most resort hotels provide fax and internet services, as do small shops – just as reliable and half the price.
International calls are very expensive, unless you use an internet phone. Mobile phones are much more reliable than landlines. In Zanzibar there is a call centre beside the post office on Kenyatta Road and another one across the road – compare prices before calling.

Regional Dialling Codes
The international dialling code for Tanzania is 255. Regional codes are as follows (omit the initial zero if calling from abroad):
Arusha 027
Chake Chake (Pemba) 024
Dar es Salaam 022
Dodoma 026
Iringa 026
Kigoma 028
Mbeya 025
Mkoani 024
Morogoro 023
Moshi 027
Mtwara 023
Mwanza 028
Tabora 026
Tanga 027
Wete 024
Zanzibar 024

International Codes
Dial the international prefix 00 and then the country code, followed by the number:
Australia 61
Canada 1
Ireland 353
New Zealand 64
South Africa 27
US 1
UK 44

Important Numbers
Directory Enquiries: 991
International Directory Enquiries: 0900
Emergency numbers: see page 316.

Tipping

Tipping is optional here. You'll never insult anyone in Tanzania by giving them a tip. Nor will you end up with New York-style rage if you fail to do so.
Rates are roughly as follows:
Porters: TSh500 per bag.
Taxis: Taxi drivers have a hard life – if the service has been good, a tip is a good idea.
Bar staff: 5–10 percent.
Waiters: around 5 percent. A Western-style 15 percent tip at an expensive restaurant would probably equate to a week's wages, so modify things a little. Leave cash, rather than adding it to the bill.
Prices rise steeply on safari, when you should be prepared to pay 6–10 percent of the total cost of the safari (minus air fares). Split this between the guide, driver, cook and cleaning staff, with more generally going to the first two.
If climbing Kilimanjaro, you need to budget around US$200. Some operators include the tips in the price of the climb (see page 175).

Toilets

The Swahili word for toilet is *choo*. Toilets are either Western-style (sit down) or Asian-style (squat). Cleanliness and facilities depend largely on what type of establishment you are in. Mid- to high-end hotels are much more likely to have clean Western-style toilets complete with toilet paper. Toilets in cheaper hotels and guesthouses, however, tend to be seatless, paperless and often squat. Public toilets are few and far between and of varied hygienic standard.
It is a cultural, and in some cases religious, practice for most locals to wash (with the left hand) after going to the toilet rather than use paper. It is also more hygienic given the tropical climate. There is usually a plastic container and a water source in the toilet for this purpose. Washing your hands thoroughly afterwards eliminates any bacteria. Keep a roll of toilet paper in your bag at all times if that is your preferred option.

Tourist Information Offices
Local
Dar es Salaam
Tanzania Tourist Board
Ground Floor, Matasalamat Building,

Time Zone

GMT+3; EST+8.
No daylight-saving time.

Samora Avenue, PO Box 2485
Tel: 022-211 1244
www.tanzaniatouristboard.com

Arusha
47 E Boma Road, PO Box 2348
Tel: 027-250 3842/3
Email: ttb-info@habari.co.tz

Zanzibar
Zanzibar Commission for Tourism,
Amaan Road, PO Box 1410
Tel: 024-223 3485-6
Fax: 024-223 3448
www.zanzibartourism.net

Abroad
In the US, Australia and most other countries the **Tanzania Tourist Board** is represented by the local embassy or high commission.
In the UK, it is represented by:
Tanzania Trade Centre
3 Stratford Place
London W1C 1AS
Tel: 020-7758 8070
Fax: 020-7758 8073
www.tanzatrade.co.uk

W ebsites

Web addresses are given throughout the book. This roundup lists a few of the most useful sources of background information on Tanzania and Zanzibar.
www.tanzania-online.gov.uk
The website of the Tanzanian High Commission in London, providing details on visa and work permits, business advice and tourist information.
www.cdc.gov
The website for the US Centers for Disease Control and Prevention, with a section on travel health. The site is updated regularly and gives detailed recommendations by region.
www.masta.org
The website of MASTA, the UK-based Medical Advice Service for Travellers Abroad.
www.tanzaniatouristboard.com
The official site of the Tanzanian Tourist Board, providing information on parks, safaris, lodges and tour operators.
www.tanzanianews.com
A classy news resource from the World News Network.
www.go2zanzibar.net
A free information and booking service for travellers who are looking to visit the Zanzibar Archipelago.
www.tanzania.go.tz
The official site of the Republic of Tanzania and Zanzibar, providing all sorts of detailed information on every aspect of the country.

TRANSPORT
ACCOMMODATION
EATING OUT
ACTIVITIES
A – Z
LANGUAGE

Weights and Measures

Officially metric, although some imperial measurements are still used.

www.arushatimes.co.tz
Up-to-date news from Arusha.
www.ippmedia.com
Tanzania's dominant media conglomerate, IPP Media, owns ITV and Radio One, in addition to this site, which provides online news features.
www.who.int
The World Health Organization's recommendations for safe travel.
www.zanzibar.net
Informative website on what to see and do in Zanzibar.
www.africatravelresource.com
UK-based tour operator offering tailor-made holidays.
www.tanzaniatourismonline.com
The online version of the current edition of the official annual publication *Tanzania Travel and Tourism Directory*.
www.marineparktz.com/
Everything you need to know about the marine parks and reserves of Tanzania.
www.tanzaniaparks.com/
Comprehensive information on Tanzania's national parks.
http://allafrica.com
Current affairs and social commentary with an archival search function.
www.africa-news.net
Website dedicated to providing alternative news coverage on Africa to that offered by the Western media; current affairs, blogs and magnificent photographs.

What to Wear/Bring

Clothing should be loose and comfortable – natural fibres help your skin to breathe in the heat. It should also be modest and respectable – people of the coast and islands are Muslim and you should keep shoulders and knees covered.

Life is generally informal, but it is a good idea to bring at least one set of smart clothes if you are travelling on business. You are advised to bring any specialist gear you may require (ie, snorkelling, hiking, camping equipment) as local supplies are limited and below par.

A hat, sunscreen and sunglasses are crucial protection from the blazing sun.

Seasonal Variations

In the rainy season (mid-March to late May), rain is consistent but not constant. An umbrella would be useful, as would sturdy hiking shoes if on a trek. Bear in mind that many routes are impassable at this time. Mosquitoes will be even more feisty too, so impregnated nets, repellents and prophylactics are even more important.

The dry season (between June and September) is the most popular time to visit. Rains are infrequent and the weather cooler; however, this is all relative – temperatures are still hot, and you may still face rain. There are fewer mosquitoes, but they are still a danger.

Beach Gear

Remember that the superb beaches of Zanzibar and Tanzania are in a conservative country. While bikinis are worn by tourists on the beaches, topless or nude bathing is not appropriate, and it is considered respectable to cover up once off the beach. Brightly coloured kangas do the trick nicely.

Bush gear

On safari, bright colours are bad news. Not only do they attract mosquitoes' attention, but vivid reds and oranges may disturb some animals as well. The best solution to wear neutral colours such as beige and khaki. Shoes need to be sturdy and ideally should cover your ankles, for protection against snakes and sharp branches. The more of your body is covered the better, as tsetse flies and mosquitoes will attack the uncovered bits. A hat, to reduce the sun's glare and increase your visibility, is essential, as is a good pair of binoculars.

Climbing Gear

As well as sturdy clothing and serious rain- and windproof cold-weather gear, you will need two adjustable climbing poles; a water pouch with a tube, carried in a day-pack; high-energy snacks; a head torch; and a medication pack with headache and diarrhoea tablets, plasters and re-hydration sachets.

Footwear

Big boots are useful in most places apart from the beach. They protect against ankle-biting snakes, and they also make for good protection on African transport, where nearly all bags end up on toes at some point. Closed shoes are recommended when walking through towns and cities as many areas are quite dirty and infections on blistered toes, etc, are commonplace. Take beach shoes for walking on sand and in the surf, where you can meet anything from rough coral to sea urchins.

Women Travellers

Travelling as a lone woman is perfectly safe and often entertaining. All Tanzanians are relatively conservative: you will be treated with respect, but the moment you are with a man, he will naturally be regarded as the decision-maker. Dress modestly and avoid skimpy clothing (apart from on the beach), particularly in eastern Tanzania and the islands, whose people are predominantly Muslim.

Be relatively formal in your dealings with men. Few African cultures have a concept of platonic friendship between the sexes, and what may be regarded as normal in Europe may well be regarded as a serious come-on here.

If you decide to have sex, remember that there is a high incidence of HIV/Aids in the local populace, and take suitable precautions.

BELOW: dress modestly in conservative Zanzibar.

L ANGUAGE

UNDERSTANDING THE LANGUAGE

Basic Rules

Swahili is rapidly becoming the international language of Africa and thereby one of the important languages of the world. Although a relatively easy language to pronounce, Swahili does require some effort for the first-time speaker. Every letter in the language is pronounced, unless it's part of a group of consonants. If a letter is written twice it is pronounced twice. Word stress almost always falls on the second to last syllable.

Vowels
a   as in "calm"
e   as in the "a" in "may"
i   as the "e" in "me"
o   as in "go"
u   as the "o" in "too"

Consonants
dh   as in "th" in "this"
th   as in "th" in "thing"
gh   like the "ch" of the Scottish "loch"
ng'   as in the "ng" of "singer"
ng   as in the "ng" in "finger"
ny   as in the "ni" in "onion"
ch   as in "church"
g   as in "get"

Words & Phrases

Yes Ndiyo/ndio
No A-a/hapana
OK Sawa
Please Tafadhali
Thank you Asante (nashukuru)
Sorry Pole
You're welcome Karibu sana
Excuse me Hodi
I don't speak Swahili Sisemba/sisemi Kiswahili (sana)
How do you say … in Swahili? Unasemaje … kwa Kiswahili?

Do you speak English? Unasema Kiingereza?
Do you understand? Unaelewa?
I don't understand Sielewi
I understand Naelewa
A little Kidogo
I don't know Sijui
Please write it down Tafadhali niandikie
Wait a moment! Subiri!
Speak slowly, please Tafadhali sema polepole
Enough! Inatosha/Bas!
Good Nzuri
Fine Salama
Where is…? …iko wapi?
Where is the nearest…? …ya (la) karibu liko (iko) wapi?
…toilet Choo…
Good morning (literally, how's your morning been?) Habari ya asubuhi?
Good afternoon Habari za mchana
Good evening Habari za jioni
Goodnight Lala salama

Emergencies

Help! Msaada (kusaidia)/saidia/njoo/nisaidie!
Fire! Moto!
Please call the police Mwite/muite polisi tafadhali
Are you all right? U mzima?
I'm ill Naumwa
I'm lost Nimepotea
(Get a) doctor (Umwite) daktari
Send for an ambulance Uite gari la hospitali
There has been an accident ajali/Pametokea ajali
He is (seriously) hurt Ameumia (vibaya)
I've been robbed! Nimeibiwa!
I'd like an interpreter Nataka mkalimani/mtafsiri

Goodbye Tutaonana/kwa heri, kwaheri (berphbk)
May I come in (to someone's house) Hodi!
Welcome! Karibu!
Reply: Salama/nzuri/safi/njema
Don't mention it Rica ederim
Pleased to meet you Nimefurahi
How are you? Hujambo (habari gani?)
Fine, thanks. And you? Sijambo, wewe? (nzuri, habari zako/yako?)
My name is… Jina langu ni (naitwa)…
I am British/American/Australian Natoka Uingereza/Marekani/Australia
Leave me alone Usinisumbue/niache
Go away! Hebu!/Toka!
What time is it? Saa ngapi?
When? Lini?
Today Leo
Tomorrow Kesho
Yesterday Jana
Now Sasa
Later Baadaye
Tonight Leo usiku
Why? Kwa nini?
Here Hapa
There Pale
Where can I find… Wapi nawesa
…a newspaper? Gazeti?
…a taxi? Teksi?
…a telephone? Simu?
Yes, there is Ndiyo
No, there isn't Sivyo

Days of the Week

Monday Jumatatu
Tuesday Jumanne
Wednesday Jumatano
Thursday Alhamisi
Friday Ijumaa
Saturday Jumamosi
Sunday Jumapili

Numbers

0 *sufuri/ziro*
1 *moja*
2 *mbili*
3 *tatu*
4 *nne*
5 *tano*
6 *sita*
7 *saba*
8 *nane*
9 *tisa*
10 *kumi*
11 *kumi na moja*
12 *kumi na mbili*
20 *ishirini*
21 *ishirini na moja*
22 *ishirini na mbili*
30 *thelathini*
40 *arobaini*
50 *hamsini*
60 *sitini*
70 *sabiini/sabini*
80 *themanini*
90 *tisiini/tisini*
100 *mia*
200 *mia mbili*
1,000 *elfu (moja)*

Months

January *Januari*
February *Febuari*
March *Machi*
April *Aprili*
May *Mei*
June *Juni*
July *Julai*
August *Agosti*
September *Septemba*

Greetings

Courtesy is rated highly in Tanzania, and greetings should not be rushed. Always shake hands if possible and pay attention to how people greet each other. If you learn nothing else in Swahili, try to master some of the following:

Greetings (to an elder/authority figure): *Shikamoo...*
...elder *Mzee*
...woman old enough to have children *Mama*
...man old enough to have children *Baba*
Reply: *Marahaba*
How are you...? *Hujambo...?*
...Sir *Bwana*
...Miss *Bibi*
Reply: *Sijambo* (or *Jambo* if you want to convert to English)
Hello *Salama/jambo* (*jambo* is mainly used for foreigners – reply *jambo* if you want to speak English, or *sijambo* if want to try out some Swahili phrases).

October *Oktoba*
November *Novemba*
December *Desemba*

Health

Hospital *Hospitali*
Clinic *Zahanati*
First aid *Huduma ya kwanza*
Doctor *Daktari*
Dentist *Daktari wa meno/Mganga wa meno*
I am ill *Naumwa*
It hurts here *Inaumwa hapa*
I have a fever/headache *Nina homa/kichwa kinamua*
I am diabetic *Nina dayabeti*
I'm allergic to... *Nina aleji ya...*
I have asthma *Nina ungonjwa wa pumu*
I am pregnant *Nina mimba*
I was bitten by... *Niliumwa na...*

Directions

Near *Karibu*
Far *Mbali*
Left *Kushoto*
On the left/to the left *Upande wa kushoto*
Right *Kulia*
On the right/to the right *Upande wa kulia*
Straight on *Moja kwa moja*
City *Mji*
Village *Kijiji*
Sea *Bahari*
Lake *Ziwa*
Farm *Shamba*
Church *Kanisa*
Mosque *Misikiti*
Post office *Posta*
North *Kaskazini*
South *Kusini*
East *Mashariki*
West *Magharibi*
Is it near/far? *Iko karibu/mbali?*
How far is...? *Ni umbali gani?*

Travelling

Car *Motokaa*
Petrol/gas station *Stesheni ya petroli/kupata petroli*
Petrol/gas *Petroli*
Flat tyre/puncture *Pancha/kuna kitundu*
My car has broken down *Gari langu limeharibika/ motokaa yangu imeharibika*
Bus station *Stesheni ya basi/kituo cha mabasi*
Bus stop *Bas stendi/pale inaposimama bas*
Bus *Basi/bas*
Train station *Stesheni ya treni*
Train *Treni/gari la moshi*
Taxi *Teksi/taxi*
Airport *Uwanja wa ndege/kiwanja cha ndege*

Aeroplane *Ndege*
Port/harbour *Bandari*
Ferry *Meli*
Ticket *Tikiti*
Timetable *Orodha ya saa*
What time does it leave? *Tutaondoka saa ngapi?*
Where do I go? *Nifikeje?*
How long does it take? *Mpaka tufike itachukua muda gani?*
How far is it? *Ni umbali gani?*
Which bus do I take for...? *Niingie katika bas gani kwa kwenda...?*
Please drive more slowly *Endesha polepole*
Stop! *Simama!*

Shopping

How much (is this)? *(Hii) bei gani/ni ngapi?*
Can I have? *Nipatie...tafadhali?*
No, I don't like it *A-a, siipendi hii/ sipendi hii*
Do you have any...? *Kuna...?*
Cheap *Rahisi*
Expensive *Ghali*
Big *Kubwa*
Small *Ndogo*
How many? *Ngapi gani?*
Receipt *Risiti*
Good *Mzuri*
Bad *Mbaya*

Restaurants

Waiter/Waitress! *Bwana!/Bibi!*
Menu *Orodha ya chakula*
Breakfast *Chakula cha asubuhi*
Table *Meza*
Bottle (of) *Chupa (ya)*
Fork *Uma*
Knife *Kisu*
Spoon *Kijiko kikubwa (large spoon)*
Napkin *Kitambaa*
Salt *Chumvi*
Black pepper *Pilipili*
Soup *Supu*
Fish *Samaki*
Chicken *Kuku*
Meat *Nyama*
Eggs *Mayai*
Vegetarian food *Wasiokula nyama*
Vegetables *Mboga*
Salads *Saladi*
Fruit *Matunda*
Bread *Mkate*
Drinks *Vinywaji*
Water *Maji*
Mineral water *Maji ya chupa*
Soft drink *Sharabeti/kinywaji baridi*
Beer *Biya*
Fruit juice *Maji ya matunda*
Wine (red/white) *Mvinyo/divai (nyeupe/nyekundu)*
Hot ginger drink *Tangawizi*
Coffee (black/with milk) *Kahawa (na maziwa/nyeusi)*
Tea *Chai*

FURTHER READING

Field Guides

Birds of Kenya and Northern Tanzania by Dale A. Zimmerman, Donald A. Turner, David J. Pearson (contributor) and Ian Willis (illustrator), Princeton University Press, 1999. A must for bird lovers.
Collins Field Guides:
Field Guide to the Larger Mammals of Africa
Field Guide to the Birds of East Africa and Guide to the Butterflies of East Africa
Field Guide to the Wild Flowers of East Africa
Reptiles and Amphibians of East Africa
Classic field guides, published by Collins and updated regularly.
The Safari Companion: A Guide to Watching African Mammals Including Hoofed Mammals, Carnivores and Primates by Richard D. Estes, Chelsea Green Publishing Company, 1999. A comprehensive guide to watching and understanding the behaviour of park life.

Wildlife

Among the Elephants by Ian Douglas-Hamilton, Penguin, 1978. Compelling account of the elephants of Lake Manyara by the king of elephant research.
Mahale: A Photographic Encounter With Chimpanzees by Angelika Hofer, Michael A. Huffman, Gunter Ziesler and Jane Goodall, Stirling Publications, 2000. Photos from Tanzania's Mahale Mountains.
Mara Serengeti: A Photographer's Paradise by Jonathan Scott and Angela Scott, Fountain Press, 2001. Breathtaking photographic study of the Serengeti and its inhabitants.
Mikumi National Park by Graham Mercer and Javed Jafferji, Gallery Publications, 2005.
My Life with the Chimpanzees; The Chimpanzees I Love: Saving Their World and Ours; In the Shadow of Man; Through a Window: My Thirty Years with the Chimpanzees of Gombe by Jane Goodall. Several titles detailing the chimp queen's life and work with the Gombe Stream chimpanzees.

Jane Goodall: Friend of the Chimps by Eileen Lucas, Millbrook Press, 1992. A touching biography of the ape-protector.
The Hunter Is Death by Tom V. Bulpin, National Book Network, 1991. A fascinating account of African hunting and game control.
In the Lion's Den by Mitsuaki Iwago (photographer), Chronicle Books, 1996. A photographic essay on the king of beasts.
Ruaha National Park by Graham Mercer and Javed Jafferji, Gallery Publications, 2005.
Saadani National Park by Rolf D. Baldus, Vanessa Beddoe and Javed Jafferji, Gallery Publications, 2007.
Selous Game Reserve by Rolf D. Baldus, Ludwig Siege and Javed Jafferji, Gallery Publications, 2005. Three guidebooks by local author and photographer.
Serengeti: Natural Order on the African Plain by Mitsuaki Iwago, Chronicle Books, 1996. A visual diary of life and death in the Serengeti.
The Serengeti's Great Migration by Carlo Mari (photographer), Harvey Croze and Richard D. Estes, Abbeville Press, Inc, 2000. One of Africa's greatest events depicted in wonderful detail.
The Serengeti Shall Not Die by Bernard Grzimek, Fontana, 1969. Where it all started; the account of the struggle to preserve the Serengeti, by the man who made it happen.
Tanzania – African Eden by Graham Mercer and Javed Jafferji, Gallery Publications, 2005. Beautifully photographed A–Z of the wonders of Tanzania.

History

Africa: A Biography of the Continent by John Reader, Vintage Books, 1999. A panoramic history of where human life began.
Africa Explored: Europeans in the Dark Continent by Christopher Hibbert, Cooper Square Publishers, 2002. The lives, journeys and impact of the 19th-century explorers.
The Africans by David Lamb, Vintage Books, 1987. Part travelogue and

part history of a continent at odds with itself. Written by former bureau chief for the *Los Angeles Times*.
Battle for the Bundu by Charles Miller, Macdonald, 1974. The East Africa campaign during World War I.
Cargoes of the East: The Ports, Trade and Culture of the Arabian Seas and Western Indian Ocean by Edmond Bradley Martin and Chryssee Perry Martin, Gallery Publications, 2007.
Empires of the Monsoon by Richard Hall, Collins, 1996. Ambitious but thoroughly readable history of the countries and trade routes surrounding the Indian Ocean.
A History of Tanzania ed. N. Kimambo and AJ Temu, Kapsel Educational, 1997. Tanzanian-written history of the country, with a refreshingly non-European angle. About the only general history to pay serious attention to what was happening before the Europeans arrived.
No Man's Land: An Investigative Journey through Kenya and Tanzania by George Monbiot, Green Books, 2003. Looking for justice in the area where conservation and land rights meet.
The Penguin Atlas of African History by Colin McEvedy, Penguin, 1997. Part of Penguin's Atlas of Human History series.
Revolution in Zanzibar: An American's Cold War Tale by Donald Petterson, Westview Press, 2002. Eyewitness account of the 1964 Zanzibar Revolution.
The Scramble for Africa by Thomas Pakenham, Abacus, 1994. Masterly unravelling of the complex politics and history involved in Europe's 19th-century land grab.
Tanzania Notes and Records. Contains great period pieces on a wide variety of topics of Tanzanian history and culture. On sale at the National Museum in Dar es Salaam and the Arusha Declaration Museum.
The White Nile by Alan Moorehead, Haperperennial Library, 2000. Tale of European exploration of East Africa in the 19th century.
Zanzibar Island Metropolis of Eastern Africa by Major FB Pearce, Gallery Publications, 2006.

Lives and Letters

African Voices, African Lives: Personal Narratives from a Swahili Village by Patricia Caplan, Routledge, 1997. A story of three distinctive villagers, told through their words.
The Leakeys: Uncovering the Origins of Humankind by Margaret Poynter, Enslow Publishers, 2001. Biography of the family of pioneering archaeologists.
The Life of Frederick Courteney Selous by JG Millais, Gallery Publications, 2001. Biography of the first of the great white hunters.
Livingstone, by Tim Jeal, Yale University Press, 2001. Authoritative biography of the greatest of the explorers.
Memoirs of an Arabian Princess by Emily Said-Ruete, Markus Wiener Publications, 1989. The autobiography of a princess from Zanzibar who eloped with a German to Europe. An intriguing historical portrait of sultan Zanzibar.
Tanzania, Journey to Republic by Randal Sadleir, Radcliffe Press, 1999. This description of life as a district commissioner in colonial Tanganyika is also a fascinating account of the road to independence.

Travel Writing

Africa Solo: A Journey across the Sahara, Sahel and the Congo by Kevin Dertscher, Steerforth Press, 1998. A crisp, clean tale of solo travel in Africa.
Going Solo, by Roald Dahl, Puffin, 2001. Autobiographical account of working for Shell in 1930s Dar es Salaam before joining the RAF.
Kilimanjaro Adventure by Hal Streckert, Kathy Wittert (editor) and Tom Tamoria (illustrator), Mission Press, 1999. A climb to Africa's roof.
Kilimanjaro: To the Roof of Africa by Audrey Salkeld, National Geographic, 2002. Accompanying coffee-table book to an Imax film on the mountain, with superb photography and authoritative text.
Livingstone's Tribe: A Journey from Zanzibar to the Cape by Stephen Taylor, Flamingo, 2000. White former resident of South Africa journeys south from Zanzibar, looking at the people of Africa, black and white.
North of South: An African Journey by Shiva Naipaul, Penguin, 1997. Written in the 1970s, this humorous tale still holds water.
Safari Living, by Gemma Pitcher, photographed by Javed Jafferji, Gallery Publications, 2005. Stunning coffee-table book on the design of

the country's best lodges and camps.
Sand Rivers by Peter Matthiessen, Bantam, 1982. A private safari in the Selous.
Tanzania: Portrait of a Nation by Paul Joynson-Hicks, Quiller, 1998. Beautiful photographs and well-written text.
A Tourist in Africa by Evelyn Waugh, Methuen, 1985. The comic novelist's journey through East Africa.

Fiction

Antonia Saw the Oryx First by Maria Thomas, Soho Press, Inc, 1993. A finely composed juxtaposition of two women: one black, one white.
Death in Zanzibar by M.M. Kaye. Penguin, 1984. Torrid romantic novel.
An Ice Cream War by William Boyd, Penguin, 1983. Grimly comic novel set during the World War I East Africa campaign.
The Snows of Kilimanjaro by Ernest Hemingway. The master storyteller turns his attention to death and the African bush, where he spent many happy hours hunting.

Feedback

We do our best to ensure the information in our books is as accurate and up-to-date as possible. The books are updated on a regular basis, using local contacts, who painstakingly add, amend and correct as required. However, some mistakes and omissions are inevitable and we are ultimately reliant on our readers to put us in the picture. We would welcome your feedback on any details related to your experiences using the book "on the road", as well as interesting new attractions, or facts and figures you have found out about the country itself. Maybe we recommended a hotel that you liked (or another that you didn't). The more details you can give us (particularly with regard to addresses, e-mails and telephone numbers), the better.
We will acknowledge all contributions, and we'll offer an Insight Guide to the best letters received.

Please write to us at:
Insight Guides
PO Box 7910
London SE1 1WE
United Kingdom
Or send e-mail to:
insight@apaguide.co.uk

Zanzibar by Giles Foden, Faber & Faber, 2002. Murder mystery wound up in the true-life events of the bombings of the US Embassies in Dar es Salaam and Nairobi.
Zanzibar Tales: Told by the Natives of East Africa by George Bateman, Gallery Publications, 2001. Collected Swahili folk tales, translated a century ago.

Other Insight Guides

The classic Insight Guide series combines in-depth features and an exploration of essential sights accompanied by vibrant photography. Insight Guides to Africa include: **Cape Town; East African Wildlife; Egypt; Gambia and Senegal; Kenya; Mauritius, Réunion and Seychelles; Namibia** and **South Africa**.

Berlitz Pocket Guides provide authoritative travel iformation in an ultra-portable format. With fold-out maps, colour-coded chapters and a handy A–Z of practical tips, they offer tremendous value for money. African titles in this series include **Cairo; Cape Town; Kenya** and **Marrakesh**.

Insight Fleximaps to African destinations include **Cairo; Cape Town; Marrakesh; Morocco; Seychelles;** and **South Africa**.

ART & PHOTO CREDITS

AKG London 21, 26, 30/31, 33, 37, 39
Alamy 70L, 149&T, 154, 179, 243
Mohammed Amin/Camerapix 23
Yann Arthus-Bertrand/CORBIS 86
Daryl Balfour/Gallo Images 101BL, 110TL
Anthony Bannister/Gallo Images 18, 102TR, 127L, 129BL, 129BR, 130TL,
Anthony Bannister/NHPA 123TL, 129TR, 131TL, 226
Peter Barker/Panos Pictures 42
Keith Begg/Gallo Images 4BR
Tobias Bernhard/Oxford Scientific Films (OSF) 134BL, 134BR
Bettmann/CORBIS 84
Trygve Bolstad/Panos Pictures 83,
Mark Bowler/NHPA 109L
Bojan Brecilj/CORBIS 27, 28
Marion Bull 160T, 248
Dan Burton 2/3, 132, 268T, 270, 271L, 271R
Camerapix 14/15, 17, 41, 44, 47, 163
Vincent Carruthers/Gallo Images 125BL
Peter Chadwick/Gallo Images 125TR
Waina Cheng/OSF 128TR
Gary Cook 68, 185T
Peter Cook/OSF 105TL
David M. Cottridge/OSF118BL
Gerald Cubitt 93L, 94TL, 94TR, 94BR, 95TR, 96TL, 97TR, 97BR, 98BL, 99TR, 99BL, 100TR, 100BL, 100BR, 101TR, 104BL, 104BR, 106BL, 106TR, 111BR, 112BL, 112BR, 113BL, 114TR, 114BL, 115TR, 115BR, 116TL, 117TL, 117TR, 118TL, 118TR, 119BL, 119BR, 127R, 128BL, 128BR, 129TL, 177, 200
Bruce Davidson/Nature Picture Library 130TR
Mark Deeble & Victoria Stone/OSF 123BR, 134TR, 135TR
David M. Dennis/OSF 123BL
Nigel Dennis/Gallo Images 111BL, 123TR,
Nigel J. Dennis/Gallo Images 113TL, 113BR, 115TL, 124BL
Thomas Dressler/Gallo Images 199T
Mary Evans Picture Library 32, 34, 35R, 35L, 36, 38, 231
David Fleetham/OSF 124TL
Michael Fogden/OSF 125BR
Dr Aron Frankental/Gallo Images 103BR
Max Gibbs/OSF back cover centre, 202T
Nick Greaves/Images of Africa 133R
Clem Haagner/Gallo Images 88/89
Lawrence Hamilton 146, 213
Roger de la Harpe/Africa Imagery 1, 4/5, 199, 269
Roger de la Harpe/Gallo Images back cover right, back flap bottom, 12, 110BR, 113TR,

Martin Harvey back flap top, 29, 82, 85, 90/91, 95TL, 96TR, 98TL, 101TL, 102BL, 104TL, 104TR, 114TL, 116TR, 116BL, 120, 128TL, 187, 192, 196, 197, 209, 220, 223. 229, 232, 256, 258T, 262, 262T
Martin Harvey/Gallo Images 95BL, 110BL, 119TL,
Robert Harvey/SAL/OSF 125TL
Mark Henley/Panos Pictures 147
Daniel Heuclin/NHPA 122BR
Paul Joynson Hicks/Jon Arnold Images 175
Gerald Hinde/Gallo Images 97TL
Arne Hodalic/CORBIS 16
Frank Hoogervorst/Panos Pictures 51
Fred Hoogervorst/Panos Pictures 138/139
Friedrich von Hπrsten/Images of Africa 77, 158, 227
Lanz von Horsten/Gallo Images back cover bottom, 108
Norman Hughes/fotoLibra 8B
Crispin Hughes/Panos Pictures 66L
Hulton-Deutsch/CORBIS 40
Richard Human/fotoLibra 50
iStockphoto.com 8T&C, 71, 75, 78, 87, 307, 313, 320, 322
Tim Jackson/OSF 94BL
Darrell Jones 58/59, 122BL, 244/245, 257, 263, 267
David Keith Jones/Images of Africa 126, 142, 228L
Jupiterimages 266
Richard Kirby/OSF 218/219
Satoshi Kuribayashi/OSF 131BL
Peter Lillie/Gallo Images 95BR, 102TL, 116BR, 130BL
Mike Longhurst/Rex Features 65, 278
My Hanh Luong-Skovmand/CIRAD 130BR
Guy Marks 81, 164/165, 173L, 173R, 175T, 176, 178, 191, 194, 212, 215
McPHOTO/Still Pictures 7T&CR
Paul Miles/Axiom 52
Ron Nunnington/OSF 102BR
Stan Osolinski/OSF 105TR
Lehtikuva Oy/Rex Features 151, 280
Oxford Scientific Films 122TR
Edward Parker/OSF 133L
Partridge Films /OSF 105BR, 134IL
Rod Patterson/Gallo Images 124TR
Caroline Penn/Panos Pictures 67
Tony Perrottet front flap bottom, 53, 66R, 136/137, 167, 249
Manfred Pfefferle/OSF 265T
Linda & Brian Pitkin/NHPA 135BL
Christophe Ratier/NHPA 76, 206
Rittener/Getty Images 24
Steve Robinson/NHPA 105BL
Alan Root/SAL/OSF 124BR
Geoff Rowswell 152
Juan Ryder/Gallo Images 4BL

Wayne Saunders/Gallo Images 224T
Anup Shah/Gallo Images 205
Melissa Shales 22, 61, 151T, 264, 265
Carlo Signorini Jones/Images of Africa back cover left, spine,79
Sean Sprague/Panos Pictures 63
Mattias Stahre 131BR
Guy Standen/fotoLibra 6CR, 74, 180/181
Stockbyte/Getty Images 324
Marie-Laure Stone/fotoLibra 9B
Tanzania Tourist Board 6T&B, 7B, 9T&C, 46, 64, 140/141, 169, 243T, 246/247, 288, 303, 308, 314
Andrew Taylor/Gallo Images 106BR
Dieter Telemans/Panos Pictures 56/57
Charlotte Thege/Images of Africa 3B, 225
Topham/ImageWorks 55, 73
Topham Picturepoint 20, 54
Tom Ulrich/OSF 117BL, 118BR
Stephen Valentine/fotoLibra 319
Alan Ward/fotoLibra 251, 253, 254T, 255
Mark Webster/OSF 135TL
Duncan Willetts/Camerapix 45, 72L
Marcus Wilson-Smith front flap top, 80L, 153, 221, 233, 242, 272
Konrad Wothe/OSF 131TR, 135BR
Ariadne Van Zandbergen 5B, 10/11, 19, 25, 48/49, 60, 62, 69, 70R, 72R, 80R, 92, 93R, 96BL, 96BR, 97BL, 98TR, 98BR, 99TL, 99BR, 100TL, 101BR, 103TL, 103TR, 103BL, 106TL, 107, 109R, 110TR, 111TL, 111TR, 112 TL, 112TR, 114BR, 115BL, 117BR, 119TR, 121L, 121R, 122TL, 150, 155, 156, 157, 159, 160, 161, 162, 166,, 170L, 170R, 171T, 172, 182, 183, 185, 186,188, 189, 190T, 193, 193T, 195, 201, 203, 204, 207, 209T, 210, 211, 214T, 216, 217, 224, 228R, 230, 235, 235T, 236, 237, 238, 239, 241, 241T, 254, 257T, 259, 260, 261
Ariadne Van Zandbergen/Alamy 258

Map Production Stephen Ramsay
© 2008 Apa Publications GmbH & Co. Verlag KG (Singapore branch

⚜ INSIGHT GUIDE
TANZANIA & ZANZIBAR

Cartographic Editor **Zoë Goodwin**
Production **Linton Donaldson**
Design Consultant **Klaus Geisler**
Picture Research
Hilary Genin, Corrie Wingate

INDEX

Numbers in italics refer to photographs

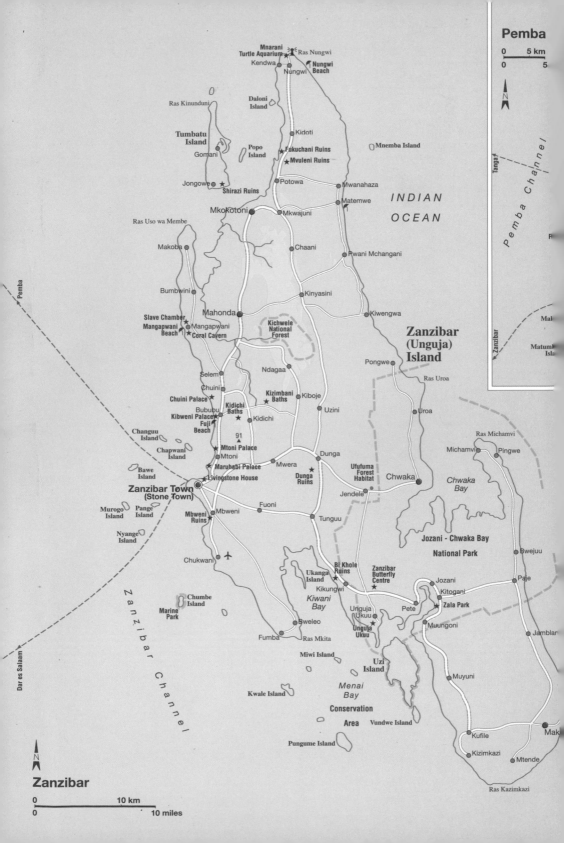

Pemba

0   5 km
0   5

N

Mnarani
Turtle Aquarium
Ras Nungwi
Kendwa
Nungwi
Nungwi
Beach

Ras Kinunduni
Daloni
Island

Tumbatu
Island
Popo
Island
Kidoti
Mnemba Island

Gomani
Fukuchani Ruins
Mvuleni Ruins

Jongowe
Potowa
Mwanahaza

Shirazi Ruins
Matemwe

INDIAN
OCEAN

Mkokotoni
Mkwajuni

Ras Uso wa Membe
Pwani Mchangani

Makoba
Chaani

Bumbwini
Kinyasini

Mahonda
Kiwengwa

Slave Chamber
Mangapwani
Beach
Mangapwani
Coral Cavern
Kichwele
National
Forest

Zanzibar
(Unguja)
Island

Pongwe

Selem
Ndagaa
Ras Uroa

Chuini
Kiboje

Chuini Palace
Kizimbani
Baths
Uzini
Uroa

Kidichi
Baths
Bububu
Kibweni Palace
Fuji
Beach
Kidichi

Ras Michamvi

Michamvi
Pingwe

91

Mtoni Palace
Dunga

Changuu
Island
Mtoni
Mwera
Dunga
Ruins
Ufufuma
Forest
Habitat
Chwaka
Chwaka
Bay

Chapwani
Island
Maruhubi Palace
Livingstone House

Bawe
Island
Jendele

Zanzibar Town
(Stone Town)
Fuoni

Murogo
Island
Pange
Island
Mbweni
Mbweni
Ruins
Tunguu

Nyange
Island

Jozani - Chwaka Bay

Chukwani
National Park
Bwejuu

Bi Khole
Ruins
Zanzibar
Butterfly
Centre
Jozani
Paje

Chumbe
Island
Ukanga
Island
Kikungwi
Kitogani
Zala Park

Marine
Park
Kiwani
Bay
Unguja
Ukuu
Pete
Jamblar

Sweleo
Unguja
Ukuu
Muungoni

Fumba
Ras Mkita

Miwi Island
Uzi
Island
Muyuni

Kwale Island
Menai
Bay

Conservation
Area
Vundwe Island

Pungume Island
Kufile
Mak

Kizimkazi
Mtende

Ras Kazimkazi

N

Zanzibar

0   10 km
0   10 miles

Dar es Salaam

Zanzibar Channel

Pemba

Pemba Channel

Tanga

Zanzibar

Mak

Matumbi
Island